REGIONAL IMPERATIVES IN UTILIZATION AND MANAGEMENT OF RESOURCES

REGIONAL IMPERATIVES IN UTILIZATION AND MANAGEMENT OF RESOURCES

India and the USSR

Edited by

S. MANZOOR ALAM

ATIYA HABEEB KIDWAI

CONCEPT PUBLISHING COMPANY, NEW DELHI

First Published 1987

Published by
Naurang Rai
Concept Publishing Company
H-13, Bali Nagar
NEW DELHI-110015 (India)

Printed in India by
C.S. Enterprises
at Hardev Printers, Mayapuri,
NEW DELHI-110064

DEDICATED TO

HIS EXCELLENCY COMRADE MIKHAIL S. GORBACHEV, GENERAL SECRETARY, CENTRAL COMMITTEE, COMMUNIST PARTY OF THE SOVIET UNION, AS A TOKEN OF OUR ADMIRATION :

FOR HIS PERCEPTIVE POLICIES AND BOLD INITIATIVES IN THE CAUSE OF GLOBAL PEACE, PROTECTION OF HUMANITY AGAINST NUCLEAR HOLOCAUST :

AND FOR PROMOTING FIRMLY INDO-SOVIET FRIENDSHIP.

—The Editors

ACKNOWLEDGEMENTS

The Editors wish to acknowledge with a deep sense of gratitude the financial and administrative support of the University Grants Commission, New Delhi, in sponsoring the participation of Indian scholars in the bi-national Indo-Soviet Seminar on Regionalisation for the Rational Utilisation, Conservation and Management of Hydro-Resources for Integrated and Comprehensive Regional Development, at Dushambe, USSR, in September 1985, and for the publication grant.

CONTENTS

SECTION THREE
POWER RESOURCES IN REGIONAL DEVELOPMENT

SECTION FOUR
PROBLEMS OF RESOURCE USE IN ARID REGIONS

SECTION FIVE
RESOURCE USE IN MOUNTAINOUS REGIONS

SECTION SIX
DEVELOPMENT AND MANAGEMENT OF NATURAL RESOURCES

LIST OF CONTRIBUTORS

S. Manzoor Alam
Vice-Chancellor, Kashmir University, Srinagar

Fatima Alikhan
Reader in Geography, Centre for Area Studies, Osmania University, Hyderabad

E.B. Alayev
Doctor of Economics, Council on Productive Forces, USSR State Planning Committee

A.B. Avakyan
Doctor of Science, Institute of Water Problems, USSR Academy of Sciences

Y. P. Badenkov
Deputy Director, Institute of Geography, USSR Academy of Sciences

A.Y. Biyalinov
Kirghiz Academy of Sciences, USSR

Sulabha Brahme
Gokhale Institute of Politics and Economics, Pune

M.A. Burkhanova
Tajik Academy of Sciences, USSR

Satyesh C. Chakraborty
Professor of Regional Development, Indian Institute of Management, Calcutta

V.A. Dukhovny
Director, Central Asian Scientific Research Institute of Irrigation, Ministry of Land Reclamation and Water Economy, USSR

K. Dzhurayev
Tajik Pedagogical Institute, corresponding Member, Tajik Academy of Sciences

G.S. Gosal
Department of Geography, Punjab University, Chandigarh

P.A. Kerzum
Institute of Pedology, Ministry of Agriculture, Tajik, SSR

U. K. Kletselman
Deputy Chairman, Council on Productive Forces, Tajik Academy of Sciences

G.V. Kopanev
Council on Productive Forces, USSR State Planning Committee

N.I. Koronkevich
Candidate of Geography, Institute of Geography, USSR Academy of Sciences

A.Y. Levintanus
Candidate of Geography, Institute of Geography, USSR Academy of Sciences.

A.M. Mamytov
Chairman, Commission on Natural Productive Forces, Kirghiz Academy of Sciences,

R.N. Mathur
Professor of Geography, Banaras Hindu University, Varanasi

H.S. Mavi
Professor and Head, Department of Agricultural Meteorology, Punjab Agricultural University, Ludhiana

K.M. Mirzoyev
Tajik Academy of Sciences, USSR

H. Mukhabbatov
Head, Sector of the Council on Productive Forces of the Tajik Academy of Sciences

S K. Negmatullayev
Director, Institute of Seismology, and Corresponding Member, Tajik Academy of Sciences

G.M. Nikolayeva
Institute of Geography, USSR Academy of Sciences

V.N. Orlovsky
Institute of Geography, USSR Academy of Sciences

K.O. Otorbaev
Academician, Kirghiz Academy of Sciences, Rector, Kirghiz State University

G.A. Privalovskaya
Institute of Geography, USSR Academy of Sciences

K. M. Saidmuradov
Chairman, Council for Productive Forces, Tajik SSR, Corresponding Member, Tajik Academy of Sciences

B. Sanginov
Director, Vakhsh Zonal Station, Corresponding Member of the Tajik Academy of Sciences

G.N. Sapozhnikov
Head of the Department, Nature Conservation and Optional Use of Natural Resources, Presidium of the Tajik Academy of Sciences, USSR

O.P. Sapov
Academician, Tajik Academy of Sciences

G.V. Sdasyuk
Doctor of Sciences, Institute of Geography, USSR Academy of Sciences, USSR

G.S. Seleznev
Tajik Academy of Sciences, USSR

K.V. Stanyukovich
Head, Sector of the Council on Productive Forces of the Tajik Academy of Sciences

L.M. Taran
Institute of Geography, USSR Academy of Sciences

I.D. Tsigelnaya
Candidate of Geography, Institute of Geography, USSR Academy of Sciences

K. U. Umarov
Head, Sector of the Institute of Economics, Tajik Academy of Sciences

Z.D. Usmanov
Academician, Tajik Academy of Sciences, USSR

E.G. Vakesman
Deputy Director, Institute of Pedology, Ministry of Agriculture of the Tajik SSR, Candidate of Sciences

S.I. Vasichikova
Institute of Pedology, Ministry of Agriculture, Tajik SSR

T.K. Vlasova
Institute of Geography, USSR Academy of Sciences

A.I. Zavulunov
Head, Sector of the Council on Productive Forces Tajik Academy of Sciences

S.K. Ziyadullaiev
Chairman, Council for Productive Forces, Uzbek USSR

PREFACE

Anthropogenic intervention for the utilization of natural resources for human use and for the progress and development of society has generated the twin processes of the intensification of resource utilization through improved technology and their rapid depletion through excessive use. The stark reality is that most of these natural resources are exhaustible and cannot be replenished.

Water constitutes one of the key resources and to a large measure determines the survival of society. The focus of the third Indo-Soviet Seminar on the management and development of natural resources held in Dushambe, Tajikistan, was on this vitally important resource. The Soviet and Indian scholars who shared their experience in the development of hydro-resources in their respective countries stressed on the level of technological achievements in controlling and conserving water resources and on the critical areas where significant gaps in knowledge exist and which preclude the optimal and most productive use of water resources.

The Russian experience clearly shows that with a strong political will the technological achievements can be profitably applied to transform an infertile semi-arid area into an agriculturally fertile belt. The transformation of the Tajik SS Republic from a deficit to a prosperous and surplus food and fruit basket of the USSR speaks eloquently for the benefit that mankind can derive from appropriate and rational use of water resources. The Russians have used their water reservoirs and hydro energy production for region forming purposes and for the development of production complexes. These have led to an integrated development of regions in the semi-arid regions of Tajikistan, Kazakastan, etc. This is not to imply that there are no negative consequences of the application of advanced technology. Both the Russian and the Indian papers do highlight that excessive use of water resources has in many areas led to the disturbance of ecological balance whether in the agricultural or in energy production belts. The negative consequences of irrigation leading to waterlogging, soil salinity and alkalinity seem to be a dominant trait of the canal irrigated areas of India. The sharing of research experiences and technology between India and USSR can help both the countries in minimising these negative consequences, in improving conservation of resources and in augmenting productivity.

The development of industrial complexes has been a major cause for the pollution of water bodies in the urban industrial belts whether in the Soviet Union or in India. The level of pollution is so rapidly rising in the water bodies of cities of the world that it demands not only bilateral but international cooperation, otherwise in the not too distant future it will constitute a major global health hazard for the fast growing urban population. While Indo-Soviet cooperation in this field should be most welcome and extremely valuable UNESCO must also intervene through its worldwide programme of MAN and the Biosphere (MAB).

This Volume on the Regional Imperatives of the Utilization and Management of Resources—India and the USSR is timely and of topical interest. It presents a realistic scenario of the problems and prospects of the development of water resources in the two great societies of the world. The papers speak of the great scientific and technological achievements in the development and utilization of water resources leading to accelerated and industrial development. The papers also give an authentic account of the acuteness of ecological problems granted by the processes of modern development in the fields of industry and agriculture. The universality of these problems calls for both bilateral and global sharing of scientific experiences and the message of this book in this regard is loud and clear.

This book is unique in the sense that for the first time a group of leading Soviet scholars have boldly set out their views in the English language highlighting their successes and failures in harnessing and managing the natural resources and particularly the hydro resources in the semi-arid areas of the USSR.

I do hope that scholars will find this volume a valuable contribution in the understanding of problems associated with utilization and management of water resource in the semi-arid regions of India and USSR.

S. MANZOOR ALAM

INTRODUCTION

The resource base in countries with vast territorial extents like India and the USSR is characterized by an uneven distribution of individual resources ; by diversity in their productivity levels and in regional resource combinations ; and by disparateness in the natural resource potential of different regions. In conditions like this, policy formulation for resource development rests on the understanding of two processes : firstly, the process of territorial differentiation in the development of natural resources and its impact on the natural environment ; and, secondly, the regional integration of technological and socio-economic factors which lead to the formation of regional production complexes.

The papers presented in this volume attempt to highlight some of the policy issues involved in the use of natural resources and outline the implications and consequences of various strategies adopted for their development in some selected regions in India and the USSR. The nature of the subject matter has forced both scholars and practitioners to transcend the boundaries of their own disciplines, whether these be social sciences like economics and geography, or, applied sciences like agronomy, plant biology or civil engineering. However, since most of the contributors are geographers, we find the geographical approach dominating in many of the papers. Emphasis of the authors has generally been on accounting for the essential natural distinctions between regions and the level and type of development which they have achieved historically. Regions have also been differentiated on the basis of landscapes, geo-complexes and eco-systems in order to outline the policies for the rational utilization of natural resources and environmental protection.

The regions on which the Soviet papers have focused are Central Asia and Kazkhastan. These regions have a varied resource base, are disparate in terms of levels of development and, hence, pose diverse issues of resource development. Central Asia is a fairly hot region and is endowed with valuable agricultural resources, specially for the production of heat loving plants. Its resources of natural gas, oil, rare metal ores and hydro-power and its desert and mountain pastures have significant economic importance. The present structure of the region's economy and the prospects for its development are closely linked with the natural resource base, a fact which gives rise to a distinct set of problems related to rational utilization of resources. The same is true for Kazakhastan which occupies about 12 per cent of the territory of USSR and has some industrial complexes of national importance.

The Indian papers are mostly topical and arguments are substantiated with the help of regional case studies which are taken from all over the country. The emphasis has, however, been on the use of water resources, both in the rural and urban settings.

We have devided the 36 papers presented in the colloquium into six sections on the basis of their analytical emphasis. In Section One we have grouped those papers which concern themselves with general issues or specifically regional aspects of resource use. In Sections Two and Three we have brought together papers dealing with hydro-resources, and power resources respectively. The papers in Sections Four and Five are more region specific and focus on the problems of arid and mountainous regions. In the last section are included papers which are essentially policy and planning oriented and deal with the management issues of resource development.

Section One focuses on the regional aspects of resource use and includes six papers which either deal with the general principles of resource use or highlight some of the problems associated with the regional development of resources as productive forces. The general scenario in the developing countries is sketched by Sdasyuk. She argues that some of our global problems have their genesis in the contradictions which are embedded in the process of social development and use of natural systems. These natural systems, due to increasing anthropogenic impact, lose their ability for self regeneration, become degraded and sometimes approach the threshold of irreversibility. Excessive utilization, which is made possible both by advanced technology and by primitive exploitation, also depletes the resource base to the extent that today we are threatened by anthropogenic abiotization of the earth's crust. The situation is more grim in the developing countries located within the tropics which are facing the twin problems of desertification and crisis in the mountains. She points out that no policies for the use of renewable natural resources on the regional basis have been evolved in these countries, although the need for coordination of their use is obvious, especially under increasing ecological stress and devastation of some types of resources in individual regions. The author, in conclusion, highlights the contributions the geographers can make since the strongest characteristic of the geographical science, in her view, is its ability to analyse regional processes and phenomena. Several schemes of regionalization are finally proposed by the author which can be meaningfully used as frameworks while resolving solutions to problems of regional development.

Alayev highlights the main principles of the regional use of resources in the USSR. These are : achievement of self reliance, protection and conservation of nature, integrated use of natural resources, intensification of resource use and unity of management. According to him the use of natural resources is an intervention of society into the natural environment in order to supply the social production by raw materials. This intervention may be rational or irrational. We have to, therefore, ensure that our plans should not only aim at effective exploitation of natural wealth but also at its economical utilization, reproduction and conservation.

Privalovskaya elaborates upon the efforts made by Soviet scholars to evolve schemes of natural-economic regionalization. Most of these schemes reflect some aspects of the interaction of economic activity with the natural environment and may be grouped into three types; firstly, those which are based on natural phenomena and their role in the economy ; secondly, those which are based on the interdependence of natural and economic phenomena, and, thirdly those which are based on economic phenomena and their impact on natural environment. Schemes which are based on the diversity of criteria used can also be identified within these broad types. These schemes help in formulating policies for the effective development of resources in the USSR which is a large country and is characterized by great diversity of natural and socio-economic phenomena.

Dzhurayev discusses the role of economic and geographical regional planning as a basis for the rational use and territorial complex based development of productive forces in the Tajik SSR. In his view the goal of regional planning is to achieve a rational geographic division of labour and a rise in the productivity of that labour. This can be done through the creation of economic geographical complexes like the Tajik Territorial production complex which includes the regions of Gusiar, Vakhsh, Kulyab and Garm. In each of these regions, distinct sub-regions, micro-regions and altitudinal belts can be identified which highlight the regional diversities and justify the regional approach to the planning of natural resources.

The last two papers in this section introduce the Central Asian economic region and the South Tajik Territorial Production Complex. Most of the Soviet papers that follow in this volume are about these regions. Kopanev introduces the Central Asian economic region which consists of the four Soviet Socialist Republics of Uzbek, Kirghiz, Tajik and Turkmen and is one of the 19 large economic regions of the country with 6 per cent of its area and 10 per cent of its population. Like the other Union Republics its constituents also have their own governments and budgets. They specialize in growing and processing cotton and other heat loving plants ; in grassland farming and in agro-based industries on the basis of which they participate as a macro-territory in the national economy. The author also highlights the place and role of macro-economic regions in national planning and discusses the principles which govern their development as an integrated regional complex.

Privalovskaya, Valsova and Taran provide a comprehensive account of the South Tajik Territorial Production Complex and outline the factors which condition its integrated regional development. South Tajikistan, former Bukhara, is one of the most backward regions of Central Asia in terms of socio-economic parameters. In terms of natural climatic conditions it lies in the zone of intra-continental deserts. The region has, however, experienced rapid economic development during the last decade because a territorial production complex, dependent on a distinct resource base of hydro-energy, bio-climatic possibilities of land development, mineral raw material and considerable reserves of labour power has been formed here during the Ninth five year plan (1971-75). A power industrial complex and an agro-industrial complex have already taken shape which form the two production cores of the region and set into motion the process of integrated regional development.

Section Two comprises of those papers which are specifically concerned with the development of water resources. Some of these papers are general and discuss the issues related either to the role of water resources in different facets of the development process or to the management of these resources. The papers coming later in this section are case studies from India or Central Asia. Koronkovich and Nikolayeva discuss the transformation of water resources under the impact of economic activity. They single out the importance of a new school of thought in hydrology which concerns itself with the evaluation and forecasting of the anthropogenic impact, both direct and indirect, of various kinds of human activity on water resources. This impact is guaged through the analysis of spatial hydrological rows, temporal hydrometrological rows or balance methods which are outlined in the paper. The authors also indicate the spatial and temporal unevenness of the allocation of water resources on a territory depending on run off, air humidity, economic activity, and industrial and domestic consumption. The problems arising out of the anthropogenic impact on water resources are also elucidated.

Levintanus comments on the Soviet experience of studying water resources in India and on the expanding scientific and technical cooperation between the two countries. He also highlights the common problems of water resource development in the two countries and suggests that regional forecasts of water consumption would help in the identification of appropriate water development strategies. He outlines the specific factors which regulate exploitation of water resources in India and in conclusion indicates a phased programme of water resource development for the country.

Mavi reviews the techniques of the measurement, evaluation and mapping of hydro-resources. After having emphasized the importance of the accurate measurement and mapping of water resources in every phase of its development, its rational use, redistribution and conservation he critically evaluates the various methods in vogue today. He concludes that most of these methods are not yet refined enough to be taken as true indicators of reality and better and more sophisticated methods have to be developed.

Mathur deals with the negative consequences of irrigation practices and suggests some preventive and remedial measures to overcome them. Taking up the specific case of northern India, he outlines the problems related to faulty irrigation practices such as water logging and soil salinity and alkalinity. He also discusses in detail, the preventive or remedial measures which could be adopted by planners in the region.

Avakyan highlights the role of reservoirs in regional development. Water reservoirs according to the author entail a prompt, multiform and radical transformation of the nature and economy of certain regions and hence their construction should precede sufficient analysis and planning. Systems analysis is an appropriate analytical tool which could be used to study the importance and impact of reservoirs. The author concludes by formulating some basic principles of reservoir construction.

The only paper in this volume dealing specifically with urban areas is that of Alam who inquires into the pollution hazards to water bodies in urban settings. Taking up the cases of Hyderabad which are metropolitan centres with significantly high rates of urban and industrial growth, the author points out that the same dynamic processes which induce resilience in the metropolitan economy by generating high rates of employment and income, also simultaneously enhance environmental pollution, and lead to the growth of industrial slums which disturbs the ecological balance of the city and expose its inhabitants to serious environmental hazards. The pollution caused by each of the industries located in these centres, as well as that caused by humans and animals is discussed in detail. This is followed by a brief survey of the eutrophication of the Dal Lake in Srinagar, Kashmir. In conclusion the author emphasises that in order to maintain the health of the urban population in India, regional planners will have to give due importance to pollution control while preparing development plans of urban regions.

Alikhan takes up the case of regionalization for the management of hydro resources and substantiates her arguments with a case study of the development of the Godavari basin in Andhra Pradesh, India. After giving a brief introduction to the hydro-resource potential in India she opens up the debate on the conflict between linguistic and economic regions and how this conflict comes in the way of regionalization for the optimum management of hydro-resources. She suggests that a compromise between the river valley and administrative boundaries can be affected by constituting River Boards to plan for the management of water resources within a regional framework at the macro level, whilst state boundaries could serve to delineate sub-regions for the purpose of planning and implementation at the meso and micro levels.

The subsequent two papers deal with the water resources in Central Asia. Tsigelnaya puts forth an estimation procedure through the method of water balance which makes it possible to single out and estimate the lithogenic links in water circulation, i.e., run-off in depth and soil moisture, and, also to estimate different sources of water resources in Central Asia. Dukhovny reviews the development of the water economy and the process of land reclamation and analyses the effect these have on the economic and ecological situation in Central Asia. He also singles out the main functions of the agencies which operate a water management complex which is a set of interlinked enterprises and units aimed at creating and utilizing water resources. He illustrates how, on the basis of optimization of basinal cycles, considered in the context of territorial cycles, progressive socio-economic and ecological development of a basin can be ensured through sophisticated irrigation.

Vaksman, Vasilchikova, and Kerzum discuss the salinization and boggying of irrigated lands in Tajikistan and the measures taken to protect them ; enlargement and proper maintenance of existing water networks in the valleys, according to the authors, should be taken up regularly. Ziyadullaiev enquires into the ways of rational use and conservation of the water resources of Uzbekistan where artificial irrigation is the basis for stable and secure farming. He is of the view that in order to increase the efficiency of social production and to provide for further development of the productive forces of Uzbekistan, both in the industrial and agricultural sectors, integrated systems of water use should be developed.

The papers in Section Three concern themselves with the situation of power resources in India and Central Asia. Chakraborty in his paper deals with the production, distribution and consumption of power for rural development in India. He traces the historical relationship between energy resources, technological development and economic growth and elaborates on the sources of energy in the country. He notes that the social base of technology in India is primitive and dominated by the usage of non-mechanical tools and implements and also primitive and manual methods of energy generation. In order to attain rapid economic growth, India has to increase labour productivity and hence has to enhance generation of energy from sources other than human and animal muscle. Indian options on energy development are, however, very limited and there are wide regional variations in the types and quantum of energy used. These variations, according to the author, are determined by the nature of technology in use in the different parts of the country and other socio-political considerations. The author also notes that there is a strong lobby in India in favour of thermal power generation based on coal and petroleum. The lobby for hydro-power, on the other hand, has been weak over the past years. This leads to a discussion of the political economy of power consumption in India in a historical perspective and to an elaboration of the changing pattern of power consumption in the rural areas.

Burkhanova discusses the utilization of power resources

in the Tajik SSR within the perspective of environmental issues. She points out the negative impacts of power industry, specially fuel power industry, which should be given special consideration while formulating development perspectives. She also emphasizes the importance of "enercology" which is the study of the interaction of energy production and ecology. Differentiating between pure and polluting sources of power, she indicates some non-conventional sources of energy, specially for low temperature supply, which can be used to advantage in the Tajik SSR.

Kletselman highlights the role of hydro-power industry in the formation of the South Tajik Territorial Production Complex (ST TPC). Tajikistan stands second in the USSR according to total resources of hydro-power and first according to hydro-power resource per unit of area. It also has the highest economic efficiency in hydro-power production. These advantages have enabled the Republic to develop an industrial agricultural production complex. Studies also indicate that in future, industries which are power intensive in production could locate beneficially in the region. The Nurek and Rogun hydro-power plants would ensure cheap supply of power to all envisaged industries.

Mirzayev, Negmatullayev and G.S. Seleznev investigate into the requirements in the construction of the earth-filled Nurek hydro-electric power station in the Vakhsh region in conditions of high seismicity, intensive deformation of the earth's crust and great and small faults. They also explain the relationship between the changes in water level and the region's seismicity which has been investigated for the first time in the USSR.

The two Soviet and two Indian papers in Section Four deal with the problems of arid regions. On a general plane, Orlovsky discusses the problem of desertification on a global scale and outlines the contributions the Soviet researchers have made to appreciate its problems and find its solution. Arid territories make up 25 per cent of the earth's land surface and provide habitation to 800 million people or 20 per cent of the world's population. Over 200 million hectares of irrigated land, or 14 per cent of the world's croplands is in arid zones.

Desertification is a complex and multifaceted process involving both general geographic aspects and socio-economic and political aspects. However, the major cause of it is man's irrational utilization of water, land and vegetation. USSR has drawn up a whole complex of reclamation measures to fight this problem. The Institute of Deserts of the Turkmanian Academy of Sciences has launched training programmes for developing countries for their graduates.

In the second paper on arid regions in the USSR, Vlasova outlines the ways of optimizing and increasing the productivity of arid farmlands. Emphasizing the necessity of radical socio-economic and political change which only can reduce the constraints in the distribution of food products among individual countries and among social layers within the countries of the world capitalist system, the author points out that the immediate task is to expand food production in the third world and to make them less dependent on food imports. Most of the Third World is beset with the "ecological-agricultural" crisis, land degradation and spreading of desertification. Vlasova outlines the severity of desertification in different countries and proposes that within arid zones the development of irrigated agriculture accompanied with appropriate measures to fight against its negative ecological consequences, is an important way of increasing the productivity of agricultural production. Such an attempt has been succesfully made in the Tajik Republic.

The two Indian papers in this section deal with water management in arid and semi-arid tracts. Brahme concerns herself with the diagnostic aspects of water management in India. The arid areas in India comprise 11.8 per cent and the semi-arid areas, 25 per cent of the total geographical area of the country. Historically some form of irrigation has been practised in these regions. However, with the progress of commercialization of agriculture during the colonial period, the author notes, the concept of protective irrigation was pushed into the background and the productive aspects attained prominence. This inevitably led to changes in the principles of irrigation water management which are harmful for some regions. During the post-independence period, however, irrigation received high priority and a number of irrigation management systems were adopted in the country according to the regional requirements. The author critically discusses some of these systems in operation in terms of surface irrigation and ground water projects and proposes guidelines for the reorganization of irrigation water management, which, in the semi-arid areas, would ensure stability of yields on all farms through protective irrigation. The author strongly emphasizes that all the infrastructural facilities needed for the realization of the full production potential of irrigated agriculture must be provided on the basis of shared capitalization rather than monopolistic appropriation as happens in the country today.

Gosal sets out to develop the prescriptive aspects of water management in the arid and semi-arid tracts of India more specifically the Central and South Western Punjab, where considerable amount of experimental research has been done by agricultural scientists. He first outlines the methods of water management in irrigation farming tracts where along with canal irrigation facilities, tubewell irrigation based on large underground water reserves has beed developed. He notes that in these areas the tendency of the farmers is to over-irrigate the crops. He suggests that optimum irrigation schedules should be prepared for major crops and uniform application of water in the fields by suitable irrigation methods should be ensured. In areas of rainfed agriculture, the author notes, the problems of water management become more challenging. Suitable crop varieties and agro-techniqnes have to be identified. Some of the techniques which hold promise for improving the yield of dry land crops in this region are moisture conservation, securing and maintaining optimum plant population, identifying the best crop sequence, water harvesting, effective soil conservation and afforestation. The author also emphasizes that 'Lab-to-Land' programmes should be taken up effectively for a comprehensive diffusion of the strategies of water management.

The papers in Section Five on resource use in mountainous regions deal with the problems of utilization, conservation and management of resources in Central Asia, Kazakhstan and

Tajikistan. Mamytov highlights the historical conditions under which the eco-systems of the mountain regions have evolved in Central Asia and how the Soviet scientists have after great research, formulated principles of mountain development. The author stresses the necessity of international cooperation which will make it possible to elaborate the scientific basis for an optimum anthropogenic impact on the utilization of mountain resources, specially pastures, forests, water and wild life. International studies of vertical zonality, with temperature and water regimes would also provide a scientific basis for regionalization and economic utilization of mountain resources.

Usmanov and Sapov in their paper provide a model of the interaction of natural and economic systems of the mountainous areas in the River Vakhsh Basin. The region has a complex geological structure and sharply dissected relief. The authors present an aggregative portrait of the natural environment of the region and then a conceptual model of the interaction of a region's nature forming components and the anthropogenic impact on them. Using the systems approach they construct what they call a conceptual "Machine of Knowledge" for a region's integrated development. It is like an imitation model of the dynamics of the natural-anthropogenic complex of the Vakhsh Basin. Anthropogenic impacts are interpreted as disruptions brought in from outside. It is possible, through this model, to foresee different ways of the development of the region's natural resources depending on the type of planned anthropogenic impact. An analysis of different scenarios allows to choose the acceptable variants amenable to the efficient functioning of the eco-systems and preservation of the environment favourable for man.

Mukhabbatov elaborates on the economic-geographical problems of mountain ranges in Tajikistan. According to him weakly developed natural economic zones like the mountain regions have to be developed and brought into productive national economic cycles in order to increase the efficiency of agricultural production in the country. Tajikistan being a mountain Republic with 90 per cent of its area under high altitude agriculture, demands special attention as it is experiencing rapid population growth. Since economic development of the mountains is both a labour and capital intensive venture, more effective ways have to be found to overcome the natural difficulties in the process of development. The major problems in the way of mountain area development of Tajikistan are remoteness, topography, fragmentation of holdings on higher slopes, and lack of production infrastructure. There is need to develop scientific patterns of crop distribution and of agricultural specialization in relation to vertical zonality. Agro-industrial complexes can also be developed based on horticulture and animal breeding.

Badenkov discusses the problems of the development of mountain regions of the USSR within the framework of the project 'mountain eco-systems' under the UNESCO programme "Man and Biosphere". He outline the problems of development of mountain regions, the most important of which are erosion, soil degradation, flows regulation and development of productive forces. He then elaborates the ecosystems of the USSR and explains how the development of resources in each of these has led to problems of ecology. A brief resume of the organization of research in the UNESCO programme is also given.

The papers in Section Six deal with different aspects of development and management of natural resources in Tajikistan and Kirghizia. Zavulunov outlines the development of natural resources and creation of Territorial Production Complexes (TPC) in Tajikistan. He identifies the local and regional TPCs and outlines the problems their planned development should, in time, solve. The mineral resources have been given great importance in the development scheme which the author proposes. Otorbaev and Bayalinov highlight the problems of development of a Regional Complex in Kirghizia. They hold that efficient regional development requires specialization of a region's productive forces in the country's economic system as well as a coordinated development of industries producing a wide range of use values and directly affecting living standards. In a backward region this is possible only through national support and through the utilization of local resources which could be natural, labour or material. Initial backwardness, however, poses problems of insufficient development of social infrastructure, which has to be overcome on a priority basis.

Stanyukovich traces the use of natural resources of the Tajik SSR on the basis of its natural landscapess. He emphasizes the importance of the study of natural landscapes because information about them can help the planners to determine where new settlements, industrial enterprises, agricultural zones and recreational areas are to be located. It will also help them in implementing measures for nature conservation and their rational use. The prerequisite in such an exercise is to develop a scheme of regionalization based on natural characteristics and natural belts. The author identifies 52 principal landscapes by belts in Tajikistan.

The intensification of regional resource use under conditions of high rural population density in Tajikistan has been studied by Umarov. The high growth rates in the Republic are due to the traditional patterns of demographic behaviour. The population is also concentrated in rural areas which have a surplus labour force. This however does not mean that there is rural unemployment because such a condition is not possible under the socialist system. It means labour resources are above the actual requirements of the agrarian industrial production and of rural social infrastructure enterprises. The solution for this dilemma is to intensify the use of regional resources, both human and natural, through integrated target programmes. Intensification here means increased return per unit of production investments with full preservation and even improvement of environmental quality. It also does not preclude expansion of the field of production through the application of recent achievement of science and technology. Emphasis in such regions, Umarov notes, should, however, be on the intensive use of labour resources and on the intensification of conditions for their reproduction. This would gradually promote conditions favourable for increasing mobility of rural population, redistribution of surplus rural labour from the rural sectors to regions of new development or to labour deficient regions of the country.

The management problems of natural resources are taken up by Saidmuradov. The experience of long term forecasting of the development of productive forces in Tajikistan shows that a thorough inventory of vegetation, mineral raw material and hydropower resources determines, to a great extent, the rational development of material resources and of social infrastructure. The author provides a detailed inventory of the vegetation and mineral resources of the Republic, which would help in formulating the current and long-term planning perspectives.

Sanginov in his paper discusses the cultivation of fine fibre cotton in the Central Asian region. Cotton has become an important industrial crop in this region since 1918, and provides raw material for many textile, food, chemical and paper industries. The fine fibre cotton grown here is, in quality, one of the best in the world. Cotton growing here has been made highly mechanized and chemicalized. Collective and state farms here have been opened up where optimal schemes of crop rotation have been introduced. Efforts are being made to increase crop capacity and fibre quality.

Sapozhnikov provides an account of the "Tigrovaya Balka (Tiger Valley)" which is a unique nature reserve located in the lower reaches of Vakhsh river in a dry sub-tropical zone. It is famous all over the world for its Tugai vegetation which has been conserved since 1938 in 48 thousand hectares of land. It has interesting features like flood-plain terraces, sand and clay deserts, dead lakes, semi desert piedmonts and a very unique sequence of flora and fauna and several eco-systems. The nature reserve is connected with Dushambe, the capital of Tajikistan, and has become an important tourist attraction.

We hope that, taken together, these papers would bring to the readers a sense of the importance of natural resources in regional development and would convince them of the need for and importance of, inter-disciplinary and cross-national research in resource planning. Three important aspects of the man-nature-resource relationship have been successfully highlighted in this volume ; firstly, the technological and economic aspect, related to gradual depletion of the earth's resource base; secondly, the ecological aspect, concerned with pollution of the environment and disturbance of natural systems ; and lastly, the socio-political aspects, highlighting the international character of the resource regimes. The papers in this volume also indicate that the deeper their authors have gone into the problems of resource development the more they have had to connect natural factors with technical progress, the depletion of natural resources, impact of industries on the environment and questions of economic development within the framework of political and social conditions in the world.

ATIYA HABEEB KIDWAI

1

RESOURCE USE—REGIONAL PROBLEMS OF THE DEVELOPING COUNTRIES

G.V. Sdasyuk

Some of the very important global problems of our time are linked with the increasing contradiction between social development and natural systems of the Earth. Owing to the ever increasing anthropogenic impact, natural systems lose their ability for self-regeneration, become degraded and sometimes approach the threshold of irreversibility. On the one hand, they get destroyed under the influence of excessive exploitation due to the achievements of the epoch of scientific and technological revolution, and on the other hand they are depleted under the impact of primitive forms of exploitation, which are still practised in most of the formerly colonial and dependent countries, which are also experiencing the "demographic explosion".

Negative man-induced trends, both qualitative and quantitative, are observed in all natural systems. One of the most threatening processes of today is the unprecedented destruction of the biotic substance of the planet—anthropogenic abiotization of the Earth's crust. Represented for more then 99 per cent by vegetation, this biota has already been destroyed by 1/3. According to some estimates, between the 1950's and the end of the 1970's the forested areas of the globe have shrunk twice (from 50 mln sq. km down to 25 mln sq. km). If the present-day trends are conserved, it will again decrease twice by the end of the century. Till the middle of the Twentieth century most of the tree felling was in the temperate belt, now there is large-scale destruction of forests in the tropical and subtropical zones. Their ecosystems are characterized by considerably lower stability. *The centre of gravity of the global ecological problems is gradually shifting more and more to the developing countries*, located within the tropics, where the resources to check these harmful processes are more limited as compared to the developed states.

All natural systems are inseparably linked and form a single biosphere. The chain relationship is quite obvious in the processes of large-scale deforestation, erosion, decline in natural soil fertility, expansion of desertification processes, disastrous natural calamities—droughts, floods, etc. Expansion of desertification, of soil degradation, and in some cases of complete destruction of the biological potential of the Earth is one of the most harmful anthropogenic-natural processes of today.

In the last half a century annually 6-7 mln ha of productive lands are subject to desertification. At the same time, the average population growth rates, which were in the 1970's—1980's at the level of about 80 mln persons will increase upto 90 mln persons by the 1990's (90 per cent of this increase is accounted for by the developing countries). Under these conditions the serious warning given by the report of the UN Conference on Desertification (Nairobi, 1977) appears quite justified : "Estimates of present losses of productive land suggest that the world will lose close to one third of its arable land by the end of the century. Such a loss during a period of unprecedented population growth and increased demands for food could be disastrous" /1, p. 3/.

Desertification became most widely spread in the developing countries, which have vast tracts of arid lands, conserve primitive traditional agricultural practices and have high population growth rates. Well-known are the catastrophic results of the Sahel drought in the beginning of the 1970's and its even more severe outburst in 1984/85, which affected the whole of the African continent, and brought tremendous sufferings to 150 mln people.

Although in other continents the scales of desertification are considerably lower, still this global process has clearly pronounced regional specifics. Investigation of the experiences of individual countries, is very valuable both for developing specific recommendations, and for more general methodological ones. Of special interest is investigation of the Indian experience, since it is the largest among the developing countries, and possesses vast experience in the field of regional planning and development, and a network of scientific-research organization.

Arid tracts account for about 60 per cent of the Indian territory, and include several types. The most arid areas are also the most backward in socio-economic respect. Rajasthan, Kutch, Kathiawar, composing the north-western, most arid zone, were in the colonial period a conglomerate of numerous, minor feudal principalities, semi-isolated from the main state, and extremely backward. Now it is the zone of low-productive agriculture—predominantly of dry farming and nomadic pasturing.

Under weak diversification of the sectoral structure of the economy in the arid regions and limited potential of few cities to absorb rural population, rapid growth of population leads to direct increase of demographic pressure on low-stability ecosystems of these territories. This process becomes clearly accelerated. Thus starting from the 1920's, population growth rates of the Rajasthan state, which includes the main part of the Thar desert area, are above the national average. This acceleration became more obvious since the 1950's, and reached its maximum in 1971-1981 period (32.36% viz the national average of 24.7 per cent). Population of Rajasthan increased from 14 mln in 1941 to 34 mln in 1981, 8 mln of this increase being during the last decade—mean population density in this state reached 100 persons per 1 km^2. India has the most densely populated arid regions in the world.

This socio-demographic processes come together with active cultivation of marginal lands, shrinking of rangelands along with growth of cattle population. The manifold increase in prices for oil products and gasoline in the 1970's produced accelerated destruction of tree-shrub vegetation (and even of root systems) for fuel used for domestic cooking. More large-scale became the use of dried manure for this purpose, thus depriving the fields of this traditional source of organic fertilizer. Thus, *anthropogenic factors of socio-economic backwardness, increased exploi-*

tation by primitive methods undermine the normal cycles of regeneration of natural resources and produce expansion of desertification processes. According to some estimates, over 70 per cent of arid areas of India are under the impact of these factors of landscape degradation. The worst situation is with rangelands, subject to extreme over-pressure of excessive animal population. It is officially recognized, that "although 13 million hectares are classed as 'permanent pastures', these areas are in fact generally without any vegetation on account of either overgrazing or encroachments"/2 p. 344/.

Traditionally, the leading economic activity in arid regions of the majority of the developing countries is animal-breeding. Rapid growth of population is accompanied by still more rapid increase in animal population ; overgrazing produces degradation of natural rangelands, which lose productivity and become the regions of desertification. According to estimates by experts, the carrying capacity of rangelands on our planet has already been exhausted. Rangelands are referred to as the most vulnerable biosystems. The impact of overgrazing on rangelands is felt increasingly in the countries of the African continents, the Near East and Southern Asia. Most rangelands are in the lower stages of degradation. They are of very low productivity, lose their runoff control capability, are subject to erosion, which sprawls to the adjacent territories. Not able to find enough "space" on scanty rangelands, animals produce destructive pressure onto other types of lands. Forest areas especially suffer much from grazing by animals.

The most disastrous ecological effects (in rates of destruction processes and in their territorial span) are produced by deforestation in mountain areas, resulting in *high-mountain desertification.* High-mountain desertification is especially dangerous, because it produces disturbance of normal regeneration cycles of natural resources not only in mountains, but on the vast adjacent plain areas, as well. Thus, the mountain areas, which are the home of only about 10 per cent of the world's population, determine the ecological situation in areas inhabited by half of the world's population.

Advanced stages of degradation are characteristic for high mountain systems of the Himalayas in Asia, for the Andes in South America and for the East-African Highland. Despite their great dissimilarities (to say nothing of the differences in the developing states located within their area) these mountain systems have similar ecological-economic problems of development, their aggregation often referred to as *crisis in mountains.* This crisis is reflected in the increased demographic pressure on high mountain ecosystems ; in the ever increasing deforestation and devegetation ; in their use for fuel ; in cultivation of more and more steep slopes, and also in overgrazing of high-mountain range lands. All this leads to soil erosion, which is especially rapid in high mountain environments, and often results therein complete removal of the soil cover.

The VI Five-Year Plan of Nepal (1980-85) stresses, that "The greatest problem facing the country today is the critical economy of the mountainous region where the majority of the people live at subsistence level. As production could not keep pace with the growth of population, the trend towards converting pasturage and forest into arable land was intensified. In consequence the ecological balance was upset, productivity was reduced and the forests of the Tarai were mercilessly ravaged by the immigrants in their reckless quest for employment and food." Moreover, for the Nepalese population wood is practically the only source of fuel. As a result of felling for fuel and clearing for arable land in Nepal forested areas have shrunk from 6.4 mln ha in 1964 down to 4 mln ha in 1980, and cover now only 1/4 of the national area, whereas it is recommended to have no less than 2/3 of area under forests in mountainous regions. If the present rates of deforestation is maintained, all the available forests in mountains of Nepal will be destroyed by the 1990's, and those of the Tarai, which have been intensively developed since the beginning of the 1950's, by the end of the century. Deforestation in combination with cultivation of steep slopes results in catastrophic onsetting of erosion. In Nepal it is officially admitted, that : "Natural calamities like soil erosion, land-slide and flood have been on the increase in the country year by year."

Destruction of forests in the Himalayas goes together with natural calamities in the Indo-Gangetic plain, the worlds largest zone of concentration of rural population, as well as in the

Brahmaputra watershed. Impact of floods in India has increased twice in the last decade. While in the beginning of the 1970's periodic floods affected on an average 20 mln ha, by the beginning of the 1980's this area increased to 40 mln ha. In India it is officially admitted, that the losses, which the country is bearing on account of the continuing degradation of its land resources are of staggering dimensions and constitute one of the important threats to its economic progress. According to information of the Ministry of Agriculture (1980), of all the area for which data are available (304 mln ha), 150 mln are subject to severe erosion, 175 mln ha, or close to 60 per cent of area are affected by active processes of degradation.

Huge scales, the need to mobilize a million strong labour army, organizational and technological difficulties, large time span of implementation of the required programmes and projects—*all this makes solution of the problems of optimal use of natural resources, of environmental conservation,* of restoration of of the disturbed cycles of reproduction of natural resources *within the Powers of the state only.* In this connection the importance of scientific perspective for planning integrated ecological-economic development in its regional aspect becomes much greater.

Indian scientists emphasize, that in India, as well as in other developing countries, no policies for the use of renewable natural resources on the regional basis have been developed, although the need for coordination of their use is obvious, especially under increasing ecological stress and devastation of some types of resources in individual regions. In the documents for the Sixth Five Year Plan it was admitted, that the efforts to upgrade environment were implemented in a discordant and fragmented way and that attention was usually focused on individual functions such as transport, water supply, power production, etc. Populated places and their activities were not analysed as a dynamic, organic whole. Now active and coordinated efforts are required for ecologically healthy planning and development of populated places.

In India numerous programmes are developed for regional development : programme for the upliftment of backward areas, which includes mountain and arid territories, special programmes for drought-prone areas, for irrigated areas, programmes for integrated agricultural developmment, etc. Some of them have an ecological component. These programmes are parallel in many aspects in their approach to solving interrelated problems of regional development. They do not however take into account the social background of anthropogenic factors of ecological degradation. There is also no adequate institutional mechanism for implementation of these programmes, as well as for their scientific substantiation.

Modern conceptions of development have become more complicated and versatile. As applied to the developing countries they become more and more related to the tasks of meeting the minimum (essential) needs of population in employment, food supply, water supply, elementary education, elementary health care, housing, and similar "primary" measures of economic and social provision. At the same time, there is a growing awareness of the inseparable relationship of the ecological-economic development. The requirements for scientific research in this field are constantly growing.

The Sixth Five Year Plan of India (1980-1985) for the first time devoted a special chapter for "Environment", where it gives a realistic estimates of the aggravated ecological situation and establishes the important scientific-research tasks in this field. It is also stressed here that the ecological component is part of any type (sector) of economic activities and planning: "The environment must not be considered as just another sector of national development. It should form a crucial guiding dimension for Plans and programmes in each sector". Along with that the negative impact of poverty of the population, on the one hand, and of economic development itself, on the other are underlined. Life of the majority of population in the liberated countries is linked with primary exploitation of natural resources, and therefore, its dependence on the state of this natural-resource base is extremely great.

However, activities for countering natural calamities, traditionally resemble fire fighting. In the 1980's it was officially stated : "The time has come for the formulation of a long term strategy for anticipating, preventing and mitigating disaster. Such a long term strategy would naturally have to form an integral part of the National Plan...." As the priority task fo such a strategy it is suggested "to bring about a scientific and rational approach in the assessment of disasters, their impact and costs of relief." It is considered an extremely important task to establish a National Institute for this purpose, which would look into totality of disaster management from the "socio-economic, agro-climatic, meteorological, administrative and engineering angles."

The suggested programme is significant. This is the response to the most urgent problems of ecological-economic development, characteristic not only of India, but of other developing countries. The social demand of the society is addressed, first and foremost, to science. As a contemporary major problem of development, it belongs to the sphere of inter-disciplinary research ; but in this case a direct "order" is addressed to the geographical science.

One of the strongest (but not always effectively used) characteristic of the geographical science is its high potential for integrating the methodolgy of regional approach to the investigation of regional processes and phenomena.

The integrated approach is required not only to develop the *integrated* regional plans of development but is also necessary to formulate *special* programmes of economic, social, ecological character (for example, to formulate plans to counteract desertification). The need for such "integration" of research and planning is accounted for by the very essence of the current anthropogenic-natural processes, by the inseparable relationship of *ecological-economic* processes of development and their strong dependence on social factors, political systems, value systems of the society, etc.

Coming now to certain methodological recommendations on formulation of regional schemes for integrated development, which aim at optimal use of natural resources, conservation and improvement of the environment, we suggest to consider the following three-fold schemes.

(1) Analysis of the major constants of development in spatial-hierarchical, and temporal aspects ;

(2) The central scheme of structure and stages of studying the major parameters of a region, formulation of alternatives for its development on this basis, as well as of recommendations

aiming to optimize decision-making and implementation ;

(3) Hierarchy of systems of regionalization for planning, of stages of development, and range of mapping scales.

It may be noted that these schemes are predominantly based on the Soviet experience of regionalization for planning and scientific substantiation for regional planning. However, the fruitful experience of the Soviet-Indian collaboration in the field of geography, which counts already over a quarter of a century, reveals, that the Soviet principles of regionalization for planning may be successfully applied in a modified form of investigation of specific conditions of the developing countries.

Scheme No. I*

DIMENSIONS OF RESOURCE ANALYSIS

Temporal Past

Present

Future

Natural Resources
Environmental
Technological
Economic
Social
Political
Institutional

Micro Mezo Macro National International

SPATIAL

Modification of Scheme 3 mentioned above

*Modification of Scheme 3.

A PLAN FOR NATIONAL DEVELOPMENT

Research Stages & Problem Definition

Goal Formulation

Analysis of Present Conditions and Forecasting of Major Development Trends

Economic

Production Specialization

Population Manpower Resources

Energy
Transport
Infrastructure

Expected Level

Resource Analysis

Material Manpower Social Potential

Level and Structure

Verification

Formulation of Alternatives

Elaboration and Assessment of Development Alternatives :

Sectoral and Integrated Programmes

Formulation of Criteria

Economic Alternatives

Territorial Production Complex (TPC)

Assessment of Alternatives

Implementation

Selection and Implementation of the System

Institutional

Problems and Objectives

Alternative Strategies

Resources

Constraints

Management

REGION AND ITS ROLE IN THE COUNTRY

Goals

Social	Ecological
Settlement Pattern	Land Use Pattern, Environmental Conditions and Trends
Social Infrastructure	Natural Hazards
Employment opportunity	
Food Supply	

Energy, Minerals, Water Land, Forest	Territorial Combinations of Natural Resources Specified in Accordance With Available Resources

---

Evaluation and Ranking of Alternative Systems and Optimization of Decision-Making

Social Alternatives Social Programme	Environmental Alternatives Environmental Conservation and Improvement Programme

---

Estimated Consequences	Plan	Implementation	Performance Evaluation

Impact upon other Systems

I. Hierarchy of System of Regions (Areas) for Planning

II. Multi-Level Planning for Integrated Development

Hierarchical Levels					
Marco	National			Country	Not larger than 1 : 1 000 000
Marco	Macro-Regional			Macro Regions General Scheme of Marco-Regional Planning	1 : 500 000
Mezo	High Level	Administrative Regions	(States)	Scheme of Town & Country Planning (T & CP)	1 : 300 000 — 1 : 100 000
Mezo		Administrative Subregion	(States Subregion)	Project of T & CP	1 : 100 000 1 : 50 000
Mezo		Industrial Node		Project of Industrial Node	1 : 25 000 1 : 10 000
Micro	Low Level	Low-Admistrative Region	District Planning	Project of Areal Plan. for Adm. Regions	1 : 50 000 1 : 25 000 —
Micro	Town & Country Planning	Town Residential Area Micro-Region (Taluka & Block) Industrial (Rural) Areas	Master Plan Taluka & Block-level Planning Master Plan Master Plan		1 : 10 000 1 : 5 000 1 : 2 000 1 : 1 000 1 : 500 1 : 5 000 1 : 2 000 1 : 2 000
Micro		Industrial Units	(Part of Techn. Proj.)		1 : 1 000
	Planning of Indust. Units & Indust. Groups	Regional (Areal) Units	Stage of Regional Planning		Scale of Maping

Extensive use of natural resources has mostly exhausted them. More intensive production, optimal use of nature including environmental conservation—this is *the new modern type of ecological-economic development*. These are the necessary preconditions for further progress and the very existence of civilization.

K. Marx wrote : "Man lives on account of nature. This means, that nature is his body, with which man has to be in permanent communication, in order not to die." This "communication", as is known, is realized, first and foremost, in labour which is the process, in which man directs, regulates and controls his own activities and the exchanges between himself and nature.

More and more true appears the opinion, that in the *society-nature* interaction, the resources and *potential* of the latter are *in the state of extreme stress, and the main reserves of development of civilization* are in *society itself*. Disturbance of normal reproduction cycles of the renewable natural resources because of extreme anthropogenic impacts, degradation of natural landscape, large-scale deforestation and desertification—threaten on a global scale and have been especially vigorously manifest in the developing countries. Geographers are urged to actively study these global problems, which have clearly pronounced regional character, and to contribute to their solution. This problem should be, apparently, referred to as *the theme of utmost priority in the system of modern geographical research*.

Specially acute and fast disturbances are characteristic of the anthropogenic-natural processes in mountain systems (which affect the vast adjacent lowland areas) and in arid regions. Problems of environmental conservation and reclamation in these regions include the need to intensify use of their natural potential, increase of production and upgrading of the level of well-being of population. These problems have *regional-integrated character*, they are organically interlinked and interdependent, thus accounting for *the need to formulate integrated regional* plans of development to solve *not only integrated problems of development, but the sectoral (ones) as well*.

Time is one of the most limited, and absolutely "non-renewable" resources of development. When studying scales and stages of degradation of natural landscapes, it is especially important to define and prevent the threshold of irreversibility. From this angle, it appears a priority task to develop methodology of forecasting these processes, and to compile "Red Maps" of the regions, which indicate the threshold state of landscape degradation, devastation and transformation of lands into "deserts".

The Soviet-Indian scientific collaboration in the field of geography, has moved on from the stage of publishing collaborative articles (1960-1966) to books on problems of regionalization and urbanization (1965-1976) to the holding of bilateral seminars on problems of regional development and rational use of nature (1976-1985) and to the study of analogous regions like mountain and arid territories. It is quite obvious, that development of these research projects of extremely high practical and methodological importance may be not only mutually beneficial, but may raise international response as well.

REFERENCES

1. *Integrated Regional Schemes to Combat Desertification Guidelines.* Centre of International Projects of GKNT. Moscow, 1982.
2. Marks, K, Engles F., Sochineniya (Collection of works), t. 23 (in Russian).
3. Mitchell B., *Geography and Resource Analysis.* Longman, London, 1984.
4. Pertsik Ye. N., Rayonnaya planirovka (Regional Planning). M., 1973 (in Russian).
5. *Report on Development of Backward Hill Areas.* PC, New Delhi, 1981.
6. *Report on Drought Prone Areas and Desert Areas.* PC, New Delhi, 1981.
7. *Sixth Five Year Plan,* 1980-1985. Govt. of India, PC, 1980.
8. *Sixth Five Year Plan,* 1980-1985, Nepal. Kathmandu, 1980.
9. United Nations Conference on Desertification. Round-up, Plan of Action and Resolutions, UN, New York, 1978.

2

MAIN PRINCIPLES OF THE REGIONAL USE OF RESOURCES

E.B. Alayev

Resource availability is a necessary condition for any development. If the territory is a material base of the political sovereignty of a state, the resources (first of all, natural resources) are material base of economic independency of a state. Simultaneously the use of resources represents the main sphere of interaction between man, economy and nature.

The notion "nature" embraces for us the set of non man-made material conditions (matter, processes, states) for the life of human society ; as opposed to society, nature is firstly an "operational basis" of its activity and development and, secondly a source of all the primary resources of social production. Man is also part of nature, but when we speak about the use of natural resources, we exclude deliberately both man and man-made creations.

Development of natural elements occurs according to natural laws. The unity between man and nature is reflected, in particular, in the fact that the same objective laws are applied to the man-made objects (constructions, buildings, machines, technological processes, etc.), but here the laws act in specific, artificial conditions which man has to reproduce continuously in order to support their functioning. From the ecological point of view the notion "nature" includes also those man-made objects which are dominated by natural laws in their functioning such as reservoirs, canals, cultivated lands, parks and artificial plantations, dams, etc.

Permanent exchange of matter between man and nature is a law regulating social production (K. Marx). These man-nature relations are embraced by the concepts "use of natural resources" and "conservation of nature". Use of natural resources is an intervention of society into nature (natural environment) in order to supply the social production by raw materials. This general term may be divided into particular terms like use of water, of land, of forests, etc.

One distinguishes rational and irrational use of resources. Rational use foresees not only effective exploitation of natural wealth, but also its economical utilization (non-renewable resources), reproduction (renewable resources) and conservation of conditions for that reproduction. This human activity is called conservation of nature (when this activity is directed towards nature) or environmental reclamation (when this activity is directed towards improvement of conditions for society and production).

"Natural resources are bodies and forces of nature which at the contemporary level of development of productive forces and of knowledge may be utilized to meet the demands of human society in a form of direct participation in the material activity" (Soviet geographer A.Mints). One distinguishes several kinds of resources such as minerals, water, land and soil, biological and territorial resources. Power resources are often considered separately. According to their specific qualities resources may be renewable and non-renewable.

Natural resources are the main material base of regional development. In some cases, deficit of natural resources may be compensated by other resources like man-power, advantageous geographical location, etc. But this is true in some specific cases only. Fortunately, almost each region possesses natural resources, although in different ways. In most cases natural resources determine specialization of a region and its participation in territorial division of labour.

The USSR has rich experience of organization of rational use of natural resources. Here some general principles are elaborated, from which we may emphasize six : self-reliance, protection, conservation, complex utilization, intensive utilization and unity of resource management.

Self-reliance is rather a national policy issue and not a regional one. Its essence consists in the reality that the Soviet Union, which emerged as the first state of workers under conditions of capitalist encirclement and permanent danger of agression and economic boycott, was obliged to prospect and to exploit practically all the resources necesssary for its economy and defence. This policy was fully justified and its validity was confirmed by the victory of the USSR over the agressor in the World War II. This principle is however still valid, despite the mutual friendship of socialist nations and participation of the Soviet in the international division of labour. Key resources important for defence capacity and stability of economy, for both modern and future periods still have to be developed on the basis of self-reliance.

Protection of nature is a leading principle in the socialist nature-use policy. "In the interests of the present and future generations, the necessary steps are taken in the USSR to protect and make scientific, rational use of the land, its mineral and water resources, and its plant and animal kingdoms ; to preserve the purity of air and water, to ensure reproduction of natural wealth, and improve the human environment" (Constitution of the USSR, Article 18). "Citizens of the USSR are obliged to protect nature and conserve its riches" (Ibidem, Articles 67). A system of juridical laws to protect the nature and its components is elaborated and approved in the USSR. In the economic policy three main methods to protect nature are practiced : rational location of projects, introduction of purification equipment ("ecoequipment"), and introduction of new nature-protecting and resource-economizing technologies ("ecotechnologies"). Each project of new construction or reconstruction is checked by environmental experts. When intervention into natural landscape (natural ecosystem) is inevitable, a principle is obeyed i.e., to transfer an ecosystem onto a new, more effective and stable level of functioning.

Conservation of nature in Russian has a narrower meaning as compared to in English. This principle is directed mainly towards stability of the global natural processes of reproduction of natural resources, especially biological ones. Creation of reserved territories (national and natural parks, reservations, etc.) has accelerated in recent decades. There is an attempt to pass from creation of isolated reservations to creation of their systems, in order to increase their regional, national and global functions.

Complex (*integrated*) *use of natural resources* is a policy of economic nature (raising of efficacy of resource use) as well as ecological nature (diminishing of wastes which deteriorate environment). Implementation of that principle meets certain difficulties, bearing in mind the sectoral (ministerial) management of economy in the USSR. Some experiments are now in practice in order to organize complex exploitation and utilization of all components of ores in major and multicomponent basins.

Intensification of the resource use is a principle which corresponds to the stage of developed socialism. It is implied in the principle of complex use. Intensification signifies the achievment of more results by using less resources. For example, multi-purpose utilization of the same natural resource (water—for supply, for power, for transport, for recreation ; forests—for industry, for recreation, for river protection, etc.). Although the USSR is the biggest country of the world still it faces the problem of intensive use of its territory, one of the most important resources given by nature.

In planning and in pre-plan investigations, one emphasizes not only the key resources, but also the so-called deficit resources, and each region elaborates a specific pattern of using the latter more effectively and profitably.

Principle of management unity in resource utilization. Implementation of this principle creates organisational prerequisites for rational exploitation. The juridical base for that exists in the USSR, for all the natural wealth. Land, its minerals, waters and forests—are the exclusive property of the state (Constitution, Article 11). The jurisdiction of the state determines the main lines and general measures for rational exploitation and conservation of mineral resources (Ibidem, Article 73). Local bodies of state authority and administration are obliged to exercise control over observance of legislation as regrads land use, and conservation of nature (Ibidem, Article 147).

For some key resources a united, centralized management is introduced ; for example, Regional agro-industrial associations (Russian abbreviature : RAPO) seek to give the main productive force—land—in the hands of a single body. Analogous measures for environment are also being undertaken.

The main principles of rational resource use in a region have been elaborated above. All of them are subordinate to the general objective i.e., to effectively provide the national economy and the society with all necessary resources without harming the friendship with the "mother nature". One should harness her natural processes for development.

[illegible] Regulation of Resources [illegible] 19

[illegible] of legislation as [illegible] in Article

[illegible] management [illegible]

[illegible]

3

NATURAL-ECONOMIC REGIONALIZATION
Soviet Experience

G.A. Privalovskaya

In the present stage of the development of human society one of the global problems is to meet its long-term requirements in different natural resources. The problem arises because of lack of balance between the constantly growing consumption of resources and the available reserves of them. The problem becomes specific also due to the fact that in the past the influence of exponentially increasing consumption of natural resorces on the environment has been underestimated. The present level of scientific and technological progress enhances large scale development of natural resources, but it does not always, and everywhere, allow to sensibly coordinate different interests of their multipurpose use. For instance, it is known that forests are the source of raw materials and fuel, but at the same time they are a regulator of the heat and water regime. Likewise water is a resource as well as a factor of increase of land productivity and of improvement of the environment. But predominantly, fuel-raw material orientation of the natural resource utilization has led to deterioration of the self-protection properties of some of them and thus the further development of fuel-power, mining and timber industries, as well as of agriculture, at the modern level of scientific and technological progress, causes deterioration of the environment.

This problem is of a distinct social character. In the USSR it is understood as a problem of overcoming natural-resource limitations, which have evolved historically under conditions of spatial disparities among the regions of active economic activity, on the one hand, and concentration of the main reserves of fuel, power, water, forest, non-ferrous ores and other resources, on the other. These resources are the natural source of production of over 90 per cent of gross product in the major sectors of industry of the USSR, on which depend the high end results of the whole economic development of the country. But it is these resources which, due to high and stable rates of annual growth of the mining industry's product (between 3 and 5%) during 20 to 25 years, that have turned out to be close to exhaustion in the most developed regions of the country. To provide for the further requirements of the economy in fuel, power and raw materials, it is necessary to develop new sources, difficult of access, in the northern and eastern regions or those at greater depths in the European USSR. This will lead to a situation when extraction of a large group of natural resources will become more expensive.

The rapid growth of industrial production on the basis of the use of fuel-power and raw material resources makes more acute the problem of providing water for the economy as a whole. In great measure the problem is aggravated further because of the natural distribution of water resources within the country, which does not coincide with the geography of its economy : in regions where there is deficit of water 70 per cent of industrial and 75 per cent of agricultural production of the country is located. The overcoming of water-resource limitations is also a complicated economic task.

An economical use of land as a specific resource, limited in its size, is becoming ever more necessary. The priority of the agricultural use of the territory is indisputable. But because of a considerable spatial overlapping of the main agricultural zone of the country and the regions of industrial development it comes into conflict with the interests of other sectors of the economy. In this respect great damage to agriculture is particularly done by mining industry. For instance, by the beginning of the 1970's, the area damaged by mining works within the agricultural zone reached 450,000,000 ha. That is why, decrease of the areas withdrawn from the agricultural cycle and their recultivation with the purpose of returning them to this cycle are among the most important tasks, associated with the overcoming of natural-resource limitations of economic development.

Regarding the above, a strict inventory and economic evaluation of natural resources becomes an all-state task. It is not an accident that during the decade from 1967 to 1977 the fundamental legislation of the USSR and of Union Republics about the use and protection of natural resources was adopted, which, in particular, foresees creation and introduction of four state cadastres—for lands waters, forests, and minerals. The cadastre, service, providing the society with knowledge about its natural-resource potential, economic evaluation and the possibilities for the use of natural resources, including legislative questions, is of paramount importance for compiling prognostic Master Schemes of an efficient use of their individual kinds and groups.

Basing on the study and evaluation of definite kinds and groups of natural resources by different regions, these schemes synthesize the results keeping in view the All-Union interests of their use. At the same time, they themselves are the initial basis for regionalization and of the evaluation of different resources, in correspondence with non-uniform possibilities and tasks of individual regions in the matter of meeting the All-Union needs. That is why such schemes are mainly aimed at co-ordination of general and regional questions of an efficient use of individual resources and of their use. The necessity to co-ordinate these questions among themselves is determined by a complex character of the problem as a whole.

In the USSR the problem of overcoming natural-resource limitations of economic development presupposes the necessity of the following : effective development of resources difficult of access and difficult to extract ; cardinal improvement of their quality and increase of their productivity ; all possible intensification of their use in the sphere of material and non-material production ; preservation of favourable environment taking into account the interests of the present population and its future generations.

The complex character of the problem requires a comprehensive approach to its solution at the All-Union, regional and local levels, and this, in its turn, preconditions the necessity to elaborate not only sectoral, but also integral resource schemes. One cannot correctly judge the efficiency of location of individual sectors without taking into account its relations with other sectors of the economy, and similar to it, it is impossible to resolve the problem of efficient use of natural resources within the framework of an individual sectoral resource scheme. In great measure this is accounted for by the fact that natural resources are distributed in space not in isolation from each other, but they form territorial combinations differing in composition, sizes and availability of resources. Within the limits of such combinations, an efficient use of certain resources may turn to be irrational for some (for instance, the use of forests is irrational for water and land resources, that of water resources—for forest and land, of mineral, for land, water and forest resources, etc.). Thus, special knowledge is needed to weaken as much as possible the conflict situations arising in a number of regions between different users of resources. The priorities may be decided upon only in the framework of integral schemes of efficient use of natural resources in order to ensure that while, meeting the All-Union needs in one resource, we do not do irreversible damage to other resources. Special targets that have been included into the annual and long-term spatial plans of economic development during the last decade is a certain step towards the creation of integral schemes of efficient use and conservation of natural resources at regional levels. The purpose of the corresponding sections of these plans is to provide for an essential lowering of the negative influence of industrial enterprises, of agriculture, transport and urban services on the environment, as well as to preserve and increase the resource potential by way of an efficient use of natural resources. This goal may be attained on the basis of co-ordination of production with the availability of natural resources and with the level of their consumption and the state of the environment in different regions of the country. But even with such a comprehensive approach, on the regional level, the problem of efficient use of nature cannot be completely solved. An integral scheme of efficient use of natural resources of the USSR as a whole is needed.

The mutual co-ordination of the All-Union, sectoral, and

regional integral schemes of efficient use of natural resources, as well as their interlinkage with different pre-plan and plan elaborations, are possible on the basis of an All-Union concept of efficient nature use, on the one hand, and on a specially worked out scheme of the country's regionalization.

The use of nature as an object of planning represents quite a heterogeneous sphere of social productive activity, directed to the satisfaction of the needs of the present and future generations in the quality and diversity of the natural environment and to the improvement of the natural resource utilization as a factor of the growth of social production.[1] This sphere includes four groups of the sectors of the economy, differing in social functions, in their relation with nature and in the tasks of the use of nature.

The resource producing sectors of the economy (geological prospecting, forestry, water economy, and some kinds of agriculture) provide for long-term requirements of society in different natural resources. Their main task in the use of nature is to achieve the utmost growth of reserves and to increase the productivity of resources, prepared for exploitation, with minimum capital investments.

The sectors of material production which rely on the development of the nature-resource potential of the country (mining and manufacturing industries, agriculture, fisheries, etc. meet the needs of society in fuel, raw materials, energy, and industrial products. Their task is to exploit as fully as possible the resources, that have already been prepared for development and extracted, without socially unjustified losses in different stages of their extraction, processing, transportation and utilization. The efficiency of resource use by these sectors is determined by the volume of final product (and in the last instance—national income) per unit of prospected or extracted resources with minimal investments.

The nature conserving sectors of the economy (forestry, water management, hydromeliorative industry and others) are to increase the quality and the diversity of environments for the benefit of present and future generations of people.

The sectors of productive and, in considerable measure, of non-productive spheres interacting with the environment in the process of realization of their different social functions, provide society with different finished products and services. In the matter of nature utilization their main task is to limit their negative influence on the environment by those threshold states beyond which, the destructive natural processes lead to irreversible changes. The last two of above four economic sectors, as objects of planning for nature use, are specific because of the time gap between the realization of capital-consuming reconstructive-transformation or nature conserving measures and the more or less remote results. Regarding this, of particular importance is co-ordination of research on the forecast of natural environment changes with the search for not only economic, but also social, effectiveness, to which the above kinds of social-productive activity could be oriented.

For such large countries, as the USSR, which within a certain social system are characterized by a great diversity of natural and socio-economic conditions, of great importance is the elaboration of the geographical aspect of the concept of rational use of nature. There is a specific need for a joint analysis of natural and socio-economic processes, phenomena, and factors determining the dynamics of space-time relations among natural complexes and territorial combinations of natural resources, on the one hand, and territorial combinations of different forms of the social organization of production in the above sectors, on the other.

A considerable difficulty in such analysis arises out of the necessity to establish limits and parameters for the spatial systems of the interaction of different kinds of economic activity with the natural environment, which would adequately reflect the space-time features of the real processes. Due to the fact, that the regional specificity of resource tasks and possible ways for their solution depend on the character of this interaction, of great scientific importance is a systems study of its space-time differentiation on the basis of specially elaborated schemes of regionalization.

Soviet geography accumulated considerable experience in elaboration of the schemes of regionalization, reflecting certain aspects of the interaction of economic activity with the natural environment. A review of this experience (see Table 3.1) shows

TABLE 3.1 : **Systematization of different kinds of natural-economic regionalization of the USSR territory**

Fundamentals of regionalization		Propertiesof regionalization	Hierarchy of systematization	Systematization of different kind of regionalization								
Principles of regionalization	Object of regionalization	Correlation of economic and natural objects	Type of regionalization	I			II			III		
		Individual features of natural and economic objects	Subtype of regionalization	1	2...		1	2...		1	2...	
	Subject of regionalization	Applied tasks determining criteria of regionalization	Kind of regionalization	ab. . .p	...	ab...p	...	...	...	...	...	ab...p
	Criteria of regionalization	Indices reflecting the criteria of regionalization	Veriant of regionalization	á... am δ... δm ń... nm	...	...	...	...		...	...	á... am δ... δm ń... nm

that the following three principal types may be distinguished in terms of the objective of regionalization : (1) regionalizations at whose bases there are natural objects, considered and evaluated from the point of view of their role in the economy ; (2) regionalizations with natural and economic objects at the basis, which are considered from the viewpoint of their correlational interdependences ; (3) regionalizations with only economic objects at their basis, which are considered either from the point of view of the impact on the natural environment, or through the prism of the influence of this very environment on themselves. Depending on the individual features of the above objects, each type of regionalization may be divided into subtypes.

Both social and applied tasks serve as subjects of regionalization. One and the same task may be resolved by one or by several types of regionalization and vice versa. One and the same type of regionalizations may be applied to the solving of several definite tasks. The latter predetermine the great diversity of criteria and correspondingly of the kinds of regionalizations of each subtype and type.

The criteria are understood as the principal features for each kind of regionalization, reflecting above all, those characteristics of objects, which are of the greatest significance for the solution of a definite task. For instance, regionalizations of the first type are characterized by priority of natural features, which clearly manifest themselves in definite specific features of different spheres and individual sectors of the economy. In the second two groups of features, are accentuated which illustrate best the density of links between natural and economic objects. In the third type of regionalization priority is given to those properties of economic objects, which allow to correctly judge the degree to which natural environment influences the trends in economic activity and economic systems and, on the contrary, the degree to which different trends of economic activity and systems affect the natural environment. The variety of such properties is reflected in the elaboration of different variants of regionalization.

Special place among the different kinds of regionalization of each type is occupied by evaluation regionalizations—cadastres, taxation, and evaluating regionalization proper. The first two are in great measure characteristic of the first type of regionalization, while the third one—of the second and the third types. Good examples of regionalizations of the first type are the numerous schemes of natural-agricultural regionalization, taking into account different natural indices for a spatial scale. In particular, well known is the experience of a natural-agricultural regionalization of the land resources of the USSR, completed on the scale of the whole country by the middle 1970's.[1,3] The principle of co-ordination of physico-geographical and agricultural approaches was put at the basis of this regionalization with a priority given to bio-ecological properties. The latter include such agroclimatic indices as the coefficient of continentality ; the sum of air temperatures above 10°C, the coefficient of annual atmospheric humidification measured by precipitation evaporation ratio, and the climatic index of biological productivity in points relatively to mean productivity of 100 points. Different combinations and values of these indices, regularly changing under certain natural conditions, serve as the basis for the working out of a multistep scheme of regionalization of the country's land stock by indices of its correspondence to the requirements of certain types of agriculture in location conditions.

The great practical value of this regionalization is, first of all, determined by the possibility of its use by the state land inventory service, for instance, in the matter of elaborating and introducing the land cadastre of the country. Besides, it allows to take into account macro-and meso-level spatial differences of the land stock according to bioclimatic productivity, which is essential for substantiating effective patterns of the development of agriculture under different natural-zonal conditions. But such regionalization does not take into account more local spatial differences in the land stock, as the basis for spatially differentiated systems of agricultural production.

Another subtype, for instance, includes different kinds of natural-meliorative regionalization. Depending on individual tasks, their leading features may be : (1) territorial differentiation of the processes of water and wind erosion and of humidification, conditioning the necessity of corresponding spatially differentiated measures ; (2) meliorative disorder of lands due to their bogging, unsatisfactory, cultural-technical state, and high degree of erosion ; (3) conditions of meliorative improvement of an area, characterized by specific geological, hydrological, engineering-geological, climatic, and other indices ; (4) the need of melioration conditioned by such physico-geographical factors unfavourable for agriculture, whose change as a result of meliorative works provides for effective agricultural production.

The most illustrative examples of regionalization of the second type are as follows :

—schemes of geological-economic regionalization by the degree of correlational dependence between the value of the nature-resource potential and its economic role, the latter having been determined by optimization criteria of the functioning of a mining enterprise ;

—schemes of agroclimatic regionalization at the scale of an oblast or Republic, reflecting different quantitative dependence of the yields of each culture on the leading agroclimatic factors ;

—schemes of ecologic-economic regionalization whose necessity is conditioned by direct and feedback links of the anthropogenic transformations of nature with economic activity of people and by the advancement of the concept of an "ecologic-economic system".

Here of the greatest difficulty is weakness of information base due to the absence in the country of an All-Union system of natural-economic monitoring. When working out integral kinds of this type of regionalization one has to rely on a coordinated analysis of a series of sectoral maps, which separately reflect the specificity of interacting natural and economic objects. And here arises the task of joining the boundaries of natural and diverse economic regions when superimposing their networks. Our experience has shown[4] that the less an area is developed, the clearer its natural boundaries ; the higher the development, the clearer delimitation of different kinds of economic activity. That is why, when superimposing different networks of natural and economic regions in weakly developed areas it is expedient to give preference to natural boundaries, in well developed areas—to the boundaries delimiting a definite type of economic development ; in areas of medium development—to both depending on the degree of similarity with neighbouring territories.

Agricultural, economic-geographical, economic-natural, and economic-nature resource regionalizations are examples of the third type. Elaboration of the last two types of regionalization is mainly associated with compilation of project sectoral schemes. As for integral regionalization, it is, on the one hand, hindred by insufficiency of elaboration (both in theoretical and in regional aspects) of the concept of use of nature and, on the other, by the weakness of the methods for integrated economic and extra economic evaluation of spatial combinations of natural resources. Without the solution of these basic questions it is impossible to create constructive schemes of an integral economic-natural and, in particular, of economic-nature-resource regionalization on the scale of the whole country and of its individual regions.

The fundamentals of the suggested variant of a scheme of economic-nature-resource regionalization (as applied to the natural resources for industry) are highlighted in a number of publications including some in English. [5,6] Here we shall give only the following explanations.

Because the character of the use of natural resources depends on a great number of different natural and socio-economic conditions and because it, first of all, influences the development of the economy, a broad approach is needed for the elaboration of a definite network of regions. It can be done by choosing the all-Union system of interaction of the economy's spatial structure with the spatial combinations of natural resources as an object of regionalization.

Differences in the character of this interaction are reflected on a map by specific features of the process of economic development (type, stage, mode of development, degree of development), which is closely connected with use of the nature-resource potential of the developed territory. That is why, the scheme of regionalization in which these specific features are taken into account may be looked upon as a time "section" of the involvement of the country's nature-resource potential in the economic use, and the boundaries of economic resource regions—as the reflection of its spatial unevenness.

The all-Union task aimed at the overcoming of nature-re-

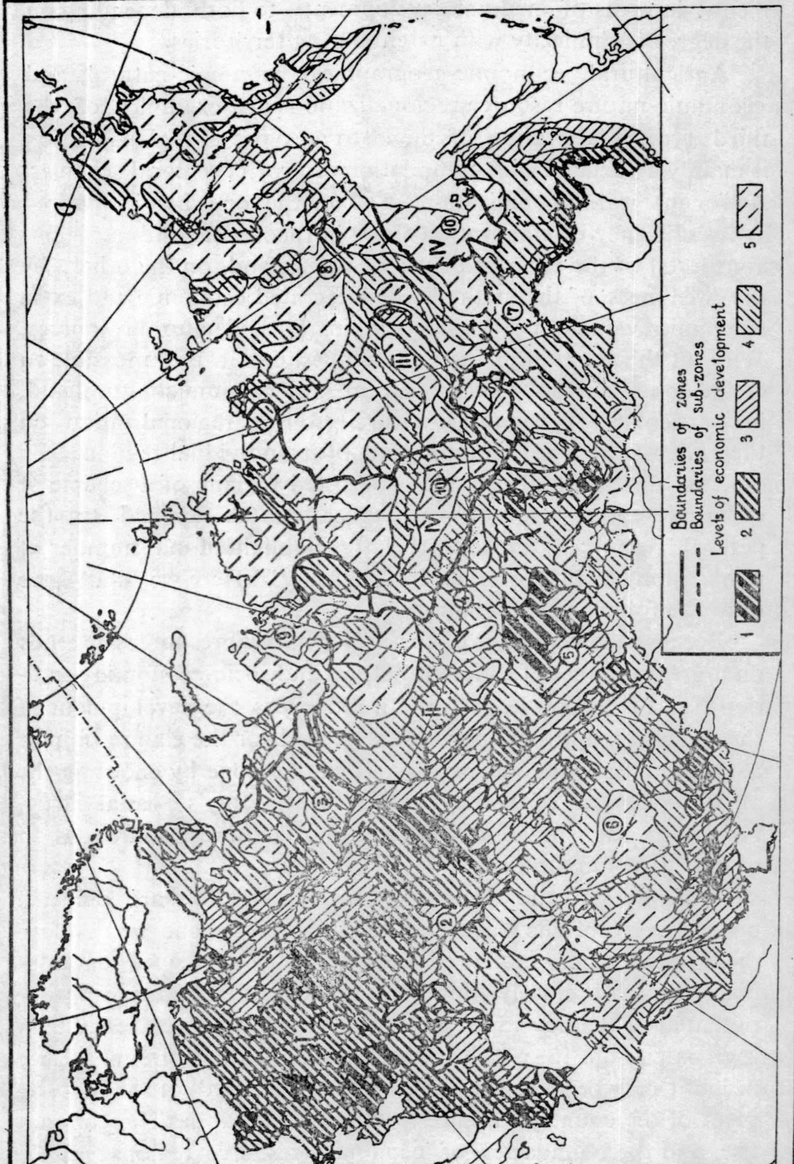

FIG 3.1 : *Level of Economic Development*

TABLE 3.2 : **Possible correlations of intensive and extensive ways of developing natural resources in the USSR***

Economic zones	Total	Economic-nature resource regions: Predominantly with intensive ways	With intensive and extensive ways: intensive predominate	With intensive and extensive ways: extensive predominate	Predominantly with extensive ways	Regions poor in resources
with developed economy	99/100	50/50.5	18/18.2	8/8.1	—	23/23.2
with developing economy	93/100	15/16.1	30/32.2	28/30.2	3/3.2	—
Perspective	34/100	4/11.8	8/23.5	9/26.5	13/38.2	—
reserve	12/100	—	—	4/33.3	8/66.7	—
Total in the USSR	238/100	69/29	56/23.5	49.20.6	24/10.1	40/16.8

*In the cardinal—the number of regions classified by economic zones, in the dominator—the percentage of regions characterized by predomination of certain ways of development of natural resources, in their total number by each zone.

source tension by all possible intensification of the use of natural resources is a subject of regionalization. But transfer to the resource saving strategy, as a basic practical line, is based on a sensible combination of intensive and extensive ways of development of natural resources. As the levels of economic development differ (Fig. 3.1), either the former, or the latter may predominate. Determination of a correct, spatially differentiated correlation of these two ways is very important for the resolving of the above all-Union task. Possible correlations of these ways in different economic zones of the country are shown in Table 3.2.

Criteria of the regionalization are expected perspectives of natural resources reproduction (growth, stabilization, decrease) when the most economically and socially efficient ways are used. It serves as basis for defining priority among the regions participating in the solution of the all-Union task.

REFERENCES

1. Gofnam K.G., Sotsialisticheskoye zemlepol' zovaniye kak obyekt upravleniya (Socialist landuse as an object of management).—*Ekonomika i matematicheskiye metody*, 1979, v. XV, No. 1.
2. Shashko D.I., Glushkova M.I., Rozov N.N.K, razrabotke prirodno-khozyaistvennogo rayonirovaniya zemel'nogo fonda (Towards elaboration of the natural-agricultural regionalization of the land stock).—Sb.nauchn. trudov Gos. NII zemel'nykh resursov , 1977, 1, 17.
3. Prirodno-sel 'skokhozyaistvennoye rayonirovaniye zemel' nogo fonda SSSR. Mashtab 1 : 8000 000. (Natural-agricultural regionalization of the USSR land stock. Scale 1 : 8000 000) ; GUGK pri Sovete Ministrov SSSR. 1984.
4. Karpukhin S.S., Privaloskaya G.A., Romashkevich G.N. Prirodno-khozyaistvennoye rayonirovaniye territorii SSSR dlay tselei aerokosmitcheskikh eksperimental 'nykh issledovaniy (Natural-economic regionalization of the USSR territory for the purposes of aero-space experimental research).—V kn. : II Vsesoyuznaya konferentsiya po ispol' zovaniyu kosmicheskoi informatsii pri reshenii issledovaniya prirodnykh resursov Zemli i okruzhayushchei sredy (materialy konferents., Moskva, 1978). M. TSNIIGAiK, 1980.
5. G.A. Privalovskaya. *Regicnal Development and the Natural Resources of the USSR Geoforum*, 1984, v. 15, N. 1, pp. 39-48.
6. G.A. Privalovskaya. *The concept of the Spatial Organization of Resource-use in Soviet Industry.—Soviet Geography*, 1984, v. XXV, No. 5, pp. 312-327.

4

ECONOMIC AND GEOGRAPHICAL REGIONAL PLANNING AS A BASIS FOR RATIONAL USE AND COMPLEX DEVELOPMENT OF PRODUCTIVE FORCES OF THE TAJIK SSR

K.Dzhurayev

Nature, economic and geographical environment, distribution of population, production of material values, ideology, culture and other factors of development of society are interrelated and interdependent dialectically and historically. Diversified historical, economic and geographical conditions and peculiarities of continents, regions, countries and of their separate parts form a basis for many-sided activity of man. The questions of distribution of labour, distribution and development of productive forces, growth of towns, settlements, of territorial relations are closely connected with peculiarities and diversity of the economic and geographical basis in conditions of a definite mode of production which determines the character of relations of production. Development of scientific and technical progress as a basis for increasing productivity of labour depends on the knowledge of natural laws and on a complex geographical and economic approach in regard to interaction of nature with production on a global, regional and local scales. "The productive force of labour", argued K. Marx, "is determined by diversified circumstances, among others by an average skill level of a worker, by the level of development of science and the degree of its technological application, by the social combination of the productive process, the sizes and efficiency of a means of production, by natural conditions" (K. Marx, F. Engels, Collected Works, v. 3, p. 20). For example, with the growth of capital investments, labour, input, technology and machines, chemical fertilizers and so on, the gross crop-yield crops in this country was 140.1 million tonnes in 1975, 223.4 million tonnes in 1967, 237.4 million tonnes in 1978, 179.2 million tonnes in 1979, and 220.0 million tonnes in 1980.

The influence of a favourable or an unfavourable year in climatic conditions and of a general natural situation on productivity of labour can be shown with examples from other sectors of the economy, country, region and republic. Therefore, alongside the complex investigations of natural conditions, resources and, peculiarities of geo-complexes, it is especially important to have their economic evaluation, as well as a geographic forecast of alternation of favourable and unfavourable years for different regions and zones. Such an approach would favour a dynamic and complex-and-proportionate development of productive forces, the growth in national income and riches of a country.

The economic and geographical basis ; the knowledge of natural and economic conditions and peculiarities of local places ; division and growth of productive labour ; planning and regulation of harmonic interrelation between society and nature are a necessary precondition for rational economic and social development and regional planning of the country, regions and Republics. Regional planning calls for a strict scientific foundation. It is difficult to avoid errors in economic and social development if the scientific, economic and geographical approach to regional planning is substituted with subjectivism, and unsubstantiated decisions.

In developing the theory of the socialist state power, V.I. Lenin was the first man to perceive in regional planning one of the most efficient means of systematic, scientifically well grounded geographical distribution of complex development of productive forces intended for greater economy of social labour and for an increase in the economic efficiency of social production. In this respect the goal of regional planning lies in a rational geographic division of labour and the rise in productivity of labour; creation of optimum (economically and administratively) regions and towns for planning; development and specialization of economy; rationalization of transport and economic ties related with the tasks of the development of the national economy, and regulation of interrelations between society and nature.

The most important tasks of scientific regional planning are creation of conditions and possibilities for opportune solution of questions of development of economy, culture, public education, public health, environment protection and ideological educational and propaganda work for the increase in labour and socio-political activity of all layers of the population in attaining social and economic goals.

The questions of rational distribution of productive forces on the basis of economic and geographical regional planning with the aim of scientific planning, management and development of national economy were repeatedly set forth also at Congresses of the Communist Party (XII-XV, XVI, XVII, XVIII, XIX, XXII, XXIV and XXVIth Congresses) which clearly shows the great importance rendered to these questions on the part of the Central Committee of the CPSU and the Soviet Government. At the XXVIth Congress of the CPSU there was stressed the necessity to provide for improvement of distribution of productive forces, bearing in mind the increase in efficiency of social production on the basis of further specialization and proportionate development of economy of the Union Republics and economic regions within the national economy of this country (Materials of the XXVIth Congress of the CPSU, M., 1981, p. 184).

As far back as in the 1930's, compelled by the economic and geographical conditions, the Tajik complex expedition of the Academy of Sciences of the USSR led by academician N.P. Gorbunov, companion-in-arms of V.I. Lenin, pointed out that "*the execution of eeonomic and geographical investigation and description of the main regions of Tajikistan is needed*" (1, pp. 236-237), because planning, investigation and development of productive forces of individual taxonomic units *starts from physico-economic and geographical descriptions*, investigations, and analysis.

In the Republic, where a powerful energetic base is being built, labour resources grow rapidly, industries develop at a high rate, and so do agriculture, transport, towns and settlements. Economic and geographical regional planning is the core of general planning as well as of rational distribution and development of productive forces.

Singling out scientifically substantiated economic and geographical regions, subregions, microregions and veritcal belts in mountainous places will assist systematic development of labour division which will fix "certain branches of production for definite regions of the country" (K.Marx, F. Engels, Coll.w., v. 23, p. 366).

Plans for economic and social development of the Republic, its regions and provinces, which are being worked out on the basis of strict scientific conceptions of planning and management of national economy for the present and for the future pose problems of all types (economic, agricultural, industrial, administrative and others) of regional planning in the Republic.

In Tajikistan, where every region represents a specific world of nature, population and economy, the improvement of regional planning is of special importance. Economic and geographical regions, subregions, microregions, etc, need to be singled out. The following are the basic factors of their formation :

1. Economic and geographical situation which noticeably influences distribution and development of productive forces.

2. Nature considered as an economic and geographical environment which conditions life and activity of population, or as a natural resource and territorial base for economic and social development. According to the Marxist-Leninist theory, it speeds up or slows down the process of distribution and development of productive forces, even without being its moving force, and at every stage of social development it puts forward specific tasks in the field of nature use. Thus, protection of nature at present is gaining all the more importance for distribution, development, specialization and complex development of productive forces of economico-geographical regions of the Republic and for the increase in

efficiency of use of natural conditions and natural resources. This is especially true of such natural conditions and natural resources of regions and belts which are open to rapid mastering and provide the greatest impact on the national economy.

Participants of the above-mentioned Tajik complex expedition of the Academy of Sciences of the USSR wrote :

> "the mountain-foot belt economically is the most important belt of Tajikistan, both as a base for foodstuffs production, and as a territory for production of fruit for exporting. The main task of the country lies in efforts directed at its conservation and development, at the increase in productivity of its high quality cultures" (1, p. 34).

3. Population as the main productive force. In conditions of the Republic the growth of population and labour resources is one of the preconditions of its economic and social development both in general and in its separate regions and provinces.

Due to the impact of a series of economic and geographical factors, the majority of population, of the Republic's labour resources are concentrated in small warm valleys which represent specific geo-complexes. Development of a powerful base of energy, industry, agriculture and of towns will lead to further essential changes in distribution of productive forces and in the use of labour resources in the regions. Organization of planned transfer of qualified and non-qualified manpower will be required for all this, and in the Republic there exist real possibilities for it. With the scientifically substantiated distribution and development of productive forces, the high density of population and sufficient labour resources will exert positive influence upon the growth rates of national economy sectors, upon formation of a branched structure of national economy, upon levelling of economic and cultural development of provinces and regions of the Republic.

4. Historic, economic and geographical development as a factor of regional planning. An economic and geographical region exists in geographical space and in time. Therefore characteristics of a region should be presented in a historico-economic

aspect. The historical phases, in the concept of an economic region, is of prime importance in the theory of Soviet economic and social geography. When studying the process of change of productive forces and development of an economic and geographical region, it is possible to reveal the forces and factors which determine the essence of the region. Having established the character and direction of action of social and economic forces, and the laws which determine development of an economic and geographical region, one can fully understand and more accurately forecast geographical distribution and development of productive forces both in separate regions and for the Republic as a whole.

5. Reasonable distribution and development of productive forces resting upon a rational use of, natural and labour resources, and of the economic and geographical environment is of crucial importance for the development of countries and regions. An economic and geographical regions, being a part of the Republic, is subjected to the influence of socio-economic factors inherent to the Republic as a whole which determine its complex development. Therefore the study of nature, economic and geographical environment, population, labour resources, towns and settlements and of transport and economic ties is of great import in the analysis of an economic and geographical region.

6. The problem of distribution and development of productive forces, forecasting of the structure of economy, the place of a region in the socio-geographical division of labour is of great value to the concept of an economic and geographical region.

Economic and geographical regions, subregions and microregions should be singled out systematically while considering the distribution and development of productive forces.

7. According to V.I. Lenin mutual production co-ordination of economic components within even a small local place finds clear cut reflection in complex development of productive forces of an economico-geographical region. In decisions of the XXIV, XXV and XXVIth Congresses of the CPSU special significance is given to geo-economic problems of formation of territorial production complexes and agricultural complexes. Creation of such complexes marks a new stage in perfection of

economic and geographical regional planning of the country, and of each and every region and Republic.

Owing to the specific character of geographical situation and orography in Tajikistan characterized by small territories (within the radius of 50 to 100 km) there can develop only different branches of mining and processing industries, agriculture and transport. Due to this geographical and economic formations, develop separately from each other, differing almost in all characteristics. Economic and geographical frames of these geographico-economic territorial units create a network of economic and geographical regions, subregions, microregions and altitude belts of the mountainous part of the Republic. For the efficient use of local natural, material and labour resources and of the economic and geographical environment there can be distinguished the following economico-geographical taxons : a large economic-geographical complex (territorial-production complex), an economic-geographical complex, an economic-geographical district, an economic-geographical region, an economic-geographical subregion, an economic-geographical microregion, an economic—geographical altitudinal (vertical) belt.

The South Tajik Territorial-Production Complex (ST TPC) is a large economic-geographical complex. At the XXVIth Congress of the CPSU there was set forth the task of constructing an electrochemical plant in the South Tajik TPC and of putting into operation of new capacities at the aluminium plant. Specifically stressed was the necessity of the beginning of construction of the Rogun hydro-electric power station and of putting into operation of the Bainazinsk hydro-electric power station. The output of electric power in the Republic was to reach up to 16.0 billion kwt/hours (Materials of the XXVIth Congress of the CPSU, M., 1981, p. 194).

The area of the South Tajik TPC is equal to 53.2 thousand sq. km, which comprises 37.2% of the Territory of Tajikistan. There live over 2.5 million people there. The complex produces more than 64% of the gross national product and about 64% of the national income of the Republic.

It is possible to single out four economic and geographical complexes within that TPC :

1. The Gissar economic-geographical complex (composed of the capital Dushanbe, the Lenino, Gissar. Tursunzade and Ordzhonikidzeabad administrative regions) with an area of about 11 thousand sq. km and with the population of over 1 mil. people.

2. The Vakhsh economy-geographical complex (the Kurgan-Tyubin region) with a population of about 900 thousand people.

3. The Kulyab economic-geographical complex (the Kulyab region) with the territory of 12 thousand sq. km and population of up to 500 thousand people.

4. The Garm (Surhob) economic-geographical complex (composed of the Faizabad, Komsomolabad, Garm and Girgatal administrative regions). Its territory has an area of 18.1 thousand sq. km and population is about 140 thousand people.

The northern part of the Republic forms the Leninabad economic and geographical complex (the region of the same name) with the area of 26.1 thousand sq. km and population of more than 1.3 mil. people.

The eastern part of the Republic embraces the Pamir economic-geographical complex (GBAO), the territory of which amounts to 63.7 thousand sq. km and population reaches the figure of about 140 thousand people.

In every economic-geographical region (complex), according to differences in natural and economic conditions, there can be singled out districts, regions, subregions, microregions and altitude belts, among which individual units have already become and still others can become geo-economic complexes of different scales and authority with the pace of economic and social development.

For example, 5 geo-economic districts can be singled out in the Leninabad economic-geographical complex : the Khodzhent, Kanibadam, Kuramin, Ura-Tyubin and Zeravshan ones. At the same time, in the northern part of the Gissar economico-geographical complex there distinctly stand out not districts, but geoeconomic regions : the Ramit, Rohati, Barzob, Khanaka, Karatag, Shirkent ones. Thus, every geocomplex has its own taxons.

The economic and geographical frames (boundaries) of development of economic-geographical complexes of different scales and authority create a system of geoeconomic districts, regions, subregions, microregions and of altitude belts, on the basis of which there should be perfected the administrative and territorial structure and economic and geographical parameters of rational distribution and development of productive forces of the Tajik SSR.

5

CENTRAL ASIAN ECONOMIC REGION

G.V. Kopanev

Four Soviet Socialist Republics : Uzbek, Kirghiz, Tajik and Turkmen constitute the Central Asian economic region. Like the other Union Republics, they have their own governments, budgets, national Emblems and Flags. All the Republics are divided into oblast (region) and primary divisions which are administrative areas. There are administrative districts in large towns and capitals.

The socio-economic development of the Republics of the Union is carried out in close cooperation and is aimed at solving national social tasks strengthening the common economic complex of the country.

The Central Asian Republics specialize in growing and processing of cotton and other heat-loving plants ; in grassland farming ; and in a wide range of industries connected mainly with the development of agriculture. They share common water and energy resources. This common specialization and sharing of resources have enabled the Central Asian Republics to participate as a macro territory in the national economy of the country.

The Central Asian Republics have an area of 1.277 thousand km^2 (6% of the area of the country) and a population of 29.8 mln people (as on Jan. 1, 1984), i.e., 10% of the population of the country. It is one of the 19 large economic regions and one of the 3 inter-republican regions, the other two being Transcaucasian and Baltic.

The division into large economic regions is connected with

the peculiarities of the social territorial division of labour ; the specificity of the natural and economic conditions and peculiarities of the historical development. These factors primarily determine the pattern of specialization of certain large regions of the country, as well as their development as a stable economic unit capable of meeting the demands of the population and the economy and performing certain functions to attain the goals of the development of the productive forces of the country

The large economic regions (except two whose administrative borders as Union republics coincide i.e.,—Kazakhstan and Byelorussia) have no administrative government bodies. The development of these large economic regions is carried on through state planning and the regulation of inter-regional economic links in accordance with the interests of the development of the economy of the country.

The large economic regions play an important role in planning, especially in the preparations of the pre-plan documents which determine the directions of further development and specialization of the regions. These plans are made in terms of the demands of the main economic tasks and the state of the technical-economic data of different resources in different regions of the country as well as the priority of their development. When the plan is worked out in detail, these tasks are distributed among the Union Republics considering the concrete socio-economic conditions in each of them.

The Central Asian region is one of the largest as far as the population is concerned. The population density here is the highest, especially in the oases region created artificially.

As to the division of social labour, the region is the main cotton producer and the main silk and astrakhan producer. It is also an important supplier of gas and of non-ferrous and rare metals. It is an important food base, providing the common national fund with southern fruit, table grapes, valuable water-melons, melons and gourds both fresh and canned. It is also a major producer of agricultural machinery.

At the same time, the region is supplied with metal, various machines, consumer goods electricity, oil and oil produce.

The economic unity of the region, common specialization and

natural resources, the unity of transport-distribution systems (of energy, gas pipe-lines, water distribution, transport) contribute to the accelerated progress of each of the Union Republics. Management and inter-republican distribution of resources are realized according to the unique plan of the social and economic development of the country by respective ministries and authorities and by republican management bodies within the Republics. Such division of functions makes it possible to provide the most effective combination of industrial and territorial planning.

The economic division of the country into large economic regions makes it possible to analyze most completely the trends and peculiarities of the territorial development, both of the country's economy and that of each individual region. It also permits the analyses of the possibilities of increasing the contribution to the division of social labour by these territorial components. It helps in substantiating the strategy of the interconnected development of the large economic regions in accordance with the tasks of the economic and social development of the country determined by the directive organizations.

The development of the productive forces of a region is firstly due to its all-Union tasks, and secondly due to the complex of social tasks it performs to completely meet the requirements of the population of the region. A complete and effective usage of the resources permits an all-round development of the economy.

The solution of these problems is obtained through the creation of production apparatus made up of various industrial and agricultural enterprises and infrastructural assets. This apparatus is realized and its functioning is ensured by means of material and financial investments through different channels. The enterprises of the Union (of energy, fuel industry, metallurgy, chemical industry, machine-building) are financed by Union ministries and served by their specialists. These large Union enterprises make up the leading part of the productive core of an economic region. The enterprises of local importance are managed by republican ministries and departments.

Union ministries are also responsible for the construction of large-scale water systems regulating water run off, its distribution over the territory and among the main consumers and above all, among vast irrigated lands. They are also responsible for port engineering and the construction of high-voltage power lines and their maintenance. Local bodies look after the distribution of energy, fuel and water within Republics.

The water distribution system includes water sources with the irhydro-schemes ; the main canals as well as transport ; energy and gas pipe-line systems with the corresponding elements of, control and distribution of industry. A complex of systems function within the Central Asian region and adjacent Kazakhstan regions. Objectivelp, Southern Kazakhstan should also have been included into the region under discussion owing to its natural and economic characteristics. However, the national border between the Republics caused the creation of a large independent Kazakhstan economic region with a complex specialization.

Large economic regions represent a new economic-geographical category performing certain functions in terms of the general characteristics of the country's economy, territorial division of labour and transport-economic links.

Central Asia occupies the most southern part of the Asian territory of the USSR. It covers the plains on the eastern coast of the Caspian sea, hilly sandy deserts (the Kara-Kum, the Kizil-Kum, The Moini-Kum, the western piedmont and mountain systems of the Pamirs and Tien Shan, the southern and eastern parts of the Ust Urt plateau, the southern coast of the Aral sea, as well as the northern slopes and piedmont plains of the Kopet Dagh.

A large part of the western region consists of plain areas, hilly sandy massives and small mountain formations, the eastern part is mountainous with very limited areas of land suitable for settlement and farming.

The climate is dry, continental, with very small amount of precipitation in the plain part and somewhat greater in the mountains. The ramified mountain system in the east of the region blocks greater part of the atmospheric precipitation forming here more than 7,000 glaciers within an area of 20,000 km^2 and giving birth to the main rivers of Central Asia.

The vast piedmont plains situated to the west of the mountain systems are most favourable for farming. They are crossed by full-flowing rivers, have rich loess soils and have been tilled by man since ancient times. It is in the valleys of the Amu Darya and Syr Darya that many ancient civilizations were cradled.

The region possesses a number of oil-and-gas-bearing provinces and rich deposits of many useful minerals including non-ferrous, rare and precious metals. According to the estimates of gas deposits, this is the second gasbearing province after Western Siberia.

The development of the region's economy is determined by the vast areas of highly fertile soils, large pasture lands, rich water and hydro-power resources, hydrocarbonic raw materials and various useful minerals.

The main factor determining the development of the economy of Central Asia however, is its people. The region is characterized by a rapid growth of labour and moral potential.

Central Asia possesses 1/5 of the pasture lands and about 1/3 of the irrigated lands of the country. At present, only a little more than 1/3 of the lands suitable for farming (if irrigated) are used in social production. It is though true that part of these potentially usable lands require priliminary melioration as to desalinization, decrease in the level of ground waters, and surface planning. Side by side with irrigated agriculture, dry agriculture is developed here on mountain slopes. Grain and fodder crops are grown on such lands but it is more effective to use them for horticulture and vine-growing. There are about 1 ml hectares of such lands and no more than 1/10 of them are used for dry horticulture and vine-growing.

The problems posed by the water distribution system are becoming increasingly important for determining the main lines of the development of the productive forces of the region. This is due to the limited water run off. Hence, the development of new lands, the distribution of large-scale industrial complexes and the development of towns require great state expenditures on the construction of the water system, the regulation of the water run off, the extraction of ground waters, the desalinization of the mineral water and the territorial redistribution of the water resources.

The Pamirs and Tien Shan have rich hydro-power resources.

These enormous gas resources have made it possible to develop the power industry here by constructing a system of thermoelectric and hydro-electric plants. The use of solar, wind and geothermal energy is becoming increasingly important for smaller scattered users.

This region occupies the third place (after Siberia and the Far East) in the country as to water power. 14% of potentially usable water power are concentrated here. The availability of water power in the south of Tajikistan is the greatest in the country (5 ml kwh per km^2 as compared with 150 thousand kwh average in the country).

In gas production, the region occupies the second place after Western Siberia. A lot of gas is sent to other regions. A number of gas fields are characterized by a high content of ethane, sulphur and other valuable components and the gas is used for producing various chemicals at the gas chemical complex in Uzbekistan. Now the second complex is being built in Turkmenia.

Central Asia is unique in various salt deposits. Large deposits of potash salts are concentrated in the south of Uzbekistan and Turkmenia (3rd place in the country), the Kazilkum desert has a major phosphorite deposit, all the territory is rich in common salt, and the west of Turkmenia (the Kara Bogaz Gol bay) is an inexhaustible source of a complex of dfferent salts. Further to the south there are policomponent deposits developed for a long time. There are large deposits of various limestones, underground waters (iodine, bromine, etc.) in the mountains and deserts of the region. Central Asia is rich in non-ferrous, precious and rare metals.

The mountain valleys and created oases are favourable for people to live there. The region possesses great potentialities to develop recreational facilities of both local and Union importance. Many historical and natural monuments, contemporary architecture and engineering constructions are unique and of interest to tourists from abroad.

The wide ranging programmes for developing new regions and new resources for extensive industrial and civil construction are accompanied with a complex of conservation measures.

However despite the great development of the productive forces of the region and construction of hydraulic engineering projects, the irrigation of lands could not help in influencing the condition of the inner water reservoirs, viz., the Aral sea and lake Issyk-Kul. Much work is being done at present to keep the water level in these reservoirs at the optimal values, to prevent anthropogenic desertification.

The main part of the population (about 3/5) lives in villages. The growth rate of population is the highest in the country. For the period between the censuses of 1959 and 1979 the rural population increased 2 times whereas in the USSR on the whole it increased 1.3 times.

The sex and age structure differs markedly here from the structures of the other regions. Younger age groups are predominant, the proportion of those able to work is lower and the difference between the numbers of men and women is better balanced.

The majority of Uzbeks, Tajiks, Kirghiz and Turkmens living in the USSR live in these territories. There are two autonomous territorial units pertaining to the Union Republics—the Kara-Kalpak Autonomous Soviet Socialist Republic with the population of about 1 million people and the Gorno-Badakhshan Autonomous Region with the population of 0.1 ml people (the former is within the Uzbek SSR and the latter within the Tadjik SSR).

The population in Central Asia is growing faster than in the other regions of the country. It is true of both the town and rural population. The ratio of the urban to rural population has changed little during the past 3 five-year plan periods.

The urbanization process is quite significant. Towns are expanding, many villages aquire the status of towns, the way of life is changing everywhere and an intensive process of rapprochement of town and village, industrial and farm labour is going on. It is manifested in different ways, one of them being the location of small industrial enterprizes, branches and shops in rural settlements.

The main part of the population work in industrialized agriculture and in agro-based industries. About 1/4 of the able population are engaged in the nonproductive sphere and a little more than 1/4 are in industry, transport and construction. Central Asia is also characterized by a high level of education, and of culture, science and health services. The region has 4 republican Academies of sciences, branches of the Union Academy of Agriculture named after V.I. Lenin (VASHNIL) and hundreds of research, design and development institutions. There are 70 higher schools including 5 universities and 356 secondary education establishments. All the capitals and large towns have Russian and national theaters.

The system of settlements reflects the peculiarities of production. It is increasingly characterized by the development of large towns and a decrease in the number of small settlements.

Fergana valley is the largest massif of settlement and about 1/4 of the population live here. The density in certain areas reaches 350 people per 1 km^2. A large massif of settlement is situated in the middle part of the Syr Darya basin, where the towns of Tashkent and Chirik are situated. Other oases are smaller, they are connected with the presence of fertile soils and water sources.

In the postwar period, due to the extensive construction of water distribution systems, a system of new oases was created in the Golodnaya, Karshi, Jizak steppes and along the Kara-Kum Canal in Yavan and Dangarin valleys. On their basis, independent regions were created in some cases (Sydarshsk, Jizak, Kashkadaryin).

At present, there is 1 town in Central Asia with a population of about 1 million people (Tashkent) and three with the population of over 500,000 people (Dushanbe, Frunze, Samarkand).

The basis of agriculture are the arable lands of vast plains and valleys which possess, when irrigated, extremely high bioclimatic potentialities compared with the other regions of the country. Practically all agricultural crops can be grown here, however, preference is given to heat loving crops which cannot be grown in more northern regions.

The main product, however, is cotton. It should be pointed out that Central Asia is the northernmost zone in the world where cotton is grown. More than half of the irrigated lands of the region are used now for cotton growing. This regional specialization in cotton production started as early as the 30's when the country faced the problem of becoming independent in cotton production. Now the USSR is one of the largest cotton producers in the world. 9/10 of the total Union production of raw-cotton is realized in the Central Asian Republics.

This cotton complex is like an organic whole consisting of allied agriculture and industries, transport, and technical and personnel training. Cotton occupies a dominating place in the economy of Central Asia. It permeates everything. All activities of economic planning and the vast majority of work collectives as well as individuals are somehow connected with the factors and conditions of the cotton complex. The cotton complex determines the economic specialization of the region and its place in the division of labour in the Union.

In addition to the cotton complex, other economic complexes have also been developed but these complexes in many respects are linked with the cotton complex.

More than 2/3 of all the irrigated lands of the region are used in the agricultural component of the cotton complex, cotton being grown on about 3 million hectares of this land.

The industrial component is represented by large enterprises of agricultural machine building, producing machines and various technology for cotton processing. The all-Union production of cotton-picking machines is concentrated here. The chemical industry producing fertilizers and chemical weed- and pest-killers for agriculture, specially for cotton is represented by a number of large factories with up-to-date equipment (Navoisk, Samarkand etc.). Cotton is processed by a wide range of enterprises and light industries located in many settlements.

About 2/3 of all the workable population of the region are engaged in the cotton complex. It is one of the largest inter-industrial complexes of the country. At present, large tracts of land are being put to cotton production on the basis of which large territorial-industrial complexes are formed. The share of fine-fiber cotton is growing in the total cotton production.

Other inter-industrial production complexes based on using rich lands are closely connected by the conditions of land and water, labour and material resources.

A large rice complex of Union significance has been recently created. For the last 2-3 five-year plan periods it has become significant in the production of rice in the country. The rice complex is situated mainly in the Kara-Kalpak ASSR and includes factories processing rice-shala and allied enterprises.

The production of fruit, grapes, vegetables, melons, watermelons and gourds has no such definite localization as cotton growing. It is scattered all over the territory of the region and is usually of subservient character. It specializes in individual kinds of this valuable produce depending on the natural-climatic conditions, traditions and customs of the population. In addition there are relatively large concentrations of vineyards and orchards. This is particularly true of mountain regions, on whose sloping lands it is impossible to grow cotton. Thus, in Tadjikistan, Uzbekistan, Kirghizia, large specialized farms have been created, uniting tens of thousands of hectares of vineyards and orchards.

Of special significance are the achievements of the agricultural sector of Tadjikistan where during the last decade, the industrial production of citrus fruit has been created by means of trench agriculture. At present, the Tadjik SSR occupies a leading place among the other Union republics as to the production of lemons.

Large pasture lands have encouraged pasturable livestock breeding. 26 million sheep are grazed on the territory of 60 million hectares of desert and mountain pastures. It cannot however be denied that these are the poorest pastures in the world. In order to feed one sheep, on the average 5-10 hectares of desert land are needed which should also be watered. This makes pasturable livestock breeding very complicated. But it is very effective. It gives the best astrachan in the world, much wool and highly vitaminized meat. The development of a livestock breeding complex involves the construction of many watering-places on pastures. A special service watering pasture has been created.

Central Asia possesses a complex water distribution system. Hence a complete regulation of river run off is necessary which is obtained by means of a system of water reservoirs of a total capacity over 50 km^3, a ramified system of canals distributing water many hundred kilometers away from the sources also supplying all the oases, production complexes and settlement systems. The unique Kara-Kum canal functions here, which is more than 1,000 km long and crosses through the Kara-Kum desert (the second largest after the Sahara) from west to east.

The problems of the development of the water distribution system have been paid special attention since the creation of the Soviet State. In the years of the first five-year plans (the 30's) the system of the Fergana canals was constructed in a very short period (less than a year) through self-help.

Earlier in this paper we discussed only the main inter-industrial complexes based on the agricultural use of land. There are, also, other branches of agricultural production : livestock breeding, silk farming, apiculture and seed growing. There are relatively small but unique farms growing a very valuable crop-liquorice, volatile-oil-bearing plants (kazanlik rose) and herbs.

The Industrial sector is represented not only by agroindustrial complexes but also by many industries and large 'flagship' enterprises in other branches specially of heavy industry.

The fuel-power complex is represented by the use of large gas fields in the lower part of the Amu Darya basin. This gas is used locally for powerful thermal power stations (Mary, Navoyi etc.) and complex processing at the gas-chemical complex. It is also represented by the Angren brown coal basin and a powerful GPS of the same name, by oil extraction on the west of Turkmenia and by a number of oil-refining plants. The system of unique hydropower plants attached to the complex water-engineering systems on the rivers of Central Asia occupies an important place in the generation of electric power. They are the legendary Nurek HPS, Toktogul HPS, Chervak HPS, Baipasin HPS and many others.

The economy of Central Asia and the south of Kazakhstan is served by a unique power system uniting all the main power stations. However, vast desert and mountain areas with small scattered users are supplied with power by means of small local hydraulic, diesel and mobile thermal power plants. Wind, solar and geothermal power plants are beginning to be used.

Having this highly developed system of power supply, the republics of Central Asia get additional electric power from

Kazakhstan.

Ferrous and non-ferrous metallurgies are represented by the Bekabad metallurgical works, Tajik aluminium plant, Kirghiz mining-metallurgical and Uzbek mining-metallurgical combines and many other enterprises.

The engineering industry produces, in addition to agricultural machines, equipment for textile industry (Dushanbe), tip-lorries (Kirghizia), refrigerators (Frunze, Dushanbe, Samarkand), elevators and cine equipment (Samarkand) and a lot of other products for the economy and the population of the region.

Industry producing construction materials is represented by the large Tokman glass plant of Union importance (Kirghizia), a number of concrete plants, concrete product plants and house-building combines.

Consumer goods such as textiles, knitted fabrics, clothing and boot and shoe enterprises, porcelain and delft-ware are manufactured by many industries in accordance with the requirements of the national everyday life. The food industry is a complicated and ramified complex of various enterprises and factories.

The industrial production is developing at a rate which outstrips the Union average. The relationship between the scales of the gross output in agriculture and industry is rapidly changing in favour of industrial production.

A powerful basis for construction has been created in Central Asia, characterized by a high level of industrialization. These are specialized large construction complexes responsible for the construction of high-head water developments, enterprises of heavy industry, as well as large general construction trusts, undertaking immense civic construction to convert towns into beautiful architectural ensembles with comfortable multistoried houses having convenient flats. Complete microregions and new towns as well as large rural settlements are constructed to meet the increasing requirements of the population and to provide the rural population with the condition of life similar to those in town.

Construction is going on everywhere. However, new large projects are concentrated, as a rule, in the regions with high natural resources concentration. Here, new large complexes of industries of Union importance with enterprises and objects serving them, are being erected along with the modern system of settlements. They are called territorial productive complexes (TPC).

According to the decisions of the XXIY, XXY, XXYI Congresses of the CPSU the South-Tajik TPC has begun to be formed in the western piedmont of the Pamirs on the basis of the development of the rich hydropower resources of the Vakhsh river. At present, the first stage has been completed—three industrial systems have been created : The Nurek system on the basis of the Nurek HPS named after L.I. Brezhnev, the Yavan system on the basis of a large electrochemical plant, and the Tursun Zade system on the basis of the Tajik aluminium plant. The complex is developing rapidly. Its second stage of development is connected with the commissioning of even a greater HPS than the Nurek HPS—the Rogun HPS. Its construction started during the X five-year plan period and developed during the current five year plan period.

The South Tajik TPC has three resource 'origins' which have made it possible to develop three most important components of the complex. These are power resources of the rivers Vahksh and Piandzh, whose development started the creation of (1) a power-industrial complex, (2) land-water resources and (3) a high bioclimatic potential allowing the development of an agroindustrial complex growing and processing fine-fiber cotton, heat-loving vegetables and fruit, high quality kinds of table grapes and citrus plants. Considerable labour resources provide for the development of a ramified complex of labour-consuming industries. On the basis of the development and irrigation of large areas of desert lands—territorial production complexes having agroindustrial orientation are created in the Golodnaya, Karshin, Djizak steppes and other regions.

6

THE SOUTH-TAJIK TERRITORIAL PRODUCTION COMPLEX (ST TPC)

G.A. Privalovskaya, T.K. Vlasova and *L.M. Taran*

This paper has been prepared for the use during the field part of the Third Soviet-Indian Symposium on "Utilization, Conservation and Management of Natural Resources for an Integrated Development".*

Today regional development, based on a comprehensive inventory of natural resources, is considered to be one of the essential factors of economic modernization and social progress. And it is no mere chance that the Soviet experience of spatial planning and regional development is of interest to developing countries.

With all the differences in the social orders and socio-economic conditions of countries of different types, one can distinguish common factors and phenomena, whose study makes effective international scientific co-operation in the study of the problems of efficient use and conservation of natural resources.

The South-Tajik Territorial-production Complex is an excellent field for studying such tasks and problems of integrated regional development.

*This paper has been prepared on the basis of booklets by G.V. Kopaneva "The South-Tajik TPC"—M., "Znanie", 1983 and by R.N. Khaidarova "The South-Tajik Territorial-Production Complex"—M., "Znanie", 1973, with the use of some additional meterials and personal observations of the author.

South Tajikistan is the former East Bukhara. Prior to the Soviet Power, this was one of the most backward regions of Central Asia in terms of its socio-economic parameters. Not without reason, East Bukhara was considered to be a backward province of the most backward feudal state—Bukhara Emirate. During the years of the Soviet Power great changes took place in the south of Tajikistan, as well as in the whole Soviet Central Asia. As a result of extensive socialist construction, a multi-sector highly developed economy has been created in this region.

The example of economic development of this territory proves once more the importance of an efficient use of natural resources in the matter of solving current socio-economic tasks.

NATURAL RESOURCES

The area of the South-Tajik Territorial-Production Complex (ST TPC) is 53.3 thousand sq. km (about 37% of the total area of the Tajik SSR). It includes the following four natural-economic zones : Gissar, Vakhsh, Kulyabian, and Garian, differing in natural resources, in the level of development, and in specialization of the economy.

1. Land-climatic resources

Contrary to the adjoining regions of Tajikistan (where 93% of the territory are mountains), within the ST TPC considerable areas are occupied by wide intermontane plains (Gissar, Vakhsh, Kulyab-Pakhar, the lower part of the Kafirnigan plain, Beshket, Yavan, and Dangrian) and low mountains suitable for agriculture. Most intermontane valleys have altitudes between 400 and 850 m. The watersheds dividing them are between 600 and 1,200 m.

Despite a relative homogeneity of climate, the natural climatic conditions in South Tajikistan, which lies in the zone of intra-continental deserts, depend on altitudinal difference. According to temperature conditions and humidity, the following four agro-climatic regions (ACR) are distinguished : Gissar, Makhsh, Kyzylsu, and Karategin-Darvaz. Their borders closely correspond to those of natural-economic zones.

The Gissar ACR occupies the Gissar valley between the ridge of the same name in the north, the Karategin and Surkku crests—in the east, and the northern slopes of the mountains of Rongon, Aktau and Babatag—in the south. Its altitudes are between 600 and 1,200 m. In the widest part of the Gissar valley the Capital of the Tajik SSR—Dushanbe is situated. Here the width of the valley reaches 20 km, and the altitudes above sea level—between 800 and 850 m. The Gissar valley is a large agricultural region of the Republic and is well provided with heat and moisture at all altitudes. The annual sum of precipitation on the average is about 400 to 700 mm. In this ACR climatic conditions allow to grow several kinds of cotton plants and to develop boghar agriculture. Grain, technical and fodder crops are cultivated here. Vegetable growing, cultivation of melons, horticulture and viticulture are very common here.

The Vakhsh ACR is located to the south of the Gissar valley, up to the crests of the Sarsaryak and Tereklitau mountains in the east. Its altitudes are between 600 and 1,200 m. The sum of active temperatures here (about 4,400°C) is the largest in the Republic, which is sufficient for cultivation of fine-fibered cotton and other subtropical cultures. The humidity conditions in the Vakhsh ACR vary : it is comparatively dry (up to 200 mm) in the valley of Kafiringan, while to the east and northeast the amount of precipitation increases and reaches its maximum (500 to 700 mm) in the Yavan valley, where boghar cultivation of grain crops is possible.

The Kyzylsu ACR is situated to the east of the Vakhsh region stretching up to Khazratishokh ridge. Abundance of heat here is combined with good humidity conditions, which are much more favourable than those of the Vakhsh region, but less favourable than in Gissar.

The Karategin-Darvaz ACR embraces practically the whole Garm zone and partially the Gissar one (the Ordzhonikidze-Abad and the Faizabad regions). It is bordered by the ridges of Karategin, Zalaikai, Peter the First and Darvaz, and in the north its border coincides with that of the Republic. Despite the high-mountain relief, the region receives a considerable amount of heat. Humidity conditions vary.

Lands suitable for location of agricultural production, of industrial enterprises and settlements are limited by mountain ridges. However, this limitation within the TPC is not so great as in the adjoining regions of Tajikistan. The area of agricultural lands (including high-mountain pastures) comprises about half of the total area of the Complex—2.58 million ha. The most productive lands—the plowed field and perennial plantations—occupy 0.53 million ha (Table 6.1). The total fund of lands suitable for irrigated agriculture is estimated to be 0.67 million ha. So far a little over half of them have been irrigated. The rest can be used if mechanical uplifting of water at considerable heights is organized (in some places up to 100 m), which may be done with the use of the energy of hydroelectric power stations created here.

Soils of the region are characterized by great diversity and specificity. Their properties, as well as the character of climate change with altitude. Depending on specific features of the temperature regime and humidity, different kinds of sierozems (gray soils) and mountain brown soils are forming. Sierozems are the most widespread types of soils of the piedmont plains. They contain between 1 and 4 per cent of humus, react well to fertilization and irrigation and are easy to cultivate. High harvests of different cultures may be secured on these soils. Uplands are occupied by mountain brown soils with a humus content between 2.5 and 4 per cent.

The Vakhsh, Gissar and Kulyabian valleys are the principal agricultural regions of not only the region under consideration, but also of the whole Tajik SSR. The most fertile soils are found here and in the Orzkhonikidze—Abad region. Of special value for the Republic are considerable areas (0.4 million ha) of boghar plowed (unirrigated) lands and pastures which may be used for growing fruit trees and grapes.

Within the Complex, considerable areas are occupied by rivers, irrigation canals, and water storage reservoirs (about 0.2 million ha). Creation of the Nurek, Rogun and other large water reservoirs, construction of new main line canals and irrigation systems will considerably increase this area.

TABLE 6.1 : **Land resources of South Tajikistan (as of 1979)**

Kind of land resources	Million ha.	Proportion in the total of the Tadjik SSR (%)
	The total stock of lands	
Area	5.33	37.4
Agricultural lands including:	2.58	57.5
plowed fields	0.50	63.2
pastures and hay fields	2.05	56.8
perennial plantations	0.03	56.8
Lands under roads, cattle passes, buildings, streets, squares, and personal plots	0.10	67.9
Water basins	0.20	70.0
Forest and shrubs	0.30	62.0
Mountains, sands, solonchaks, and other lands, which are not used in agriculture	2.15	30.5
	Lands suitable for irrigation	
Total	0.67	63.8
Irrigated	0.40	64.5
Reserve for irrigation	0.27	62.9

Water resources

Regarding water power resources, the territory of the South-Tajik Complex is the richest region. Every square kilometer of it may produce 5 million kwhr of electric energy against the country's average 150 thousand kwhr. Within the STC over 7% of potential water power resources of the USSR are concentrated.

The upper reaches of the Amu Darya river is a peculiar "generator" of water resources. Not less than 2/3 of the water run-off, coming from the glaciers of the Pamirs and giving life to the Republics of Soviet Central Asia, flows through the territory of the South-Tajik TPC. "Keys" to its regulation are here. They are represented by a system of complex hydrotechnical structures, connecting the use of rivers for producing energy with irrigation. Water storage reservoirs of this system are able to provide regulated water run-off, which increases the irrigation potential of the river approximately by 1/5 and, in combination with other water economy measures, allows to expand the areas of irrigation in the basin of the river and of its tributaries nearly by 500 or 600 thousand ha., bringing the total area of irrigated lands to 5 million ha.

The main sources of water of the ST TPC and of the neighbouring territories of the Gorno-Badakhshan Autonomous Oblast, hydrographically united with it, are the rivers of Vakhsh, Pyankzh, Kafiringan with its tributaries and small rivers of the Gissar ridge. The large rivers of South Tajikistan have a mixed glacial and snow alimentation. 80 or 90 per cent of their annual run-off forms during the period of melting of snows and glaciers. Such a run-off regime corresponds to the regime of water consumption in the irrigated agriculture of the region which has for many centuries developed in the basin of the Amu Darya.

The rivers of Kyzylsu, Yakhsu, Ilyak, Yavansu and a number of others, on the resources of which the irrigation of the region's lands to a considerable degree depends, are of snow-rain alimentation. The main part of the water here accumulates in the time of spring floods, a very short period—through March-May. The rest of the year, i.e., during 8 to 10 months the level of water is very low. For providing water to the developing regions, industrial centres, and created agricultural-industrial complexes the necessity of creating an interbasin re-distribution system of the run-off of the rivers most abounding in water arises. For instance, constructions have begun to be erected for transferring part of the Varzob river run-off along the Gissar canal into the basin of Surkhan Darya, from the Pyandzh—to the basin of Kyzylsu, from the Vakhsh—to the Yavan and Dangarin valleys.

The water resources of the Kafiringan basin are not yet fully regulated. In the total annual run-off they are in excess, but in July-September they are in deficit.

The Yavan and the Obikkik valleys do not have necessary resources of water and take it from the Vakhsh river along a special tunnel 7.5 km in length and with the capacity of 65 cu. km a second. The use of the water resources of the Pyankzh river is difficult because of complicated orogenic-geological conditions. On the whole, the territory of the Vakhsh zone is best provided with water. A number of large hydroelectric power stations of the Vakhsh cascade are being built there, and it is possible to create a powerful Pyandzh cascade, whose hydro-electric power stations will produce 100 billion kwhr a year. This will considerably surpass the amount of electric energy produced at present in the whole of Soviet Central Asia.

The hydroelectric power stations built in the South of Tajikistan are multipurpose : they will be able to meet the requirements of water for irrigated cultivation and at the same time will provide cheap electric energy. Alongside the construction of unique hydroelectric power schemes on the Vakhsh river, measures are also taken to increase the seasonal regulation of the run-off of Kyzylsu, Yakhsu and other rivers, by building a number of main line canals.

Besides the resources of the surface water, within the region there are considerable reserves of underground (fresh and mineralized) waters. The operational reserves of fresh water suitable for drinking, for household and industrial use, as well as for irrigation comprise about 1 cu.km. The region of the ST TPC is rich in different mineral waters whose diversity is conditioned by specific geological-structural and hydrogeological conditions. In the number of mineral springs Tajikistan occupies one of the leading places in Soviet Central Asia. Within the territory under consideration various springs have been found : from cold to hot, from fresh to very salty and greatly differing in the mineral and gas composition.

Almost all the mineral springs are concentrated on the southern slope of the Gissar ridge and are represented by siliceous nitrogen warm waters (Khodzha-Obi-Garm, Obi-Garm, Tamdy-Kul', Yavros and others) by hydrosulfide sulfate-chloride sodium waters (Shaambary), and by cold, carbonate ones (Sangkhog). Mineral waters with valuable properties are most important for creating resorts. The medicinal importance of the waters increases due to the content in them of radon, hydrogen sulfide, nitrogen and other gases Very important are also muds found on the bottoms of salty lakes. These resources serve as a favourable prerequisite for the creation of a large All-Union medicinal-resort zones. A large water storage reservoir of the Rogun hydroelectric power station built at the height of the Issyk-Kul' lake (1,300 m), in combination with deposits of radon waters and with favourable natural climatic conditions (a considerable amount of atmospheric precipitation —between 500 and 600 mm) allows to form here a sanitary-rehabilitation zone of a regional and even All-Union significance, which will service not only the regions of Soviet Central Asia, but also those of Kazakhstan and Siberia. It will benefit from it proximity to Dushanbe (about 100 km).

Mineral raw material resources

Utilization of mineral raw material resources is one of the principal factors in the formation of the South-Tajik Territorial-Production Complex. Fuel-power resources of the ST TPC are represented by oil and gas. The explored deposits of gas, coal, oil shales and peat are not great and industrially not very significant. Explorations of oil-and gas-bearing deposits in South Tajikistan have shown five large tectonic zones—Dushanbe, Vakhsh, Kafirnigan, Obi-Garm, and Kulyabian. Over 120 anticlinal structures bearing oil and gas have been discovered, in which there are three gas (Komsomol'sk, Andygen, and Kyzyl-Tumshuk), three oil (Kichik-Bel', Akbash-Adyr, and Kurgancha) and one oil-gas (Shaambary) deposit. At the end of 1970 geologists proved that the Upper Cretaceous deposits in the Kulyab zone on the Beshtentak structure are gas-bearing. Extraction of oil and natural gas in South Tajikistan began in 1964. In 1970 the output of natural gas was 318,000,000 cu.m and that of oil—132,000 tonnes.

The major consumers of natural gas at present are the Vakhsh Nitrate Fertilizer Plant, the Dushanbe Thermoelectric Power Station, and the Dushanbe Cement Plant. Part of the extracted gas is used by population for domestic purposes. The needs of the STTPC in natural gas are not met by the local output. Due to this, the Resolutions of the 24th CPSU Congress provided for construction of a main gas pipeline 300 km long, piping the Afghan gas to Dushanbe.

In terms of the explored reserves of raw materials for chemical industry, South Tajikistan occupies one of the leading places in the Republic. The creation of chemical industry in the STC has become possible thanks to huge reserves here of salt, limestones, and dolomites and to the availability of cheap electric power.

Carbonate rocks (limestones and dolomites) and salt are the principal mineral raw materials for chemical industry. By its explored reserves of limestones and dolomites the STC occupies one of the leading places in the Soviet Union. Of the 11 deposits of common salt 3 have been explored, the rest are not studied enough yet. Total reserves of common salt may provide for the requirements of large chemical enterprises in this raw material.

The ST TPC also has considerable reserves of mineral raw materials used in the production of building materials. Dozens of deposits of clays and loams are used for producing brick, porous clay filler, limestones, and dolomites. Lime, gypsum, sand-gravel, building and facing stones are also available.

A convenient combination of these deposits and their location near the sources of cheap electric power permitted an expedient construction of the Yavan Electro-Chemical Combine. Its raw material base includes the limestones of the Tsuskhur deposit, the dolomites of the Yavan and the common salt of the Tut-Bulak deposits, whose reserves will provide for the needs of the Combine for many decades. The salt available in this region is practically unlimited.

Within the ST TPC raw material used for aluminium has been found. These are the nepheline syenites of the Turpi deposit. They are a complex raw material, whose processing will allow to use its components and to produce alumina, cement and a number of chemical products. The region also has the potential for development of a tungsten industry. Of considerable interest is the Maikhurin tungsten deposit, situated near the southern slope of the Gissar ridge. Its ores are complex, containing, besides tungsten, zinc, cadmium, and indium, which makes them still more valuable. Exploration of this deposit continues revealing great possibilities for its industrial use. A highly profitable mining enterprise may be created here.

POPULATION

The South Tajik Territorial-Production Complex is situated

in the densely populated region of the Republic. As of January 1,1981, 2,623,000 people lived here, including 909,000 in cities and 1,714,000 in rural areas. The mean population density of the ST TPC comprises 49 persons per sq.km, which is twice as high as that of the Republic as a whole. However, the population is irregularly distributed within the ST TPC. It is predominantly the lower parts of the valleys of large rivers that are intensively developed and densely populated. The slopes and the highlands are populated much more sparsely or there are no permanent settlers at all. The main mass of people live in the Gissar and the Vakhsh valleys, containing about 78 per cent of the region's population (Table 6.2). These two valleys have the highest population density—between 60 and 90 persons per sq.km. The Garm zone is sparsely settled, as its greater part is occupied by mountains. Here the population density is no more than 6 persons per sq.km., while its share in the total population of the Complex is a little over 6 per cent.

TABLE 6.2 : **The growth dynamics and the distribution of population within the South-Tajik Complex (ST TPC)**

Zones	Population numbers as on the beginning of year, thous. people			1981 as compared with 1926 (times)	Population density, persons per 1 sq.km (1981)
	1926	1959	1981		
Garm	251.3	47.7	116.6	0.5	6
Gissar	170.3	531.4	1240.4	7.3	90
Vakhsh	26.3	420.3	799.1	30.4	62
Kulyab	183.2	230.1	466.8	2.5	38
Total within the TPC	631.1	1229.5	2622.9	4.2	49

As compared with other Republics, the population growth in Tajikistan is high. But the south of Tajikistan occupies a special place in this respect : the economic development of the vast fertile lands of the Vakhsh valley and of the adjoining areas since the 1920s has drawn population from other regions of the Republic (especially from the mountainous one), as well as from densely populated regions of Uzbekistan. As a result, the rates of population growth increased further. On the whole, from 1926 to 1980 the population of the Republic increased 4 times, while that of South Tajikistan—4.2 times. The ratio of the STC in the total population of the Republic increased from 61 per cent in 1939 to 66 per cent in 1981.

Very high were rates of population growth in the Vakhsh valley (over 30 times during the period from 1939 to 1980), and low in the Garm zone, where even the absolute population decreased. The reason for such a situation was, first of all, migration in the 1940s and 1950s of mountain people to the Gissar and Vakhsh valleys, which to a certain degree also reflected on the development of the economy of this mountainous area. Beginning with the 1970s, the total number of population in this zone has somewhat increased, although it is still lower than in 1939.

The growth of population numbers of the ST TPC in the last 15 or 20 years has, first of all, been due to natural growth, which is 3 times as high as the country's average. Mechanical growth has also been of some importance, as the large industrial enterprises constructed here required qualified workers and specialists, which have not always been available in the Republic.

Construction of large industrial enterprises conditioned high rates of urbanization. Industrialization of the economy and development of the diverse natural riches of the area promoted a rapid growth of industrial personnel and, consequently, development of cities. In the Vakhsh and, especially, in the Kulyab zones the numbers of urban population in the period from 1926 to 1981 increased correspondingly 43 and 95 times. The ratio of urban population in the southern part of the Republic increased from 15% in 1939 to 34.6% in 1980 and the ratio of rural population decreased accordingly. Cities serve as focus points (multifunctional centres) of perspective group systems of settlement. At present within the STC there are 8 cities and 27 settlements of an urban type. They have formed differently. Such cities as Kulyab, Regar (Tursunzade), Ordzhonikidzeabad, and Kalininabad have been built as centres of large agricultural regions in the years of socialist construction. Nurek and Yavan developed as settlements in the areas of natural resource development. Among the cities there are also those which in the past have evolved as handicraft-trading centres (Kurgan-Tyube). During the years of creation of the STC all of them have considerably grown.

Particularly high are the rates of population growth in the Capital of the Republic—Dushanbe. In 1926 its population was about 6,000 people, in 1939—83,000, and at present—over 500,000. By the growth of population Dushanbe occupies one of the first places in the Soviet Union. Rapid urban growth also characterizes the industrial centres of the Complex such as Kurgan-Tyube, Kulyab, Nurek, Tursunzade, and Yavan.

It is known that the process of urbanization goes on in different ways : due to migration of rural population to cities, inclusion of rural settlements into the city boundaries, and a direct employment of rural population by the enterprises in near-by cities. All these are present in the Complex. The process of urbanization is accompanied by development of group systems of settlements, which creates the most favourable conditions for erasing socio-economic and cultural differences between the city and the village. The role of the group systems of settlement continuously grows and embraces an even greater number of settlements.

Despite the decrease of the share of rural population in the total population, and contrary to other regions of the country, Soviet Central Asia and, in particular, South Tajikistan are characterized by a considerable absolute growth of rural residents. However, the process of urbanization obliterates more and more the division into urban and rural population. In rural areas the number of small settlements decreases though some of them are enlarged. The creation of large administrative-economic centres and improvement in socio-cultural services also goes on. These progressive changes spread everywhere. Most kishlaks have been rebuilt and have changed their appearance.

ECONOMY

For the years of the Soviet power immense transformations have taken place both in the South of Tajikistan and in Central

Asia. The first impulse came to this territory by the legendary Vakhshstroy. The latter solved a concrete economic problem—it helped to ensure the country independence in relation to cotton. At the same time it was of enormous social value. It changed the way of life of a dekhanian, the character of his labour. New steps, new stages followed transforming the image of the republic.

Creation of the South-Tajik territorial production complex is associated with Resolutions of the XXIY CPSU Congress, March 1971, envisaging commissioning of the first aggregates of the Nurek hydro-electric power station ; of capacities at the aluminium plant and of the electro-chemical combine. By the beginning of the ninth five-year plan period (1971-1975), i.e., by the time of the decision of the formation of a large TPC of Union significance in the South of Tajikistan, the major bulk of the economic potential of Tajikistan was concentrated in this region.

Formation of the South-Tajik TPC has a distinct resource basis : large and highly effective reserves of hydroenergy, high bioclimatic possibilities of land development (though their areas are limited) and a significant reserve of labour resources. These three factors cause respective development of its three most important production components : complex of energetics and ener gy-consuming productions connected with the necessity to ensure employment of quickly growing labour resources. Inter-sectoral complexes technologically and economically interconnected among themselves form the production core of the South Tajik TPC.

Power-industrial complex

The South Tajik TPC has no large prospected fuel resources, therefore at present as well as in the future hydro-power stations will provide for the energy requirements of the region. The plans of the power-industrial complex on the basis of hydro-energy resources of the Vakhsh river was implemented in the sixties by the Council on the Study of Productive Forces (SOPS) at the State Planning Committee of the USSR and SOPS of the Academy of Sciences of the Tajik SSR. Before this the energy requirements of the region were provided from small hydro-power plants on the Varzob river (the Varzob cascade) with a total capacity of 25 kw-hrs and the cascade of the Vakhsh hydropower plants (Golovnaya, Tsentralnaya, Perepadnaya). The development of water resources of the Amu-Darya river and the high economic effectivity of hydropower plants open still wider possibilities of hydroenergetic construction within the framework of the STC and the creation of new electrical energetics.

The first stage of formation of the South-Tajik TPC was the construction of the core of the complex late in the sixties. This core is the Nurek hydropower station. The first two aggregates of the Nurek hydropower plant were commissioned in 1972 and the last tenth aggregate in September of 1979. In spite of the fact that the Nurek hydropower plant began to use all its capacity only late in 1979, the expenditures for its construction was returned already by the end of 1980, when its electrical energy output became 10 billion 515 million kw-hrs.

The dam of the plant, 300 m high, built of local building material (sand, pebble-stone, stone) is the highest in the world. It is constructed in the narrowest place of the river—the Pulisangin gorge. The plant building whose major part is submerged under the water, rises at the foot of the mountain. The building incorporates 9 hydro-power aggregates 300 thousand kw each. Numerous tunnels bringing water to the station penetrate through the unapproachable rocky banks of the Vakhsh river. In the station region alone their length reaches 36 km.

The Nurek water reservoir is 10.5 billion m^3 in capacity (the useful volume is 4.5 km^3, not operational "dead"—6 km^3). It is a powerful means in maintaining the regime of the river run-off and allows to produce not only more than 11 billion kw-hrs of electrical energy each year but to irrigate additionally more than half a million hectares of cotton field on the lands of Tajikistan, Uzbekistan and Turkmenia. Along the Dangarin tunnel, 30 km long, the water from the Nurek water reservoir flows down to the sunny Gissar valley. No other such hydropower plant has been constructed in the world in mountain conditions. Unusual conditions of construction—high seismicity (magnitude 9), tightness of the construction site created a lot of difficulties. Since it was the first venture of its type the design of the

Nurek hydropower plant had to be corrected several times. Now the experience gained by constructors allows to erect similar hydrotechnical constructions much more quickly (see Table 6.3).

TABLE 6.3 : **Main indices of the largest hydro-power plants on the STC rivers**

Name of the plant	Useful volume of the water reservoir km³	Stated capacity mln kw	Comments
	VAKHSH Cascade		
Rogun	8.6	3.6	under construction : total volume of water reservoir 11.7 km³
Shurob	0.02	0.75	under design
Nurek	4.5	2.7	built : total volume of water reservoir 10.5 km³
Baipaz	0.02	0.6	under construction
Sangtudin	0.1	0.8	under design
Golovnaya	0.02	0.2	built
Perepadnaya on the Vakhsh canal		0.03	built
Tsentralnaya		0.02	built
TOTAL	13.26	8.7	
PYANDZH Cascade (the most promising hydro-power plants)			
Kokchin	0.2	0.4	planned to be designed
Moscow	0.04	0.8	planned to be designed
Dzhumar	1.3	2.0	planned to be designed
Dashtidzhum	10.2	4.0	planned to be designed
TOTAL	11.74	7.2	planned to be designed
	On the Kafirnigan and Varzob rivers		
TOTAL	Insignificant	2.3	A cascade of hydro-power plants on the Varzob river is built
ALTOGETHER	About 25	18.2	

The capacity of the Rogun hydro-power plant water reservoir will reach 11.7 km^3, the useful volume being 8.5 km^3, the "dead" (unreworked volume)—3.2 km^3. The Rogun plant will supply 13 billion kw-hrs of eletrical energy to the united energetic system of Central Asia.

In the lower reaches of the river 8 km from the Rogun hydro-power plant the Shurob hydro-power station is planned to be built in the future. This small hydro-power station of 750,000 kw will function in co-ordination with the Rogun hydro-power plant. It will render a favourable effect on the regulation of the water run-off in the zone of operation of all Vakhsh hydro-power plants. A direct effect of regulation is estimated as 1 billion kw-hrs of electrical energy.

Near the Nurek hydro-power plant, in the lower reaches of the river, the Baipaz hydro-power plant is being completed. Its capacity is not great—600,000 kw. The classical scheme of construction of a hydro-power plant with drainage of the river bottom for a construction site via a tunnel was rejected. Instead, a concrete wall was built, separating, a small zone from the Vakhsh river-bed. There a foundation area is being made for the station building. Annual output of electrical energy when operating at full capacity will amount to 2 billion 8 million kw-hrs.

Commissioning of the Nurek hydropower station determined the beginning of large energetics of the Tajik SSR. A powerful energetic base allowed the development of large energy-consuming projects such as the aluminium plant in Tursunzade—the main consumer of electrical energy of the TPC and the Yavan electrochemical plant.

Creation of the energetic-industrial complex of the South-Tajik TPC rendered a decisive effect on the appearance and growth of new towns and urban settlements. Three small kishlaks were transformed into the well-built modern town of Nurek which has a population of about 23,000 and is growing with very quick rates. The town of Tursunzade (the former Regar) and the kishlak Yavan were transformed into industrial centres. The population of the former has doubled in 15 years and that of the latter has increased 5 times. Ordzhonikidzeabad whose population has more than doubled in 20 years is within the sphere of influence of the complex. A settlement for the workers of the Rogun hydro-power plant is also under construction.

Agroindustrial complex

In the seventies when the ST TPC began to be formed in a planned way intensive development of agriculture went on. With the increase of the sowing areas by 4 per cent, production of cotton increased in nine years by 195 times, of potatoes —three times, of vegetables and fruit-twice, of grapes—1.4 times and of silkworm cocoons—1.2 times (Table 6.4).

TABLE 6.4 : **Development of agriculture in South Tajikistan**

Basic indices	1970	1979	1979 against 1970 % Tajik SSR	STC
Sowing area of all agricultural crops (thousand hectares)	507.6	528.2	104.4	104.0
Livestock of cattle by the end of the year (thousand heads) total	694.6	820.7	117.2	118.2
including :				
cows	260.0	310.3	119.0	119.3
sheep and goats	1447.4	1742.3	116.4	120.4
Agricultural products output in collective farms and state farms (thousand tons)				
raw cotton	572.1	664.8	124.3	116.2
grain	141.8	196.3	157.8	138.4
potatoes	21.1	63.9	229.8	302.8
vegetables	54.5	111.8	217.6	205.1
fruit	27.1	51.4	164.9	189.7
grapes	47.7	65.7	162.6	137.7
cocoons	1227	2109	163.6	171.9

The territory of the complex is one of the largest irrigated regions. Irrigational Engineering Systems that receive water from the Vakhsh canal are established and function. This canal built during the first five-year plan period brings 190 m^3 of water to the field each second. The main components of this system are : Dzhilikul, Kafirkala, Kumsangir, Mardassa. On the basis of the Baipaz hydro-power plant erected in 1968, Yavan-Obikink irrigating system was constructed and is operating with a tunnel of 70 m^3/ sec of capacity and two main-line canals. It is necessary to point out that from 1972 special delivery of water from the Nurek water reservoir is carried out for irrigation purposes during the drought period. It amounts to 2.5 billion m^3 per year. A more complete use of the Nurek water reservoir will change the economic image of formerly waterless Dangarin steppe, since the construction of the Dangarin irrigation tunnel is planned to be accomplished in the near future. Upon the construction of the Rogun water reservoir large massives of lands will be irrigated in the Garm natural-economic zone.

In the agroindustrial complex a leading part is played by growing and processing of raw cotton especially of the fine-fibre variety. Already at present the region is one of the main suppliers of this product.

The STC yields 8% of cotton produced in the country and 1/3 of its fine fibre growth. A specially favourable combination of land-climatic resources with possibility of developing irrigated land farming contributes to the development of fine-fibre cotton. As is known the conditions for the development of fine-fibre cotton growth in the USSR are limited because our cotton areas are situated in the very North of the cottonzone of the world. These conditions usually yield mid-fibre growth. Fine-fibre cotton plant may be cultivated in the very Southern regions of Central Asia in the South of Tajikistan and in the adjacent regions.

Thus a cotton production complex was formed on the territory of South-Tajikistan involving cultivation and primary processing of raw cotton and its seeds. This complex occupies the plain territory of the Gissar, Vakhsh, Kyzylsui and Yakhsui valleys. Cotton industry must be also included into the cotton complex. By 1970 its enterprises processed about 10% of the cotton fibre produced in the region.

On the basis of processing cotton seeds butter-fat (creamery industry has been created, occupying the leading place in the food industry. A greater part (75-80%) of the product of this sector, i e., cottonoil—was exported out of Tajikistan. Specialized enterprises appeared that served and are serving the cotton production complex. These are the manufacture of agricultural machines (harvesters, harrows) and overhaul of agricultural machinery.

In South Tajikistan along with cotton-growing horticulture and viticulture as well as production of dried and canned fruit and grape wines is important. Part of this product is carried away to other regions. Further development of boghar (unirrigated) horticulture and viticulture may play a major part in the agroindustrial complex. Mountain slopes are good for this purpose.

During the last few years, it has been possible to ensure production of good table and commercial varieties of grapes and southern fruit. There are good prospects for the development of trench growing of citric plants.

Thus in spite of the limited area of cultivable lands in the territory of South Tajikistan there are immense possibilites for the development of an agroindustrial complex with many sectors. However high crops are often restricted by mountain slope erosion, salinization and swamping of irrigated soils.

Salinized soils and solonchaks occur nearly in all irrigated Tajik oases. In 1960 30% of ths area of irrigated lands of the republic had soils salinized to some extent. During the recent years, as a result of a number of land-reclamation measures the area of salinized soils on irrigated lands reduced to 9% of the total area. However this phenomenon has not been totally eliminated. In particular, salinized soils were preserved in the Vakhsh valley. Such soils do not practically exist in the Gissar valley.

According to the last estimates of the Soil Science Institute of the Tajik Ministry of Agriculture, byliquidation of salinization of irrigated soils alone 65 thousand tonnes of raw cotton may be additionally produced in Tajikistan including 30 thousand tonnes of fine fibre cotton. It is equal to the cultivation of approximately 26 thous ha of new lands. Expenses for land-reclamation of one ha of formerly irrigated lands are 5-10 times less than those for cultivation of 1 ha of new land for cotton.

Organization of reserved territories

At present there are two reserves in Tajikistan—"Tigrovaya Balka" and "Ramit". Within the territory of the South-Tajik TPC in the lower reaches of the Vakhsh river there is a tugay reserve "Tigrovaya Balka". Its area is about 42,000 ha. This reserve was established by the Statement of the People's Comissariat of Land Farming of November 4, 1938. In 1977 the reserve was included in the important reserves of the Union and of the world.

The "Tigrovaya Balka" reserve has the unique tugay-desert complex of vegetation, widely distributed formerly over all the river valleys of the desert zone of Central Asia. This vegetation includes : azidovnik, turanga, tamarisk, reeds and meadows. There are many dead lakes on the territory of the reserve. They are the former Vakhsh river beds which are now filled with water during floods. Lakes are rich in fish, one may come across a large number of waterfowl in winter.

The most valuable representative of the animals of "Tigrovaya Balka" are tugay, deer and dzeren. Here in Tajikistan we managed to produce the posterity of dzerens. No doubt the reserve is playing an extremely important part in production of rare endangered animals. Efforts are also being made to preserve the reserve "Tigrovaya Balka"—a unique corner of subtropic wild nature of Central Asia that has survived almost untouched till now.

7

TRANSFORMATION OF WATER RESOURCES UNDER THE IMPACT OF ECONOMIC ACTIVITY

N.I. Koronkevich and *G.M. Nikolayeva*

The research into the transformation of water resources is becoming increasingly topical. It is important to single out a new school of thought in hydrology—the anthropogenic one, which deals with the evaluation and forecasting of the impact of various kinds of human activity on the river flow and other kinds of water resources.[2] It should be emphasized here that in this approach account has to be taken not only of the activities that have an immediate effect on water resources (various branches of the water economy, such as irrigated agriculture, industrial and public water supply and the regulation and diversion of water), but also of those activities which have an indirect influence on water resources, through soil, vegetation and other natural components like non-irrigated agriculture, forestry, expanding urbanized areas.

In order to gauge the magnitude of the anthropogenic impact on water resources (usually of the river network), three groups of methods are applied : (1) analysis of spatial hydrological rows and their conditioning factors ; (2) analysis of temporal hydro-meteorological rows ; (3) balance methods. [1,8,9,10] The first group involves methods comparing the river runoffs of two or more regions or river basins, differing in the character of economic activity over a given period of time (for instance, over the period of the estimation of normal runoff). The methods pertaining to the second group involve the comparison of the river runoff of a certain region or river basin over two or more periods differing in the character of economic activity. A combination of these methods is the "reconstruction" of the natural runoff through equations of multiple correlation with meteorological factors over a period of intensive economic activity and for a period when no such activity was taking place. The difference between the actual and reconstructed runoffs characterizes the value of anthropogenic change. The balance methods are based on the estimation of river runoff according to its components with an account of the impact produced on them by anthropogenic factors, which in their turn are obtained through experimental research in the field as well as water statistics.

Each of the methods singled out has its advantages and disadvantages therefore to obtain more reliable conclusions it would be wiser to apply several methods. Of much interest are combined methods, in particular the one which considers temporal hydrological rows of two or more river basins simultaneously. In gauging the integral anthropogenic impact on the river runoff of many regions in India and the USSR it is expedient to compare the runoff of a certain river at its exit from the mountains, or some other territory little affected by economic activity, with the runoff in this river's outlet, after it has crossed territories characterized by an intensive anthropogenic impact on water resources. This method is best applied in India and Soviet Central Asia in conditions where the bulk of the runoff is formed in mountainous regions hardly changed by human activity, whereas the major anthropogenic impact occurs on flat country.

The anthropogenic transformation of water resources is determined by the natural and economic peculiarities of a region or country. Table 7.1 provides a comparative balance estimate of water resources in separate regions and river basins in the USSR and India as well as the land water resources in the world in general. The table makes use of data provided in works [3,5,6,9] cited in the paper. According to Table 7.1 India has far greater specific (in milimetres of layer) indicators of

TABLE 7.1 : **Comparative balance estimation of water resources, mm**

region	area mln. km^2	precipitation P mm	total river runoff R mm	surface component of river runoff S mm	underground component of river runoff U mm	gross wetness of territory W mm	evaporation E mm
USSR	22,4	500	198	152	46	348	300
Basins : Dnieper	0,50	625	106	66	40	559	519
Don	0,42	560	70	55	15	505	490
Volga	1,4	642	187	136	51	506	455
Ob	2,9	521	134	90	44	431	387
Yenisei	2,6	415	238	163	75	252	177
Lena	2,5	325	203	140	63	185	122
Amur	1,9	480	185	155	30	325	295
Syr-Darya	0,22	457	66	41	25	416	391
Amu-Darya	0,23	106	63	42	21	64	43
India	3,3	1030	449	344	105	696	591
Basins :							
Ganges-Rajmahal	0,98	1073	502	383	119	690	571
Manvnadi-Hirakud	0,08	1424	700	665	35	757	724
Narbada-Garudeshvar	0,09	1136	444	408	36	728	692
Godavari-Manjra mouth	0,06	775	125	95	30	680	650
Penner-Nellore	0,05	681	65	49	16	632	616
Luni-Chitalvana	0,06	379	38	29	9	350	341
Earth's land	132,3	834	294	204	90	630	540

runoff resources, as well as soil moisture (gross humidification of territory), than the rest of the world and particularly the Soviet Union. This means that provided equal anthropogenic impacts, the proportional change in India's water resources will be less. Out of the total world river runoff resources of 38,830 km^3 a year, the USSR commands 4,350, while India—1590 km^3 a year. In per capita terms river runoff resources in India (around 3,000 m^3) are 6 times lower than those of the USSR, and 4 times lower than the average world figure.

The spatial and temporal unevenness of the allocation of water resources on a territory is obvious. One has only to compare the water balances of different river basins and regions. In the USSR the highest water supply available is in the northern and mountain regions in India—it is in the mountain regions. Conversely the most populated territories in the USSR are the southern forest zone, the forest-steppe and steppe regions as well as desert oases and ; in India, most of the flat country. These regions have comparatively scarce water resources, while at the same time they are the major water consumers. However, these territories can to a great extent meet their requirements in water due to transit runoff formed in lesser populated regions.

The temporal unevenness of water resources, the river runoff in the first place, is manifested in seasonal differences, as well as in fluctuations from year to year and from one water cycle to another. The indicator of the degree of natural regulation of the river runoff is the ratio of the value of the subsurface component to the total river runoff. An analysis of Table 7.1 shows that in this indicator both India and the Soviet Union are behind average world figures. The problem of artificial runoff regulation by surface and subsurface reservoirs is therefore particularly vital for these countries. When deciding on the question of the need of runoff regulation, however, it is essential to compare the natural flow regime with the diagram of water consumption. In the USSR the greater part of the runoff in most rivers takes place during the relatively short period of spring flooding, when the snow, which had fallen in the winters, rapidly melts. The main demand for water, however, comes during the dry summer. The only exception are several rivers in the Far East and the mountain regions. Thus, in Central Asia the period of intensive melting of glaciers and snow beds largely coincides with the period of the highest water demand. In India many rivers reach their highest water content at about the same time when demand for water is at its peak. But even provided such coincidence, the need for artificial runoff regulation remains due to the following reasons : (1) the lack of synchronism in runoff fluctuations (in natural conditions) and water demand ; (2) the unfavourable effects of excessive flooding ; (3) the need to solve water problems in water scarce years at the cost of the years with a better water situation.

Low air humidity is another feature of natural conditions which affects water consumption. The higher the humidity deficit, the more water evaporates, especially in irrigated farming, and the more anthropogenic changes occur in water resources.

But of course, the transformation of water resources is chiefly determined by the character of economic activity. The largest water consumer, both in the Soviet Union and in India, is irrigated farming. But the USSR irrigates annually less than 20 million hectares, while India 55 million hectares[7]. The USSR plans to be irrigating in 15-20 years 30-32 million hectares, but India will also expand its areas under irrigation. Moreover, in India, unlike in the Soviet Union, irrigated lands are utilized several times a year most of which are under such a water-intensive crop as rice. Hence, the wide discrepancies in water consumption for the needs of irrigated farming : in the USSR is 150 km^3 a year, while in India the figure is several times greater. In the USSR the share of industrial and domestic water consumption is bigger than in India. These types of consumption of water resources have a relatively minor effect on their quantity, since 5-20% of the gross water consumption is irretrievably lost and 70-80% goes in irrigated farming. However, industrial and domestic water consumption are the main threat to the quality of water resources, since the waste-water dumped into rivers and reservoirs is the main source of there pollution.

Water consumption by irrigated farming, industry and the

population of towns and cities is usually taken into account in water statistics and generally provides good material for the estimation of their impact on river runoff and other water resources. The most specifically required information here is of the quantity of regeneration water off irrigated land. On the other hand, several types of economic activity, although having an impact on water resources, are not covered by water statistics, as we have already mentioned. These types have an indirect effect on water resources. To take account of this effect, the results of observations at hydrological stations are required. We are not able to provide a detailed structure of the impact of economic activity on river runoff in the case of India. But its complexity is evident when considering the present and prospective impact of different types of human activity on river runoff in the Soviet Union (Table 7.2). The table is based on the calculations of one of the authors of this paper.[4] Figures for 1980 have been taken for the estimation of present transformations. For a 20-30 year perspective the most cautious variant was adopted of population growth and economic development, with due account of the most marked trends in water economization and in the optimization of water resources management. According to other estimates, runoff transformation in the perspective might be 1.5 to 2 times greater. Changes in total runoff can be determined more exactly than those in its components. Thus, when estimating the changes in the stable component of runoff, the assumption was made that the component's increase is identical to reservoir live storage, while the irretrievable withdrawal of the runoff is attributed to the low-flow period. The first of these assumptions overestimates the value of the stable component of runoff, while the second underestimates it. But in the final analysis, the distortion of the actual change of stable runoff is relatively minor.

An analysis of Table7.2 shows relatively minor contemporary changes in the total river runoff in the USSR (less than 5%). However, it is significant that these changes fall in the most populated regions of the country (oases of Central Asia and Transcaucasia, the southern parts of the European Soviet Union and of West Siberia, Kazakhstan), which have limited water resources. Water problems are particularly urgent here today, more so, as the above mentioned regions are unique in the ecology with respect to seas and lakes, which are either enclosed or weakly connected with the world oceans. Their water balance is being upset (seas : Caspian, Aral, Azov ; lakes : Sevan, Balkhash, Issyk Kul). The decrease in water resources, their pollution, the fall of the water level in a number of enclosed seas and lakes, their salinization with its harmful implications for nature and the economy, are factors which have precipitated the issue of diverting part of the runoff of the Northern and Siberian rivers to the Southern Soviet Union.

TABLE 7.2 : **Present and prospective decrease in river runoff in the USSR under the impact of a complex of anthropogenic factors, km^3/yr**

Type of economic activity	Present change		Prospective change	
	total river runoff	stable component	total river runoff	stable component
Non-irrigated farming	—20	—3	—29	—6
Drainage	+6	+5	—5	—
Forestry	+4	—3	+6	—3
Growth of urbanized territories	+16	—2	+25	—4
Runoff regulation	—18	+480	—25	+900
Irrigation	—127	—127	—180	—180
Municipal economy and industry	—21	—21	—30	—30
Average total	—160	+330	—240	+680

Most changes in the river runoff are due to irrigated farming. Water resources are much less affected by measures designed to enhance productivity of non-irrigated farming (such as diverting overland runoff on the fields to soil moisture resources) and by other types of impact on river runoff. But they may be very significant for individual regions. For example, in the Don basin, 70 per cent of whose watershed has been plowed, measures to increase non-irrigated farming productivity have led to a

10-15 percent fall in the river runoff. Anthropogenic impact, however, does not always have the same effect on water resources. Some types of it lead to higher river runoff. This concerns primarily the growth of urbanized territories (regions occupied by cities, roads and other areas with firm soil). The most important result of anthropogenic impact on water resources is probably the change in the structure of river runoff, rather than a change of the total runoff. Although various, types of economic activity have a different effect on the ratio between the flood and the stable runoffs, in the long run, however, the resources of the latter increase, chiefly due to the creation of reservoirs. It follows from Table 7.2 that in the USSR stable river runoff has grown, due to flood runoff, by one third. In prospect its resources may become at least twice greater. Runoff regulation is the universally recognized method of solving water problems. There are however, such drawbacks as the entailing flooding of land and the need to retain, on ecological cosiderations, elements of flooding regime on the rivers.

It should be emphasized in general, that the scale of anthropogenic impact on water resources is increasingly constrained by the need to protect the environment and its separate elements. This concerns mostly the following problems : protection of water from pollution ; decrease of area of flooded and underflooded land during hydraulic engineering construction ; degradation and salinization of soil cover during irrigation. In India, the savannah rice irrigation turned the 'regurs' into gray rice soils with poorer agronomical properties. Chernozems in the USSR require very careful flooding in order to avoid adverse effects. The USSR tackles the problem of reducing land flooding and underflooding by shifting most of the hydraulic engineering construction to sparsely populated or mountainous regions. An urgent and universal problem is the prevention of a qualitative exhaustion of water resources as a result of their pollution. The USSR has worked out scientific principles for a radical solution to the problem. There is to be no further dumping into the rivers and reservoirs even of reclaimed waste water, since it too is a source of pollution.[9] There is to be large-scale introduction of low-waste and non-waste production technologies, recirculating water supply with a complete cycle, water recycling, etc. Many appropriate measures are already being carried out.

Of course, many problems of anthropogenic impact on water resources have not been fully solved. The most urgent of these are : the expansion of the network of water balance stations ; the monitoring of the state of the environment's water element ; the improvement of methods of estimating the anthropogenic impact on water resources and its implications for nature, economy and population ; elaboration of measures for the optimization of water resource management with due place for conservation.

REFERENCES

1. Koronkevich N.I. "The estimation of the change in a torritory's water balance under the impact of human activity". In *Methods of Research into a Territory's Water Balance and the Mapping of its Elements.* Moscow Institute of geography. USSR Academy of Sciences,1973, pp. 117-96.
2. Koronkevich N.I. "The hydrology of anthropogenic direction : theory and research methods". In : *Anthropogenic Changes in Water Resources.* Moscow. Institute of geography, pp. 5-24.
3. Koronkevich N.I. "The characteristics of water resources". In : *Natural Resources of the Russian Plain in the Past, Present and Future.* Moscow. Nauka. 1976.
4. Koronkevich N.I. "The forecast of the state of water resources without diverting part of the runoff". In : *The Impact of Runoff Diversion on Natural Conditions.* Moscow. Institute of geography. 1982, pp. 88-105.
5. Nikolayeva G.M. "The zonal peculiarities of the water balance structure in South-East Asia". Izvestia AN SSR (geography series). 1974. ♯ 6
6. Nikolayeva G.M., Chernogayeva G.M. *The Water Balance of Asia.* Moscow. Sovetskoye Radio. 1977, p. 116.
7. Levintanus A.Y. "Water resources and water consumption in India : present state and the forecast for 2000". *Izvestia VGO.* 1981. ♯ 5.
8. Lvovich M.I. *Man and Water.* Moscow. Geografgiz. 1963, p. 568.
9. Lvovich M.I. *World Water Resources and their Future.* Moscow. Mysl. 1974, p. 448.
10. Shiklomanov I.A. *Anthropogenic Changes in the Water Content in Rivers.* Leningrad. Gidrometeoizdat. 1979, p. 303.

8

THE SOVIET EXPERIENCE OF STUDYING INDIAN WATER RESOURCES

A.Y. Levintanus

The stable and long standing interest of Soviet scholars and specialists in the study of Indian water resources and its development is conditioned by the similarity of water problems typical of both countries, the Indian experience in the field of irrigated farming and the, expanding scientific and technical cooperation between India and the USSR.

The problems, posed by water resources in India and the Soviet Union, are caused both by natural and by anthropogenous factors. More than 70 per cent of the area in the USSR lies within the zone of unassured farming—excessive precipitation or scanty rainfall. Water erosion affects some 60 million ha where the crop yield is reduced by 40-60 per cent. Therefore, various agrotechnical and institutional measures aimed at regulating river flow acquire particular importance.

Regional imbalances in terms of precipitation distribution in India are even more striking. The Thar desert in the North-West where in some areas the average annual rainfall comes to just about 100 mm is situated in the same latitudes as the valley of mighty Brahmaputra in the North-East enjoying the world record of 10-11 m, rainfall in an average year. As much as 60 million ha (20 per cent of all land resources) in India are susceptible to chronic droughts while 20 million ha are flooded annually. In this context major endeavours for optimal utilisation of water resources become vital.

Though both countries are relatively rich in water resources (annual run-off in the USSR is estimated to be of the order of 4,700 cu. km and in India—1,900 cu. km) their exploitation is hampered by uneven spatial distribution of resources. Eighty-four per cent of the surface flow in the USSR is carried by the rivers to the Arctic and Pacific oceans and only 16 per cent of the discharge comes to southern and south-western regions where 75 per cent of the population and 80% of industrial and agricultural output of the country is concentrated. The situation is especially grave in the republics of Central Asia and Kazahstan, many parts of which lack perennial rivers.

The basins of the Ganga, Indus and Brahmaputra account for 2/3 of the surface water resources of India, the Ganga alone holding more water than all the rivers of the peninsular India. In the Brahmaputra valley per capita water resources amount to 28 thousand sq. m while in the basins of the Krishna and Penner in southern India only 400 sq. m.

Recent years witnessed aggravation of water problems in the USSR and India caused by anthropogenous modifications of river flow. Among them are the land reclamation measures, including irrigation and drainage, which embrace dozens of million of hectares. Withdrawal of water for various purposes in the USSR reduced annual run-off of the Dnieper, the Don, the Ili, the Syr Darya and the Amu Darya by 17-25 per cent. In the years of low water level this figure increases to 40-60 per cent. In India the century-old exploitation of southern rivers in irrigated farming resulted in complete utilisation of water resources of the Krishna, Cauvery and Penner which are the major rivers of the region. Similar situation is characteristic of the northern part of the country where the utilisable flow of the Sutlej, Yamuna and Ganga rivers has been practically fully diverted to the fields.

Spatial imbalance of water supply and water consumption was the main reason for numerous water transfer schemes undertaken in both countries. At present operating canals in the USSR redistribute about 60 cu. km of water. The length of the world's longest Karakum irrigation canal is 1,000 km. Among the long-term, large-scale projects of this kind, mention should be made of augmenting the Volga river resources by the flow of northern rivers ; water transfers from the Ob and the Irtysh rivers to the arid tracts in Kazahstan and Central Asia and creation of the National water grid.

India enjoys a wide experience in constructing unique hydrotechnical facilities securing transfusion of water for hundreds of kilometres. The 505-km long Western Yamuna irrigation canal, was one of the first major venturies of this sort and today projects of water transfer have been launched in all the main river basins of the country. Several years ago the Government of India sanctioned the commencement of the huge project envisaging the interlinking of water surplus basins of the Northern and Central India with arid and semi-arid regions in the south of the country.

The Indian experience in water resources development aroused interest among the scholars of our country as far back as the beginning of the Twentieth century, most attention being focused, naturally, on the art of irrigation.[6] The first monographs, devoted to this subject, analysed differentiation of water consumption in the most agriculturally advanced zone of India—Indus-Gangetic plain and attributed the disparity to the availability of water resources in its eastern and western parts (II).

Political independence of India and the beginning of the Soviet-Indian economic cooperation in the mid 1950's were marked by the new stage in the Soviet indological studies. Several power projects were built in India with engineering assistance of the USSR in the late 1950's. During the 1950's a number of papers on Indian hydro resources were published[2,24]. This period was also notable for the voluminous publications on the geography of developing countries in the Institute of Geography of the USSR Academy of Sciences. A series of books, compiled there, dealt upon the regional geography of India with special reference to water resources [1,7,15,16,17].

The papers published in the late 1960's were devoted to the Indian achievements in the field of irrigation [3,4] and also to the complex geographical survey of the river system and utilisation of water resources [18,19,20]. Besides, the Soviet and Indian economic geographers published joint monographs on regionalisation of India, based on spatial association of natural resources, specifically of water [26,27].

Scientific contributions of the 1970's covered a wide range of problems pertinent to water resource development in India. The Institute of Geography of the USSR Academy of Sciences had elaborated an effective set of methods for assessing water resources on the basis of water balance approach [12,13,14]. The Ministry of Land Reclamation and Water Resources Development of the USSR compiled a review of irrigation works undertaken in India[5]. The All-Union Institute of Scientific and Technological Information had undertaken complex investigations of water resources and related problems in India [21,22,23].

The late 1970's was the period when the advanced level of Indo-Soviet geographical collaboration was achieved and it was manifested in conducting of joint seminars on regional development. The first seminar (1978) was devoted to overall methodological problems concerning research in regional development; at the next one (1980), dealing with the problems of renewable resources, several papers analysing the role of water resources within social and economic development of India were submitted [25,33,34]. The third seminar of 1985 is focused on the problem of rational utilisation and conservation of water resources. This fact highlights the concern which both countries feel towards optimal functioning of hydrotechnical systems and its economic geographical substantiation. In the USSR the October (1984) Plenum of the Central Committee of the CPSU called for fuller harnessing of the water potential for the benefit of agroindustrial complexes. In India the targets of the Sixth Five-Year Plan (1981-85) confirmed government's intention to utilise irrigation potential completely by 2000 AD.

Among the researches, made in the 1980's on water resources of India, the outlook for water consumption both on the national and regional levels has acquired special significance. The reason for that lies in expansion of human economic activity in India which is accompanied by progressive exploitation of utilisable surface and ground water resources and expansion of water scarce areas. By the beginning of the 1950's the total volume of water utilised in India was about 160 cu. km (95 cu. km surface and 65 cu.km ground). Thirty years later this amount rose to 500 cu. km, i.e. more than 50 per cent of the utilisable potential (in the USSR—20 per cent, the world average figure—10-15%).

The overall magnitude of water withdrawals in 2000 AD is forecasted to be as high as 996 cu.km and as low as 727 cu. km (Fig. 8.1). Both projections are based on intercalculation of two groups of estimates made by the Indian scholars : Scenario A representing low rates of water consumption, and Scenario B—high rates of water consumption.

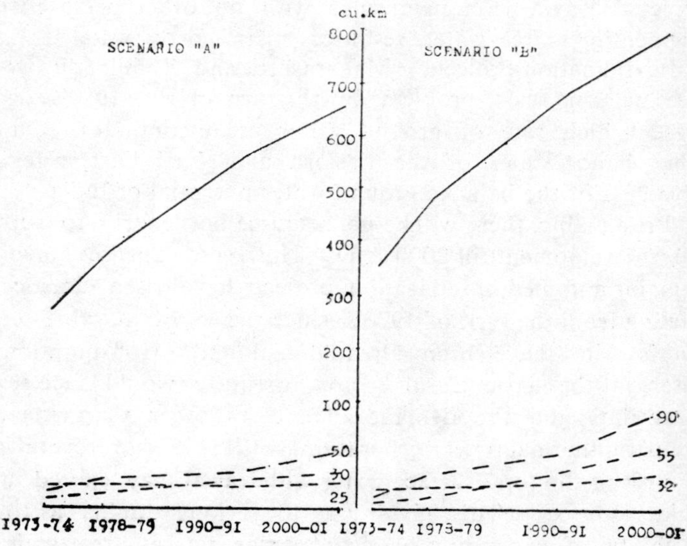

Water consumers

———Agriculture

—. .—Thermal ant atomic energetices

—.—Industry

———Population

Fig 8.1 : ***Dynamics of Water Consumption in India uptill 2003 A.D.***

The demand-supply situation for 2000 AD does not seem to be very comfortable. By the turn of the century ground water will be fully utilised and as a matter of fact the entire ground water resources seem to be committed to domestic and agricultural purposes. Regional disparities in terms of ground water consumption are great. Gujarat, Punjab, Haryana,

Rajasthan states in the West and the North-West, where the ground water availability is low, have harnessed a vast proportion of the potential and it is likely to be fully utilised by the middle of the current decade. For instance, in Gujarat exploitation of ground water reservoirs has increased at an unprecedented rate during the 1970's : the annual extraction amounted to 6,9 cu. km against the natural recharge of 4,9 cu. km[31] . As a result secular water resources of Saurashtra have been depleted leaving the peninsular with no other perspective of augmenting scarce water resources than costly water transfer and desalination projects. Maharashtra and Tamilnadu would face the same set of problems by the turn of the 1980's if the present high rate of ground water intake continues. On the other hand, states of the Eastern and North-Eastern regions have 90% of the balance ground water potential of India.

Presumably, there will be no resource bottlenecks to surface water development till 2000 A.D. However, expenses involved in major and medium irrigation projects have risen drastically, starting from the turn of 1970's, since the most suitable construction sites have been already exploited. Consumption of water in the agricultural sector in future would face severe constraints and the demand of sectors other than irrigation (industry, thermal power generation) will also rise severalfold. As a result the total surface water withdrawal may exceed utilisable resources. This gives rise to serious doubts as to the feasibility of expanding irrigated areas on a large scale as proposed by the government.

Projections of water consumption in 2000 AD reveal that the situation on the national level forebodes approaching water famine in several areas ; (1) The South : the Krishna, Cauvery, Penner basins ; (2) The West : the Sabarmati, Luni basins ; (3) The North : the Sutlej, Yamuna, Ganga basins. Thus differentiation of water strategy within the river basins is assuming great importance. However, regional differentiation brings fruit only in combination with national programmes of optimal utilisation of surface and ground flow.

India has gained world-wide experience in tackling the most sophisticated water problems. Unfortunately, realisation of such projects has been mainly confined to local and subregional territorial level. As the Indian scholars admit, lack of coordination of water management policies among states and river basins has reduced the efficiency of numerous schemes undertaken and has restrained the overall development of water resources. Besides, developments have been carried on a project-by-project, ad hoc, approach without long-term comprehensive planning. Certain proposals for overcoming water scarcity were made without due regard to regional priorities of utilising water potential and resources availability of the next 10-20 years.

To outline a scientifically grounded water strategy it is necessary to make a regional forecast of water consumption, i.e. estimate the tentative date when ultimate water potential of the major river basins is fully utilised. We have made an attempt to approach the solution of this problem with regards to specific factors regulating exploitation of water resources in India [8,9,10].

The following set of indices, typical of the major river basins, has been considered :

—Dynamics of population.

—Utilisable water resources.

—Current situation with water resources development.

—Quantity of surface waters that would have been used by major and medium projects under construction or proposed.

—Irrigation demands of agriculture.

—Perspectives of industrial and power development.

Besides, taking into account the vital importance of interstate cooperation in water resources utilisation for India and also regarding the problems of subcontinental cooperation in exploiting the Indus, Ganga and Brahmaputra, some "non-conventional" indices have been employed :

—Interstate disputes on shared water resources and,

—Water resource development of international rivers.

Analysis of correlation between indices made it possible to outline four types of river basins (judging by the tentative date of full utilisation of ultimate surface water potential) : basins of immediate utilisation of water resources (1980-1985), basins where water resources will be fully utilised in the nearest future (by the turn of 1980's), basins of perspective utilisation of water resources (by the turn of 1990's) and basins of reserved utilisation of water resources (after 2000 AD) (Fig. 8.2). In addition,

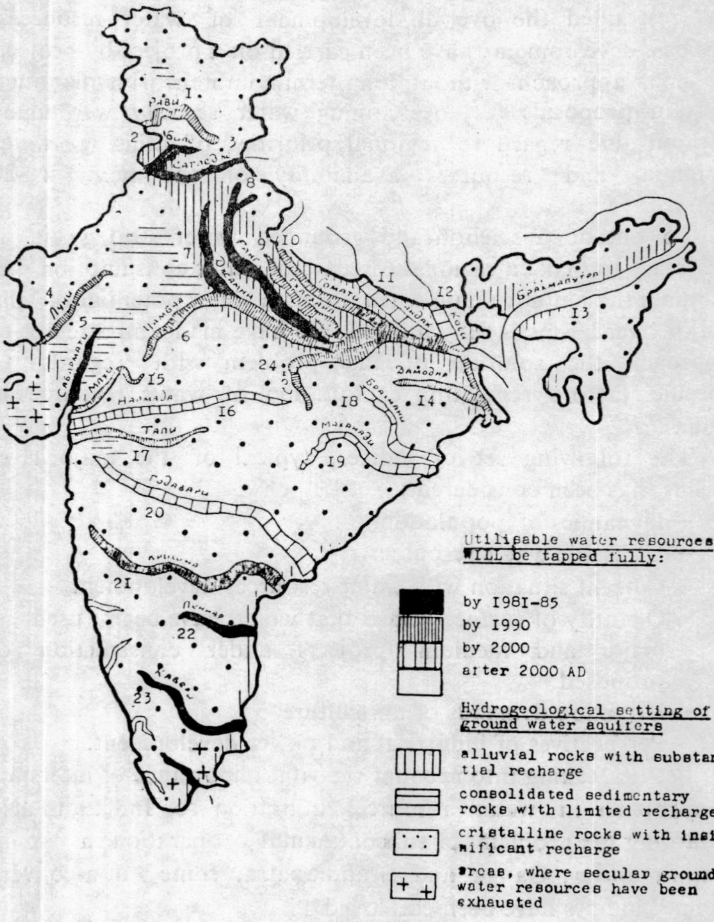

Major rivers

I—Ravi, 2—Beas, 3—Sutlej, 4—Luni, 5—Sabarmati, 6—Chambal, 7—Yamuna, 8—Ganga, 9—Ghaghara, 10—Gomati, 11—Gandak, 12—Kosi, 13—Brahmaputra, 14—Damodar, 15—Mahi, 16—Narmada, 17—Tapi, 18—Brahmani, 19—Mahanadi, 20—Godavari, 21—Krishana, 22—Penner, 23—Cauvery, 24—Son

FIG 8.2 : *Approximate Stages of Water Potential Utilisation in India—Period of full Exploitation of River Flow*

basins of the first two types with limited scope of utilising surface flow are subdivided into three subgroups in accordance with ground water situation : basins where ground waters have been fully tapped (>90% of ultimate potential), basins where a substantial portion of ultimate ground water potential has been developed (50-90%), basins where ground waters have been moderately exploited (<50% of ultimate potential).

The starting point for the classification mentioned was the correlation between the quantity of utilisable surface water resources and their actual exploitation at the beginning of 1980's. The correlation prompted a twofold classification : basins of "immediate" and basins of the "nearest future" types. As for other basins they have been grouped on the basis of extrapolating irrigation potential development. Due to limitation of data on all the irrigation projects we have confined the study to major and medium schemes and considered some 500 irrigation works of this scale.

At the beginning of the 1980's the major and medium projects provided 46% of irrigation potential created. Their spatial distribution reflects regional maturity of water resources utilisation quite adequately. In the basins of "immediate" type, where most part of irrigation potential was developed in pre-colonial and colonial periods, utilisation of water resources has begun (with some exceptions) with minor works (weirs, tanks) and only later they proceeded to major and medium projects. In other basins the post independence pioneer exploitation of water resources has been provided, as a rule, by major projects.

Ultimate irrigation (project capacity) of major and medium works was taken as an index of maturity of water resources development within the boundaries of a given river basin. It is noteworthy that ultimate irrigation of major and medium projects under operation, being 7,06 million ha in the basins of "immediate" type, decreases to 4,14 million ha in the basins of the "nearest future" type, and further, to 2,07 million ha in the basins of "perspective" type and 0,37 million ha in the basins of "reserved" type. River basins of "perspective" and "reserved" types are well defined by low irrigation demands of agriculture. Besides, delineating the basins of "perspective" type, we have been guided by the factor of interstate disputes on shared water resources which have withheld much needed development on several rivers.

A major part of water resources in the basins of "immediate" type was utilised prior to independence. After 1947 new irrigation works have tapped the remaining water potential and any future increase of irrigated areas may be possible only through modernisation of existing projects. In most basins of the "nearest future" type, projects under operation have utilised a substantial part of water potential. However, the climax of water resources development there will be timed to the 1980's when projects under construction and the first stages of those proposed become operational. In pre-independence period and during the first Plans water consumption within the basins of "perspective" type had a limited scale. Mass construction of medium and major projects started there during the Third Five-Year Plan (1961-1965) and later. Ultimately irrigation by the projects under construction and those proposed would promote utilization of a certain portion of water potential. Acceleration of irrigation development is likely to take place after 1990. Within the basins of "reserved" type, the scope of construction of major and medium projects is very limited and incomparable with that in the rest of the country.

On the basis of prognosis of utilisation of water potential, we have proposed a variant of perspective water strategy which includes 3 main stages :

Stage I—Optimal utilisation of local surface and ground water resources (duration—5-10 years)

The prime target of this stage is alleviation of water problem within the basins of "immediate" and the "nearest future" types (1980-1985 and by the turn of 1980's). Among the measures that are to be taken, priority should be given to those which do not require settlement of complex technological, financial and organisational issues, i.e. to projects envisaging increased efficiency of utilisation of local surface and ground water resources. In other words, it is necessary to maximise returns per unit of water consumed in every sector of the economy. As a matter of fact, this set of measures is part and parcel of water resources development in *every* river basin of India, *but* in the basins of "immediate" type it becomes the imperative since there is practically no time for alternative policies in the face of forthcoming water famine.

As far as 90 per cent of water withdrawn in India is consumed in agriculture alone, most attention should be paid to saving resources in irrigated farming. In water scarce areas the attempt should be made to maximise benefits from whatever little precipitation the region gets. This could be achieved if crop varieties suitable to local pattern of humidity (aridity) and water availability are chosen. In general, the choice of crops for specific areas, depends on local temperature, type of soil and precipitation. In the Indian context the latter factor turns out decisive in most cases. Therefore in river basins with limited scope of augmenting water resources, irrigation should become a supplementary source of water in addition to rainfall, that should meet the basic requirements of water for crops. To achieve this goal the crops in an irrigated command should be chosen from amongst those which are natural to the area under rainfed conditions of the local agro-climatic zone. The choice of crop structure, optimal for every agro-climatic zone, promotes high yields and productivity and moreover—ensures substantial saving of irrigation water.

While exploiting the resources of river flow it is necessary to increase the co-efficient of water utilisation. Among the measures of this kind, mention should be made of reducing water losses in distributary irrigation network, application of progressive irrigation methods and full utilisation of created irrigation potential. As little as half of the water supplied from the headworks reaches the farmer's field, the rest of it being lost in percolation and evaporation, in channels and water courses. Lining of channels (as the Indian case proves) makes it possible to reduce the losses more than twice. The prevailing methods of irrigation, for instance flooding, are quite wasteful in application of water. Experiments with sprinkler and drip irrigation proved their efficiency for Indian conditions.

Conjunctive use of surface and ground water resources is assuming special importance in irrigation : ground water can be fed into canals ; it can be used directly for irrigation during periods of canal closures. Effective exploitation of ground waters becomes vital in many areas of the country. In Maharashtra, for instance, even full exploitation of utilisable surface flow would facilitate irrigation of only 26% of cultivated areas. Under such conditions the state has no other alternative but to develop ground water resources intensively especially as they can provide irrigation in those parts of Maharashtra where other methods of irrigation are not applicable.

Finally, sizable increase in irrigated areas may be achieved through speedy completion of projects under construction and better functioning of the distributary system. Deficiencies and drawbacks in this field result in low efficiency of existing works. In 1974 the Government of India set up Command Area Development Agencies, special managing authorities within irrigation commands of major projects in order to elaborate and implement plans of fuller utilisation of water resources. Developments of the last decade proved that a promising organisational form of integral management of irrigated farming has been introduced. It encompasses a wide range of measures for optimal utilisation of local surface and ground water resources in agriculture. Such agencies have been created in all the river basins of "immediate" type, allowing for improvement of water consumption in these water scarce areas. Diffusion of this innovation and successful implementation of the targets proposed would secure increased efficiency of water resources utilisation in India.

Stage II—Complex water resources development (duration—15-20 years)

In order to augment water resources in the basins of 'immediate' and the "nearest future" types priority should be given to maximisation of returns per unit of water of the existing water supply network. As for the river basins of "perspective" type, Stage II of the water strategy envisages fuller utilisation of their vast untapped potential with the help of organisational and institutional measures. One of the most important reasons for that is the contradiction between the necessity to make effective use of water and lack of complex approach to water resources development within the basins in question (mainly in Central India). This problem substantially impedes exploitation of river flow all over the country but in the basins of "perspective" type it is the main reason for chronic underutilisation of water potential.

Major rivers of India flow through the territory of several states : the Ganga drains 8 states, the Indus and its tributaries —5, the Godavari—5, the Narmada, Krishna, Cauvery—3-4 states. It is natural that regional cooperation among the riparian states acquires national significance. Nevertheless, this principle has not yet become the guideline of general application. Under the Indian Constitution each state has exclusive powers within its territorry to exploit natural resources, water in partieular. It is not seldom that riparian states prefer to construct their own water works than to organise joint projects. "The large number of water disputes withhold much needed development on several rivers and have caused considerable loss to the national economy."[29]

Water conflicts have assumed especial magnitude in the major basins of "perspective" type—the Narmada and Godavari. Numerous times the riparian states had to suspended their progress in water resources development. As far back as in 1960's the Central Government mediated to settle the disputes but it took not less than 10-11 years to arrive at compromise agreement and overcome stagnation in the development of water related sectors.

With the background of mounting water scarcity in the country, interstate disputes and lack of complex approach to utilisation of water resources have put numerous obstacles to the progress of the Indian economy. The Indian economists assessed that as much as 20 million ha of irrigation potential is lacked up in legal wrangles. The opportunity cost of the loss due to this delay in decision-making is formidable. India loses, on an average, 34 million tonnes of cereals. The amount is sufficient to feed an additional population of 170 million.[30] Whatever the solution, a river water controversy may achieve for an individual state, national interests demand that this solution must also assure to the country, as a whole, the maximum benefits possible from the river.

For the last 5 years the interstate regime among the states concerned came into full effect nearly on all the rivers of "perspective" type through the mediation of the Central Government. Accordingly, it became possible to employ regional approach to promote the progress of the economy of these areas with poor productive forces and overall socio-economic backwardness. The regional pattern of development may also facilitate coordinated utilisation of water potential within the river basins, optimal structure of land use, and rational structure of water consumption. It should be mentioned that for some basins such as the Narmada, Mahanadi, Brahmani, Baitarani, master plans have been already compiled but not realised because of interstate disputes.

Water resources development may serve as a catalyst of transforming the economy of river basins of "perspective" type. Apart from radical improvement in water resources exploitation, the plans of complex river basin development envisage overcoming the century old backwardness of the areas populated with tribes and minor ethnic groups, fuller utilisation of the local natural resources, improvement in employment of population, diffusion of agricultural innovations, etc.

Stage III—Water resources transfer

By the turn of the century India would practically tap the entire utilisable water potential of the major river basins. Approaching 2000 AD the country is facing grave necessity of searching for extra sources of water while conventional forms and methods of water supply have been nearly exhausted. Water scarcity in many regions of India and abundance of underutilised river flow in the basins of "reserved" type justify implementation of projects of interregional water transfer. Successful execution of these schemes depends not only on technical solutions but also on radical revision of efficiency criteria, applied to traditional water supply systems. Huge investments, required for water transfer projects, make the unit cost of water transferred too high to consider at present this method of augmenting resource supply efficient. Nevertheless, at the background of mounting water crisis at the national level new methods and technologies assume particular economic and social significance, since they would take the major burden of providing the Indian population with the vital resource, i.e. water.

The schemes, elaborated by the Ministry of Irrigation of India and by prominent Indian specialists, proposes to link mighty Brahmaputra with drought-effected areas of the Thar desert in the West, basins of the west flowing rivers of peninsular India with basins of the east flowing rivers (the Krishna, Penner, Cauvery) and to connect these two systems by a longitudinal canal. The scheme envisages complex transformation of the national environment and improvement of economic ties among various regions on the basis of water resources development.

Technical solutions to this complex set of problems need a valid scientific backing, geographical in particular. This is the field where the joint Soviet-Indian investigations can make a practical contribution. Soviet-Indian collaboration in regional studies, including the problems of water resources, exceeds the limits of bilateral relations. The experience of two great States which enjoy a variety of landscapes and a wide range of regional development patterns and which have gained abundant knowledge in solving the most complicated water problems is assuming international importance.

REFERENCES

1. Batalov, A.L., Knyaginskaya L.A., Sdasyuk G.V., Yajnaya Indiya (Southern India). Moscow : Mysl, 1966.
2. Boldirev, A.A., Ilyin, A.N., Novikov Yu. M., *Ispolzovanye vodnih resursov Indiyi* (*Utilisation of Water Resources of India*). Leningrad : Gosenergoizdat, 1961.
3. Dunin-Barkovsky, L.V., Irrigacionnoye stroitelstvo v Indiyi (Irrigation construction in India). In *Vodohozyastvenniye problemy stran Azii* (*Water resources development problems of Asian countries*), Moscow : Nauka 1969.
4. Zaparyi, M.L., Ispolzovanie v Indiyi podzemnih vod dlya orosheniya (Utilisation of ground water for irrigation in India). In "*Vodohozyastvenniye problemy stran Azii*" (*Water resources development problems of Asian countries*), Moscow : Nauka, 1969.
5. Zonn, I.S., Nesterov, I.A., *Melioratsiya i vodnoyr hozyaistvo Indiyi* (*Land reclamation and water resources development in India*). Moscow : CBNTI Minvodhoza SSSR, 1976.
6. Irrigatcionniye sistemy Indiyi. Tchertejy k otchotu po poezdke v Indiyu ingenera putey soobtcheniya Ostrovskogo v 1906 g. (Irrigation systems of India. Draughts supplied to railway engineer Ostrovsky's account of his trip to India in 1906). SPb, 1907.

7. Knyaginskaya L.A., Zapadnaya Indiya (Western India). Moscow : *Geografgiz*, 1959.
8. Levintanus, A. Yu., Regionalnye problemy i perespectivy vodopotreblenya v Indiyi (Regional problems and perspectives of water consumption in India). Izv. AN SSSR, ser. geogr., 1981, N 4.
9. Levintanus A. Yu , Vodnye resursy i vodopotreblenye v Indiyi : sovremennoye sostoyaniye i prognoz na 2000 g. (Water resources and water consumption in India : present situation and forecast for 2000 AD). Izv. VGO, 1981, N 5.
10. Levintanus, A. Yu., Sostavlenye regionalnogo prognoza pri analize resursnoy situatsii rayonov starogo osvoyeniya (Formulation of regional forecast while analysing resource situation within economically advanced regions). In "Sovershenstvovaniye prirodopolzovaniya / geografitchesky aspect/" (Improvement of environmental management/ geographical aspect/). Moscow : Nauka, 1983.
11. Metchnikov, L.I., Tsivilizatsiyi i velkii istoritcheskiye reki (Civilisations and great historic rivers). Moscow : Golos truda, 1924.
12. Nikolayeva, G.M., Tchernogayeva G.M. Balansovaya otsenka vodnykh resursov Azii (Balance accessment of water resources of Asia), -Izv. AN SSSR, ser. geogr, 1974, N. 6.
13. Nikolayeva, G.M., Tchernogayeva, G.M., Karty elementov vodnogo balansa Azii (Maps of water balance elements of Asia). Izv. AN SSSR, ser. geogr., 1974, N 2.
14. Nikolayeva, G.M., Tchernogayeva G.M., Vodniye resursu Azii (Water resoures of Asia). In "*Resursu of economitcheskogo razvitiya stran Azii i Afriki*" (*Resources of economic development of the Asian and African countries*). Moscow : Nauka, 1979.
15. Oskolkova, O.B., Severnaya Indiya (Northern India). Moscow : Geografgiz, 1958.
16. Oskolkova, O.B., Tsentralnaya Indiya (Central India). Moscow : *Geografgiz*, 1961.
17. Pulyarki, V.A. Kashmir. Moscow : *Geografgiz*, 1956.
18. Sdasyuk, G.V., Vodnye resursu Indiyi i ih ispolzovanye (Water resources of India and their utilisation). — Mirovaya economika mejdunarodniye otnosheniya, 1965, 1965, N 8.
19. Sdayuk, G.V., Zeki Indiyi i ih khozyaystvennoye znatcheniye (Rivers of India and their economic importance)". In "*Vodnye resursu i Vodohozyastvenniye problemy stran Azii*" (*Water resources and Water resources development of Asian countries*). Moscow : Nauka, 1967.
20. Sdasyuk, G.V., Problemy kompleksnogo ispolzovaniya rek Indiyi (Problems of complex utilisation of Indian river). In "*Vodohozyasivenniye problemy stran Azii*" (*Water resources development problems of Asian countries*). Moscow : Nauka, 1969.
21. Tolokonniva, A.A., Zemelniye i vodniye resursu zarubejnoy Azii (Land and water resources of foreign). Itogi nauki i tenhnike. Seriya geogr. zarub. Staran. Moscow : NINITI, 1972.

22. Tolokonnikova, A.A., Vodniye resursi i ih izutchennost (Water resources of India and the state of their study). — *Geografitchesky sbornik N 5.* — NINITI, 1975.
23. Tolokonnikoya, A.A., Vodniye resursi i osnovniya vodohozyastvenniye problemy Indiya (Water resources and major water resources development problems of India). Itogi nauki i tekniki. Seriya geogr. zarub. stran. Moscow : Nauka, 1977.
24. Yaroshenko, F.D., Eenrgetitchskiye Indiyi i ih ispolzovaniye (Energy resources of India and their utilisation). Moscow : Izd-vo AN SSSR, 1957.
25. Arunachalam, B., Development of regional hydro-power potential within the framework of a national energy policy. New Delhi : Jawaharlal Nehru University, 1980.
26. Economic regionalisation of India. Problems and approaches. New Delhi : Office of the Registrar General, 1968.
27. Economic and Socio-Cultural Dimensions of Regionalisation. New Delhi : Office of the Registrar General, 1972.
28. Government of India. Ministry of Irrigation. Annual Report 1880-81. New Delhi, 1981.
29. Gulhati, N.D., How to tackle river water controversies. *Commerce.*
30. Lahiri, A.L., A long-range perspective for India. Water resources : 2000 AD. Baroda : ORG, 1975.
31. Mistry, J.F., Purohit, M.U., Environmental impact of Ukai-Kakrapar project, Gujarat, India. *Indian Journal of Power and River Valley Development*, 1982, 32, N 8.
32. National Workshop on the integrated development of the Ganga-Brahmaputra-Barak basin. Bhagirath, 1979, 26, NI.
33. Qureshi, M.H., Optimum utilisation of renewable resources of Punjab. New Delhi : Jawaharlal Nehru University, 1980.
34. Reddy, N.B., Reddy, D.N., Problems of agricultural development in arid and semi-arid regions. New Delhi : Jawaharlal Nehru University, 1980.
35. Sixth Five Year Plan 1980-85, Government of India. Planning Commission. New Delhi, 1981.
36. Sukhwal, B.L., River water management and water disputes in India. *National Geographer*, 1979, 14, N 2.
37. Ummat, R.C., From Brahmaputra to Cauvery. *Eastern Economist*, 1980, 75, N 4.

9

MEASUREMENT, EVALUATION AND MAPPING OF HYDRO RESOURCES

H.S. Mavi

Water is a scarce resource. The demand for water is increasing at a staggering rate making it more scarce. The accurate measurement and mapping of water resources is, therefore, of paramount importance in every phase of resource development, its rational use, redistribution and conservation. The sound schemes for flood control, irrigation development, power generation and water supply need quantitative measurements and mapping of the distribution of rainfall, run off and ground storage. The continuous measurement of the rate of changes in run off and safe yield occurring due to the interference by man are also the pre-requisite for water resource development schemes. An upto-date information of various parameters of water balance is essential for the operational management of reservoirs and for the hydrological forecasts. These measurements are essential in the prediction of the consequences of artificial changes in the regimes of rivers, ground water basins and lakes. The mere measurements of the various components of the hydrological cycle are not sufficient, a uniformity of the standards of measurements is also desired for the comparison and selection of the projects for the regional development and conservation of the hydroresources. The methods of measurements should not only be accurate enough to the desired levels but they should also be uniform and have undergone a thorough test to prove their reliability and usefulness in practice.

Rainfall, run off and ground reservoir are the sources of fresh water and evaporation and evapotranspiration are the processes through which the water is lost to the atmosphere. The common methods used in India for the estimation of water resources and water loss are evaluated in this paper.

RAINFALL

Rainfall is the principal component of the hydrological cycle. Its various characteristics like amount, variability and distribution, both in time and space, have a profound influence on the economic, social and cultural activities of man. The accuracy of rainfall measurement determines the degree of accuracy the other components of the hydrological cycle could be measured. The measurement of its various characteristics has, therefore, been attempted much before the measurement of other components of the hydrological cycle.

Rainfall at a point

Measurement of rainfall at a point is made with raingauges which are recording type as well as non-recording type. The non-recording type rain-gauge used in India is a simple metallic or a fibre glass cylinder that is emptied at regular intervals to measure the catch. With this type of raingauge it is possible only to measure the amount of rainfall for a particular interval of time. The recording type raingauge measures the amount of rainfall, its timing and intensity. The raingauge used by the India Meteorological Department is of syphon type.

Errors of measurements at a point location with both type of raingauges are considerable because of poor exposures and strong winds. For an individual storm the error recorded may be as much as 30 per cent. Errors for long term averages are, however, of smaller magnitude.

Rainfall over an area

There are several methods (Fig. 9.1) employed to measure the average amount of rainfall over an area. Among these, the

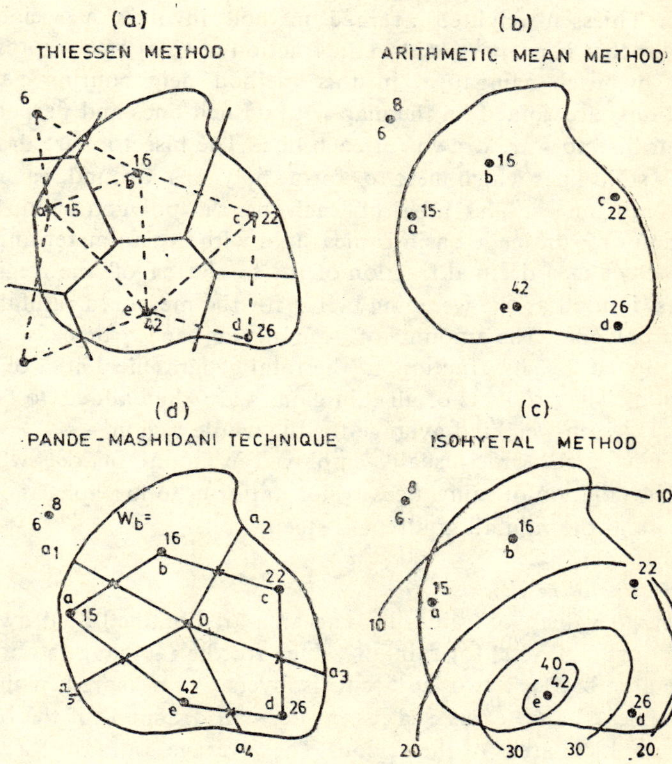

FIG. 9.1 : *Average Areal Rainfall Measurement*

arithmetic average, Thiessan and iso-hyetal methods are universally known.

1. *Arithmetic average*

The arithmetic average of rainfall of all the raingauge stations in a region is worked out and is taken as the rainfall of the region. This method is used in those areas where the topography is plain and most of the rainfall is of cyclonic nature and its gradient is not steep. This method is the simplest, quickest and the easiest method of measurement of rainfall.

2. *Thiessen-weighted average*

The Thiessen-weighted average method involves a weighing factor that is proportional to the fraction of total area represented by each raingauge. In this method neighbouring gauge stations are joined on the map with dashed lines and perpendicular bisectors are drawn for each line. The bisectors are drawn with solid lines which meet to form polygons around each of the raingauges. The area of each of the polygon within the region or a drainage basin is measured with a planimeter and is expressed as a decimal fraction of the total area of the region. This is used as the weighing factor for the measured rainfall in that polygon. The amount of rainfall at each gauge is then multiplied by its fraction of the total geographical area of the region. The products of all rain gauges are then added to form the Thiessen-weighted average for the whole region.

This method is usually employed in mountain areas where the installation of raingauges is not uniform, topography is uneven and the rainfall gradient is steep.

3. *Isohyetal method*

Average values of rainfall for an area are obtained by drawing contours (isohyets) for rainfall values for the raingauge stations. The area between two adjacent isohyets is measured with a planimeter and expressed as a decimal fraction of the total geographical areas of the region. The average rainfall for the area between two isohyets is the mean of two isohyetal values. This mean value is multiplied with the fractional area between the two isohyets. The inbetween contour area weighted rainfall values are then added to obtain the isohyetal average precipitation for the region.

4. *Pande-Mashidani Technique*

Pande and Mashidani (1978) proposed a method for determining the average annual rainfall of a basin. It is based on assumptions similar to those of Theissen. The step-wise procedure in reference to Fig. 9.1-d is as follows :—

Step 1 —Join the adjoihing rain-gauge stations by straight lines and establish the mid points of these lines.

Step 2 (a) —Establish the approximate geometric centre (o) of the area.

Step 2 (b) —Join the established centre with the points established in Step 1 and extend the resulting lines to the boundary of the basin.

Step 3 —Weight of the station (w) is measured by the product of the length of the adjacent lines.

Step 4 —The average precipitation for the basin (Pavg) is then calculated by summing up the weighted precipitation ($w_a P_a \, . \, w_b p_b \ldots W_n P_n$) and dividing this by the sum of the weights. The equation is

$$\text{Pavg} = \frac{\sum_a^n P_a w_a + p_n w_n}{\sum_a^n w_a + w_n}$$

where n = number of stations

p_a = rainfall amount of station a in cm

w_a = weight of station a in cm = $oa_i \times oa_i + 1$

w_n = weight of station n in cm = $oa_n \times oa$

The authors evaluated the method for several basins in different countries including India and the results were compared with arithmetic mean, the Thiessen and isohyetal methods. The results obtained are very close to the isohyetal method.

The advantage of the method is that it is much simpler than the Thiessen method and can be easily computerized. This method of rainfall measurement is most appropriate for those areas where rainfall gradients are very steep.

The accuracy with which rainfall can be measured depends upon the topography of the area, the type of rainfall and the density of the network of raingauge stations. Because of these factors, a measurement method most appropriate for one particular region may be quite inappropriate for another region. Thus a choice of the precipitation measuring method for a region has to be made by keeping in view the topography of the region, the type of rainfall and the net work of raingauge stations.

Rainfall for agriculture operations

Procedures and methods for the measurement and mapping of Indian monsoon rainfall characteristics like commencement of effective rains, wet spells, dry spells and withdrawal of effective rains have been put forward by numerous workers. Raman (1974), Ashok Raj (1974) and Stern and Coe (1982) have proposed various methods for the measurement of monsoon characteristics for the planning of various agricultural operations. Reddy (1985) developed a methodology for the measurement of monsoon rainfall characteristics in the Punjab for the planning of sowing operations and irrigation scheduling.

Onset of effective monsoon

The commencement of a 7 day spell satisfying three conditions is defined as the date of the onset of effective monsoon in the Punjab. These conditions are :

1. The first day's rain in the 7 day spell should not be less than 'e' mm, where 'e' is the average daily evaporation for the months of June and July.
2. The total rain during the 7 day spell should not be less than 'x' mm, where 'x' is the amount of rainfall which brings the top 30 cm soil layer to the field capacity. Here 'x' is equal to the total soil moisture content (in terms of depth) at field capacity in the top 30 cm soil layer.
3. Atleast three out of these seven days must be rainy days with not less than 2.5 mm of rain on each day.

The 7-day spell is chosen because it is compatible with the average life-cycle of a disturbance in the monsoon season (Raman, 1974). The first day's rainfall is taken as more than average daily evaporation, because rain only in excess of this will contribute to soil moisture after meeting that day's evaporative demand.

Withdrawal of effective monsoon

The withdrawal of effective monsoon is defined as the date after the last wet spell of the season on which the available moisture content in the top 50 cm of the soil falls to zero. To calculate this, a simple water balance equation is used. The equation is written as :

$$W_n = W_{n-1} - E_n$$

where

W_n = water balance on n^{th} day after the last spell of rain

E_n = Crop evapotranspiration on n^{th} day (mm/day)

W_{n-1} = water balance of $(n—1)^{th}$ day

$$W_{n-1} = M - \sum_{1}^{n-1} E$$

where

M = Available soil moisture content in the top 50 cm soil layer

$\sum_{1}^{n-1} E$ = Total evapotranspiration upto $(n—1)^{th}$ day after the last wet spell.

Wet spells

A wet spell is defined as a rainy day with 'x' mm of rainfall or a 7-day spell with total amount of rainfall equalling to 'x' mm or more with the condition that three out of these 7 days must be rainy days with rainfall more than 2.5 mm on each day. In this criteria 'x' is the amount of rainfall which brings the top 50 cm soil layer to the field capacity. The water holding capacity varies with the type of soil, so does the value of 'x'.

Based upon these criteria, the spatial and temporal characteristics of monsoon rains observed at various stations in the Punjab are mapped in Fig. 9.2

RUN OFF

Several graphical methods and empirical formulae connecting run off with rainfall have been established in India for

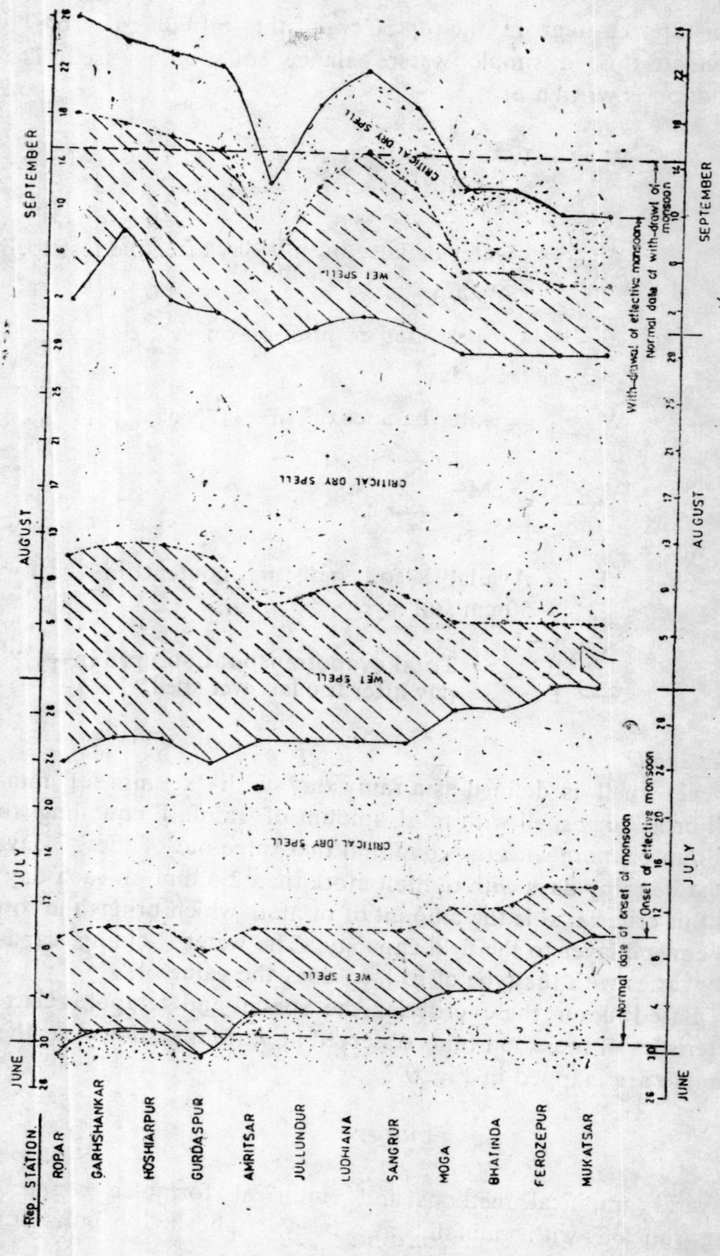

FIG 9.2 : *Temporal and Spatial Distribution of Monsoon Rains in Punjab*

measuring run off. Most of these are based on actual experiments and observations on small catchments.

Graphical techniques

Shenoy (1964) has listed three graphical methods which were developed long back in India but which are still in use.

The oldest method is that of Alexander Binne who studied the relationship between run off and rainfall in a small catchment area of Madhya Pradesh. The results are expressed in the form of a monogram.

The second graphical method was developed by W.L. Strange in South India where he classified the catchments into three categories namely, bad, average and good and presented the relationship between run off and rainfall in the form of separate curves for each category of catchment.

Sir Claud Inglis (Shenoy, 1964) developed two separate formulae correlating run off with rainfall for the hilly and plain catchment areas of Maharashtra.

Formula for the hilly catchment is :

$$R = 0.85\ P - 12$$

Formula for the plain catchment is :

$$R = \frac{(P-7) \times P}{100}$$

Where R and P are run off and rainfall (inches). Both the formulae are expressed in the form of curves.

Apart from graphical techniques, a number of empirical formulae have also been proposed. Some of these formulae are very simple and the input data is only for rainfall.

1. *Raghunath formula*

Raghunath *et al.* (1969) used an equation to measure the run off for a unit rainfall per unit area.

The regression equation is :

$$R = 0.4564\ PA^{-0.0837}$$

where R is annual run off in cm

P is annual rainfall in cm

and A is catchment area in sq. kilometers.

2. *Slope area method*

The slope area method (Khosla, 1979) is used to measure the run off in a river by multiplying the cross sectional area by average velocity of the whole stream. The velocity is measured by the Mannings formula which is given as :

$$V = \frac{R^{\frac{2}{3}} \quad S^{\frac{1}{2}}}{N}$$

where R is hydroloc mean depth

$$= \frac{\text{Area of the cross section}}{\text{perimeter}}$$

S is slope of the water surface

and N is roughness coefficient.

The method gives approximate measurements and is used in areas where actual measurements are not possible due to sudden rise and fall of floods.

3. *Khosla's formula*

Khosla found a relationship between rainfall and run off (Rao, 1979) which has been extensively used in determining the run off in Indian rivers. The formula is :

$$RA = PA - X{\cdot}TA$$

where RA is annual run off

PA is annual rainfall

X is constant for a given catchment

and TA is mean annual temperature

Khosla suggests that annual run off should be computed by summing up the monthly run off which should be calculated as :

$$Rm = Pm - Lm$$

$$RA = \sum_{1}^{12} Rm = \sum_{1}^{12} Pm - \sum_{1}^{12} Lm$$

where RA is annual run off in mm

Rm is monthly run off in mm

Pm is monthly run off in mm

Lm is monthly loss in mm

$= 4.8$ Tm where Tm $> 5°$C

and Tm is mean monthly temperature in °C.

Estimates of annual run off in the Indian rivers with Khosla's method are of the order of 1,672,500 m.cu.m. as against the

Central Water and Power Commission's calculations of 1,881,000 m.cu.m.

Based on actual discharge observations and measurements of catchment areas of the major river basin systems of India, a relationship between the two has been established (Rao, 1979) which is shown graphically for river basins having high, medium and low rainfall (Fig. 9.3). The average yield under these three situations can be summarized as :

1. River basins with predominantly high rainfall—65.0 m.cu.m. per 100 sq.km.
2. River basins with medium rainfall—45.0 m.cu.m. per 100 sq.km.

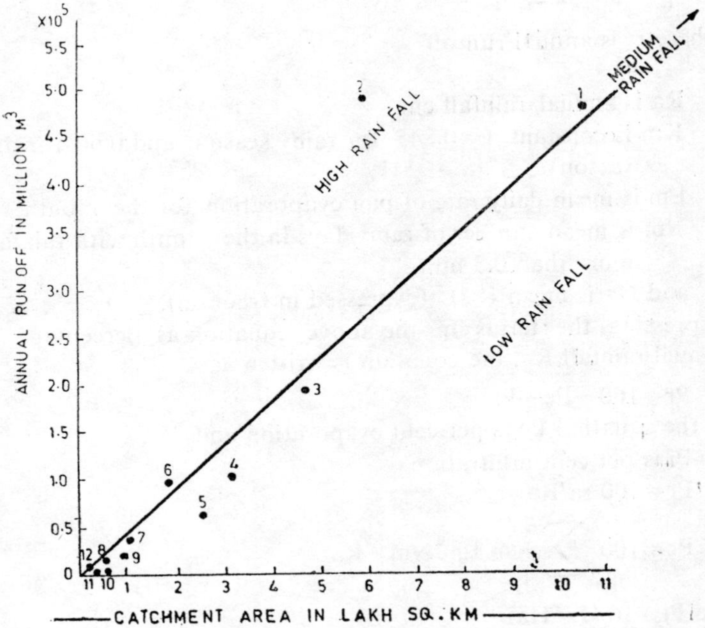

1. GANGA, 2. BRAHMAPUTRA, 3. INDUS, 4. GODAVRI, 5. KRISHNA, 6. MAHANADI, 7. NARMADA, 8. TAPTI 9. CAUVERY, 10. MAHI, 11. SABARMATI, 12. SUBARNREKHA

FIG. 9.3 *Catchment and Flow of Indian Rivers* (Rao, 1979)

3. River basins with low rainfall—25.0 m.cu.m. per 100 sq.km.

Making use of these values the run off from all the rivers of India totals to 1,645,000 m.cu.m. This figure is remarkably close to the calculations with Khosla's formula which is so far considered as the acceptable figure by the Central Water and Power Commission (Dakshinamurti *et al.*, 1973).

4. *Antarkar's method*

Antarkar (1979) gave the following equation for the measurement of annual surface flow in India. The equation is

$$r_a = Ra - \sum_{1}^{12} Km\ Em\ Nm - 0.18\ Ra\ (1 - Ha)$$

where r_a is annual run off

Ra is annual rainfall cm

Km is constant (=0.845 for rainy season and 0.60 for dry season)

Em is mean daily rate of pan evaporation for the month

Nm is mean number of rainy days in the month with rainfall more than 0.3 mm

and Ha is mean R.H. (expressed in fraction).

Expressing the terms in the above equation as percentage of annual rainfall Ra, the equation is written as

$$Pr = 100 - Pe - Pi.$$

In the equation Pe is per cent evaporation and

Pi is per cent infiltration

$$Pr = 100\ ra/Ra$$

$$Pe = 100 \sum_{1}^{12} Km\ Em\ Nm\ /\ Ra$$

and $Pi = 16\ (1 - Ha)$.

With this equation Antarkar estimated and mapped (Fig. 9.4) the surface run off for the country. Area weighted run off for the country with this equation works out to be 50 per cent. These figures agree well with the estimates made by certain other agencies. The method, however, does not take into account contribution from snow melt.

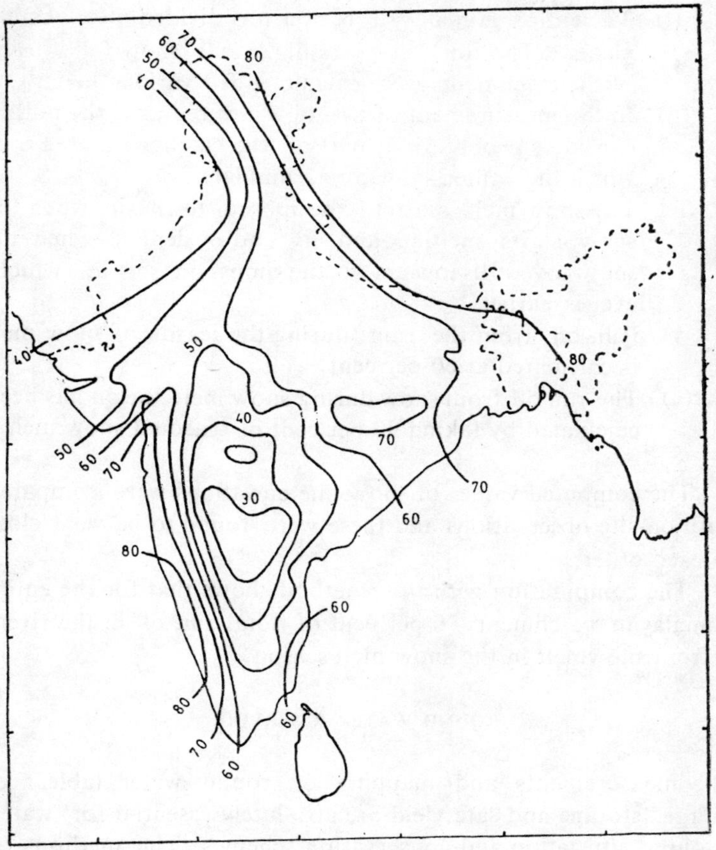

FIG. 9.4 : *Distribution of Runoff as Percentage of Annual Rainfall in India*

Snow melt

Not many serious attempts have been made to measure the snow melt run off in India. Among the very few measurements of snow melt in Himalayas is that of Gulati (1972). While Making an assessment of the role of snow and ice in the hydrology of India, Gulati computed the annual contribution by snow to the annual run off from Himalayan catchment. In doing so he adopted the following procedure :

(i) The entire Himalayan region was divided into 9 catchments. The amount of rainfall and snow fall in each of the catchments were calculated for various heights.

(ii) In the measurement of the snow covered area the author considered only that part of the catchment area over which the winter snowfall accumulates.

(iii) The snow melt season is supposed to begin when the snow starts melting and its end is defined when the snow cover disappears or the monsoon sets in, whichever is earlier.

(iv) Run off from the rains during the season of snow melt is calculated at 60 per cent.

(v) The run off from snow during snow melt season has been calculated by taking 90 per cent of seasonal snow melt.

The computed values of snow line elevations were compared with on-site observations and these were found to be very close to each other.

The computation with this method shows that for the entire Himalayan catchment 10 per cent of total run off in the rivers is from snowmelt in the snow melt season.

GROUND WATER RESERVOIR

The measurements and mapping of ground water table, recharge, storage and safe yield are absolutely essential for water resource utilization and conservation schemes. The methods of ground water measurements have not been standardized to the same extent as the methods of other hydrologic measurements like those of rainfall and run off. Some common methods used in India are briefly discussed here.

Ground water recharge

The primary source of ground water recharge is rainfall. However, in areas like Punjab, Haryana and Western U. P., where a net work of perennial canals has been laid, a substantial amount of ground water recharge takes place from the canal net-work. The measurements of ground water recharge from rainfall infiltration and seepage from canals, rivers and streams have been made for different areas of India.

Recharge from rainfall

The amount of rainfall infiltrating into the soil depends upon soil permeability, land gradient, vegetation cover, moisture content of the soil and intensity, frequency and duration of the showers. Studies conducted in Punjab (Sehgal, 1978) indicated that on an average, one third of the water added to the soil surface in the year percolates to the water table. Several empirical formulae have been proposed to estimate the ground water recharge from the rainfall.

1. *Jacob's method*

The effective average rate of precipitation with this method is determined by multiplying the cumulative departure from progressive average by a pre-determined coefficient and then adding each to a constant. Jacob's method has been used and evaluated in Western U.P. (Sehgal, 1978), where it has been found that 21.5 per cent of the precipitation goes to the water table.

2. *Chaturvedi's method*

Chaturvedi (1944) worked out an equation for the effective recharge of ground water from precipitation in the areas of western U.P.

The equation is :

$$Rp = 2.0\ (R - 15)^2/^5$$

where Rp is rainfall penetration
and R is rainfall in inches.

3. *Bhattacharya's method*

Bhattacharya *et al.* (1953) proposed an equation of ground water recharge from the rainfall. The equation is :

$$Rp = 1.35\ (R-14)^{\frac{1}{2}}$$

Rp is annual recharge and
R is annual rainfall.

4. *Sehgal's method*

Based on a detailed statistical analysis, Sehgal (1978) derived an equation for the average annual recharge in Punjab. His equation is

$$R = 2.5\,(P - 16)^{\frac{1}{2}}$$

where R is the annual recharge and
P is the annual precipitation.

5. *Singh's formula*

A refined equation has been put forward by Singh (1978) for determining the ground water recharge in the Doon Valley of U.P. The equation is :

$$QR = [\,Cr - (Ro + Et)\,]\,Ac$$

where QR is the volume of water available for recharge
Cr is contributing part of rain
Ro is direct run off
Et is evapotranspiration and
Ac is area of catchment.

The calculations with this method estimate 44 per cent of total rainfall towards ground water recharge as against 21.5 per cent with Jacob's formula, 18.1 per cent with Bhattacharya's method, 19.8 per cent with Chaturvedi's equation and 29 per cent with Sehgal's equation.

The rate of rainfall infiltration in the soil depends upon soil permeability, intensity and duration of rainfall, geology, physiography and vegetation cover. These methods, however, do not take into account all of these parameters, therefore, they give only rough estimates of recharge. Further, these methods do not take into account the deep percolation from irrigation, although the areas in which these relationships are established are heavily irrigated.

The measurements with these methods in different parts of the country suggest that no formula is good enough to be used for the entire country because the ground water recharge varies from basin to basin due to variations in rainfall intensity, geology, topography, evaporation and run off.

6. *Antarkar's formula*

Antarkar (1979) has estimated the ground water recharge with an equation which is written as :

$$im = C\left[Rm - 1.4\,(n_m - N_m)\right](1 - H_m)$$

where im is infiltration for the month

C is a constant of proportionality

Rm is rainfall in the month

nm is number of days in the month with rainfall more than 0.3 mm

Nm is the total number of rainy days in the month and

Hm is the mean relative humidity in the month expressed as fraction.

For the years as a whole, the infiltration in the soil is given as :

$$ia = C\sum_{1}^{12}\left[Rm - 1.4\,(n_m - N_m)\right](1 - H_m)$$

The author further simplified the equation for easy computation of the annual values of infiltration (ia) by taking the mean annual values of rainfall and evaporation. The simplified equation is :

$$ia = C\,Ra\,(1 - Ha)$$

where Ra is mean rainfall for the year for India

Ha is mean annual relative humidity

C = 0.18. It is calculated on the basis of the mean rainfall of India (115 mm), mean ground water storage (9% of rainfall) and mean R.H. (50—55%).

Using data for climatological station of India pertaining to rainfall and relative humidity, the author measured the ground water recharge with the above equation.

7. *Raghava Rao's method*

Raghava Rao *et al.* (1969) broadly measured the annual ground water recharge from the rainfall by classifying the rocks and other geological formations of India into 7 categories. The percentage of rainfall infiltration in each type of the rock formation in presented in Table 9.1.

TABLE 9.1 : **Percentage of rainfall infiltration to ground-water body in different rock types and formation in India**

Rock type/formation	Percentage rainfall infiltration to ground water body
1. Hard rock formations and Deccan trap	10
2. Consolidated rocks (sand stone)	5-10
3. River alluvia	15-20
4. Indo-Gangetic alluvium	20
5. Coastal alluvia	10-15
6. Western Rajasthan dune sand	2
7. Inter montane valleys	15-20

Source : Raghava Rao *et al.* (1969).

Based on these percentages, the total annual probable recharge to the ground water reservoir from rainfall is estimated at 37.11 million hectare meters. In certain areas the recharge estimates on the basis of the rates given in the above table have agreed very well with the estimates of recharge based upon actual water table rise.

Recharge from irrigation channels

The measurement of seepage losses in irrigation channels is a very complicated problem. This measurement is, however, very important in areas like Punjab and Western U.P. in ground water resource assessment because it is an important source of ground water recharge. The seepage has also rendered big chunks of land water logged. The measurements of seepage losses in the main canals of Punjab therefore attracted attention as early as the second half of the last century.

1. *Wood's formula*

This was the first scientific formula tried in Punjab for the seepage measurement (Sehgal, 1978). It is written as :

$$q = C.a.d.$$

where q is absorption in cusecs/million sq. ft.

C is constant varying from 1.20 to 1.33

a is reduced wetted perimeter of the channel section

and d is the depth of water in feet.

2. *Higham's formula*

Higham's formula as given by Sehgal (1978) has been used for long for the measurement of seepage loss from canals in the Punjab. The formula is :

$$q = C\sqrt{\frac{d}{10^6}}\ WL$$

where q is losses by seepage in cusecs for a length of canal

C is a constant and its value is 3.5

d is depth of water in the canal in feet

W is width of water surface in canal in feet

and L is length of canal section in feet.

The measurement of seepage from old canals in the Punjab are made with this method and are officially used by the State Irrigation Department. The average loss of water through seepage estimated with the method is 8 cusecs per million sq. ft. of wetted area.

3. *Method used in Bhakra canal*

In the Bhakra canal system of Punjab and Haryana, the following formula (Singh, 1978) has been used for determining seepage losses in the unlined canals.

$$S = 0.0133 \ L \ Q^{0.5652}$$

where S is total losses

L is length in thousand feets

and Q is discharge in cusecs.

4. *Method used in Pakistan*

Singh (1978) has given a formula used in the Punjab province of Pakistan to measure seepage losses in unlined canals for the ground recharge.

The formula is :

$$K = 5 \ Q^{1/16}$$

where K is absorption loss in cusecs per million sq. ft. and

Q is discharge in channels in cusecs.

The ground water recharge measurements made with these empirical methods in the Punjab vary 6 cusecs per million sq. ft. of wetted perimeter for a channel with a discharge upto 120 cusecs to a loss of 8 cusecs per million sq. ft. for channels upto 2000 cusecs discharge. Assuming the losses on the lower side i.e. at 6 cusecs per million sq. ft. of wetted areas, the annual ground water recharge from the canals, minors, distributaries and water courses in the Punjab State is estimated at 5.55 million acre feet.

SAFE YIELD

The estimation of safe yield from the underground reservoir is of vital importance in areas like Punjab where the number of tubewells for irrigation is increasing at a phenomenal rate. The safe yield is the amount of water which can be withdrawn from the reservoir without producing any undesired effect like a permanent fall in the water table which makes the pumping cost prohibitive and render the shallow tubewells dry.

Different methods have been used to estimate the safe yield in different drainage basins of India. The methods are discussed in detail by Sharma *et al.* (1975).

1. *Hill's method*

Data required for computing safe yield with this method are ground water observations and extent of annual withdrawal. In this method, it is assumed that the water supply to the basin is almost constant. Annual change in ground water level is plotted against annual draft and a straight line can be fitted to the points. The draft corresponding to the zero change in ground water level from this straight line is read and defined as safe yield.

2. *Harding's method*

The retained inflow in a basin is plotted against annual change in ground water elevations. A straight line is fitted to the plotted points. The retained inflow corresponding to zero change in water table depth is the safe yield. This method assumes that draft on the basin is reasonably constant.

3. *Method of zero net ground water-level fluctuation*

If the ground water level at the beginning and end of a period extending to several years is the same, the average annual net draft on the basin is a measure of safe yield.

4. *Method based on Darcy's Law*

In basins where the inflow is lateral and direction is known, the safe yield is calculated by Darcy's Law.

The cross sectional area is determined from geological cross-section, the permeability co-efficient from pumping tests and hydraulic gradient by actual observations. The method is best for the confined equifers having unidirectional flow.

5. *Method of specific yield and rise of water table from June to October*

Most of the rainfall in India is during the monsoon period. Rise of ground water-table from June to October gives the net recharge due to rainfall. Increase in ground water storage due to average least rise of water-table for the period of record is worked out as above, which is available ground water potential safe for pumping.

6. *Computer simulation of the ground water*

In a study in the Bist Doab basin of Punjab (Kaushal *et al.*, 1982), a computer based ground water basin model based upon Tyson Waber polygonel node system was used to study the response of water table to the increased extraction as well as on the increased recharge on the whole basin. In this study the basin was divided into 30 polygons using Thiessen's method. There are 12 water modes in the Sutlej and Beas rivers. The response of water table with 10, 25 and 50 per cent increased extraction was studied (Fig. 9.5). The model identified the areas where increased extraction through the installation of more tubewells will result in lowering the water table and will create some serious problems in water management. The model output and the historical water table data have matched reasonably well for a period of three years.

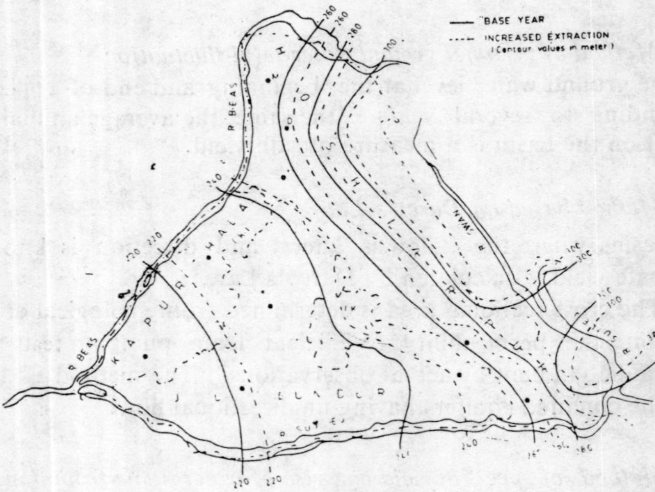

FIG. 9.5 : *Jullundur Bist Doab Water Table Contours with 50 per cent more Extraction*

EVAPORATION AND EVAPOTRANSPIRATION

Evapotranspiration plays an important role in every phase of water resource management and great efforts have been made to find out means to measure it directly. However, with the techniques developed sofar, it is difficult to obtain measurements which are truly representative of the natural conditions. Almost all the instruments and empirical formulae used in India and referred to in this study cannot be regarded as very satisfactory for this purpose. Therefore, suitable corrections must be applied to adjust the evaporation measured by these instruments to the actual evaporation from a specific surface. Numerous physical methods and empirical formulae have been proposed for the measurement of these hydrological phenomena.

Several evaporimeters are used in India for the estimation of evaporation. Some of these devices are assumed to measure evaporation with acceptable accuracy.

1. *Floating pans*

These pans are made to float in water bodies with suitable rafts. Water loss measurements from these pans are similar to those of the surrounding water surface. The installation and operations of these pans are costly. Moreover, their operation becomes difficult when the wind is strong.

2. *Can evaporimeters*

Can evaporimeter is a metallic pan usually 22 cm in diameter and 30 cm in depth. These are filled with water to a particular level and each day the loss of water is replenished with a graduated cylinder. Because of the sensible heat flow to the metal these pans give inflated values of evaporation.

3. *U.S. weather bureau pan*

The US Weather Bureau A class pan is widely used in India for measuring evaporation. It is 120 cm in diameter and 25 cm in depth. It is placed over a wooden block 10 cm height. The drawback of this pan is that the sensible heat flux from the sides and bottom results in increased evaporation which gives inflated values.

4. *Sunken pans*

Many research workers engaged in water management studies use sunken pans for measuring evaporation. The common sunken evaporimeter is 60 cm in diameter and 55 cm in depth. A hollow cylinder of 15 cm diameter is attached to the main pan with the help of a connecting tube. The pan is burried in the ground and the water surface is kept close to the earth surface. The water evaporated on each day is added with a graduated cylinder.

5. *Lysimeters*

A net work of weighing lysimeters have been installed in all the agroclimatic regions of India to measure the rate of evapotranspiration from the crops. The dimensions of these lysimeters are 130 × 130 cms with a depth of 69 cm. Below 69 cm depth there is a false chamber of 15 cm which retains the percolated water which is pumped out. These lysimeters are capable of measuring evaporation and evapotranspiration for short intervals of time. They also give additional information on dirunal patterns evapotranspiration, energy partitioning and the relationships between transpiration and soil moisture tension. The drawback of the lysimeters is the high cost of their installation and their immobility.

6. *Pichi evaporimeters*

The pichi evaporimeter consists of an inverted graduated tube filled with water and a filter paper clamped over its mouth. The instrument is kept in the Stevenson Screen. A pichi evaporimeter is not a very reliable instrument because it over-estimates the effects of wind while underestimates the effect of solar radiation. Moreover, it gives highly inflated values.

For practical purposes, it is the knowledge of evaporation from large surfaces of water bodies, crop fields, bare soil or catchment areas which is more desired. There is a close relationship between the size of the evaporating surface and the rate of water loss. The rate of evaporation is fairly independent of the size of measuring bodies under high humidity conditions. However, when the air is dry the size of the pan greatly influences the rate of evaporation. Thus in order to make the use of the measurements taken from these a relationship between the measurements from these pans with some standard instrument mesurements must be known.

The performance of four types of evaporimeters was evaluated (Fig. 9.6) under the Punjab conditions (Singh, 1978) assuming the US Weather Bureau pan as the standard. The pitch evaporimeter gave highly inflated values of evaporation while the sunken pan gave sub-normal values. The measurements with evaporimeter were found to be close to the US Weather Bureau pan.

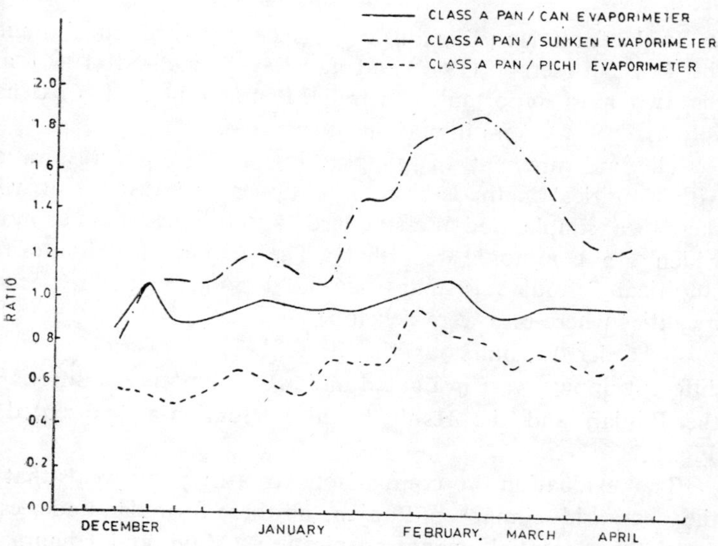

FIG. 9.6 : *Ratios of Evaporation from a Pan to Evaporation from Different Evaporimeters*

Empirical methods

The empirical methods used in India for the measurement of potential evapotranspiration fall in three groups. In the first group are those with a single input. In the second group are those with two to three meteorological parameters while in the third group are those having all the pertinent parameters.

The formula used with a single input is that of Thorthwaite (1948). Till recently this has been in use by geographers and climatologists in many parts of the world including India. The input in the formula is air temperature.

Formulae with solar radiation and temperature as inputs are those of Jenson and Haise (1963), Turc (1954), Stephen and Stewart (1963), Priestly and Taylor (1972) and Grassi (1964). The first one has been widely used by various investigators in India.

Formulae with air temperature and humidity, solar radiation and humidity and day length and vapour pressure are those of Papadakis (1965), Makkink (1957) and Hamon (1961) respectively.

In the formulae using all the pertinent meteorological inputs, the Penman method (1948) and Van Bavel's method (1966) are the two most important. In India, Penman method is extensively used by workers in various disciplines.

The measurement of evaporation and evapotranspiration with empirical methods has a great appeal, because majority of these are simple and use standard climatological data as input which are commonly recorded. The major limitation of the empirical formulae is that they hold good in the respective localities where they were developed.

In order to find out the best fit, several formulae using different inputs were evaluated under the climatic conditions of the Punjab and the results of this evaluation are presented in Fig. 9.7.

The evaluation in comparison to open pan reveals that in the semi-arid climate of Punjab, all these formulae under-estimate the potential evapotranspiration (Mavi and Chaurasia, 1980). The greatest departure from the open pan evaporation is estimated with Thornthwaite and Hamon's methods, both of which estimate about 65 per cent of open pan evaporation.

On annual basis Makkink method underestimates by 45 per cent while Stephen's and Stewart method under-estimates by 40 per cent as compared to open pan. Grassi and Turc methods estimate within 80 per cent of open pan for 8 months in the year. Even the Penman method which is most extensively used in India, underestimates by about 25 per cent on an annual basis.

The closest to open pan values are the estimates with Papadakis and Jensen and Haise methods. The monthly patterns of estimation are also in tune with open pan. The annual estimates with Papadakis method are hardly 10 per cent less than with those of the open pan method. The estimates with Jensen and Haise method are also close to pan values.

The fundamental drawback of all these empirical estimates is that except for a small period during the monsoon, the estimates are always low. The maximum deviation is during the extremely hot and dry summer months. This seems to be because of the fact that in none of these methods, the role of advective energy associated with westerly winds during the summer months could be taken into account. Even the Penman method, the only one with wind as input fails to account for the exact contribution of advective energy. This may be due to the reason that majority of these have been proposed in those climates where advective energy is not a very important phenomena.

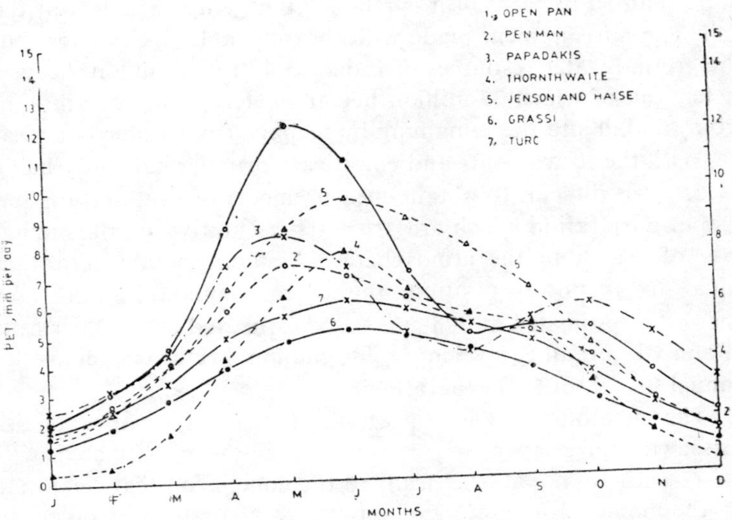

FIG. 9.7 : *Mean Daily Potential Evapotranspiration (PET) at Ludhiana Computed with Various Methods*

Hydro resource assessment at national level

Some but not all methods discussed here have been used to measure the hydro resources at the national scale. With the best methods available, the annual average normal rainfall over

India is estimated at 120 cm equivalent to 370 million hectare meters of water. Many methods are being used for run off measurements but none of these can be said to be fool-proof. Whereas the estimates of Central Water and Power Commission place the surface water of India at 188 million hectare meters, the lowest estimates are 144 million hectare meters. The surface water estimates with Khosla's method are 167 million hectare meters representing about 47 per cent of the annual rainfall. Estimates with Antarkar's method are very close to this figure. Khosla's estimates are accepted to be more reasonable. About 110 million hectare meters of annual run off goes to the ocean and is not available for utilization.

The assessment of ground water resources at the national level is a very complex problem. It is estimated that 80 million hectare meters of water seeps down in the soil annually and more than 50 per cent of it is retained by the upper layers of the soil. The measurement made with the available techniques put the ground water resources of India at 42 to 44 million hectare meters out of which 37 million hectare meters is the contribution from rainfall and the remaining by seepage from water courses.

With the instruments and empirical formulae currently being used, it is difficult to obtain measurements of evaporation and evapotranspiration which are truly representative of the actual loss of water to the atmosphere. Assuming pan evaporation equal to evapotranspiration, the average annual loss of water has been estimated at 228 cm. It is estimated that 32 per cent of annual rainfall equivalent to 120 million hectare meters is the annual loss through evaporation.

The methods of quantification of the water resources discussed in this paper and the water resources estimated with these at the national level leads to the conclusion that majority of the methods used are not yet refined enough to be taken as final. Since water is the most precious resource and its demand is increasing at a fast rate, its availability has to be precisely quantified and mapped for resource development, distribution and conservation schemes. This, in turn, is possible if more sophisticated techniques and refined tools for its measurement are developed to replace the methods which have doubtful accuracy and lack a scientific base.

REFERENCES

Anonymous, Climatological Atlas for Airmen, Poona, 1943.

Antarkar, V.N., Water Availability in India and its Variability—A Meteorological Approach, *Vayu Mandal*, July-Dec., 1979, 39-44.

Ashok Raj, P.C., Onset of Effective Monsoon and Critical Dry Spells, IARI, *Res. Bull.* No. 11, New Delhi, 1979.

Bhattacharya, A.P., Penetration of Rain Water to Ground Water Table in Doabs, West of the Ganga River, U.P.I.R.I. Tech., 1953, Memo No. 24.

Chaturvedi, R.S., Investigation of Ground Water Resources in the Kali Nadi—Nim Doab, U.P.I.R.T. Tech., 1944, Memo. No. 14.

Dakshinamurti, C.A., A.M. Michael and Shri Mohan, Water Resources of India and their Utilization in Agriculture, Water Tech. Centre, IARI, New Delhi, 1973.

Gulati, T.D., Role of Snow and Ice in the Hydrology of India, The Role of Snow and Ice in Hydrology, *Proc. Banff. Symp.*, Vol. II, 1972, 610-623.

Hamon, W.R., Estimating Potential Evapotranspiration, Amer. Soc. Civ. Engin. Proc. *Jour, Hydrol Div.* 87 (Hy-3), 1961, 107-120.

Jensen, M.P. and H.R. Haise, Estimating Potential Evapotranspiration from Solar Radiation, Amer. Soc. Civ. Engin. Proc. Jour. Irrig. and Drin. Div. 89 (IR-4), 1963, 15-41.

Kaushal, M.P., S.D. Khepar, V.V.N. Murty and S.K. Sondhi, Research Digest 1971-1981, Department of Soil and Water Engineering, COAE, PAU, Ludhiana, 1982, 171-181.

Makkink, G.F., Testing the Penman Formula by means of Lysimeters, *J. Inst. Water Engin.* 11, 1957, 277-288.

Mavi, H.S. and R. Chaurasia, An Evaluation of Empirical Methods of Computing Potential Evapotranspiration in Punjab, National Seminar on Agro Climatology, Deptt. of Agronomy, Tamil Nadu Agri. Univ. Coimbatore, 1980, 70-78.

Pande, B.B. Lall and G. Al Mashidani, A Technique for the Determination of Areal Average Rainfall, *Hydrological Science Bulletin*, 23.4.12/78, 1978, 445-453.

Papadakis, J., Potential Evapotranspiration, *Buenos Aires*, 1965, p. 54.

Penman, H.L., Natural Evaporation from Open Water, Bare Soil and Grass, Proc. Roy. Soc. (London), A. 193, 1948, 120-145.

Raghava Rao, K.V., T.S. Raju and V. Ramesam, An Estimate of the Ground-water Potential of India—First Approximation, *Soil and Water Management Symposium*, HAU, Hissar : 6, 1969.

Raghunath B., D.C. Dass, Shrinivas and V. Lakshman, Relationship Between Rainfall and Run-off from Sub-watersheds in Nilgiris, Eighth Annual Meeting of Indian Soc. Agric. Engg., Pant Nagar, 1969.

Raman, C.R.V., Analysis of Commencement of Monsoon Rains over Maharashtra State for Agricultural Planning, IMD Scientific Report No. 216, 1974.

Rao, K.L., *India's Water Wealth : Its Assessment ; Uses and Projections*, Orient Longman, 1979.

Reddy, Sitarami, C., A Study of Pattern of Rainfall Distribution in the Punjab during Monsoon Season with special reference to the onset and withdrawal of Effective Monsoon Season and the Nature and Magnitude of Dry Spells, 1985, M.Sc. Thesis (unpublished), PAU, Ludhiana.

Sehgal, S.R., Water balance, rainfall, run off, evapotranspiration recharge, surface inflow, outflow, utilizable potential. Land and Water Management in the Indus Basin (India), *Proc. of Symposium*, Vol. I, PAU, Ludhiana, 1978, 61-78.

Sharma, R.P., S.R. Sehgal and A.D. Gulati, Techniques and Methods for Development and Assessment of Ground Water Resources, Annual Review Session, C.B.I.P. Bhubneshwar, Feb. 1970, 1975, 31-37.

Shenoy, R.C., Methods Used in India for Estimating and Forecasting of run off and floods from rainfall, Third Inter-regional Seminar on Hydrology, Methods of Hydrological Forecasting for Utilization of Water Resources, Bangkok, 1964, 130-134.

Singh Surjit, Studies on Evapotranspiration on Wheat, 1978, M.Sc. Thesis (unpublished), PAU, Ludhiana.

Singh Gurcharan, Ground Water Recharge from Canals and other Water Conveyance Systems, Stream Flow and Equifer Storage, Land and Water Management in the Indus Basin (India) *Proc. of Symposium*, Vol. I, PAU, Ludhiana, 1978, 79-86.

Stern, R.D. and R. Coe, The Use of Rainfall Models in Agricultural Planning, April. Met. 26, 1982, 35-50.

Thornthwaite, C.W., An Approach Towards a Rational Classification of Climate, *Geogr. Rev.* 38, 1948, 55-94.

10

NEGATIVE CONSEQUENCES OF IRRIGATION PRACTICES
Preventive and Remedial Measures

R.N. Mathur

INTRODUC TION

The oceans, covering about 71 per cent of the earth's surface, contain as much as 97.5 per cent of the earth's total volume of water. The rest is distributed as : ice caps and glaciers—1.9 per-cent, subsurface water—0.5 per cent, and lakes, riversand atmosphere—0.1 per cent. In fact, liquid fresh water in a readily usable form, amounts to less than 0.5 per cent, most of it found as subsurface water (Nace, 1969, p. 9).

Occurrence of this limited utilizable water, is highly variable in space and time. Its quality too is deteriorating rapidly with increasing use by man. Further, its use often involves high percentage of loss or wastage.

Irrigational use accounts for more than 75 per cent of the world's total use of water. With only about 15 per cent of the world's cultivable land under irrigation at the present, and with rapidly increasing demands for food and fibre, the need for rational utilization, conservation, and management of this highly limited resource can hardly be overemphasized.

Scientific management of water resources involves the collaboration of geographers, engineers, hydrologists, meteorologists, crop scientists, soil scientists etc. Interdisciplinary studieslike those of 'soil—water—plant' and 'irrigation—drainage—water quality' interrelationships have thus been made possible. The concern of geographers is largely with the spatial patterns emerging from interaction between human activities and occurrence of water under varying environmental conditions.

Water management in irrigation aims at achieving maximum efficiency in its use in terms of crop production per unit irrigation water, per unit area and per unit time. This involves proper understanding of the influencing environmental factors. For example, reclamation of an area made saline by previous uncontrolled irrigation could be achieved by a balance of water table decline by pumping, combind with application of just enough irrigation water to allow leaching without waterlogging.

India is the second largest irrigated country with about one-fifth (38 million ha) of the total irrigated area of the world. Irrigation accounts for more than 90 per cent of the total water use of the country (Chaturvedi, 1976, p. 47). However, faulty irrigation practices, causing wastage of water, often lead to environmental problems or negative consequences like water-logging, and soil salinity and alkalinity, the latter often being a consequence of the former. Further, water pollution from irrigation is becoming significant in the country on account of increasing use of fertilizers, pesticides and herbicides carried in solution by irrigation water.

As a result, agricultural production in the country has lagged behind its irrigation potential. In fact, during the period 1951-81, the latter has increased from 22.6 to 58.6 million ha as against the former which increased from 55 to only 130 million tonnes. Further, only about one-fourth of the cultivated land has been brought under irrigation so far with the development of about one-half of the irrigation potential. Thus, there is urgent need for introduction of conservation practices in the management of irrigation water. The approximate shares of the different means of irrigation are : canals—40 per cent, wells and tubewells—38 per cent, tanks—15 per cent, and others—7 per cent.

The problems related to faulty irrigation practices shall now be considered, mainly in the context of northern India, followed by an account of their remedial and preventive measures.

WATERLOGGING

An agricultural land is said to be waterlogged when its productivity or fertility is adversely affected by a rise in ground water level. A balance generally exists between the inflow of water (the amount of water entering an area by infiltration, seepage, incoming surface and subsurface flow etc.) and the outflow (the amount of water leaving the area by evapotranspiration, seepage, outgoing surface and subsurface flow, puming from wells etc.), with due allowance for any change in storage.

The balance gets disturbed by any change in the hydrological conditions in the area. A new balance would ultimately be established under the changed conditions, with or without any undersiderable consequences, depending upon the degree of change. Waterlogging in an irrigated area, due to increase in inflow from irrigation water, as compared to outflow, is actually a manifestation of man's increaing interference in the hydrological cycle. It adversely affects crop yield, and may lead to such ill effects as soil salinity and alkalinity, growth of wild flora, and decline in community health.

A rise in ground water level may lead to fall in crop production by : (i) cutting off normal air circulation as soil pores in the root-zone get saturated with water, (ii) adversely affecting the transpiration process with decreasing osmotic pressure difference, and (iii) reducing the formation of soluble nitrates in the soil, useful as plant nutrients, since a fall in oxygen supply hampers bacterial activity necessary for fixation of atmospheric nitrogen in the soil.

In the alluvial soils of the Indo-Gangetic Plain, the root-zone of crops generally extends to 0.5 m below the ground. Crop yield in such cases would therefore be affected by waterlogging when ground water, under the influence of capillarity, rises to within 0.5 m of the ground surface. The fine grained soils, characterised by large capillary rises, as compared to the course grained soils, would obviously be more prone to the evil.

The thickness of the capillary fringe in the region is from 0.5 m to 1.0 m above the water table. Thus, waterlogging would occur when the water table is within a depth of 1.0 m (0.5 m+0.5 m) below the ground in the former case and 1.5 m

(0.5 m + 1.0 m) in the latter.

The deep-rooted plants would be more susceptible to the problem than the shallow-rooted plants. The critical depths of water table at which yield of certain crops in the region would be adversely affected are : wheat—0.9 to 1.2 m, barley—0.9 m, gram—0.9 m, sugarcane—0.3 m, rice—0.6 m, cotton, maize and millets—1.5 to 1.8 m, fodder crop—1.2 m, and lucerne—2.1 to 2.4 m.

Causes of waterlogging

Faulty irrigation practices, responsible for wastage of water, may lead to waterlogging, often in combination with factors like seepage from canal system, and inadequate drainage. The problem would thus vary in intensity in space according to the relative significance of the influencing factors.

Areas affected by waterlogging

In India, the problem has, of late, assumed serious proportions with the shifting emphasis from protective to intensive irrigation for attaining greater agricultural production. It affects an area of above 6 million ha, out of the country's total area of 328 m ha. In adjoining Pakistan too, it has affected an area of about 2.5 m ha, out of its total area of 81 m ha, and is increasing by 20,000 to 40,000 ha per year (Simons, 1967, p. 54).

The worst affected tracts in India are mainly in the irrigated command areas of river—valley projects like the Bhakra-Nangal (in Punjab, Haryana and Rajasthan), the Kosi (Bihar), the Gandak (Uttar Pradesh and Bihar), the Sarda (Uttar Pradesh), and the Chambal (Rajasthan and Madhya Pradesh). They suffer mostly from wastage of water by over-irrigation in different combinations with factors like seepage from canal system, poor drainage due to almost flat topography, obstruction to natural drainage, and frequent flooding by streams. The lowlying rice growing coastal belts in the eastern and the southern parts of Peninsular India also face the problem, due mainly to poor drainage.

Anti-waterlogging measures

Anti-waterlogging measures aim at reducing the inflow or

increasing the outflow of water from the affected area. The former are mainly preventive in nature, for example, checking of application losses, lining of canals and water courses, and provision of intercepting drains along canals ; whereas the latter are mainly remedial, for example, provision of drainage, improvement of natural drainage, and pumping from wells. However, there has hardly been any attempt in the country so far towards planned implementation of the measures.

Preventive measures

(i) *Checking of application losses*

Application losses account for about 17% of the water supply reaching a field (National Irrigation Commission, 1972). These losses are mostly due to faulty irrigation practices, and can be reduced by measures like volumetric charging for water to check over-irrigation; provision of field irrigation channels so that each field would have direct access to irrigation water, thereby avoiding irrigation by inundation from field to field as it leads to non-uniform distribution of water amongst the fields and causes loss of water as well as fertilizers ; grading and shaping of fields to provide for proper alignment of channels and field drains ; consolidation and rectangulation of land holdings, mainly for reducing the length of irrigation channels and increasing the effectiveness of field drains ; adoption of suitable methods of irrigation, including drip and sprinkler irrigation, according to prevailing crop, sol, and water availability conditions ; irrigational scheduling, including the time and depth of irrigation ; rotational supply of water ; and adoption of appropriate cropping patterns and soil management practices for making the best use of available wates, thereby avoiding any wastage.

Implementation of the above measures necessitates an integrated development of land and water resources. An ideal areal unit for the purpose would obviously be a river basin. This has led to the formulation of 'Command Area Development Programme' (CAD) by the Government of India in 1974.*

* See : Central Water Commission, 1981. *Report* on the Status of Irrigation Development in India through Major, Medium, Minor and CAD schemes.

It has not only hastened the utilization of the created irrigation potential but has also increased the agricultural production per unit of land and water in the command areas.

The programme incorporates 76 irrigation projects covering a total area of 15 m ha and has several Command Area Development Authorities, comprising multidisciplinary agencies, associated with the task of development of land and water resources. The Programme lays special emphasis on the conjunctive use of surface and ground water resources.

The engineering advantages of consolidation and rectangulation of holdings, the most significant land-reform measure related to checking of application losses, although indirectly, becomes evident from a perusal of the case study of an area in village Pakhrauli in Rae Bareli district in Uttar Pradesh (Sinha and Borah, 1980). The area covers 120 ha, out of which 97 ha was brought under consolidation. Realignment of irrigation and drainage channels was carried out in accordance with the topographical features of the area and the whole operation was completed in a period of about 3 years. The average size of holdings before consolidation was 0.35 ha, varying between 0.05 and 3.00 ha, and the individual plots, rather much scattered, were as small as 0.01 ha.

The highly significant impact of consolidation on irrigation water management in the area becomes obvious from a comparison of the pre-and post-consolidation conditions, given below : the first figure stands for the former and the second for the latter.

(1) Length of irrigation channels (m/ha)—140 ; 85
(2) Length of drains (m/ha)—153 ; 140
(3) Length of roads (m/ha)—37 ; 60
(4) Distance of the remotest plot from the irrigation channels (m)—50.80 ; Negligible
(5) Distance of the remotest plot from the field drains (m)—50.60 ; Negligible
(6) Area occupied by the channels and drains (percentage of the field area)—4.70 ; 3.85
(7) Area occupied by the roads (percentage of the field area)—1.00 ; 1.55

(8) Length of field bunds or embankments (m/ha)—1,000 ; 375.

(ii) *Linking of canals and water courses*

In the north Indian Plains, about 45 per cent water entering the head of an unlined canal is lost in transit at different stages, that is, 17 per cent from main canal and branches, 8 per cent from distributaries, and 20 per cent from water courses (National Irrigation Commission, 1972). However, in Punjab, seepage losses from unlined main canals amount to 115 ha m per year per 1 km length, as reported by Dakshinamurti *et al.* (1973, p. 100) whereas, for the same area, Punmia and Lal (1975, p. 615) give a figure of 2.44 cumecs per 1 million m^2 of wetted perimeter. For the unlined distributaries in the state, the former authority mentions a figure of 38.24 ha m per year per 1 km length of the channel.

Seepage from unlined canals has effected a significant rise in water table in the Indo-Gangetic Plain. For instance, in some canal irrigated tracts in Punjab, the water table has risen by as much as 7 to 9 m above the long-term levels recorded since 1895 during the pre-canal irrigation period (Pereira, 1973, p. 186). Further, well marked rises, in the water table accompanied by waterlogging and salinization, have been recorded in the Bhakra Command Area (2.71 million ha) due to seepage from the 4,800 km of the canals carrying a total discharge of 353 cumecs at full capacity.

Lining of canals for checking seepage losses involves heavy expenditure. It is, therefore, resorted to on a selective basis only and that too mostly in highly permeable soils or in high water table areas. The lining material commonly used in the country is brick or tile laid in cement mortor and also, in some cases, stone masonry or cement concrete. But the use of other materials like asphalt, synthetic rubber, plastic, bentonite etc. is at best in an experimental stage.

(iii) *Provision of intercepting drains along canals*

Provision of intercepting drains along canals as an anti-waterlogging measure is to drain away the subsoil flow of water from the canal, thereby checking the rise of water table. The drains, both surface and subsurface, run at right angles to the direction of ground water flow. In a hilly country, they could ideally be located along the foot-hill zone where infiltration from the hill-side enters the adjoining flat land. Their distance from the canal should be such that, while they intercept seepage and percolation, they do not draw water directly from the canal. This would mainly be judged by the difference in level between the canal water level and the adjoining water table.

Remedial measures

(i) *Provision of drainage*

Provision of a suitable drainage system is another anti-water-logging measure as it tends to increase the outflow of surface and subsurface water from the affected area. In fact, an efficient system of surface drains permits a quick flow of rain and excess irrigation water so that infiltration is reduced to the minimum. When deep enough, they also serve a seepage drains, carrying away the infiltrated rain and irrigation water, and thereby checking any rise in water table. The drainage problem in the country is quite acute in the Indo-Gangetic Plain due mainly to factors like flat topography, frequent floods, canal irrigation, and obstruction to natural drainage.

Land grading which provides for continuous land slope towards field drains situated at the lower end of a field, alongwith land consolidation, are important aspects of a drainage improvement programme whereby each field would have direct access to drainage channels. The slopes generally range from 0.1 to 0.5%—the flatter slopes being suitable for heavy clayey soils and the steeper ones for lightsandy soils.

The 'check-basin' method of irrigation, largely prevalent in the country, is hardly conducive to efficient surface drainage since it tends to ponding of surface water in the basin. On the other hand, 'border-strip' and 'furrow' methods of irrigation provide better surface drainage and need to be increasingly adopted in the country.

Subsurface drainage is generally poor in soils with low permeability and high water table. In such cases, the imminent rise in water table from infiltration of rain or irrigation water could be checked by installing subsurface drains or tile drains

Apart from being more effective than surface drains, they do not hinder agricultural operations nor cause any loss of valuable cultivable land. The tiles in the drain are laid in a continuous line, at a depth of about 1.2 to 1.6 m below the ground and give a slope towards the open drainage ditch or outlet which ultimately carries away the water. The tiles commonly used are 30 cm long and 10 to 12.5 cm in diameter and laid end to end with loose joints so that the infiltrating water, entering the tile-line at each joint, could be easily drained away.

The nature and extent of drainage required and the proper location for the drain and its outlet could be quickly though tentatively determined by a superimposition of the surface and water table contour maps of the area. This would also throw light on the areal extent of the part of the drainage basin contributing runoff to its lowlying waterlogged area, as well as the severety of waterlogging, the direction of surface and subsurface drainage, and the depth of water table below the ground.

(ii) *Improvement of natural drainage*

Improvement of natural drainage serves as an anti-waterlogging measure as it leads to removal of obstructions in the natural flow of water. The concerned operations include removal of silt and of obstructions from aquatic weeds or other vegetative growth, and adjustments in the gradient of channels. Also, any obstruction from embankments, constructed for flood protection, or for canals, roads, railways etc., could be removed by suitably remodelling them wherever possible. In fact, due to faulty planning, they often run across the direction of natural drainage. However, little can be done if the obstructions are due to natural causes like impervious clayey subsoil layers, rocky strata, or 'hidden ridges', like the 'Delhi-Lahore ridge' underneath the alluvium in the north-western part of the Indo-Gangetic Plain.

(iii) *Pumping from wells*

Pumping from wells helps the anti-waterlogging operations by increasing the outflow of water from the affected area. The water table is thus brought down to the safe level by the removal of excess ground water. For example, the rice fields in the

Kuttanad region in Kerala, extensively waterlogged during the monsoon season, have been reclaimed by using propeller pumps for removal of excess ground water.

Further, in the Jagadhri Tube-well Scheme in Haryana, a battery of 384 tube-wells have been installed along the Western Yamuna Canal, including its main branch canal, to pump out excess ground water from the waterlogged area. The pumped out water is then conjunctively used to augment the discharge of the canal by about 17 cumecs. Being at a safe distance from the canal, the tube-wells are not drawing canal water by induced seepage.

The phenomenon of induced seepage has, however, been noted in the case of the Upper Ganga Canal in Meerut district of Uttar Pradesh. A battery of 30 feeder tube-wells, with a discharge of 0.085 cumec each, have been installed along the canal, primarily for supplementing the discharge of the canal during the lean months. The wells, situated at a distance of 125 to 365 m from the canal, have been found to be drawing canal water by induced seepage (Kathpalia, 1955 ; Sharma *et al.*, 1961).

SOIL SALINITY AND ALKALINITY

Soil salinity and alkalinity occurs due to disturbance of the salt balance of the soil. In India, the evil occurs mostly in the arid and semi-arid regions since rainfall is not adequate enough to leach or wash away the soluble salts from the soil. Also, prevalence of high temperatures promotes excessive evaporation of water from the soil, thereby increasing its salt content. Many investigators have put forward the view that aridity conditions in these regions have developed mainly as a result of the disturbance of the ecological balance by human activities. The salt problem is thus believed to be largely a man-made phenomenon.

Further, introduction of irrigation in the country has often brought new lands under the evil due to disturbance of the salt balance whereby more salt is brought into the area as compared to that being removed from the area, either due to waterlogging, as noted earlier, or by the use of saline irrigation water, or under their combined influence. As a result, some areas in

Gujarat, Rajasthan, Punjab (mainly Ferozepur, Bhatinda, and Sangrur districts), Haryana (Rohtak, Gurgaon, Mohindergarh and Hissar districts), Uttar Pradesh (Agra and Mathura districts), the Union Territory of Delhi etc. have been rendered infertile.

Capillary rise of ground water and its subsequent evaporation results in the deposition of dissolved salts, mostly of sodium, calcium and magnesium, in the root-zone or even on the ground. In the latter case, the incrustation of salts is known by such local names as 'reh', 'kallar' or 'thur'. Heavy clayey soils, with their low permeabilities, are more prone to the problem on account of their extremely slow leaching action. Also, presence of any hard '*kankar*' (a nodular form of impure calcium corbonate) bed in the subsoil augments the problem by impeding the drainage.

Accumulation of salts in the root-zone adversely affects plant growth by reducing the capacity of the roots to absorb water and nutrients from the soil. Further, adsorption of sodium salts ont he soil, when the water used for irrigation contains high proportion of sodium salts in solution, may alter the physical condition of the soil, thereby retarding plant growth.

However, irrigation water with moderate salinity could be used if there be adequate drainage and if enough irrigation water is applied so that some of it goes through the soil profile and is ultimately drained out of the area, thereby maintaining the water table sufficiently below the root-zone. It would be desirable too to adopt a cropping pattern wherein salt tolerant crops like cereals, are grown in preference to legumes. However, it would be even more profitable to grow fodder crops than cereals since straw yield is less adversely affected than grain yield.

Saline soils

In saline soils, electrical conductivity of the saturation extract is more than 4 umhos/cm at 25°C and the exchangeable sodium percentage is less than 15. The pH value is generally less than 8.5. The excess soluble salts in the soils may be removed by leaching so that they may again become normal soils. Therefore, they do not pose any serious problem to agriculture.

These soils are recognised by the presence of white crusts of salts on the ground. The soils are generally flocculated due to presence of excess salts and absence of significant amounts of exchangeable sodium. As a result, their permeability is equal to or higher than that of similar non-saline soils.

Akali soils

On the other hand, in the case of alkali soils, found mostly in the arid and semi-arid regions, the exchangeable sodium percentage is greater than 15 and conductivity of the saturation extract is less than 4 umhos/cm at 25°C. The pH values range between 8.5 and 10. The soils have low permeability since the colloids swell when wet due to high sodium concentration. This impedes infiltration of water whereby most of the rain falling on them is lost as runoff.

Areas affected by salinity and alkalinity

In India, the saline and alkali soils mainly occur in the arid or semi-arid tracts in the northern plains in Rajasthan, Punjab, Haryana and Uttar Pradesh, in the irrigated '*regur*' or black cotton soil region in Peninsular India, and in the coastal alluvial tracts which face intrusion or inundation by sea-water.

It is estimated that about 25 million ha land in the country is affected by salt problems. The main states. in decreasing order of the area affected, in million ha, alongwith corresponding percentages in terms of the state's total area, are : Uttar Pradesh—1.3 m ha, 4.4 per cent; Gujarat-1.2 m ha, 6.4 per cent; West Bengal—0.85 m ha, 9.7 per cent ; Rajasthan—0.73 m ha, 2.1 per cent ; Punjab—0.69 m ha, 13.5 per cent ; Maharashtra—0.54 m ha, 1.8 per cent ; Haryana-0.53 m ha, 12.1 per cent ; Orissa—0.41 m ha, 2.6 per cent ; and Karnataka—0.41 m ha, 2.1 per cent.

The severely affected areas in Uttar Pradesh occurs in the Ganga-Yamuna and the Ganga-Gomti doabs. Except for in the south-west, comprising most of Mathura and Agra, and parts of Etah and Mainpuri districts, where the problem is mainly of salinity, the bulk of the affected areas, in the districts of Aligarh, Etawah, Kanpur, Unnao, Pratapgarh, Hardoi, Rae Bareli etc., suffer from alkalinity.

Preventive and remedial measures

Soil salinity and alkalinity, resulting from waterlogging, can be checked by adoption of the preventive anti-waterlogging measures, as discussed earlier. However, reclamation in such cases involves the use of remedial measures. For instance, in the case of saline soils, the salts are leached below the root-zone by applying sufficient irrigation water and keeping the water table deep enough by pumping or by drainage so that the salts do not reach the root-zone, thereby allowing the plants to freely derive their nutrients. If salt content in the lower layers be higher than that in the surface layers then provision has to be made for subsurface drains.

Reclamation of alkali soils is relatively more difficult since they have low permeability and require the replacement of excessive exchangeable sodium by calcium. They have, therefore, to be treated with amendments like gypsum, pyrites, calcium chloride, sulphur etc., or by organic material such as manure and molasses or leguminous crops like '*dhaincha*' (Serbania aculeata).

Further, deep ploughing helps in the development of root system in the subsoil, thereby speeding up the downward movement of water. Also, a crop of rice, after application of gypsum, with adequate use of manures and fertilizers to provide for nitrogen, phosphorus, potassium and zinc, hastens the reclamation process. Thus, adoption of proper soil management practices and cropping patterns are important aspects of the process.

CONCLUSIONS

The environmental problems arising out of wastage of water from faulty irrigation practices, often in combination with the other contributory factors, could certainly be minimised, if not altogether eliminated, by an integrated development of land and water resources, preferably with a river basin as the basic areal unit for planning. So far, the development in the country has mainly been on an ad-hoc project-by-project basis.

As regards the use of water for irrigation the water resource development plants should lay emphasis on judicious application of water on the farm, including proper timing of irrigation according to changing plant requirements, suitable cropping patterns and soil management practices for high water use efficiency, efficient water conveyance system, provision of proper drainage for removal of excess water, and conjunctive use of surface and ground water resources.

REFERENCES

Central Water Commission. 1981. *Report on the status of irrigation development in India through major, medium, minor and CAD schemes.*

Chaturvedi, M.C. 1976. *Water : Second India Studies*, Macmillan, New Deihi.

Dakshinamurti, C. *et al.* 1973. *Water resources of India and their utilization in agriculture*, Indian Agri. Res. Inst., New Delhi.

Kathpalia, K.N., 1955. Some aspects of losses in Upper Ganga Canal. *Jl. Central Board of Irrigation and Power*, Vol. 12, No. 4, pp. 590-599.

Nace, R.L. 1969. World Water inventory and Control. In: *Introduction to Geographical Hydrology* (Ed. R.J. Chorley), Methuen, London.

National Irrigation Commission. 1972. *Report of Irrigation Commission*, Vol. I, Ministry of Irrigation and Power, Govt. of India, New Delhi.

Pereira, H.C. 1973. *Land use and water resources*, Cambridge Univ. Press, Cambridge.

Punmia, B.C., and Lal, P.B.B. 1975. *Irrigation and water power engineering*, Standard Publishers Distributors, Delhi.

Sharma, H.D. *et al.* 1961. Experimental studies on induced infiltration from canal by adjacent well and the effects of partial penetration on well efficiency, *Tech. Memo. No. 31-R.R. (S-16)*, U.P. Irrig. Res. Inst., Roorkee, India.

Simons, M. 1967. *Deserts : The problem of water in arid lands*, Oxford Univ. Press, London.

Sinha, C.P., and Borah, R.C. 1980. The evaluation of an Alkali Soil Reclamation Project at Pakharauli in Uttar Pradesh, *Proc. Inter. Symp. on Salt Affected Soils, Karnal, India*, Feb. 18-21, 1980.

11

THE ROLE OF RESERVOIRS IN REGIONAL DEVELOPMENT

A.B. Avakyan

Reservoir construction is one of the few fields of human activity that entails prompt, multiform and radical transformations of nature and economy of certain regions. Reservoirs, or man-made lakes, serve a basis for water use and regulation. They are one of the most important factors changing geographical environment in many river basins of the world. After World War II reservoir construction acquired global character. All over the world the number of reservoirs has increased 4 times, and their total volume—10 times, during the last 30 years. In Latin America their volume has increased 35 times, in Africa—60, and in Asia—90 times. All the world's largest reservoirs have been constructed during this period. More than 30,000 man-made lakes are under operation on the Earth at present. Their total volume exceeds 6,000 cu km and the surface totals almost 400,000 sq km.

Construction of reservoirs has resulted in changes of natural conditions on the territory of 700,000 sq km. Infrastructural changes, caused by population resettlement and reorganization of the national econony enveloped the area of 1.5 mln sq km, which makes up nearly half of the territory of India, one of the largest countries in the world.

It goes without saying that the transforming role of man-made lakes manifests itself mainly in the places where they are located. Being the key to many water management problems, reservoirs eliminate or attenuate certain contradictions caused by the development of the national economy. On the other hand, man-made lakes themselves cause new conflicts between certain branches of the water economy, that make different demands on the character and degree of runoff regulation, reservoir parameters, bed preparation, operation regime, time of construction, conditions of initial filling, location and structure of hydroschemes. Conflicts within certain branches of the national economy also arise, because reservoirs have both positive and negative effects on every branch of the water economy, except hydraulic power engineering. The development of water management practice, construction of reservoir cascades and interbasin connections aggravate certain intra-and interbranch conflicts. In all these cases reservoirs cause undesirable consequences for the areas where hydraulic structures themselves are located and also in their lower pools.

The area affected by large man-made lakes totals thousands of square kilometers, stretching over hundreds and thousands kilometers along the river course. Consequences of reservoir construction manifest themselves differently in various natural zones and economic regions.

Economic role and effectiveness of man-made lakes are determined primarily by their geographical position. The latter influences their parameters, direction and intensity of the development of various natural processes, reservoir preparation, structure of water management complex, operation regime, etc. The direct interdependence between various natural and technological and economic factors manifests itself most clearly in construction and multipurpose use of reservoirs. Therefore, geographical conditions should be taken into account for the purpose of selecting an optimum solution of water management problems in every region.

The USSR and India are among the 5 countries of the world possessing the greatest number of man-made lakes including those with the volume exceeding 100 mln cu m. Table 10.1 shows the number and some parameters of such reservoirs.

TABLE 10.1 : **USSR and India greatest number of man-made reservoirs**

Country	Number of reservoirs with the volume exceeding 100 mln cu m	Total full volume of reservoirs (cu km)	Correlation between the total reservoir volume and the territory of the country mln c um / thousand sq km	Correlation between the total reservoir volume and the population of the country mln cu m / mln people
USSR	241	1,274	57	4,700
India	202	227	69	332
USA	766	779	83	3,357
Canada	139	771	77	32,104
China	147	237	25	237

Reservoirs differ from natural freshwater bodies in terms of the following characteristics :

(a) reservoir construction violates sharply the relative equilibrium in nature leading to bank and bed reformation, rising of groundwater level, surfacing of peats, changes of fauna and climate in the shore zone, etc. ;

(b) all processes develop differently in different zones of the reservoir (in the zone of backwater decline, in the near-dam zone, etc.) ;

(c) reservoir construction entails radical changes in the economy of neighbouring regions and in the valleys downstream from the dam ;

(d) parameters and operation regime effecting the development of certain processes are determined by people, i.e. the level and profundity of our knowledge influence the direction and intensity of natural processes ;

(e) reservoirs are included in two systems of inter linkages—natural and social—and are subjected to the influence of various elements of both these systems.

Moreover it should be borne in mind that the number of man-made lakes increases every year, and this process will continue, while the number of natural water bodies remains invariable.

The necessity of reservoir construction at present and in the near future is determined by the following economic and social factors :

(a) water supply of industrial regions, cities, towns, and thermal power stations ;
(b) river runoff regulation in water deficit regions for the purpose of irrigation and water allocation to new tracts of land and reclamation of irrigated lands ;
(c) runoff regulation promoting multipurpose use of river hydro-power resources, turning rivers into comfortable deep-water-ways ;
(d) flood control in the valleys of rivers with sharp flow fluctuations ;
(e) interregional water transfer ;
(f) construction of recreational zones near some towns and resorts ;
(g) re-regulation of water discharge in lower pools of large hydropower stations according to the schedule that meets in the best way the demands of water transport, irrigation, fishery and timber-rafting.

It is only on the basis of system analysis that we can appraise the economic importance of reservoirs, both as an aggregate and separately for each of them. During reservoir construction and operation, multiform after-effects of suggested projects should be thoroughly analysed, such as the choice of parameters, measures on reservoir bed preparation, etc. Every large reservoir should be regarded from different standpoints, i.e. :

—as a storage of water, the important resource for many branches of the national economy ;
—as an object improving or deteriorating water quality ;
—as a flow regulator transforming river regime *in the*

direction favourable for many branches of water economy;

—as a source and accumulator of hydraulic power, capable of carrying peak loads, of regulating frequencies and providing emergency reserves ;

—as a water surface, used for water transport, fishery, recreation ;

—as a land consumer (inundation, water-logging, shore reformation) ;

—as an object allowing us to increase the area of arable lands by means of irrigation, flood control inter regional water transfer ;

—as an object, changing nature and economy of river valleys, deltas, inland seas, lakes and estuarien zones of seas.

The influence of Reservoirs on nature is multiform. It may be direct or indirect, positive or negative. It may manifest itself immediately or after many years after the man-made lake is constructed. This influence also depends on intrasecular and other climatic fluctuations, that can attenuate or aggravate the reservoir effect on climate, hydrological, hydrogeological and other processes.

Reservoirs influence various elements of the environment : hydrological regimes up and downstream the dam (right up to the river mouth) aquatic and terrestrial ecosystems, objects of national economy, social and economic conditions of human existences, etc.

Reservoir parameters (surface, volume, depth, length. width), its plan configuration, composition of rocks forming its bed and banks, the character of its regulation, its operation regime, climate fluctuations—all this is of great importance for changes in natural processes and the directions of these changes in the upper pools of hydraulic structures. The character and scales of variations in the flow (diurnal, weekly, seasonal and year-to year) have a considerable influence on changes of hydrological regime and the natural conditions in the lower pool.

Reservoir construction is aimed at changing many environmental elements. In this case a man-made lake is regarded as a means of nature transformation and economic development.

Among such planned transformations we single out :

—improvement of hydrological network ;

—seasonal, year-to year, weekly and diurnal runoff redistribution, creation of water surface in the interests of various branches of the national economy ;

—concentration and accumulation of hydropower resources ;

—transformation of hydrological regime for the purpose of rational land-use (saving flood-plains from excessively frequent or long-term floods, etc.) ;

—drawing of non-productive lands into national economy by means of water resource accumulation and creation of more productive aquatic media (fishery and pisciculture) ;

—attenuation or complete elimination of disastrous natural phenomena, such as floods, droughts, sedimentation of lakes and bays, etc. ;

—improvement of natural conditions in adjacent areas : making the climate mild, creation of a special network of water bodies, etc.

At the same time reservoir construction and operation leads to a number of undesirable and, as a rule, inevitable, environmental changes. However we have to reconcile ourselves to this fact. It is necessary to develop and implement complex measures on conceivable attenuation of negative after-effects.

The most significant negative effects of reservoir construction and operation on the environment are as follows :

—inundation of lands ;

—reformation of reservoir bed and banks ;

—erosion of river bed and banks downstream from the dam (and in some cases—sea-shores near deltas), resulting from detention of solid river runoff in the man-made lake ;

—rising of the groundwater level, causing water-logging and bogging up of lands ;

—transformation of vegetation and soils under the influence of water-logging and microclimate changes (intensification of winds, increase of air humidity, etc.) ;

—changes in the dwelling conditions of fauna in river valleys ;

—radical changes of aquatic fauna in the stream itself, the latter being transformed from a river into a reservoir with slow current velocity changing as a result the dwelling and breeding conditions of various aquatic organisms particularly of fish ;

—changes of water quality resulting from the slowing-down of current velocity, decrease of water self-purification capacity, excessive growth of blue-green algae and other factors.

The above changes are usually negative from the view-point of environmental protection. However it should be emphasized that reservoir effect on nature is multiform and discrepant.

Reservoir construction effects landscapes of river valleys and lake hollows. On big rivers, water-bodies resembling lakes, 10-20 km wide and hundreds of kilometers long appear instead of a river bed, its width varying from several hundred meters to 1-3 kilometers. The maximum depth of flat-country reservoirs is 20-40 m. In foothill and mountain regions it may achieve 100 or even 200-300 m. Water surface of large reservoirs is comparable to that of biggest natural lakes.

Downstream the landscape of the reservoir river valley also changes, especially during seasonal and long-term flow regulation.

Disappearance of peaks or complete cessation of floods lead to the decrease of flood-plains. Changes of solid flow regime results in river bed erosion directly downstream the reservoir and in variations of river bed processes in deltas. River valley landscapes change considerably when the whole of the flow or its greater part is diverged by derivational canals to the neighbouring river basins.

Reservoir processes are determined mainly by the character of water interchange, which causes constant runoff output flow, intensive turbulent mixing, thermal stratification, water mineralization and aeration, as well as hydrochemical, hydrobiological and other peculiarities. Reservoir water interchange is subjected to seasonal and year-to-year variations, depending on the amount of water, the character of water use, etc. Current velocity in reservoirs is 10 times slower than in natural water bodies.

Complicated transformations of river water masses occur. The basic parameters of water masses remain practically unchanged from season to season and from year to year. So do the general principles of their distribution in the man-made lake.

Variations of hydrological regime (levels, current velocity, currents, waves, solid flow and so on) in the upper and lower pools of hydraulic structures influence hydrobiological processes inside water bodies, that leads to formation of specific biotopes and biocenoses in reservoirs.

Landscape and hydrological regime variation are of great importance for the nature of adjacent areas. Reservoir interaction with the environment (particularly with the nature in the catchment area directly adjacent to the reservoir, as well as territories, lying downstream from the reservoir), differs greatly from the interaction between natural rivers and the environment. These distinctions are different for plain and mountain regions and for various latitudal and altitudal geographical zones.

Microclimatic changes occur due to the appearance of water masses accumulating and returning much heat, large water surface and other factors, that manifest themselves above the man-made lake itself and in the adjacent area. These changes envelop practically all the elements of climate-radiation balance, air temperature, humidity, wind regime, etc. The influence of large reservoirs spreads over a comparatively narrow riverside zone (not more than 10-15 km wide). However, significant reservoir effect on climate is exerted in the zone 1-3 km wide.

Changes of climatic and hydrological conditions raise the groundwater level in the adjacent areas, entailing their bogging up, changes in soil mineralization and its transformation, leading to peat-bog formation. Vegetation transforms, which manifests itself in excessive growth of hydrophyle plants. The conditions of animal dwelling change, particularly of aquatic and semi-aquatic furbearing mammals and waterfowl. The scale of these changes is appreciable. Thus the total area of lands, subjected to water-logging on the banks of USSR man-made lakes is estimated at hundreds of thousand of hectares. More than 50% of reservoir banks were re-formed. Many examples of this can be given.

Significant environmental changes are also observed on territories lying downstream the reservoir, neighbouring to the rivers with regulated flow. On some of them (the Volga, Irtysh, Syrdaria, and others) these changes threatened to become irreversible, but were averted due to the construction of special water releases from the upstream reservoirs (the Kuibyshev, Bukhtarma, Chardara). These waters restored the natural flood regime to some extent. For example, 70-130 cu km of water is sent every spring into the Volga lower reaches for the purpose of water supply of the Volga-Akhtuba flood-land in the interests of pisciculture (the volume of water depending on the year—dry or wet).

Man-made lakes influence modern tectonic processes promoting the occurrence of earthquakes, intensifying their frequency and aggravating them.

Changes of water quality resulting from reservoir interaction with the environment are very important. They have a considerable effect almost on all the types of water use, changing physical properties of water, its salt balance, concentration and forms of biogene elements, as well as quantity and distribution of phyto-and zooplankton. Sedimentation of suspended solids, increase of water transparence occur during river flow transformations in the reservoirs. Dissolved oxygen concentration in all big man-made lakes is favourable for aquatic organisms, although it does not achieve full saturation. The absence of dissolved oxygen is observed on the water-sediment interface under the conditions of marked thermal stratification.

At the same time when river water with high content of biogene elements flows into a reservoir, its self-purification is violated, particularly when the excessive growth of blue-green algae is observed. This is explained by a lower current velocity in man-made lakes as compared to rivers.

Every group of reservoirs has its own effect on the environment. Large and largest man-made lakes (with the volume exceeding 50 cu km and surface—5,000 sq km) exert irreversible effect on the adjacent areas. Besides, their influence often spreads over dozens and hundreds of kilometres downstream the dam, causing stable changes in river bed regime, solid flow and processes of coastal delta formation. The effect of large man-made lakes (with the volume exceeding 1 cu km and surface—100 sq km) mainfests itself in the river valley and adjacent areas.

A relatively prompt stabilization of the interaction with the environment is typical of medium and small man-made lakes. Although in this case the main environmental changes taking place, are not irreversible. Small and medium reservoirs have moderate negative effect on nature and the national economy. This allows us to recommend their construction practically everywhere.

On the basis of the negative after-effects of reservoir construction, we may classify them in two groups : those inherent to reservoirs themselves, and those caused by the violation of operational rules such as inopportune accommodation of certain objects of the national economy to the new hydrological conditions, as well as by low level of design works.

Under the conditions of increasing land values. acceleration of the economic development of river valleys and the influence of other socio-economic factors, the possibility of constructing large (particularly very large) man-made lakes is either absent or limited in the greater part of the world. In the future mainly small and medium reservoirs will be constructed, allowing us to meet the constantly increasing demands in water, made by water supply, fishery, recreation, etc.

The Bhakra reservoir on the Sutlej river (a tributary of the Indus river in the State of Punjab, India), is a classic example of the role of man-made lakes in regional development. This reservoir is also known under the name of Gobindsagar. Its total volume is 9.9 cu km, useful volume—7.4 cu km, surface—168 sq km. The reservoir was filled in 1963—1967.

The importance of its role in the economic development of the region is unquestionable. Its water irrigates desert regions in Punjab, Haryana and Rajasthan. The area of its irrigated lands can be increased up to 1.6 mln hectares. The reservoir construction saved 0.5 mln. hectares of land from floods. The hydropower station with the installed capacity of 1 mln kW, provides cheap electric power for municipal economy and industry. Navigation conditions improved along the greater part of the river course.

Reservoir construction effected fish stock : reophyle fish disappeared, instead, limnophyle fish widely spread. Fish catches increased more than 10 times in the river reach, turned into a reservoir. A few very profitable carp-breeding farms were organized. The dam and man-made lake favoured the development of tourism, international as well, promoted by the creation of recreational infrastructure, construction of motor highways on the reservoir banks. These highways connected the reservoir with other recreational centers in the inner Himalayas. Bathing, canoeing, wind-serfing and other kinds of aquatic sports attract more and more tourists every year.

The reservoir is constructed in an economically developed region. 375 villages with the population of 36,000 people were subjected to various effects of reservoir. 63 villages were completely inundated, as well as the town of Bilaspur, its population amounting 5,000 people who received full indemnity for their lands, houses, fruit-trees and wells. New arable lands were prepared instead of inundated ones. Population resettlement was thoroughly thought of and properly organized. It took place gradually, stage-by-stage, and thus caused no conflicts. A new town and comfortable villages were built instead of old ones.

Since dam construction disturbed traditional age-old timber-rafting of valuable tree species, timber trans-shipment was organized from the river to the funicular railway, which delivered the timber to the Nangal railway station. Nangal was turned into a large timber-trans-shipment center with the population of several thousand people. The Bhakra reservoir caused multiform environmental changes, connected mainly with the cessation of floods. Microclimate also changed in the near-shore zone : the average maximum summer temperature fell by 4.1 to 4.3°C, the average diurnal temperature by 1.5 to 3.0°C. During the cold season the water mass exerts warming effect on air (its temperature rose by 5.0 to 8.0°C). The temperature of surface water layers in the reservoir rose by 1.0 to 2.0°C during warm seasons, and by 6.0 to 8.0°C during cold seasons, as compared to the temperature of surface water layers in the river.

99 per cent of sediments accumulates in the reservoir. The amount of sediment varies from 16.4 to 51.7 mln cu m, in

different years. The average annual volume of silting is 0.05 per cent. Therefore, under the present hydrological conditions in the catchment area the man-made lake will exist for several hundred years

One of the least favourable effects of reservoir construction is the inflow of clarified water mass into irrigation canals, that caused intensive growth of aquatic plants, which did not grow there before, since the water was turbid. Now that the water is clarified, the canals are overgrown with algae. Their manual and automatic cleaning proved ineffective. Herbicides could not be applied with this purpose for some ecological reasons. Experiments showed that the only way out was to drain the canals regularly for a period of 2-5 days. Reservoir construction also had negative effects on some species of river flora and fauna. But on the whole, the Bhakra dam and reservoir can be rightfully characterized by the words of Jawahar Lal Nehru, who called them "A modern temple of revived India".

One can ennumerate other reservoirs, both in India and in the USSR, that exerted multiform effect on the environment. One of them is the Nurek reservoir on the Vakhsh river. This is one of the world's largest man-made lakes, constructed in a mountain region. Its total volume is 10.5 cu km, useful volume —4.5 cu km, surface—98 sq km. Its filling began in 1972. The Vakhsh flow regulation and the rise of the water level by 300 m made it possible to irrigate another 600,000 hectares of fertile lands in the Karshinsk and Kzyl-Kum Steppes and on the Dangarin Plateau. The Nurek hydroelectric power station with the installed capacity of 2.7 mln kW and the annual power production of 11.4 billion kWh is an important element in the power system of Central Asia. Runoff regulation improved the navigation conditions on the Amudaria and in the lower reaches of the Vakhsh. The reservoir banks are picturesque, they attract many tourists. Waters of the Nurek reservoir inundated 6,800 hectares of arable lands, which caused the resettlement of 1,500 people. Reservoir cascades are of primary importance for regional development. There are several such cascades in the USSR, among them the Volga, Dnieper, Angara, Yenisei and some others are the largest and most famous.

Let us now briefly analyse the role of the Volga reservoir

cascade. The Volga basin plays an outstanding role in the USSR national economy. Some 25 per cent of the population and 25 per cent of industrial and agricultural production is concentrated there. Water transport of the region carries out 70 per cent of the total river carriage on inland waters. The greater part of timber is rafted there, too. 50 per cent of all the fish and 90 per cent of sturgeon are caught in the Volga-Caspian basin. At present, the Volga and its largest tributary, the Kama, are transformed into a cascade of reservoirs, which are used multipurposely. Power production and water transport are the main beneficiaries of this water resource system (WRS). In the lower reaches of the Volgat here are other WRS beneficiaries, besides the ones mentioned above i.e., agriculture and pisciculture. However, it should be noted that reservoirs provide excellent conditions for the development of various branches of the national economy, that are not yet fully realized.

Hydropower stations of the Volga cascade are of great importance. Their installed capacity exceeds 12 mln kW, and their annual power production totals 40 billion kWh, that makes 1/5 of the total power produced by all the hydroelectric power stations of the USSR. Large stations of the cascade serve bases for the Power Grid of the European USSR. They take part in carrying peak loads and provide frequency and emergency reserves in the Power Grid, thus saving thermal power stations from operation under favourable regimes.

4,000 km of the Volga-Kama stream are turned into a waterway with a unified depth of 4 m. This allows us to use there ships of 2,000-5,000 tons displacement, instead of those with 600-1,000 tons displacement, used before. Reservoir construction provides the possibility to irrigate some 8 mln hectares of land in the Volga basin and to allocate water to 10 mln hectares of fertile chernozem and chestnut soils.

The reservoir cascade provides water supply to industrial centers, cities, towns, villages, thermal power stations. Thus, the Ivankovo reservoir helped to solve the problem of water supply of Moscow for many years. A special canal diverts water from the Gorkiy reservoir to the town of Ivankovo. The role of the Volga reservoir cascade in water supply is constantly increasing.

Some 30,000 tons of valuable species of fish is annually caught by collective fisheries and angles. Reservoirs are also very important for recreation. Millions of people, inhabiting the Volga basin, spend their vacations and week-ends on reservoir banks, mainly on those situated in the suburbs of Kazan, Ulianovsk, Tolyatti, Saratov and Volgograd. Reservoir shoals are rich in aquatic plants, which can be used as fodder. However, it should be mentioned that reservoir construction resulted in the inundation of 1 mln hectares of arable lands and thousands of people had to be resettled.

The experience in reservoir construction and operation, both in the USSR and abroad, allows the author to formulate some basic principles of reservoir construction :

(1) The necessity of implementing in advance multiform and detailed investigations of economic significance and efficiency of every reservoir. One should take into account all the positive and negative effects of the reservoir on nature and the national economy, both in the future and during its filling and the first years of operation, in the adjacent and far-away areas. In some cases all the calculations and measures should be carried out, taking into account multipurpose use of the reservoir along the whole river course, as well as in the neighbouring lakes and seas.

(2) The necessity of developing and implementing complex measures of reservoir bed preparation and the reconstruction of the economy in the zone of reservoir influence. Various projects should be studied on the basis of system analysis. Reservoir projects should be developed using regional planning schemes, which, in their turn, should envisage reservoir construction. Water surface planning and engineering measures on the reservoir should be carried out, when a man-made lake is projected. Economic social and ecological factors should be taken into account, special attention being paid to preservation of ecological balance and water quality. The area of valuable inundated lands should be reduced to a minimum.

(3) The dynamics of natural and anthropogenic factors should be taken into consideration, emphasis being laid on hydrotechnical construction in the river basin and possible measures on interregional water transfer. Prerequisites for the construction of reservoirs, their parameters, preparation and operation regime should be regarded as units of one chain where everything is interdependent.

(4) Reservoir construction should be considered expedient, if its total effect on the economy, in the interests of which it is constructed, defrays for the rated period, capital, operation and maintenance costs. However, the final decision can only be taken after an analysis of all non-economic factors, social, ecological, aesthetic, etc.

REFERENCES

1. Avakian, A.B., *Modern problems of construction, multipurpose use and investigations of reservoirs.*—Vodnye Resursy, 1982, No. 6, (in Russ.).
2. Avakian, A.B., Sharapov V.A., *Reservoirs of the USSR hydropower stations.* 3rd edition. Moscow, "Energiya", 1977 (in Russ.).
3. *Man-made lakes : their problems and environmental effects.* Washington, D.C., Amer. Geophys. Union, 1973.
4. Matarzin, Yu. M., Bogoslovskiy B.B., Matskevich I.K., *Handbook on the special course of reservoir hydrology*, in 5 series, Perm, 1977, 1978, 1982, 1984 (in Russ.).
5. Rao, K., Palta B., *Great man-made lake of Bhakra*, India—In : Man-made lakes, Washington, 1973.
6. *Reservoirs of the world.* Moscow, "Nauka", 1979 (in Russ.).
7. Vendrov, S.L., *Problems of transforming the USSR river systems. Leningrad*, "*Gidrometeoizdat*", 1979 (in Russ.).
8. N. Rubin, N.M. Warren , *Dams in Africa*, London, Frank. Cass., 1968.

12

POLLUTION HAZARDS TO WATER BODIES IN URBAN SETTING

Problems in Micro Planning

S. Manzoor Alam

INTRODUCTION

Industrial pollution hazards have of late magnified and have consequently emerged as major micro level planning problems in the metropolitan settlements of India. Our attention has been focused tragically on this problem by the recent grim tragedy in Bhopal where over two thousand innocent men, women and children lost their lives and thousands have been affected by diverse types of lung and bronchial diseases, by the leakage of poisonous methyl isocyanate gas. These pollution hazards, besides affecting human lives are also likely to obliterate and annihilate our rich architectural heritage as well if we do not take immediate and adequate precautionary measures to protect the lives of our people and their achievement. In this study attention has been focused on pollution hazards in metropolitan Calcutta and Hyderabad, and the Dal Lake of Srinagar which is considered as one of the most scenic lakes of India and is of great tourist attraction.

METROPOLITAN HYDERABAD

Metropolitan Hyderabad is experiencing a dynamic phase of

growth through accelerated industrialisation and high order tertiary development. This is highlighted by the following Table 12.1.

TABLE 12.1 : **Metropolitan Hyderabad**

Metropolitan Hyderabad Indicators	Socio-Economic Growth Pattern Period	
	1951	1981
Population (in million)	1.025	2.187
Industrial growth	1960	1977
No. of medium and large scale industrial units	13	100
No. of persons employed in large and medium industrial units	13,760	55,409
Capital invested (in Rs. million)	80.16	1541.00
	1966-67	1981-82
Per capita income (Rs.) per month	50.00	297.00
Proportion of migrants to total population	24.4	28.0 per cent

These dynamic elements of growth together with the inflow of petro-dollars from the Gulf countries have caused significant increase in the purchasing power of even the lower income groups. While on the one hand these dynamic processes of growth induce resilience in metropolitan economy by generating high rate of employment and high income, they also simultaneously enhance vulnerability consequent upon environmental pollution caused by discharge of industrial effluents, and multiplication of slums which exist under conditions of extreme poverty and squalor. These factors combine together to disturb the urban ecological balance and expose the metropolitan population to serious environmental hazards. In the following paras the vulnerability of metropolitan Hyderabad to pollution hazards has been examined briefly.

Industrial effluents and pollution

Hyderabad city has a diversified industrial base, dominated by engineering, chemical, textiles and food processing industries. These industries discharge colossal amount of industrial wastes which are released into lakes, rivulets and rivers. Ten of these industrial units viz. Indian Drugs and Pharmaceuticals Limited, Hindustan Aeronautics, Indian Detonators, Hindustan Machine Tools, Hyderabad Asbestos, Hyderabad Chemical and Fertilizers, Electronics Corporation of India, Hindustan Cables, Bakelite Hylam and Nuclear Fuel Complex contribute over 80 per cent of the total industrial wastes that flow out of the industrial units of metropolitan Hyderabad. These effluents contain strong concentration of organic matter which cause the depletion of oxygen from fresh water. The level of oxygen depletion was assessed by conducting the Biological Oxygen Demand (BOD) test. The Biological Oxygen Demand test of the effluents of selected industries reveals the astonishing fact that 19 of the 26 reporting industrial units have BOD values above the tolerance level of 30 mg/l (Fig 12.1).

The effluents of 38 industrial units were subjected to Chemical Oxygen Demand (COD) test. for many organic compounds do not decompose within 5 days' duration of BOD tests. The results of COD test are as such more precise and equally revealing. Under COD tests effluents of 26 out of 42 industrial units are above the range of tolerance i.e., 250 mg/l (Fig. 12.2).

These two tests signify the point that pollution through industrial effluents is of significant magnitude in metropolitan Hyderabad and calls for effective preventive measures. These effluents are being treated by the industries concerned but are obviously not diluted enough as to prove harmless. Since these are discharged in open drains, rivers, rivulets and tanks they lead to wide spread ground and surface water pollution.

Pollution and Nuclear Fuel Complex Industry* (NFC)

Among the industries located in Hyderabad, Nuclear Fuel

* Account on the pollution hazards due to NFC is based on the documents obtained from A.P. Pollution Board.

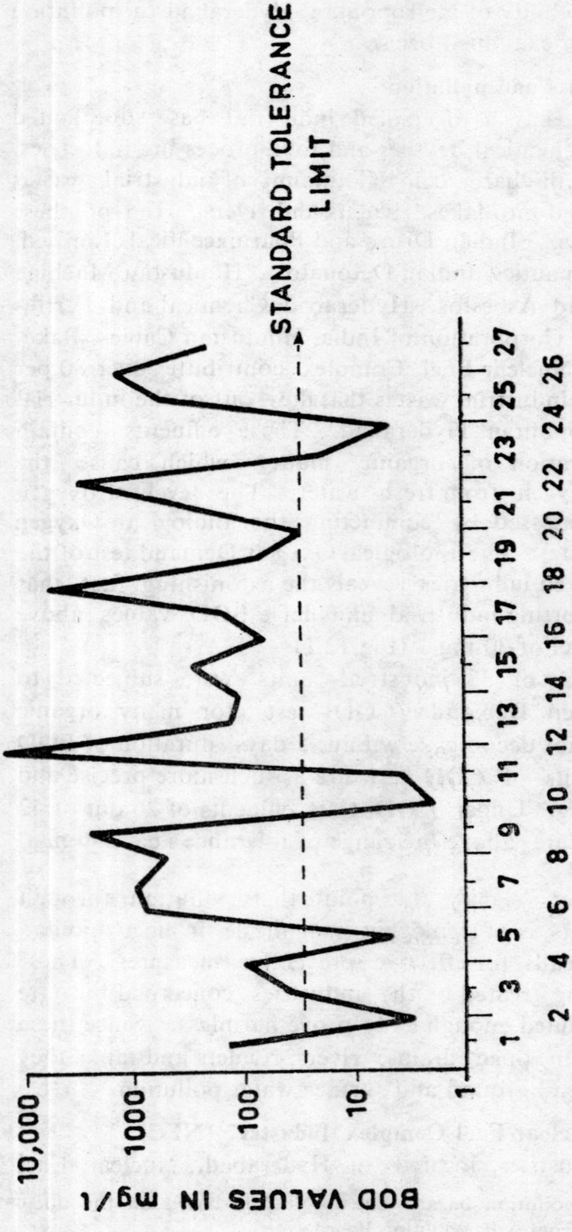

FIG. 12.1 : *Metropolitian Hyderabad BOD Values in mg/l of Industrial effluents*

Source : A.P. Pollution Control Board and National Environment Engineering Research Institute (Hyderabad)

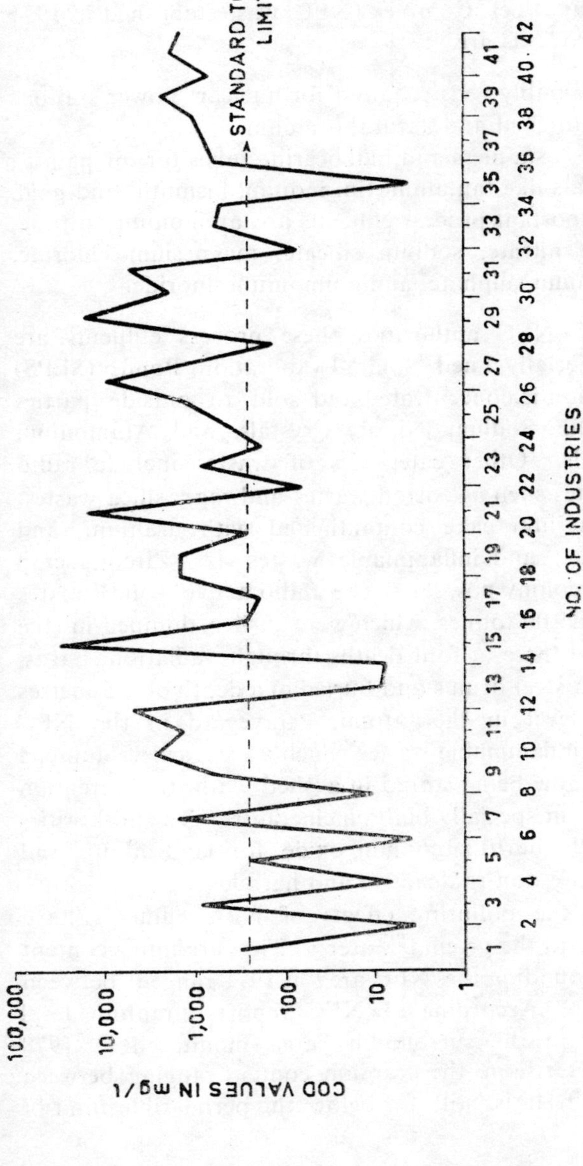

FIG. 12.2 : *Metropolitan Hyderabad COD Values in mg/l of Industrial effluents*

Source : A.P. Pollution Control Board and National Environment Engineering Research Institute (Hyderabad)

Complex is one of the most hazardous since it exposes the population of Hyderabad city and suburbs to radiation hazards. In view of this it is being dealt with in greater detail in order to appreciate the degree and level of radiation risk involved.

The Nuclear Fuel Complex (NFC) was established in 1971 and its main products are :

(1) Fuel assembly rods required for nuclear power stations using enriched and natural uranium ;
(2) Seamless, stainless and ball bearing tubes for oil paints ;
(3) Materials like tantalum, tin, indium, bismuth and gold. The important process effluents are ammonium nitrate, sodium nitrate, sodium silicate, magnesium chloride, ammonium sulphate, and ammonium fluoride.

According to NFC authorities these process effluents are "all taken to specially lined Solar Evaporation Ponds (SEPS) where the solution is concentrated and sold to outside parties as byproducts like Sodium Nitrate Crystals, and Ammonium Sulphate Crystals. Other categories of wastes include radio active solid wastes such as cotton wastes and rags, silica wastes, silica and magnesium cake contaminated with uranium, and calcium fluoride ; and inflammable wastes viz. Zircon scrap turnings and zircolony powder. The radio active solid wastes weighing around 100 tonnes, which were earlier dumped in the open and caused three or four deaths through radiation burns, are now filled in steel drums and buried at a depth of 2.5 metres below ground level in the atomic graveyard in the NFC premises. The inflammable wastes which were earlier dumped in the open are now being stored in a shed with the intention of burning them in specially built cincinerators. The authorities propose to use the burnt zirconium oxide for land filling and claim that they are non-radioactive and harmless

It seems that the polluting effects of NFC effluents have percolated down to the ground water : The uranium content in the wells surrounding the NFC area in 1971 ranged between 0.3-3 micr-gm/lit. According to NFC reports uranium level in all the wells in the surrounding area monitored in 1978 showed a distinct rise in the uranium content ranging between 11-50 micr/gm/lit. It is still far below the permissible limit of

2,000 micr-gm/lit. Nonetheless the trend is distinctly towards increase and calls for prompt preventive measures. Within a radius of 2.5 kilometres of NFC site the risk of ground water pollution has also magnified due to the rise in well water of nitrates and fluorides contents above permissible limits. This is largely due to the use of nitrates contaminated effluents for watering the plants in the NFC Campus.

	Mg/Lit Nitrate	*Mg/Lit Fluoride*
Mariguda	68.0	3.5
Mallapuram	135.0	2.0
Ashoknagar	74.0	1.95
Uppal	115.0	5.6
Habshiguda	395.0	4.25
Bakshiguda	343.0	1.3
Kushaiguda	87.0	1.5

If this rise in the level of nitrate and fluoride continues it may be a source of serious health hazard in future.

It may be observed that due to precautionary measures adopted by NFC the radiation hazards have minimised, nevertheless the fact remains that Hyderabad city is now exposed to radiation hazards which may aggravate in future if adequate preventive measures are not guaranteed.

Industrial effluents and surface water pollution

The polluting effect of these colossal amount of industrial effluents is abundantly reflected in the quality and character of the waters of the rivulet Kalvar, which passes through the Kukatpally-Balanagar Industrial area and drains into Hussain Sagar Lake. That the river is polluted is obvious from the murky colour of its water and the foul smell which persists all along its bank. In order to determine scientifically the degree of pollution in the rivulet Kalvar, Ravindra (1981) analysed its pollution load by estimating the values of ammoniacal nitrogen, nitrates, COD and BOD (Table 12.2). The table indicates strong presence of nitrates, and gradual increase of ammoniacal nitrogen. The COD and BOD values indicate that the river is getting progressively contaminated from a point near IDPL in Moosapet to the Hyderabad Public School near Begumpet, where it attains the maximum degree of contamination. Groundwater in this area is also polluted. A well, located adjacent

TABLE 12.2 : **Evaluation of Pollution Load of Certain Water Samples of Industries Belt of Kalvar River Basin**

Location	Nitrites	Ammonical Nitrogen	COD ng/litre	BOD mg/litre	Remarks
1. River Sample near IDPL Musapet (R_2)	Present	20.00	59.06	38.0	Polluted
2. River Sample at Balanagar Darga (R_3)	Present	30.00	149.60	84.0	Polluted
3. River Sample near Begumpet	Present	40.00	202.76	125.0	Polluted
4. Ground Water Sample of United Potteries, Musapet (17° 23′ 30″ : 78° 25′ 54″)	Present	8.00	38.00	23.0	Polluted
5. Ground Water Sample at Balanagar Darga (17° 27′ 30″ : 78° 27′ 21″)	Slight Traces	9.11	7.87	4.6	Slightly Polluted
6. Ground Water Sample from Hyderabad Public School, Begumpet (17° 25′ 34″ : 78° 27′ 42″)	Present	12.00	86.62	52.0	Polluted
7. Borewell Water from Nath Laboratory (17° 28′ 10″ : 78° 27′ 42″)	Slight Traces	0.23	5.00	3.4	Slightly Polluted
8. Khaithalpur Kunta	Present	18.00	55.12	36.0	Polluted
9. Well adjacent to Khaithalpur Kunta (17° 27′ 58″ : 78° 23′ 58″)	Slight Traces	0.15	7.87	4.8	Slightly Polluted

to the polluted Kalvar river, at Balanagar Dargah indicates low level pollution, but the degree of groundwater pollution rises significantly near Begumpet. On the whole however surface water in rivulet Kalvar is much more polluted than ground water in the adjacent area.

The river Kalvar drains into the Hussain Sagar lake which is located between Hyderabad and Secunderabad. Prior to the sixties the water in the lake was crystal blue but now because of the discharge of industrial effluents it is totally turned murky and its surface is invariably covered by the water hyacinth weeds. The industrial wastes which discharge into this lake are either "partly treated or untreated...include phenols, heavy metals, organic dyes, silt and sewage" (Suxena-Zafar, 1979). Consequently it is now transformed from crystal blue fresh water lake to a cess pool infested with strong cover of Eichhornea crassipes (water hyacinth) and other hardy weeds. The water of this lake is now marked for high concentration of inorganic and organic salts. Suxena and Zafar noted "high concentration of nitrates 1.13 mg/l and phosphate 0.43 mg/l indicating high level of eutrophication... The water contained several heavy metals e.g. mercury 0.016, zinc 0.95 mg/l, copper 0.4 mg/l, chromium 0.03 mg/l and lead 0.5 mg/l" (Suxena, Zafar—p. 13). In this lake heavy metals are absorbed in the hardy weeds and lodged in the lake bed which on analysis yielded as much as 152 mg mercury, 395 mg. zinc. 464 mg copper, 110 mg chromium, 145 mg lead in a kg. of dried soil." Its Composite Trophy Index (CTI) which measures level of pollution, is between 10-15 suggesting thereby that the lake water is highly polluted, is of extremely low quality and totally unfit for human consumption. Only a few decades ago Hussain Sagar was an important source of drinking water to north Hyderabad.

Man and agriculture as factors in pollution

While the rivulet Kalvar and the lake Hussain Sagar testify to a high degree of industrial pollution, the river Musi and the neighbouring lake of Mir Alam reflect pollution due to high density of human population and agricultural operations. Kanteshwar Raj (1980) has made an extensive study of the zoo

TABLE 12.3 : **Average Concentration of Some of the Chemical Factors (in PPm) during 1973-75**

Station & Year		Dissolved Oxygen	Oxidizable Organic Matter	Free Ammonia	Albuminoid Ammonia	Nitrates	Nitrites	Phosphate	Chlorides
I	1973-74	12.433	0.86	2.2189	3.132	0.128	0·058	0.03725	95.46
	1974-75	10.316	0.678	1.305	1.498	0.259	0.026	0.0437	82.729
	1973-75	11.375	0.769	1.762	2.315	0.1935	0.042	0.0404	89.094
II	1973-74	0.875	2.509	11.543	5.272	0.119	0.054	0.26	141.78
	1974-75	0.366	2.475	11.711	4.169	0.186	0.026	0.7164	106.07
	1973-75	0 62	2.492	11.627	4.7205	0.1525	0.04	0.4882	123.92
III	1973-74	1.16	1.682	9.673	4.723	0.1067	0.0704	0.199	159.46
	1974-75	1.166	1.897	8.001	3.484	0.108	0.085	0.564	135.029
	1973-75	1.16	1.791	8.837	4.103	0.10735	0.078	0.3811	147.24
IV	1973-74	4.116	1.53	6.19	4.263	0.102	0.1428	0.125	185.6
	1974-75	3.108	1.62	8 398	2.947	0.099	0.0649	0.445	151.279
	1973-75	3.612	1.575	7.294	3.605	0.1005	0.1038	0.285	168.439

Source : Kanteshwar Raj : The ecobiology of zoo planktons and allied organisms of the river Musi, Hyderabad (India) with special reference to water pollution Ph.D. thesis, unpublished, 1980.

planktons and allied organisms of the river Musi and has also made a physio-chemical and biological analysis of its water. The river Musi passes through the heart of the town and separates the walled city of Hyderabad along the southern bank from its northern extension. The scholar selected four stations for physiochemical analysis of water. Two were located along densely populated area viz. Chaderghat and Amberpet and one each on the western and eastern peripheries. The results obtained are tabulated in Table 12.3. It is highlighted by the table that stations 2 and 3 which are located in areas of high population concentration "show very high concentration of free ammonia, albuminoid ammonia, chlorides and high values or oxidisable organic matter." In contradistinction are "low concentrations of free and albuminoid ammonia, oxidisable organic matter, phosphates and chlorides" in station I which may be regarded as unpolluted site. Station 4 shows a moderate level of pollution with "significant decrease in the concentration of oxidisable organic matter, free and albuminoid ammonia as well as phosphates. The chloride values are quite high at this station which may be attributed to the drainage water which seeped in the river from the adjoining area" (Kanteshwar Raj—op. cit.). It may thus be concluded that stations II and III which are located close to the densely populated areas received sewage discharges and are grossly contaminated. This high concentration of oxidisable and nitrogenous compounds at these sites indicate pollution due to decomposition.

Comparable to this level of river pollution is the pollution in the lake of Mir Alam near the Nehru Zoological Park. This lake was constructed in 1806 and was for quite sometime used to supply drinking water to the walled city. It has now ceased to be a source of water supply and its water is now unfit for human and even animal consumption. Suxena and Zafar point out that "due to aging it has silted heavily and maintains calcareous water which is rather hard for human consumption." It has been estimated roughly that during the period 1965-79 its chloride content has increased at the rate of 1.46 mg/l/year. It receives large quantum of nitrate from the surrounding agricultural fields, and also of silicate from the floor wash of the nearby filter beds. Consequently it maintains, round the year, a fairly high level of nitrate 0.66 mg/l and silicate 17 mg/l which are "harmful to both human and animal consumption" (Suxena-Zafar, 1979, p. 7). Its Composite Trophy Index (CTI) has been assessed to range between 8-10 which indicates a fairly high order of pollution.

This brief analysis focuses attention on the growing hazard of surface water pollution in metropolitan Hyderabad due to industrial effluents as well as human and agricultural factors. We have also observed that the city is now exposed to radiation hazards as well. The State Pollution Control Board does exercise some control but it is not effective enough to minimise, much less eliminate, the polluting effects of industrial wastes and human filth. If the city and state planning authorities fail to contain pollution, it may emerge in the next decade or so, as a major health hazard and threaten the survival of the elements of resilience in the metropolitan system.

Calcutta metropolitan district

The pollution hazards of Calcutta metropolitan are of far greater magnitude and of more serious proportion than metropolitan Hyderabad because of its much larger scale of industrialization and larger size of population. This is being highlighted in the following paras.

The Calcutta Metropolitan district stretches over a distance of 100 kms. from Kalyani in the north to Budge Budge in the South. It contains a population exceeding 10 million and has a high concentration of large scale jute, engineering, chemical, leather industries etc. This straggling metropolitan district is also interspersed in certain segments with large patches of intensively cultivated lands. These industries discharge excessively large quantum of industrial effluents and the agricultural fields consume enormous quantity of fertilizers and pesticides. These together pollute extensively the surface water in the Calcutta Metopolitan District. The intensity of pollution by the use of fertilizers and pesticides is highlighted by Tables 12.4

Note : This section of the chapter relies heavily on the Comprehensive Pollution Survey and Studies of Ganga River Basin in West Bengal published by Central Board for the Prevention and Control of Water Pollution (1982).

and 12.5 which illustrate the quantity of inorganic manures and toxic pesticides consumed in the Ganga Basin of West Bengal.

TABLE 12.4 : **Consumption of Inorganic Manures in the Ganga Basin by Sub-Basins in West Bengal**

Sl. No.	Name of District	Fertiliser input in tonnes Nitrogen N	Phospherous P	Potassium K
1	2	3	4	5
Basin : Ganga*				
Sub-basin : Mahananda-Atrai-Ganga				
1.	Maldaha	3,600	660	1,595
	Sub-basin: Bhagirathi-Hugli (also including Subarnarekha & Creeks)			
2.	Birbhum	10,300	968	1,577
3.	Murshidabad	8,600	968	2,324
4.	Bardhaman	17,500	1,407	2,324
5.	Nadia	8,000	1,188	1,826
6.	Purulia	900	484	332
7.	Bankura	6,700	968	1,909
8.	Hugli	13,900	1,144	2,158
9.	Medinipur	8,700	1,100	1,992
10.	Haora	3,000	660	1,079
11.	Calcutta	—	—	—
12.	24 Parganas	11,500	1,012	2,407

*Areas outside Ganga basin included to present districtwise figures.

TABLE 12.5 : Consumption of Some Toxic Pesticides by Districts in Terms of Active Ingredients in Kg. (1979-80)

District	Pesticide				
	DDT	BHC	Lindane	Endo Sulfan	Aldrin
Maldha	—	7894	—	819	—
Birbhum	Data	Not	Available	....	
Murshidabad	646	16775	106	2592	852
Bardhaman	84	8240	5	445	650
Nadia	78	256	43	3282	80
Purulia	306	1557	—	30	10
Bankura	264	3201	7	—	47
Hugli	8010	19117	1381	2157	1397
Medinipur (W)	—	26951	—	143	208
Medinipur (E)	—	19051	16	100	9
Haora	—	1091	—	—	—
24 Parganas (N)	13122	131876	131	2297	853
24 Parganas (S)	—	6992	—	—	—

Source: Comprehensive Pollution Survey and Studies of Ganga River Basin in West Bengal (1982) Central Board for the Prevention and Control of Water Pollution.

Human and animal pollution

The human and animal factors are perhaps the greatest pollutors of the environment of the Calcutta Metropolitan District. This is borne out by the fact that coliform pollution due to faecal contamination is a more serious and difficult problem to handle in maintaining the quality of water in the CMD. The Eschirichia and Aerogenes (also known as Entrobacter) are the major coliform (bacterial) species. It is believed that some, though not a majority, of coliform species are pathogenic. Since Eschirichia species occur only in the gut of warm blooded animals, their presence in water is an indication of faecal contamination. They consequently lead to the spread of such virulent diseases as gastro-entritis, typhoid, cholera, etc. by a host of pathogenic bacteria. Pathogenic viruses are responsible for diseases such as poliomyelitis, meningitis, respiratory diseases, hepatities etc. In view of this bacteria containing characteristic of waste water, doctors and scientists conversant with pollution problems advise against the direct reuse of waste water for drinking purposes. It has been estimated that domestic waste water contains 100 million coliform per 100 ml and 7,000 viral particles per 100 ml—Viruses being more resistant to disinfection than bacteria, may persist in water after disinfection process (chlorination etc.) which destroy all pathogenic bacteria (Pavoni & Perrich—1977).

From the human source the pollution is primarily in the form of organic load and the BOD may be the convenient form of measurement of the quantum of generated pollution load.

Domestic

Towns	BOD (kg.)
Durgapur	11,068 kg.
Bhatpora	8,172 kg.
South Dum	5,342 kg.
Haora	17,977 kg.
Calcutta	1,60,006 kg.
South Suburban	6,838 kg.

Among the districts of West Bengal in the Ganga water Basin the Calcutta Metropolitan District tops the list with a staggering BOD load of 1,60,006 kg. Among the Sub-basins the largest quantity of pollution load is contributed by the Hugli bank (Fig. 12.3).

The Calcutta Metropolitan District with its disproportionately large human population, its extremely high density of cattle population, primarily in feedlots, generates enormous amount of pollution load from these sources. A lot of waste from these khatals is allowed to be washed into sewer and also moves directly into the river because of the large swine and cattle population along the river side.

Industrial pollution

The pollution load of industrial waste in the CMD includes both organic and inorganic materials, the latter consisting of

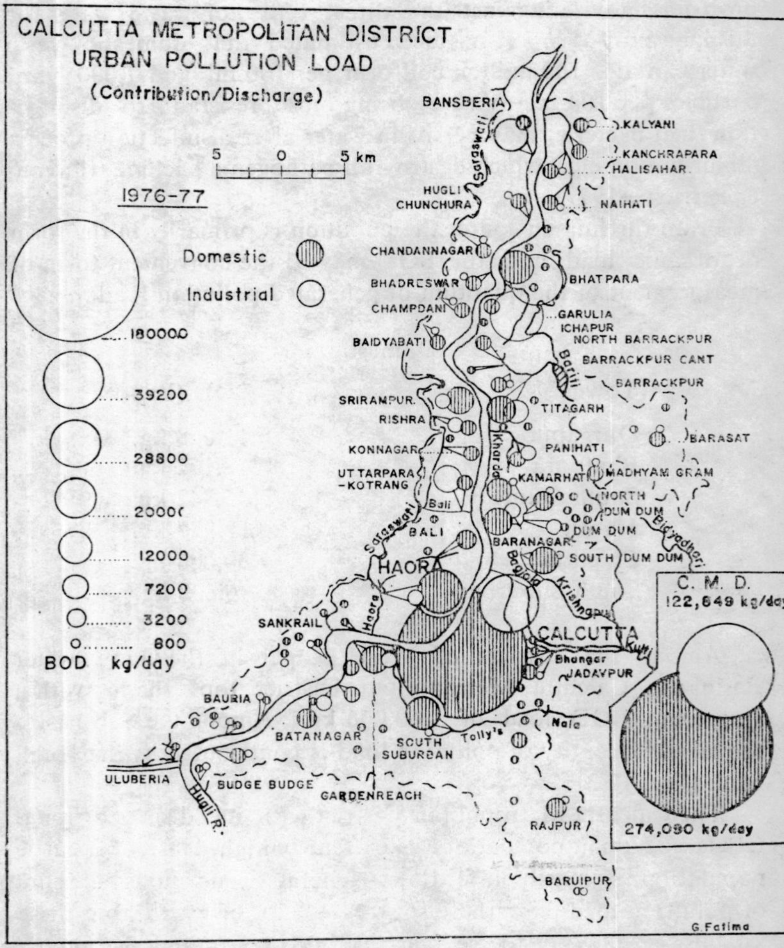

FIG. 12.3 : *Calcutta Metropolitan District Urban Pollution Load*

many metallic and non-metallic substances. Of the metallic load, lead (Pb), Arsenic (As), Mercury (hg), Chromium (Cr), Selenium (Se), and the non-metallic loads, phenol, cyanide, petro-chemicals and pesticides specially organo-chlorines are highly toxic to mammals and fish. Estimates of total industrial waste water generated are difficult to make as water consumption by selected industries varies almost 100 fold. There are over 5,500 major, minor and cottage industrial units in the Ganga Basin in West Bengal, of which only 285 may be taken as significant waste water generators.

The total industrial BOD load in waste water is highest in Calcutta (29,802 kg/day) followed by Bhatpora (23,719 kg/day), Garulia (22,501 kg), Bansberia (12,734 kg) Titagarh (7,209 kg) and Ranigang (6,300 kg) (*See* Fig. 12.2).

The total industrial BOD load in the CMD is 1,22,849 kg/day, and domestic BOD of 2741,090 kg/day is more than double the industrial which may be largely due to its large urban population exceeding 10 million (1981). The corresponding domestic water supply and waste water figures for the CMD are 1,181,583 KLD and 787,696 KLD respectively plus industrial waste water of 1,435,304 KLD approximately. These figures thus emphasise the intensity of industrial waste water pollution in the Hoogly river of the Ganga Basin. The high turbidity of water in this segment keeps the availability of sunlight at an extremely low level thereby limiting the autotrophic tendencies which aggravate eutrophic conditions.

Analysis of the sample waters of Bhagirathi and Hooghly rivers

On the basis of water samples analysed from (May 1980 to July 1981) it may be observed that the BOD (mg/l 5 days at 20°C) in the Bhagirathi segment has so far remained well below (i.e. 0.3 to 2 0) the tolerance limit set by ISI (3.0 for both B and C). The higher values are recorded in the dry season when the flow in the river becomes low.

In reference to the Hugli segment the findings as yet are rather confusing. Some queer figures have crept into the analysed results. While Patta gives the figure 2.4 and Ulubeira 3.5, the corresponding figures for Kalayani is 13.5, Dakshineshwar 41.5 and Diamond Harbour 30 0. These are rather high figures since the general monthly figures are low. It is obvious therefore that the water here remains substantially polluted for one reason or the other which is also confirmed by NEERI figures for BOD (1977-78) at Patta is 0.5 to 1.8 and at Garden Reach is 1.3 to 3.6.

This analysis of the sample water also reveals an excessively high presence of total coliform organism at (1500-460,000 MPS/100 ml) compared to ISI prescribed tolerance limit (500 for B and 5,000 for C) MPN (Most Probable Number). The alarming situation is doubly magnified by the presence of the high level of faecal coliform organism which is definite indication of large scale faecal contamination of the water. The NEERI figures for total coliform 2,900-155,000 $\frac{\text{MPN}}{\text{100 ML}}$ and faecal coliform 2,400 to 100,000 MPN/100 ML (1977-78) within a stretch of the Hugli from Tribeni (near Bansberia to Birlapur (near Budge-Budge) also testify to a high degree of pollution. It has, however, been observed that despite this high degree of pollution the quantity of dissolved oxygen (DO) is as yet favourably high and constitutes a redeeming feature.

But when we consider the BOD/COD ratio it reveals a critical situation. The ratio is, in most cases, below 0.08 and in all cases below 0.2. This ratio should be well above 0.6 (preferably 0.8 or higher) to indicate fair biotreatability of the water. The very low ratio everywhere along the Hugli is indicative that even acclimatization for biological treatment of the waste would not solve the problem of high pollution in Hooghly river of the CMD (Rao-Datta, 1979).

Dal lake

The Dal lake is one of the most scenic lakes of India. It is located in the heart of the city of Srinagar, the capital of the Indian State of Jammu & Kashmir. It receives its supply of fresh water mainly from Harwan spring in the North and Shalimar, Nishat and Chashme Shahi springs on the east. It drains into the river Jhelum.

Srinagar is located at a height of 1,584 meters above the main sea level. It is the summer capital of the State of Jammu & Kashmir. It is a town of great tourist attraction becaue of its pleasant summer, scenic charm, handicrafts and Moghal Gardens. Functionally it is dominated by the tertiary sector including trade and tourism. Its industries are of small scale and mainly of cottage industries type and are, therefore, by and large non-pollutant. Yet it is an eutrophic lake and has remained so far a long time (Das, 1970). This has been largely due to the following factors :—

(i) formation of more and more vegetable lands and consequently sinking of water surface area ;

(ii) growth of population on the islands and consequent expansion of villages giving rise to encroachment on a rapid pace ;

(iii) pollution of the waters of the lake by the tourists who live in house boats as well as by the locals who live permanently within the Dal premises, in small hamlets.

As vegetable prices are rising and demand for vegetable is on the increase the vegetable growers are ever on the look out for the expansion of their fields on the Dal Lake. The reclamation is an art with which they are very well conversant. The substance for this reclamation is the Dal weed. These weeds are collected by local methods dumped on grass mats (RAD) and sunk or are made to float in a submerged condition in the waters of the Dal. Occasionally these semi-floating lands are fixed in position by plantation around. Year after year further weeds are dumped till the floating lands sink more and more downwards and ultimately touch the bottom surface of the Dal. After sometime the plantation is felled and vegetables are grown on this land. If not checked the Dal lake will be swamped by floating vegetable gardens (Mir, 1983).

All along the foreshore of the lake there has been an enormous increase in human settlements, hotels and guest houses. Garbage and human wastes from these settlements and buildings are directly dumped into the lake. In addition the raw sewage and sullage from the 900 houseboats and innumerable doongas in which the tourists live are also directly poured into the lake (Qadri, 1985).

Encroachment on the lake has been proceeding for a considerable period of time and of late the pace has accelerated. It has been pointed out that "out of the original 21 km^2 of the lake only 10.5 km^2 are under open water whereas the rest of the 10.5 km^2 are being reclaimed to form floating gardens 4.2 km^2 ; marshes 2.9 km^2 and land 3.4 km^2 " (Qadri, 1985). This is authenticated by the Survey of India maps which reveal that between 1856-1964 the lake has shrunk by 13.25 km^2 at an average annual rate of 0.08 sq. km. In the last 13 years the rate of shrinkage has further increased to 0.22 km^2 per year. This has been largely due to heavy encroachment of business houses, ho'els, floating garden and also due to accelerated rate of silting.

These factors have caused enormous increase in the coliform and bacterial population in the lake and the decomposition of the garbage and human wastes demand BOD at a rate faster than its replenishment which results in hypoxic conditions.

An analysis of certain basic characteristics of the Dal waters reveals a significantly high level of eutrophication. The parameters which clearly signify this fact are :—

(i) Morphometric features ; (ii) increased oxygen content in the surface layer ; (iii) hypolimnetic oxygen deficit ; (iv) increased specific conductivity ; (v) the pattern of assimilation curve and (vi) increased values of phytoplankton production (Vass, 1980).

An analysis of the chemistry of Dal lake reveals that its water is alkaline and slightly buffered (Zutshi-Vass, 1978). The pH ranges from 7.4—9.6 and shows significant seasonal fluctuations. The frequency of pH recording adove 9 units has been significantly high. It testifies to a high degree of eutrophication of the lake waters. The dissolved oxygen concentration of surface water range from 7.2 to 17.6 mg/l. The Nagin basin of the Dal develops a climograde oxygen curve during spring which is shifted to positive heligrade in summer. The bottom water during this period recorded only 13% oxygen separation which is an indication of higher trophic level.

The chief causative factor for this change being enrichment due to run-off from floating gardens and habitation coming up on the sides of these lakes. The Dal lake thus constitutes an interesting example where man not industries has been the principal polluting factor.

CONCLUSION

These three case studies do stress the point that industrial pollution has assumed menacing proportions in the metropolitan cities of India. The problem is further magnified, when, due to inadequate sewerage and sewage disposal system even in metropolitan cities, the cattle and human waste also combine with industrial effluents to pollute the metropolitan environment to such an extent as to constitute a major health hazard. In order to maintain the health of Indian cities urban and regional planners will have to consider this important factor while preparing a balanced integrated development plan of the city and its region.

REFERENCES

Alam, S. Manzoor, Vulnerability and Resilience of Cities—the case oj Hyderabad—UNESCO Pilot Project, 1983, pp. 58-69 mimeographed.

Central Board for the Prevention and Control of Water Pollution, New Delhi, *Comprehensive Pollution Survey and Studies of Ganga River Basin in West Bengal*, 1982.

Das, S.M., Ecology of Dal Lake—Kashmir India (170), *Kashmir Science*, Vol. VII, Nos. 1-2, pp. 16-24 (A Science Journal of University of Kashmir), 1978.

S.I. Elyas, L. Shanti Kumar and Y.S. Murty, Bacteriological Criteria to Assess Raw and Drinking Water Quality, 1983 (unpublished paper).

Mir, G.R., When do we take the first step—Paper submitted in a Seminar on Dal Lake, 1983.

National Environmental Engineering Research Institute, Progress Report on Remodelling of Sewage Treatment Works of Twin Cities of Hyderabad-Secunderabad upto the period ending 31 March, 1980 (Mimeo).

Pavoni, J.L., and J.R. Perrich, Evolution of Waste Water Treatment Alternatives, *Handbook of Water Quality Management Planning* Ed. J.L. Pavoni, New York, 1977, pp. 90-100.

Qadri, Yasin, Effects of Urban Pressure and Pollution of Ecology of Dal Lake—An Overview (mimeographed)—Paper presented in Northern Command Nature Workshop, JLY : 1985, pp. 1-12.

Raj Kanteshwar, The Ecobiology of Zoo Planktons and Allied Organisms of the River Musi, Hyderabad (India), with special reference to Water Pollution, 1980, Ph.D. thesis, unpublished.

Rao, M.N. & A.K. Datta, *Waste Water Treatment*, Calcutta, 1979, p. 338.

Ravindra, Hydrogeological Investigations of Kalvar River Basin—Hyderabad Urban and Ranga Reddy Districts, 1981, 1980, Ph.D. thesis (unpublished).

Suxena, M.R. & A.R. Zafar, Assessment of the Industrial and Organic Pollution, Biological Production and the Rate of Eutrophication of the Lakes of Hyderabad (mimeo), Department of Botany, Osmania University, 1979

Vass, K.K., On the Trophic Status and Conservation of Kashmir Lakes *Hydrobiologia*, vol. 68, 1980, pp. 9-15.

Zutshi, K.K. Vass, Limnological Studies on Dal Lake Chemical Features, *Indian Journal of Ecology*, Vol. 5, No. 1, 1978, pp. 90-99.

13

REGIONALISATION FOR THE MANAGEMENT OF HYDRO-RESOURCES

A Case Study of the Development of the Godavari Basin in Andhra Pradesh

Fatima Alikhan

INTRODUCTION

Water is one of the most vital and abundant resources among the natural resources of the earth. However, a major part of it, found in the oceans, is not fit for direct consumption by man, animals or plants. The cheif sources of fresh water are the rivers and lakes which by their very nature are highly localised on the earth's surface. Ground water is another important source of fresh water and its distribution is widespread, though it is more difficult to assess groundwater reserves accurately.

Water is necessary in every aspect of life, but in India, it has been used most extensively for agriculture as more than seventy-five per cent of the Indian population lives in rural areas (Census of India, 1981) and is mainly dependent on agriculture. Thus despite the fact that India is well set on the path towards industrialisation, her water resources will continue to be used primarily for agriculture in the forseeable future.

Apart from agriculture, large amounts of water are needed for domestic purposes in rural and urban settlements, for industries, for the generation of hydro-electric power, as a cooling agent in thermal and nuclear power stations and for navigational purposes. Finally, water is an essential ingredient in maintaining the overall health of the environment. Therefore the proper management of water is of crucial importance particularly as most of the country is dependent on rainfall which is concentrated in three to four months of the year.

THE HYDRO-RESOURCES OF INDIA

India has 14 major rivers with catchment areas of 20,000 sq. km. and above ; forty-four medium sized rivers with catchment areas of between 2,000 and 20,000 sq. km ; and, numerous minor rivers with catchment of less than 2,000 sq. km. The total flow in all river systems of India, was calculated as 1672.5 thousand million cu.m. (or 60104.6 Tmc). Underground resources, though not properly surveyed, are broadly estimated as being 333 thousand million cu.m. Upto 80 per cent of the water-flow in Indian rivers occurs in the four monsoon months from mid-June to mid-October. For the rest of the year, there is inadequate or no water supply. Therefore since time immemorial, the storage of water has been essential for meeting the various needs throughout the year. At the time of India's independence in 1947, the total effective storage capacity in various basins excluding small tanks was 18,000 million cu. mts. Three decades later, it had increased to 147,000 million cu. m. Rao (1975), notes that even this is far less than the storage capacity in developed countries with similar potential and requirements. This is perhaps due to the fact that a large proportion of India's hydro-resources is concentrated in the rainy north eastern part of the country, a large part of which is lost to the sea without being used.

The satisfactory conservation and development of any scarce resource calls for a co-ordinated strategy and an integrated policy, the absence of which can lead to a waste of resources, and, an imposition of limitations on the benefits which might otherwise have accrued. The Irrigation Commission, appointed by the Government of India in 1969 to look into the question of future irrigation development in the country, advocated an integrated policy for the conservation and development of hydro-resources and noted that there was a need to pay attention to all aspects of hydro-resources management which included irrigation, drainage, navigation, flood control, hydro-electric power generation, water supply for industrial and domestic use, land reclamation, control of water pollution from human, animal and industrial wastes, pisciculture, recreation and the control of groundwater levels, if any of these factors were attended to without regard to their effects on the others, serious conflicts or losses could result (Report of the Irrigation Comission, 1972, Volume I).

The planning of hydro-resources has to be related in space to a defined area or region and a river basin has traditionally been the natural unit which lent itself ideally for such planning. A river basin with its well-defined water-shed boundary and close inter-relationship between surface and ground water resources within it, has often presented itself as the ideal economic resource region for the planned management of water and other resources located within it. But in recent years the large-scale inter-basin transfer of waters having become technically feasible and economically attractive, the concept of a river-basin needs to be redefined to include not just the valley and delta but also the command area. In India the planned development of river basins also has to take account of the fact that the major Indian rivers flow through more than one State, resulting in a competition for their waters not only between the various users within a State but also between the riparian States.

ECONOMIC AND ADMINISTRATIVE REGIONALISATION FOR THE MANAGEMENT OF HYDRO-RESOURCES

The delineation and articulation of economic regions in geographic terms has proved to be an aid in the process of planned development. But in the Indian situation, Sdasyuk (1961) has rightly observed that the formulation of economic regions has been a process of conflict with the consolidation of linguistic States and their aspirations for economic parity on the one hand, and the growing integration of the country's economy as a whole on the other. She continues that it reflects similar experience in the USSR if the word 'linguistic' were to be substituted by its Soviet analogue 'nationality' (Sengupta and Sdasyuk, 1961). On the other hand, Gerasimov (1961) noted that the two situations were not very comparable observing that India differed markedly from the Soviet Union in natural conditions, social structure, historical background, demographic problems, etc. This, he considers, questions the applicability of the Soviet experience to the Indian situation in the field of economic regionalisation. But he added that despite these differences, the multi-ethnic and multi-linguistic character of the population, common to both India and the Soviet Union, with some common features in the techno-economic development of these countries, opened up opportunities for the fruitful application of a number of methods developed and tested in practical planning in the USSR, to the Indian conditions.

Yet, despite the implicit recognition of economic regionalisation as a base for economic planning in India its implementation has not taken concrete shape. On the contrary, the re-organisation of the States on a linguistic basis promoted the economic consolidation of these States by strengthening intra-State production-economic links and the integration of their economy (Sengupta and Sdasyuk, 1961). Linguistic States have thus emerged as objectively existing economic regions with well-defined borders, which have to be taken into account while planning for the management of resources including hydro-resources. The evolution of the linguistic States into economic regions has been further reinforced by the federal nature of the Indian Constitution which decrees that the utilisation of water, land and forest resources be under the jurisdiction of State Governments. In the case of the major rivers of India which flow through more than one State, the development of a river valley region therefore involves the coordinated functioning of a number of States and has been a source of conflict between States.

The development of a river basin involves the optimum use of water available in the basin as surface or groundwater, together with the development of lands in the basin. Man's use of the land by way of cultivation, irrigation and drainage, deforestation, afforestation and grazing, urbanisation, industrialisation and highway construction etc., in turn have a bearing on water yields, stream-regimes, ground-water recharge, flooding, sedimentation and water quality. Hence the rational management of hydro-resources requires that attention be paid to all these factors. In the case of inter-State rivers, the optimum management of hydro-resources may involve locating works in one State, while benefits accrue wholly or partially to other States. Secondly, functions like water-shed management, pollution control, the fostering of fish and wild-life etc. by their very nature demand a coordinated plan for the entire river valley region. When a fragmented approach is adopted, the available resources cannot be put to the best use.

The need to have coordinated plans for river valley regions found expression in the enactment of the River Boards Act in 1956 which empowered the Union Government to establish River Boards to advise State Governments on the regulation and development of inter-State rivers. Differences over the sharing of river waters between several States led them to withhold their consent to the formation of River Boards and the proposal to set them up was virtually dropped in the 1960s. Since then, most of the river waters disputes have been settled through the awards of various Tribunals set up to solve the problems of sharing of river waters. The recent establishment of a national Ministry of Water Resources is a welcome step in the direction of better management of water resources as it will provide a much-needed national perspective. It is particularly relevant today when the possibility of inter-basin transfer of waters offers the nation an escape from the cycles of flood and drought, e.g. the Ministry could plan and oversee the implementation of a coordinated strategy for the management of the water resources, over an entire river basin regardless of intervening State boundaries. Its recommendations could be adopted by each riparian State for implementation in its own section of the basin. The following part of the paper describes the hydro-resources of the River Godavari, one of the major Indian rivers, which flows through five States and shows what has, and is being done, to manage the water and other resources occurring in the lower half of the river basin located in the State of Andhra Pradesh which may be said to constitute a resource-cum-planning region.

THE GODAVARI BASIN

A hydro-resource region

The River Godavari is the largest of the peninsular Indian rivers and flows through five States. It rises in the Nasik district of Maharashtra, 80 kms. from the Arabian Sea coast and after flowing for 1,465 kms. joins the Bay of Bengal in Andhra Pradesh. It has a catchment area of 3,12,812 sq. km. spread over five States [Table 13.1].

Unlike the situation in most other river basins, the main river in the Godavari Basin carries only about 25 per cent of the total volume of water, the rest being contributed by its tributaries. The important tributaries are the Pranhita, Indravathi, Sabari, Wardha, Penganga and Purna which join the river on its left bank and the Manjira, Maner and Pravara which join it on the right bank. Of these, the only tributary that lies exclusively in the State of Andhra Pradesh is the River Maner. After flowing for about 1,335 km. the Godavari cuts through the Eastern Ghats in Andhra Pradesh, flowing through a narrow gorge 130 km. from the sea. The maximum discharge of water is 80,137 cu.mecs. and the minimum is 42 cu. mecs. The average annual yield at Dowleshwaram is 105,000 cu.mecs (K.L. Rao, 1975, p. 82). At Rajahmundry, 97 km. from the Bay of Bengal, begins the vast delta, consisting of a wide belt of river-borne alluvium, gradually extending into the sea.

TABLE 13.1 : **River Godavari : Percentage of catchment area in different states**

S. No.	State	Percentage of Catchment Area
1.	Maharashtra	48.6
2.	Madhya Pradesh	20.7
3.	Karnataka	1.4
4.	Orissa	5.5
5.	Andhra Pradesh	23.8
	TOTAL	100.0

Source : Irrigation Commission, 1972.

As pointed out already, hydro-resources constitute the most important resources in a tropical country where almost 80% of the people are dependent on agriculture. As such the most important resource of the Godavari Basin is water. Apart from the abundance of water, the Godavari Basin in Andhra Pradesh is rich in other natural resources, particularly mineral and forest. Besides having almost all the proved reserves of coal in Andhra Pradesh, which are also the largest deposit outside the Chota Nagpur Plateau, the region has limestone and iron-ore deposits. Recent explorations have shown the presence of natural gas and petroleum deposits too. The Godavari Basin also has, by and large, a rainfall higher than the State's average and is mainly under forest. Yet despite their abundance and diversity, the natural resources of the region have not been adequately developed and it remains a backward region settled mainly by a tribal population. The backwardness of an area rich in resources can be the outcome of neglect due to its location on the periphery of administrative regions (Sdasyuk, 1961, p. 13). This seems to be confirmed from which shows that the Godavari Basin lies straddled across the borders of the States of Andhra Pradesh, Madhya Pradesh, Maharashtra, Orissa and Karnataka which may have subjected it to the neglect common to peripheral areas. Another contributory factor as noted by Khan et al. (1983), could be the ad hoc nature of the developmental programmes so far. These problems can be tackled if the river basin could be viewed as a region, and its resources managed in an integrated manner on the basis of long term plans.

One of the earliest plans for the integrated development of the Godavari Basin was prepared by the Commerce and Industries Department of the Government of the former Hyderabad State (Slaughter, 1944). It put forth a development plan for the Godavari Basin based on the potential of the region as a "centre of gravity of hydro-thermal exploitation" (Slaughter, 1944, p. 41). The plan identified among other things, industrial development possibilities in the Godavari Basin, based on the availability of coal, hydro-electric power, lime-stone, clay and iron-ore, as also the development of agriculture based on the expansion of irrigation facilities. Due to the re-organisation of the State boundaries along linguistic lines soon after, the plan was not implemented as it was conceptualised.

Almost forty years later, a second report has been prepared for the Government of Andhra Pradesh (Khan et al., 1983), for the integrated resource development of the Godavari Basin in the State. This Report also views the Godavari Basin in the State as a resource region, with mineral, forest and population resources complementing the hydro-resources of the river basin. It also recommends that the resources of the Godavari Basin should be developed within the framework of a long-term, integrated plan.

THE GODAVARI BASIN IN ANDHRA PRADESH

More than half the course of the River Godavari lies in the State of Andhra Pradesh, the basin extending over eleven districts in the northern part of the State (Table 13.2). Of these, the three districts of Adilabad, Karimnagar and Nizamabad ; large parts of Medak, East Godavari, Warangal and Khammam ; and, very small portions of other districts like Hyderabad and Rangareddy are located within it. The former districts are hilly and forested (Khammam, 48 per cent and Adilabad, 43 per cent under forest), and also have large proportions of their population belonging to the Scheduled Tribes (Adilabad 17 per cent, Khammam 24 per cent). Almost half the population of Andhra Pradesh (24.5 million) lives in these eleven districts, though densities vary greatly from the sparsely populated, hilly and forested districts of Adilabad and Khammam (102 & 109 persons per sq. km. respectively) to the wholly urban district of Hyderabad (10,325 persons per sq. km.). Eight of the twenty Class I towns of Andhra Pradesh are located in the Godavari Basin, including the State capital Hyderabad, (pop. 2.5 million) and its second largest city Vishakapatnam (pop. 5,94,000). But the districts of Adilabad, Karimnagar, Medak and Khammam, lying entirely or largely within the basin, have no large urban centres and have small proportions of their population living in urban areas (Medak 12 per cent, Karimnagar 16 per cent, Khammam 17 per cent and Adilabad 19 per cent urban). These districts are also backward with comparatively low

TABLE 13.2 : **Godavari basin in Andhra Pradesh : Selected geographic, demographic and economic indicators, by districts 1981**

S. No.	District	Area (Sq. Km.)	% Area in Basin	Population (millions)	Density (per Sq. Km.	Tribal population: % of State Tribal Pop.	Tribal population: % of District Pop.	% Literates	% Urban	Class I Towns (pop. in '000's)	% Area Under Forest
1	2	3	4	5	6	7	8	9	10	11	12
1.	Adilabad	16,128	100	1.6	102	8.6	16.9	19	19	—	43
2.	Khammam	16,029	52	1.8	109	13.5	23.9	26	17	—	48
3.	Karimnagar	11,823	100	2.4	206	1.9	2.5	22	16	—	22
4.	Warangal	12,846	53	2.3	179	9.2	12.7	24	17	1. Warrangal 336	22
5.	Nizamabad	7,956	100	1.7	211	2.8	5.3	22	19	1. Nizamabad 183	21
6.	Medak	9,699	85	1.8	188	2.2	3.8	22	12	—	10
7.	Rangareddy	7,493		1.6	211	2.3	4.6	29	24	—	9
8.	Hyderabad	217	2	2.2	10,325	0.5	0.6	58	100	1. Hyderabad 2500	
9.	E. Godavari	10,807	67	3.7	343	4.5	3.9	35	22	1. Rajahmundry 267 2. Kakinada 226	26
10.	W. Godavari	7,742	20	2.9	369	2.1	2.3	38	21	1. Bheemavaram 102 2. Eluru 168	10
11.	Vishakapatnam	11,162	25	2.5	226	4.8	6.1	28	32	1. Vishakapatnam 594	34
Basin Districts		111,904	63.5	24.5	219	52.4	4.8	—	—	8	— —
Andhra Pradesh		275,068	25.8	53.6 million	195	100	—	30	23.2	20 towns	—

Source : Compiled from Census of India, 1981, Series 2, A.P. Provisional Population Tables.

levels of literacy (Adilabad 19 per cent, Karimnagar, Medak and Nizamabad 22 per cent literates each) compared to State average (30 per cent).

Thus it becomes clear that a large part of the Godavari basin is hilly and forested with a low density of population and low levels of literacy and urbanization. This is in direct contrast to the tremendous resource potential of the region.

THE HYDRO RESOURCES OF THE GODAVARI BASIN AND THEIR UTILISATION IN ANDHRA PRADESH

Though the mineral deposits and forests in the Godavari Basin are very important resources, the most prominent resource is water. As already mentioned, the river flows through five States, but its course in Andhra Pradesh is the longest, being 770 km out of a total length of 1,465 km. Thus, though Andhra Pradesh's share in the basin is only 23 per cent (Table 13.1) the State's share of the main river's course is fifty two per cent. This comprises the lower part of the river into which two thirds of the basin drains. The potential for utilising the waters of the Godavari in Andhra Pradesh is therefore greater than the State's share in the basin would imply. The Godavari Water Disputes Tribunal which gave its award in 1979, awarded Andhra Pradesh, 43,547 mil. cu.m. (1,495 Tmc) as its share of the river waters. This includes 17,245 mil.cu.m. (592 Tmc) already being utilised in 1982 under existing schemes and 1,427 mil.cu.m. (49 Tmc) which have been committed for use through projects under way. Thus 854 Tmc or 57 per cent of the State's share of the Godavari waters remained to be utilised, for which numerous schemes have been proposed or are being investigated to ensure that optimum use is made of this precious resource.

The water resources of the Godavari Basin have been used in the region since time immemorial for irrigating lands by traditional means like tanks and wells, but these were minor irrigation schemes tapping the small streams of the basin and serving small areas. The first major scheme to be undertaken to harness the Godavari waters was the Godavari Delta Project in 1847. This was followed by the Nizamsagar Project in the 1930's and Sriramasagar Project in 1960's. Though they, together with some other smaller projects, utilise the Godavari waters to benefit vast areas, there is still tremendous scope to utilise this precious resource better. The following part ofthe paper reviews briefly the major projects on the River Godavari and its tributaries in Andhra Pradesh.

MAJOR PROJECTS ON THE RIVER GODAVARI BASIN IN ANDHRA PRADESH

The Godavari barrage or the cotton barrage

The nineteenth century saw the advancement of technology that led to the harnessing of major rivers throughout the world. In India, the construction of weirs and barrages for irrigation and flood control were undertaken on the rivers Cauvery, Ganges, Indus, Krishna, Godavari, etc. At this time the lower reaches of the River Godavari, including the vast delta were located in the former Madras Presidency and this area which today forms one of the granaries of the country, was subject to the vagaries of the monsoon as well as to devastating floods from the untamed river. The first major development scheme, to harness the hydro-resources of the Godavari was therefore designed to provide irrigation facilities to the delta and resulted in the Godavari Anicut which was concieved and executed by Sir Arthur Cotton in 1847. The weir (long. 81.45, lat. 16.55) consisted of a gigantic barrier, about 6 km wide across the River Godavari at Dowleshwaram (population 25,912, 1981), 8 km. downstream of Rajahmundry (population 267,749, 1981). Here the river branches off into the Gowthami and Vasistha rivers which branch further downstream into seven major streams. In 1982 the Godavari Anicut was replaced by the Cotton Barrage. The three canals taking off from the Barrage not only irrigate the areas in the Godavari Delta but also provide for inland navigational facilities. The barrage also serves the purposes of a highway between the districts of East and West Godavari. Before the construction of the Barrage, about 28,000 hectares of land were imperfectly and irregularly irrigated in the delta. The construction of the Barrage and development of the canal system had facilitated the irrigation of 1,75,200 hectares of land initially. Over the decades, the irrigation and drainage systems were perfected and problems ironed out. By 1887, the extent of cultivation under the Godavari Delta System increased to 3,21,600 hectares and at present about 4,86,000 hectares are being systematically irrigated in the Godavari Delta.

In the 1960s the weir started showing signs of deterioration owing to ageing as well as to the extra strain imposed due to increased pond level and the immediate construction of a barrage 40 mts. upstream of the old weir. The new Cotton Barrage inaugurated in 1982 consists of 4 arms which total about 6 kms in length.

The Nizamsagar Project

Eight decades after the construction of the Godavari Barrage and the development of the delta system a number of projects were undertaken on the major tributaries of the River Godavari in the former State of Hyderabad. The most prominent among these was the harnessing of the River Manjira, an important tributary of the River Godavari, draining the semi-arid agricultural region of Telengana. This project as conceived of by Nawab Ali Nawaz Jung Bahadur, the Chief Engineer of Hyderabad was to have consisted of :

(a) the Nizamsagar Dam located on the River Manjira about 160 km. north of the city of Hyderabad ;
(b) the Devanur Dam to be constructed 200 km upstream of the Nizamsagar Dam to control silting of the Nizamsagar Dam; to generate 25 MW of power, and to supply water to Hyderabad.

But due to a lack of resources consequent to the outbreak of World War II the Scheme was never completed in its entirety and only the Nizamsagar Dam was constructed. Though proposals for the Devanur Project were put forth once more after the war, the re-organisation of the State boundaries, made it unfeasible, as the dam site would now have been in Andhra Pradesh while submergence would have been in Karnataka. The Manjira Scheme in its totality had provided for the most optimum utilisation of the available water. The shelving of the Devanur Dam resulted in the rapid silting of the Nizamsagar Dam whose storage capacity was reduced from 157 mil. cu.m. (26 Tmc) to 349 mil. cu.m. (12 Tmc) and has now been increased to 524 mil. cu.m. (18 Tmc) after increasing its height. Such problems encountered in utilising river waters highlight the need for the establishment of an organisation at the national level, empowered to plan for the most rational use of river waters while the implementation may be entrusted to the States.

The Godavari Valley Project

One of the most exhaustive schemes for the development of the Godavari basin in its totality was put forth by the post-war Planning Department of the former State of Hyderabad, constituted in the 1940's on the lines of a similar department in the Government of India. The Department undertook investigations for the agricultural and industrial development of the Godavari Basin based on the development of irrigation and power. A Godavari Valley Authority was constituted with Nawab Ali Nawaz Jung Bahadur as its Chief Commissioner. The project was to have been completed in about a decade. In the first phase, the project envisaged the generation of thermal power at Ramagundam to be utilised for pumping water from the River Godavari to provide immediate facilities for irrigation through canals taking off from the river. A dam was to be constructed on the River Kaddam, a tributary of the River Godavari to provide water for a canal taking off from the north bank. A power plant was envisaged at Kishtapuram (now in Maharashtra), to generate about 50,000 K.W. to supplement the thermal power and an additional 5,000 K.W. were to be generated from the water stored at the Kaddam Dam. The water let out into the river after generating power was to be picked up again by throwing a weir across the river at a point where the River Kaddam entered the Godavari and irrigation canals were to be aligned from here, to irrigate lands in Adilabad, Karimnagar, and Warangal districts.

The utilisation of the water resources of the River Godavari by the generation of hydro-electric power and the provision of cooling water to the thermal plant at Ramagundam was to have provided the power for the creation of an industrial city at Mancherial in Khammam district as the industrialisation and further growth of Hyderabad city was deemed unsuitable from the point of view of availability of water and power. The problem of acute water scarcity being faced by the industrialising city of Hyderabad today, amply justifies the fears and foresight of the planners in the 1940's.

The re-organisation of the State boundaries consequent to the formation of the new State of Andhra Pradesh on linguistic lines led to the reviewing of some of the proposals and to a modification of other proposals, as the proposed sites of the Godavari Valley Project were now distributed between the new states of Andhra Pradesh and Maharashtra (formerly Bombay). The Kaddam Dam was the first part of the original scheme to be executed. Started in 1949, the Kaddam Dam was completed by 1962 and irrigates 26,305 hectares in the backward Adilabad district. But the proposed dam at Kishtapuram, and, the pick up weir below, were instead combined at the Pochampad Damin Andhra Pradesh in the Sriramsagar Project, Stage I.

The Sriramsagar Project

This project plans to utilise about 5,825 mil.cu.m. (200 Tmc) of water. The Project envisages the construction of the Pochampad Dam, the Lower Maner Dam, the Kakatiya Canal (Godavari South Canal) the Lakshmi Canal (High Level South Canal), the Saraswathi Canal (Godavari North Canal) and an extension of the Kaddam Canal. The Pochampad Dam is across the River Godavari near Pochampad village (long. 78°. 20′ East ; lat. 18°. 58′ North) in Nizamabad district, 5 km. upstream of the Soan Bridge on the Hyderabad-Nagpur National Highway, and about 200 km from Hyderabad. It will irrigate 4,11,000 hectares as per the latest modified estimates, in Nizamabad, Karimnagar, Warangal and Adilabad districts of Telengana region, in Andhra Pradesh. In addition, it is to supply drinking water to Warangal (population 336,018), and also supply water to the National Thermal Power Corporation. The Sriramsagar Project, Stage-I was cleared by the Government of India in 1964, to irrigate 2.28 lakh hectares under the Kakatiya Canal upto the River Maner. Since the command area could not be localised upto Maner, the Kakatiya Canal was extended beyond Maner from 146 km. to 224 km. upto Huzurabad, by constructing a reservoir across the

River Maner. Subsequently the canal was extended further upto 235 km. to supply water to Warangal town which had an acute and chronic problem of water shortage.

The Sriramsagar Project under A.P. Composite-II envisages the extension of the Kakatiya Canal from 235 km. to 349 km. upto River Musi in the basin of the River Krishna, in Nalgonda District. The Sriramsagar Project has not yet been completed in its entirety, but the main dam across the Godavari at Pochampad, the Lower Maner Dam at Karimnagar and the Kakatiya Canal with lining have been completed upto 235 km, i.e., water has been released for Warangal. An irrigation potential of 213,000 hectares has also been created. During 1984-85 water was released into minor irrigation tanks through this canal to irrigate about 40,000 hectares of crops stricken by drought in the districts of Karimnagar and Warangal. The Saraswathi or the Godavari North Canal, 47 km. upto River Kaddam has also been completed and water was released during 1984-85 to feed the Kaddam Reservoir to irrigate standing crops under the Kaddam Canal. Earth work on Lakshmi Canal is under progress.

The completion of the rest of the Sriramsagar Project envisaged under A.P. Composite-II comprises the following :

(a) the Kakatiya Canal from 235 km. to 349 km. upto River Musi in the Krishna Basin ;
(b) improvements to the Kaddam Canal for stabilising the existing command area ;
(c) excavation of the Saraswathi Canal tail reach from 77 km. to 153 km.

When completed, the Sriramsagar Project will be one of the major irrigation projects in India and a boon to vast areas of semi-arid, drought prone lands of Telangana in Andhra Pradesh.

Brief description of selected projects proposing to utilise godavari waters in Andhra Pradesh

As mentioned already, the various existing projects and those under construction will together utilise only 43 per cent of

Andhra Pradesh's share of the Godavari waters. Proposals for the utilisation of the remaining 57 per cent have to consider the fact that though a large amount of water is available for utilisation, most of it is located in the mountainous, rainy and densely forested middle section of the river where the massive contributions by the tributaries Pranhita, Indravati and Sabari (Fig. 13.1) lead to a four-fold increase in the water in the main river. In this middle section, there is little likelihood of a great demand for water for irrigation and other purposes in the near future, for as noted earlier, it is a sparsely populated area with a mainly tribal population and little cultivable land. On the other hand, the demand for water is practically unlimited in the upper section of the Godavari basin in Andhra Pradesh, consisting of the semi-arid, agricultural region of Telangana and in some of the coastal areas in the lower section not covered by the existing irrigation schemes. The increasing water requirements of the large urban centres in the basin, like Hyderabad and Vishakapatnam, have also to be considered, their future growth being dependent on assured and sufficient supplies of water. Thus plans for the future utilisation of the Godavari waters have rightly taken into consideration the varied needs of the entire region. Some of the proposed projects were first put forth more than four decades ago by the Governments of the then States of Hyderabad and Madras and were not executed due to several reasons. These have now been put forward in modified forms, keeping in view the changed State boundaries, improvements in technology, changed requirements etc.

Some of these proposed projects like the Polavaram and Inchampally Projects and the Yellampally Dam will now be briefly described here.

The Polavaram Project

The Polavaram Project is a modification of the Rama Pada Sagar Project which was investigated in the mid-1940s by the then government of Madras State and could not be undertaken due to political problems. The project is to be located 3 kms. upstream of Polavaram (lat. 17°. 13′ East and long. 81°. 46′ East) a taluq headquarter in West Godavari District, 34 km.

above Rajahmundry and 42 km. above the Godavari Barrage. It will be a terminal major project across the River Godavari and will be located just before the river emerges out of the Papikonda Gorge in the Eastern Ghats and enters the coastal plains. The erstwhile Madras Government had plans to take water from here right upto Madras city, with dams across the rivers Krishna and Pennar, but though the plans have been modified due to the re-organisation of the States and the formation of Andhra Pradesh, the revised Polavaram Project also provides for the diversion of 2,330 mil. cu.m. (80 Tmc) of water to the River Krishna. The Project envisages the following benefits :

(1) Irrigation facilities for 162,000 hectares under the Left Main Canal in the districts of East Godavari and Vishakapatnam and 129,000 hectares under the Right Main Canal in the Districts of West Godavari and Krishna.
(2) Supply of water to the rapidly industrialising port city of Vishakapatnam (population 594,259) as well as to villages and towns enroute.
(3) Navigation facilities upto Vishakapatnam.
(4) Generation of power upto 1,000 MW.
(5) Diversion of water to River Krishna at Vijaywada for irrigating vast drought-prone areas in Karnataka and Maharashtra (35 Tmc) and in Rayalseema, Telangana and coastal areas of Andhra Pradesh (45 Tmc.)

Inchampally Project

This Project will be a joint project between the States of Andhra Pradesh, Madhya Pradesh and Maharashtra and will be an example of cooperation among the riparian States. The Inchampally Project will utilise 4,225 mil. cu.m. (145 Tmc) of the Godavari waters mainly to produce power but also to irrigate 120,000 hectares of land. The Inchampally Dam will be located in an underdeveloped area, 12 km. below the confluence of the Indravati with the Godavari, at Inchampally village, in Karimnagar District, 124 km. from Warangal, the nearest district headquarters. The project will generate 660 MW of power to be shared by the three States of Andhra Pradesh, Madhya Pradesh and Maharashtra in the proportion of 27:38:35. Within Andhra Pradesh, the districts of Khammam, Warangal and Mahbubnagar will benefit from the irrigation facilities.

The Yellampally Dam

Investigations are underway to formulate a proposal to construct a dam across the Godavari at Yellampally village 7 miles upstream from Mancherial. This dam will utilise 760 mil. cu.m. (26 Tmc) to supply water to Hyderabad as well as to the industrial town of Ramagundam (population 12,118) located 15 km. downstream, but at a higher elevation.

The city of Hyderabad is located on the River Musi, a tributary of the River Krishna on which it has depended for its supply of water since it was founded over four centuries ago. Rapid industrialisation of the city, fostered by the new State of Andhra Pradesh of which Hyderabad became the capital in 1956, has led to vast increases in the city's population in the last two decades. Traditional sources of water supply which were adequate till recently have now become insufficient for the industrial and domestic needs of the growing city. Though the River Manuira, a tributary of the River Godavari has been tapped at Sangareddy 64 km. away and another dam is being constructed at Singur, 60 km. upstream of Sangareddy, these sources will together fall short of projected needs by the turn of the century, by sixty per cent (Alam, 1984). Therefore it becomes imperative to tap sources which will provide the city's water requirements for not just the immediate future but for a longer period of time. Though water can be brought to Hyderabad from dams on the River Krishna also, it is as well to remember that the Krishna waters allocated to Andhra Pradesh are being almost fully utilised, whereas there is no such problem regarding the availability of the Godavari waters. Thus the Yellampally Dam will fill a vital need by providing an assured supply of water for the growing needs of Hyderabad. The Project proposes to pump water from Yellampally to the lower Maner Dam and from thence to Shamirpet Tank, on the northern outskirts of Hyderabad, where water will be stored and pumped to the city.

CONCLUSION

River valley regions offer the best scope for the optimum management of hydro-resources, yet in the formulation and implementation of development plans in a federal structure such as India's, State administrative boundaries cannot be easily ignored. Since their formation, the linguistic States of India, with their strong regional aspirations have been emerging as economic regions. Thus the apportioning and utilisation of waters of the large multi-State rivers has been a source of continuing conflict. Intra-State conflicts have also to be contended with, particularly as the traditional river basins consisting of river valleys and deltas have been enlarged with the addition of new command areas. The conflicts between regional and national interests and between States can be reconciled by an organisation at the national level that can transcend the limitations of administrative boundaries in planning for the optimum utilisation of hydro-resources of river valley regions. The recent formation of a national Ministry of Water Resources raises hopes that these conflicts can be resolved in the best interests of the various States, the nation and the environment. Such a national authority can plan for the management of the hydro-resources of large inter-State rivers within a regional framework at the macro-level, whilst at the meso-and micro-levels the State boundaries can serve to delineate the sub-regions for detailed planning and implementation. This will ensure the optimum management of hydro-resources in a comprehensive manner from social, economic, environmental and other aspects, leading to a maximisation of regional welfare, for as Dr. K.L. Rao (1976) expressed it "perhaps no other facet of human endeavour confers such large and widespread benefits as water resources development and sustained and continuous research is needed to meet increasing demands and challenges."

REFERENCES

1. Ajit Kumar Singh, 'States as Planning Regions' in *Indian Journal of Regional Science*, Vol. IV, No. 1, 1972, pp. 48-58.
2. Alam, S.M., Vulnerability and Resilence of Cities : The Case of

Hyderabad (India), UNESCO Pilot Project, 1984, Mimeo, Hyderabad.

3. Bandman, M.K., Optimisation of the Spatial Structure of the Economy of a Region and its Parts in A.G. Aganbegyan ed., *Regional Studies for Planning and Projecting—The Siberian Experience*, Mouton Publishers, The Hague, 1981.
4. Census of India, Provisional Population Tables, Paper I of 1981 supplement, Series 2, Andhra Pradesh, Director of Census Operations, Andhra Pradesh, 1981.
5. Gerasimov, I.P. *Preface, Economic Regionalisation of India : Problems and Approaches*, P. Sengupta and Galina Sdasyuk, 1961.
6. Government of Andhra Pradesh, Perspective Plan in Respect of Irrigation in Andhra Pradesh, Irrigation and Power Department, Hyderabad, 1981.
7. Government of Andhra Pradesh, Report of the Commission for Irrigation Utilisation, Volume I & II, Hyderabad, 1982.
8. Khan, Waheeduddin, Prakasa Rao, V.L.S. et al., "Integrated Resource Development in the Godavari Basin", Preliminary Report prepared for the Commissioner, Godavari Development Authority, Centre for Economic and Social Studies, Hyderabad, 1983.
9. National Remote Sensing Agency, Satellite Remote Sensing Agency Survey of Natural Resources of Andhra Pradesh, Project Report, Volume-I, Secunderabad, 1978.
10. Prakasa Rao, V.L.S. & L.S. Bhatt, "A Regional Framework for Resource Development", *Bombay Geographical Magazine*.
11. Rao, K.L., *India's Water Wealth, Its Assessment, Uses and Projections*, Orient Longman, New Delhi, 1975.
12. Report of the Irrigation Commission, Volume-I, II & III, Ministry of Irrigation and Power, New Delhi, 1972.
13. Sengupta, P. and Sdasyuk, Galina, Economic Regionalisation of India : Problems and Approaches, *Census of India*, Monograph Series Volume-I, No. 8, New Delhi, 1961.
14. Slaughter, E.W., *The Godavari Industrial & Agricultural Development Plan*, H.E.H. The Nizam's State Railway Press, Hyderabad, 1944.
15. United Nations, *River Basin Development, Policies and Planning*, Volume I & II, Budapest, 1976.

14

THE WATER RESOURCES OF CENTRAL ASIA
Estimation Procedure

I.D. Tsigelnaya

A striking feature of Central Asia is the uneven distribution of the river network over its territory. There are only a few rivers on the vast plains that account for 70 per cent of the territory of Central Asia. Only Amu Darya and Syr-Darya—the largest rivers in Central Asia—cover many hundreds of kilometres of desert expanses.

Unlike the plains the mountains in Central Asia are cut up by a well ramified river network consisting of more than ten thousand rivers. All Central Asia's water resources are formed in the highlands.

The fact that mountain structures are hard to reach, means that their natural conditions have not been studied adequately enough. The same can be said with respect to water resources. The clearest picture of all the sources of water resources can be obtained only through the method of water balance, a method which makes it possible to single out and estimate the lithogenic links in water circulation i.e., runoff in depth and soil moisture, and to estimate different sources of water resources.

The water balance in the mountainous regions of Central Asia, situated thousands of miles from the oceans, is shaped in strongly marked continental conditions. The continentality, characteristic of entire Central Asia, serves as a backdrop, violated by a complex orography which determines the climatic differentiation.

The high mountain ranges, which spread out latitudinally, prevent the cold air mass from the north from penetrating into the southern regions. The climate in the high plateaus, which are subject to heating during the day and to cooling at night, is strongly continental and dry. High mountain ranges are characterized by more humidification and less temperature fluctuation. There are sharp fluctuations in the climate and the physical and geographic conditions in hollows and valleys. In the Fergana, Gissar and Panj valleys the maximum temperature for the summer is 45°C. But the winters there are cold, due to the accumulation in the hollows of cold air masses which sink down from the surrounding mountains.

The mountain ranges, spread out longitudinally (the Academy of Sciences range, the Akshiyrak range and others), serve as a barrier for air currents from the west. This brings about precipitation, chiefly in the form of snow, on the western slopes of the ranges. The precipitation level rises dramatically in mountain junctions. By intercepting at times all the moisture brought from the west they render dry the hollows and valleys lying beyond them. Despite their great height the high uplands surrounded by mountain ranges are extremely poor in moisture. In the Western Pamirs, for one, the annual precipitation level at heights over 3,500 m is less than 100 mm.

The same diversity can be found in the mountains in the case of soils and vegetation. An intricate complex of landscapes has been shaped here, ranging from deserts to alpine meadows. A peculiarity of highlands is the combination of longitudinal and altitudinal zonalities. In some cases this may lead to major discrepancies in the basic natural components within one and the same territory and on equal altitudes, while in other cases this may lead to their similarity at different altitudes. This peculiarity has a major impact on the water balance structure.

To study the water balance of Central Asia's highlands use was made of an equation system suggested by M.I. Lvovich (1959, 1963 ; Water balance, 1969), which has the following form :

$$P=R+E,\ R=S+U,\ U+E=W,\ W=P-S,$$
$$P=S+U+E,$$

with : P—Precipitation, R—total river runoff, S—surface runoff, U—under ground runoff into the rivers, E—total evaporation, W—gross wetting of the territory.

Since in the case of mountainous regions, the estimation of ice runoff is of particular significance, we broke up the surface runoff into the snowmelt and glacial components (S' and G).

A study of the water balance and its peculiarities in the mountains should proceed from the dependence on the basin's average weighted altitude. It is a fact that the runoff formation in the mountains is determined by the altitudinal zonality of the natural conditions. That is why the study of the regularities of river runoff distribution in the mountains, as well as of the other water balance elements, is based on its connection with the altitude. The altitude above the mean sea level reflects the complex of physical and geographical conditions of altitudinal zonality. As a rule, greater altitude entails better conditions for the condensation of atmospheric moisture and greater atmospheric precipitation, lower air temperature, less evaporation and greater river runoff. In other words, a change in the altitude brings about changes in the entire complex of natural conditions and consequently in the humidification conditions and the correlation among the water balance elements. But the character of these conditions is not uniform within a mountain system and is different for its various parts, depending on the specific altitudinal natural zones. Hence, the relationships between water balance elements and the altitude should be set for individual territories within which the structure of the prevailing forces and influencing factors remain relatively uniform. The boundaries of these territories should correspond to the natural ones established during physical and geographic regionalization.

In studying the water balance of mountainous territories, one has to keep in mind the extreme scarcity of data on atmospheric precipitation, especially in high-altitude areas.

The alluvial benches where "karasus", take their source have been poorly studied. Their yield is apparently small and has a minor share in the water balance of mountainous Central Asia. According to estimates by V.F. Shlygina (1965), the "karasu" runoff on the northern slope of the Zailiysky Ala Tau accounts for 6-10 per cent of the income part of the balance. According to V.L. Schultz's estimates (1965), the share of the runoff in the alluvial bench zone of the Fergana Valley is a mere 3 per cent of the valley's overall runoff.

In estimating the income part of the water balance (precipitation) use was made chiefly of a map drawn up under the supervision of O.A. Drozdov. Some corrections were made to it based on research which took into account the inaccuracies of gauging precipitation by pluviometers. Research carried out in recent years demonstrated that the error in gauging solid precipitation in regions with strong winds may reach 80-100 per cent. But according to all specialists, precipitation in the mountains of Central Asia occurs in conditions close to calm. The comparison of the average monthly speed of wind with that during precipitation, carried out at the Alaarcha and Tuya-Ashu stations, showed that the average monthly speed of wind is 2—2.5 times greater than that during precipitation (Grigoriev, Tsytsenko, 1969). To specify the amount of solid precipitation we apply the generalized correction factor for solid precipitation (Ks) obtained for the northern slope of the Zailiysky Ala Tau by I.S. Sosedov (Mansurova, Sosedov, 1969). The application of this apparently regional dependence for the entire mountainous Central Asia is rather conditional but the results of available studies in other mountain regions provide ground for belief that we do not make a big error by using this dependence. The values of the corrections are as follows: 1,500-2,000 m—1.11 ; 2,000-2,500 m—1.16 ; 2,500-3,000 m—1.20 ; 3,000—3,500 m—1.30. To determine the amount of solid precipitation we used the available regional dependencies on the altitude of the share of solid precipitation in its annual sum. The correction for solid precipitation is minor and does not exceed its annual amount (Melikishvili, 1967 ; Litovchenko, 1971).

The figures for the precipitation in the glacial zone at the altitude of the glacier feeding boundary have been corrected on the basis of studies conducted by A.N. Krenke (1982). His calculation of the precipitation at the glacier feeding boundary involves, the determination of the value of the summed ablation which at this glaciological level equals accumulation. To calculate the ablation we used the formula of V.G. Khodakov and A.N. Krenke (1966) :

$$A=(T_{av.sum.}+9.5)^3 ,$$

where A is the summed ablation value ; and $T_{av.sum}$ is the average summer air temperature.

Having excluded the landslide and drift strom factors and assuming that liquid precipitation at this glaciological level is insignificant, we get the annual precipitation in a first approximation.

Central Asia is one of the driest regions in the Soviet Union, but its mountainous parts are, as a rule, well humidified. Due to the elevation of air masses and the ensuing orographic aggravation of the fronts, there is substantial precipitation on the windward mountain slopes—in certain places over 1,500-2,000 mm a year. Apart from the orographic aggravation of the fronts, an important part in the genesis of precipitation is played by the inbursts of cold arctic air from the Kara and Barents seas, which contributes to a more active elevation of humid air in the foothills. As a rule, there is substantial precipitation on all peripheral slopes of mountains with any kind of exposition. The western and south-western slopes face the humid western air current, while the northern slopes attract the air masses moving from the north. All the windward mountain slopes and valleys cut deep into mountain countries or are protected by high mountain ranges, which intercept most of the atmospheric moisture and are very dry. Also peculiar is the precipitation distribution in such closed hollows as the Fergana, Issyk-Kul and Susamyr. There is significant discrepancy in the humidification of their western and of their eastern parts. The eastern parts are much better humidified than the western ones, which is due to the impact of the complicated relief on the passage of the fronts.

Among the northern slopes of Tien Shan, the Kirghiz range gets the most precipitation i.e., up to 900 mm. The open slopes of the Kirghiz range get more precipitation than do the deep valleys. On open slopes the annual sum of precipitation grows by 33 mm for every 100 m of altitude, while in the valleys the precipitation gradient falls up to 10 mm for 100 m of altitude.

Among the regions with the highest annual precipitation i.e., up to 2,000 mm, are the western spurs of Tien Shan (the Pskemsky, Ugamsky and Chatkalsky ridges) and the western slopes of the Zavarshansky and Gissarsky ridges. In the Vakhsh valley annual precipitation falls to 1,000 mm, while in the narrow canyon-shaped Zaravshan valley it falls to 350 mm. As we have already said, the internal regions of mountain countries and closed hollows have low precipitation : Western Pamir, less than 100 mm, the Syrts (dry highlands) of Tien Shan—250-350 mm and the Susamyr hollow and the Alaysk valley—300-350 mm.

The total river runoff was calculated by means of a map of the runoff of rivers in mountainous Central Asia. In drawing up the map we used data collected from 1935 to 1980 on the runoffs of nearly 450 rivers. Around 75 per cent of all the rivers have watersheds with an area less than 1,000 km^2. The poorest runoff data is on river basins which are located either low (average altitude under 500 m) or high (average altitude 400 m and more). The chosen calculation period to determine the annual normal runoff includes cycles of dry-and-wet years. However, it should be said that there is no full synchronism among the cycles. The period does not include the driest year —1917—and the wettest year—1921— which were extreme for most of the rivers. Regular runoff observations of a majority of rivers were started much later. The extension of observation rows for basins-analogues for such a long period of 18 years may therefore lead to greater error in determining the normal runoff.

The relation of the runoff to the average weighted altitude of the watersheds, which served as a basis for the map, was extrapolated in such a way so as to get a picture of the change in the runoff with the altitude within the entire altitudinal spectrum of the territory under consideration. For the upper limit we take the average weighted altitude of the region of glacial ablation. This glaciological level involves the runoff formed in the glacial zone. For the lower limit we take an altitude at which the runoff is subjected to an active anthropogenic impact.

A certain regularity can be traced in the distribution of river runoff on the territory of mountainous Central Asia : the greatest runoff occurs in basins situated on the slopes of peripheral ridges of the southern, south-western and western expositions, i.e. watersheds open to humid air masses. Much smaller is the runoff from the slopes of peripheral ridges of the north-eastern and eastern expositions. The effect the exposition has on the runoff can be seen in the case of the Kashka Darya basin. In this basin at an equal average altitude the watersheds become less aquiferous as we proceed in clock-wise direction, starting with the southern slope of the Karatepe ridge which lies in the southern part of the basin. At an average weighted altitude of the watershed of 1,600 m. the runoff from the southern slope of the Karatepe ridge reaches 500 mm. In the watersheds of Kashka Darya proper and Djina Darya it reaches 150 mm, in the Tanhaz Darya basin — 70 mm and in the Yakkobag Darya and Guzar Darya basins it is less than 70 mm. Such a fall in the runoff is due to the change in the exposition, which makes the watersheds less accessible to humid air masses. The lowest runoff can be observed in basins lying deep inside mountain systems. They involve rivers of Central Tien Shan and Eastern Pamir.

The highest runoff can be found in the basins of the southern slopes of southern peripheral ridges, the tributaries of Kafirnigan, Vakhsh and Surkhan Darya. At an average weighted altitude of 3,000 m the runoff reaches 1,200-1,300 mm, and at an altitude of 3,500 m it exceeds 1,500 mm. There is high runoff in the basins of the rivers Chirchik, Pskema, Ugama, Koksu and others. At an average altitude of 3,000 m it reaches 900 mm. In Central Tien Shan (the middle part of the Naryn river basin) the runoff does not exceed 300 mm. In Eastern Pamir the runoff fluctuates between 60 and 100 mm. Also low is the runoff of the western part of the basin of lake Issyk Kul, a mere 100-120 mm. In its eastern part, however, the runoff reaches 800 mm. An average runoff of 30-50 mm is characteristic, as a rule, of watersheds with an average weighted altitude of under

1,000 m.

Surface, subsurface and ice runoffs have been calculated on the basis of data obtained from studies of over 250 river basins. The share of each of the components was determined by the method of hydrograph break-down. Out of the long rows of observations we chose four years corresponding to two having an average water content, water-poor (75-80% of available supply) and water-rich (20-25% of available supply).

In Central Asia the relationship among components of the total river runoff during the year has the following pattern : from November to February the rivers are fed by underground waters of the active water exchange zone, in March in the lower parts of the basin the snow starts melting, but the seasonal snowmelt runoff is still so small that subsurface feed remains the basic one. Subsurface feed rises by June due to snowmelt and greater liquid precipitation. In July—September the rivers are fed by underground, ice and snow (in early July) waters of the glacial zone.

It should be said that due to low solum depth and high water permeability of orogenic soils, there is an almost total lack of surface rainfall runoff. Rain water reaches river beds very fast, but not before travelling underground. An analysis of the formation of rainfall runoff conducted by O.P. Scheglova (1960) for the entire Central Asia demonstrated that its share in the annual runoff is low and does not exceed 10 per cent.

When determining runoff components through the hydrograph breakdown method the greatest difficulties arise in finding a maximum position of the runoff. In mountain regions, where the underground waters of the main aquifers are not hydraulically linked to the river, use can be made of A.F. Makarenko's method (1948), which takes into account the dynamism in the runoff of gravity springs from the main aquifers drained by the river. The dynamism factor (the ratio between the maximum and minimum spring runoffs) changes with the altitude from 1.5 (at an altitude of 2,000-2,200 m) to 4 (at an altitude of 3,000-3,500 m).

For the glacial component we have taken the runoff produced from the melting of seasonal snow in the ablation area and the feeding area, as well as from the melting of old ice in the ablation area. The date for the start of ice runoff is determined according to a dependence showing the change with the altitude of the dates when the snow cover comes off in the non-glacial part of the basin.

The share of the underground component in the river runoff varies between 27 and 70 per cent, and the average figure for mountainous Central Asia is slightly more than 40 per cent. The higher the location of the watershed, the smaller is the share of the underground component in the total runoff. This is quite understandable, since at high altitudes there are frequent outcrops of rock which is of low accumulative capability and the poor soil cover is of low absorbability.

In the basins of rivers with average weighted altitudes ranging from 1,500 to 2,000 m (Guzar Darya, Kashka Darya and others) over 50 per cent of the runoff reaches the rivers underground. For the mountain regions of Central Asia in general the largest share of underground runoff has been found in basins with average weighted altitudes of 2,800-3,000 m, i.e. areas with a developed forest-grassland-steppe belt and where underground water frequently comes up to the surface in the form of springs. In regions with karstic activity it is practically impossible to trace the change in sub-surface runoff.

The share of the surface runoff in the total river runoff varies from 73 to 30 per cent. The average figure for mountainous Central Asia is 60 per cent. As a rule, the higher the watershed, the greater is the share of surface runoff (with the exception of karst regions).

The share of the glacial component in the total runoff fluctuates between 5 per cent (Tupolang river, Zarchub settlement) and 83 per cent (Seldara river with source from under the Fedchenko glacier). As a rule, the share of glacial feed is 22-25 per cent.

The total evaporation differs drastically depending on the place : from 30-50 mm in Western Pamir and 100-150 mm in the syrts of Tien Shan up to 500-600 mm in the Fergana valley The dependence of total evaporation on the altitude which we obtained for the worst studied regions is rather approximate, since the determination of precipitation proved to be a problem. Total evaporation falls with the rise in the altitude, which is quite understandable, since the higher we go, the lower the air temperature and the lower the humidity deficit.

The water balance pattern for several river basins is given in Table 14.1. The maps drawn up of the water balance elements made it possible to apply the balance method when estimating the water resources in the mountain regions of the three Central Asian republics-Uzbekistan, Tajikistan and Kirghizia (Table 14.2).

Tajikistan is the richest in water resources. Not only has it got the greatest volume of runoff, it also has the best figures for the relative value of runoff depth. The local water resources in Kirghizia however are not as rich, in Uzbekistan they are still less. Less than 10 per cent of the region's runoff is formed in the mountains of Uzbekistan. Nevertheless, due to the transit runoff of Syr-Darya and Amu Darya, which carry water from the other republics, Uzbekistan has substantial water resources. An important indicator in determining the amount of water resources is sub-surface runoff. Since this is the most stable of the river runoff components, it characterizes that part of river water resources which do not require regulation for utilization. But on the other hand, in conditions of Central Asia, where the main consumer of water-irrigable farming requires water in the vegetation period, much use is made of surface runoff fed by ice or snow, since the period of its formation coincides with the time when irrigation is at its peak.

The following figures should provide a picture of the water resources formed in the mountainous part of Central Asia :

precipitation	— 205.6 km^3,
total river runoff	— 113.7 km^3,
surface runoff	— 68.2 km^3,
sub-surface runoff	— 45.5 km^3,
evaporation	— 91.9 km^3.

TABLE 14.1 : **The water balance of some of the river basins in the mountain regions of Central Asia**

River	Region	Basin area km²	Average weighted altitude of basin m	Precipitation mm	Runoff					Evaporation mm
					total	Surface		Subsurface		
					mm	mm	%	mm	%	
1	2	3	4	5	6	7	8	9	10	11
Tosor	Terskey Ala Tau northern slope	324	3190	440	246	116	47	130	53	194
Cholponata	Kungey Ala Tau southern slope	75	3420	800	820	229	44	291	56	280
Shamsi	Kirghiz ridge northern slope	457	2850	960	350	172	49	178	51	610
Nishbash	Kuraminsky ridge north-western slope	141	1980	670	513	282	55	231	45	157
Borolday	Borkoldoy ridge northern slope	1360	1050	612	246	153	62	93	38	366
Sayramsu	Ugamsky ridge northern slope	444	2181	1300	504	242	48	262	52	796
Maydantal	Ugamsky ridge southern slope	471	3015	1500	1027	657	64	370	36	473
Kashka Darya	Zarafshansky ridge, southern slope	468	1823	981	366	149	41	217	59	615

TABLE 14.1 (Contd.)

1	2	3	4	5	6	7	8	9	10	11
Yakkobag Darya	Alaysky ridge north-western slope	504	2700	1224	422	243	58	179	42	802
Shirabad Darya	Kugitang Tau ridge eastern slope	2950	1495	392	79	44	56	35	44	313
Sangardak Darya	Baysun Tau mts. south-eastern slope	920	2286	1000	507	279	55	228	45	493
Takob	Gissarsky ridge southern slope	75	2390	1457	1005	620	62	385	38	452

TABLE 14.2 : **Balance estimate of water resources in the mountain regions of Uzbekistan, Tajikistan and Kirghizia**

(numerator—km^3, denominator—mm of layer)

Republic	Area km^2	Precipitation	Runoff			Evaporation	Gross wetting of territory	Factors	
			total	surface	sub-surface			total runoff	river feed by underground waters
Uzbekistan	83,6	37,6/450	10,6/127	6,4/76	4,2/51	27,0/374	31,2/323	0,28	0,14
Tajikistan	142,0	68,0/480	53,4/376	32,0/221	21,4/155	14,6/104	36,0/259	0,79	0,60
Kirghizia	197,5	100,0/506	49,7/252	29,8/151	19,9/101	50,3/254	70,2/355	0,50	0,28

REFERENCES

1. Grigoriev, A.A., Tsytsenko, K.V., On the accuracy of determining atmospheric precipitation. In : *Problems of Water Management*, 14/ Hydrology/, Frunze, Kirghizstan, 1969.
2. Krenke, A.N., *Mass transfer in glacial Systems on the territory of the USSR*. L., Hydrometeoizdat, 1982.
3. Krenke, A.N., Khodakov, V.G., *Glacial surface melt and air temperature Materialy glyaziolog.* issled. M., 1966, n 12.
4. Litovchenko, A.F., Results of the studies into the accuracy of precipitation estimates in the mountains. Hydrology issues in Mountain regions. Alma-Ata. Kaz. University, 1971.
5. Lvovich, M.I., *Land Water Balance.* Materialy k 3 syezd Geogr. obsh. L., Nauka, 1959.
6. Lvovich, M.I., *Man and Water.* M., Mysl, 1963.
7. Makarenko, A.F , *Underground feed of Rivers.* Trudy labor. hydrolog. problem AN USSR, 1948, v. 1.
8. Mansurova, E.P., Sosedov, I.S., Experience of precipitation estimate in the mountains of Zailiysky Ala Tau. In : *Hydrophysicalresearch in the Mountain Regions of Kazakhstan.* Alma-Ata, Nauka, 1969.
9. Melikishvili, O.E., Certain results of the estimation of main systematic errors in gauging atmospheric precipitation. Soobsh. AN Gruz SSR, 1967, v. 46, n 3.
10. M., Nauka, *Water balance of the USSR and its transformation*, 1969, 338 pp.
11. Shlygina, V.F., The formation of underground waters of cones of debris on foothill plain of Zailiysky Ala Tau, Trudy Instituta geologii AN KazSSR, 1965, v. 14.
12. Scheglova, O.P., *River feed in Central Asia,* Tashkent, TashGU, 1960.

15

THE DEVELOPMENT OF WATER ECONOMY AND LAND RECLAMATION AND ITS EFFECT ON THE ECONOMIC AND ECOLOGICAL SITUATION IN CENTRAL ASIA

V.A. Dukhovny

With the development of civilization, water economy, as an industry involved in creating and utilizing water resources, kept expanding its sphere of activity to become a generally active and essential part of the economy and a condition for the existence and progress of society. Water resources are involved in all biogenous processes without exception, but at the same time they form and transform numerous natural conditions, undergoing changes themselves, the degree of which depends on the intensity of their impact on the ecological situation as a whole.

Today, in the late 20th century, the utilization of water resources in the arid regions has approached the volume of the resources available and the gap between supply and demand is widening. In his search for a solution to the problem of achieving sufficiency in food and the raw materials for industry, man directs his efforts to maximize the efficiency of water utilization. In the arid zones this is more so because the remarkably fertile land of these zones, when reclaimed, will turn into blossoming oases. If we add to this that these regions have a labour surplus as well as various mineral resources for the development of industy, the need to solve the problem of water supply in arid zones becomes apparent.

In this country the development of the water economy and land reclamation in Central Asia is a matter of constant concern of the government. Already at the very beginning of Soviet rule, in 1918, a decree was passed, introduced by Lenin, providing for the irrigation of 500 thousand hectares of land in Turkistan. Since then drastic changes have affected not only irrigated lands, but also the economy of the entire Central Asian region, which is a graphic example of the efficiency of the social economic development of a water management complex in arid zones.

In our understanding, a water management complex (WMC) is a set of enterprises and units with links between them, aimed at creating and utilizing water resources. This whole set is dynamically developing in certain natural conditions, which themselves, in this connection, are undergoing constant change.

The main links within a branch and within the entire WMC are aimed not only at the interaction with the region's economy, but also at continued development of water and land resources. In conditions of the arid regions, land resources become a basis for the economy only if irrigation is provided. That is why greater farming areas and productivity are directly related to water resources dynamics (Fig. 15.1).

Within the WMC we can single out the functions as shown in Table 15.1 :

When considering the diagram of interrelations among the functional components within a branch and a WMC (Fig 15.1) it becomes clear that despite their seeming difference, they are closely linked in their natural and industrial amalgam.

It is expedient to draw the boundaries of a water management complex along those of a natural exogenous system—within the limits of the boundaries of a river basin. The three basic components—formation, conservation and planning, should act within these river basin differences ; while utilization, reproduction and exploitation of irrigation systems should act at the level of territories subjected to the influence of water management measures.

TABLE 15.1 : **The main functions of operational bodies in water management complexes**

Function	Purpose	With the help of what facilities, measure
1	2	3
Creation of water resources for utilization	Bringing natural resources of rivers, lakes and other sources into a state which would meet society's requirements in quality, quantity and location	Reservoirs. Inter-and intra-basin diversionary canals. Intake structure. Dams
Water resources conservation	Maintenance of required water quality and the prevention of an adverse effect of anthropogenic processes on water resources	Monitoring stations and posts ; a system monitoring duty and draining of water in basins. Purifying installations. Flushes
Maintenance of inter- and intra-economic irrigation canals and installations	Supervision over the state of installations, ensuring of the set mode of operation ; prevention of destruction and damage	Irrigation canals, installations on the means of water metering
Distribution of water among various types of consumers (agriculture, industry, etc.)	Meeting demand in water of water-consumer organizations	The same
Water management and intra-economic water distribution	Transfer of water for technological needs within an enterprise, including the system of enterprise division, transport and water supply	Canals, installation means of water metering

Improvement of irrigation techniques	Introduction of progressive irrigation methods, drawing-up of recommendations for enterprises, their equipment with the necessary facilities, assembly, launching with adjustment and maintenance	Sprinkler systems irrigating machines drip and sub-surface irrigation, mobile pipes
Maintenance of system and installations in working order	Organization of preventive maintenance to ensure constant high performance of water management installations	Maintenance system
Monitoring of the state of land reclamation. Reconstruction of irrigation systems	Enhancement of natural fertility of land. Greater technical level of irrigation systems, better state of reclamation, cutting back on irrational utilization of water	Headers, drainage, observation network laboratories, soil expeditions
Creation of water management systems and their expansion in the process of construction	Introduction of new land, facilities and systems	Construction base industry, organization

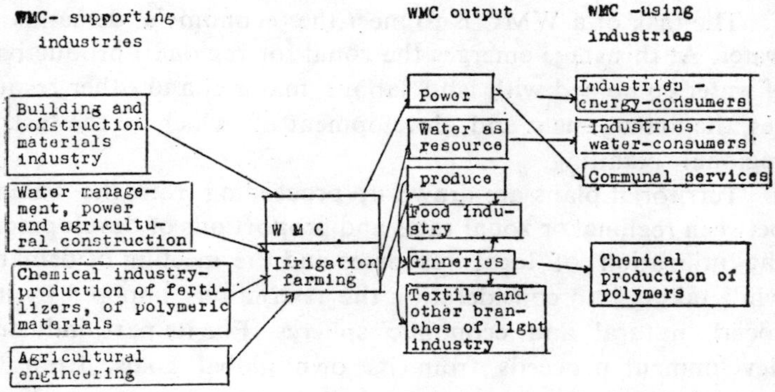

FIG. 15.1 : *Diagram of impact of WMC links on the economy of the arid zone*

The WMC structure should be likewise divided into two levels—the level of formation and conservation (the basinal level) and the level of utilization and consumption (the territorial level). Such a dual structure has two clearly defined aspects, natural ecological and economic.

From the point of view the first aspect, the basis for the two WMC levels are two biogeocenosis cycles, the basinal and the territorial, characterized by undisturbed or disturbed anthropogenic activity in the watershed area and close interaction. On the other hand, a river with its tributaries as an axis of industrial management and a major source of water resources, should ecologically fit in with the economic demands of the development of adjoining administrative territories. Thus, the problem of planning WMC development is determined through the linkage of industrial and territorial planning based on the analysis of the basin factors of the development of industries and regions.

Water management and reclamation proceed from the fact that the reproduction, creation and conservation of water resources, the adjustment of the regime of water sources to meet society's demands in water, are all industrial functions which should be managed on a national scale and should proceed from the overall unity of water resources, and the ommon property of water.

The task of a WMC is to meet the economy's demands in water. At this stage emerges the zonal (or regional) productivity of water combined with land, labour, material and other resources, the management and development of which is the task of regional planning.

Territorial plans are drawn up proceeding from the balance between regional or zonal rates and proportions of development; the utilization of local resources and the meeting of demand, while taking into consideration the restrictions imposed by the social, natural and economic spheres. For its part, industrial development proceeds from its own global goals, from the tasks faced by the economy, taking into account the optimization of the utilization resources for industries and the prospects provided by technological progress. At the same time it is necessary to take into account the economic goal of the industry, the creation of the necessary conditions for meeting the demands in water of the economy as a whole, as well as for solving the problem of irrigation.

To achieve an optimal combination of the industrial and territorial levels of WMC development, the development potentials in different regional zones of a basin should be juxtaposed. This should be linked to the distribution of funds for the reproduction and utilization of water resources inside these zones. A maximum economic effect should be achieved within the basin's boundaries.

The creation of a WMC in Central Asia is based on a large natural and socio-economic potential. Favourable climatic conditions (much sun, the great amount of warm cloudless days), soil conditions (splendid sierozem, meadow and newly irrigated soils with great fertility reserves, well conditioned and rich in calcium and potassium), and hydrological conditions make it possible to take in two harvests a year on vast areas of land and to grow such heat-loving plants as cotton, rice, grapes, all kinds of vegetables, fruit, melons and even citric fruits, provided there is irrigation.

Another essential contributing factor precipitating the need for irrigated farming and for an entire WMC in Central Asia is the rapid population growth. By the end of the century the region's population will have increased by 60 per cent and the region will account for 80 per cent of the increase in the entire country's able-bodied population. Among the region's demographic features are the high stability of the rural population, its low migration and high skill in using the advantages of irrigation for growing crops. Finally, the region has a high energy potential and large discovered reserves of oil, gas, and minerals.

These potentials provide all the necessary conditions for the development in Central Asia of the entire WMC, including irrigated farming, backing industries (engineering, mineral fertilizer, chemical industries), as well as processing industries (ginning, light, textile, canning, food, etc).

In the forty years from 1940 to 1980 the area of land under irrigation grew in Uzbekistan from 2.0 to 3.4 mln. ha or by

TABLE 15.2 : **The rates of growth of gross produce in the Republics of Central Asia and Kazakhstan**

(Base Year 1940) mln. roubles, numerator (1955 prices), denominator%

Republic	YEAR						
	1940	1950	1960	1965	1970	1975	1980
Uzbekistan	1145	1551	2238	2754	3472	4062	5277
	100	135	195	240	303	355	461
Tajikistan	260	271	438	623	771	928	1107
	100	104	168	240	296	357	426
Turkmenia	209	296	398	499	691	845	1005
	100	142	190	239	331	404	481
Kirghizia	316	353	676	742	911	1094	1194
	100	112	182	235	288	346	378
Kazakhstan	928	1402	3955	3652	5670	5199	7204
	100	151	426	394	611	560	776
Overall	2858	3873	7605	8270	11515	12128	15787
	100	136	266	289	403	424	552
USSR	39737	39455	63128	71019	87082	90675	98070
	100	99	150	179	219	228	247

169 per cent in Tajikistan from 0.32 to 0.6 mln. ha or by 186 per cent, in Turkmenia from 0.37 to 0.94 mln. ha or by 252 per cent, in Kirghizia from 0.8 to 0.95 mln. ha or by 131 per cent and in Kazakhstan from 1.0 to 1.93 mln. ha or by 193 per cent ; the overall increase was from 4.5 to 7.9 mln. ha or by 775 per cent. Over the same period in the country as a whole areas under irrigation increased from 6.1 to 17.5 mln. ha, that is by 287 per cent. Nevertheless, gross growth rates of produce over the same period grew by 552 per cent in the case of Central Asia and Kazakhstan, as against the 247 per cent of the country as a whole. Thus, land productivity due to irrigation was growing twice as fast in the region as in the country as a whole. Over the same period the overall water intake to meet all the demands in the economy of the region increased from 52.3 km^3 a year to 146.7 km^3 or by 280 per cent. The increased growth rates of agricultural and industrial production contributed to the sharp rise in water utilization in the region, which more than doubled.

WMC development was not confined to the expansion of links of irrigated farming only (Fig. 15.2)., but have effectively extended to all the industries with the exception of mining, forestry, fuel industry and pasture husbandry. The rest of the industries act either as water consumers or users or suppliers and processor of the WMC's primary product.

Table 15.3 shows the increase in the growth of water consumption by different branches of the economy over the same period as was considered in the previous table.

TABLE 15.3 : **The distribution of water consumption among branches of the Economy in Central Asia**

(*numerator—% to the appropriate year, denominator—% to 1940*)

Consumer	1940	1960	1970	1975	1980
Industry	4.6 / 100	7.0 / 180	8.5 / 378	10.7 / 411	6.1 / 393
Communal services	0.4 / 100	0.4 / 125	0.5 / 225	1.6 / 642	3.0 / 1.433
Agriculture	9.4 / 100	91.4 / 114	89.6 / 193	85.2 / 160	88 / 209
Fishery	1.0 / 100	0.9 / 120	1.1 / 239	1.8 / 342	1.7 / 412

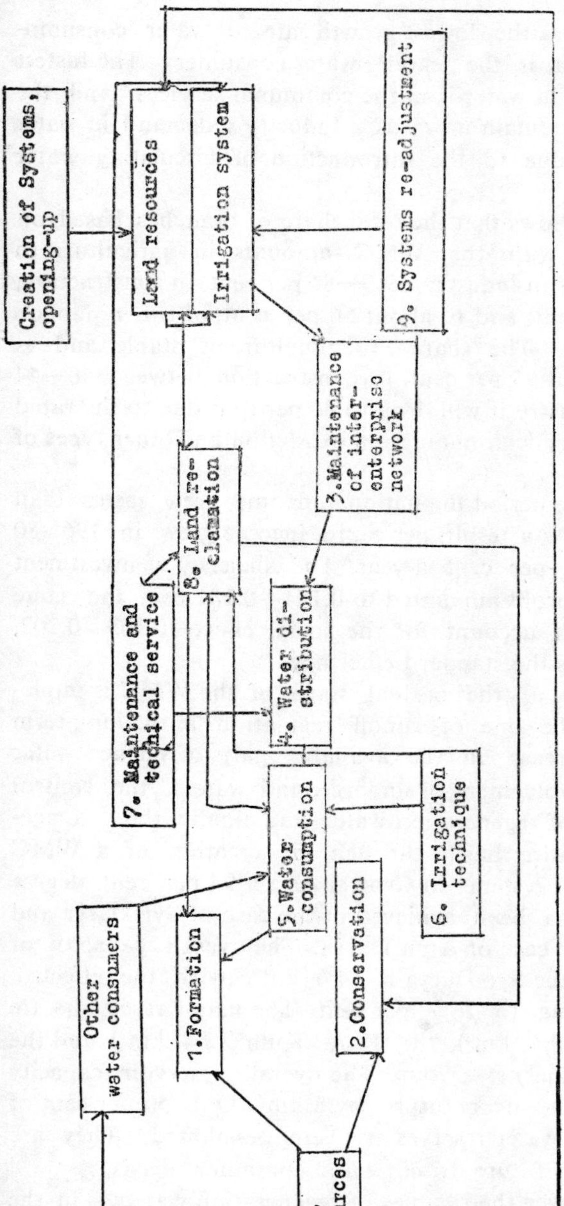

FIG. 15 2 : *Diagram of functional links within a WMC*

Agriculture has the slowest growth rate in water consumption, although it is the leading water consumer. The fastest growing demand in water is in the communal services, and the trend is likely to remain upwards. Industry's demand in water will be falling due to the introduction of circulating water supply.

An analysis shows that the total share of branches based on and connected with the WMC amounts in agriculture to 95—96.7 per cent in industry, 59.9—86 per cent, in construction, 36.1—48.2 per cent, and to about 56 per cent, of the republic's total production. The share in agriculture is stable and is likely to remain at 95 per cent, in construction between 40—44 per cent, in industry it will drop to 40 per cent due to the rapid growth of the chemical, mining, oil extraction and other types of industries.

Over the same period the national income grew faster than the population. As a result, per capita income grew in 1965-80 from 8.4 to 14 per cent a year. The efficiency of investment in WMC in net profit amounted to 0.134+0.181 over the same period, and with account for the social effect—0.163+0.202, which far exceeds the standard efficiency.

The progress of the basinal stage of the WMC is implemented along the line of runoff regulation in the long-term aspect, the increase in the available part of surface water resources, the involvement of underground waters, the control over the regime of regeneration water, and finally the management of the entire basin through the creation of a WMC automatic control system. In Central Asia a 94 per cent degree of regulation has been achieved in the case of Syr-Darya and 86 per cent in the case of Amu Darya. The overall capacity of reservoirs along the Syr-Darya is 34.6 km^3, with the effective storage amounting to 26.7 per cent. The major reservoirs are the Toktogul (19.5 km^3), the Kara Kum (3.4 km^3) and the Chardaryin (5.6 km^3) reservoirs. The overall reservoir capacity is to grow in the near future by 8 km^3. Only 50 per cent of the underground water reserves are being exploited. They are being withheld for future drinking and communal needs.

The control over the regimes of regeneration waters is in the planning stage, particularly since the launching of the Syr-Darya basin and the Amu Darya basin automatic control systems. These water management complexes, expect efficient interaction and forecasting of all the linked water resources in the formation, utilization and operational management.

The development of the WMC's territorial stage proceeds along two lines—the irrigation of new lands and the reconstruction of lands already under irrigation. The irrigation of new lands makes it possible to involve into the sphere of production the huge potentials of the unused land in the arid regions and at the same time create jobs for the surplus labour in the densely populated regions. It will also increase food supplies to the rapidly growing population. Since most of the new land in the region is desert, a special complex method has been worked out and introduced in Central Asia to irrigate and develop land. This method was first tried out in the Hungry steppes, where in a relatively short period of 29 years, 500 thousand hectares of land were developed in the republics of Uzbekistan, Kazakhstan and Tajikistan. The method is based on the creation of territorial industrial complexes where priority is given to irrigated farming.

Under this method the irrigation and development of land and the construction of most of the infrastructure facilities are conducted according to a single design and plan. There is one client, as a rule, and the work is done by one organization which bears full responsibility from the blueprint stage to the stage of the final product. Due to this method, the investments were repaid in the early stages of the development of the complex, i.e., in about fifteen years from the start of the construction.

The above mentioned methods were applied during the development of other large areas of land in the Karshin steppe, in south-west Uzbekistan, in the lower reaches of the Amu Darya, in the Kara Kum canal region in Turkmenia and in the Yavan Obikinksk valley in Tajikistan. On the whole over one million hectares has been developed using this method in Central Asia.

The links determining the productivity of the WMC's territorial stage, are based on a number of factors : whether the branches making up the WMC have a social and industrial infrastructure and are provided with material supply ; the linkage of branches ; the area of land under irrigation and its productivity, and available water supply for irrigated farming.

Proceeding from the goals of increasing WMC productivity per unit of water it is necessary to constantly boost the produce of irrigated farming on the existing land and irrigate and develop new lands. Irrigated farming can be improved through the further introduction of capital funds, the construction of housing, recreation facilities, development of municipal services, more efficient and skilled management, better seed-growing as a result of mechanization, higher labour efficiency and the introduction of a regionalized system of farming. On the other hand, an essential part of this process is the reconstruction of irrigation systems (the switchover to sophisticated systems, the increase in the available water supply and higher efficiency of the systems), improved land reclamation, the cutting down on harvest losses incurred through salinization and bogging, and relief smoothing to achieve better humidification. Sophisticated systems make it possible to reduce operating expenses, enhance the irrigation system's capacity and cut on the expenses in farming production. Finally, the main effect of the reconstruction are the reduced specific water expenses per hectare, which in conjunction with the other factors gives a sharp boost to the productivity of irrigated land per unit of produce.

The great amount of work carried out to date along these lines brought about a dramatic improvement in the indicators for water management and farming. In 1966-80 Uzbekistan performed the reconstruction of its irrigation network on an area of 1.3 mln. ha, capital planning on 634 thousand ha and reclamation on 2.2 mln. ha. As a result, the efficiency of the irrigation network grew from 48 to 61 per cent, 2.6 mln. ha, of land has been fully reclaimed and the yield of raw cotton grew by 0.7 to reach on average 3.254 t/ha.

The present stage of reconstruction provides for minimal water expenses per unit of harvest. With this in mind, proposals have been drawn up on the complex reconstruction of irrigated lands. The reconstruction's efficiency, apart from increasing the productivity of the existing lands, would make it possible to release water resources through rational management, which in its turn serve as a boost for new irrigation.

Water management and reclamation bring about changes in the two kinds of biogeochemical cycles (biogeocenoses) formed in natural conditions—territorial (minor) and basinal (major changes).

In the arid zone natural territorial biogeocenoses are characterized by low productivity, which due to humidity deficit is always several times lower than the potential created by climatic, energy and soil resources. That is why irrigation has such a drastic effect on the intensity of the cycle, and this requires careful control over the changes in the components of balances and natural conditions.

With the development of irrigation in the arid zone, constant changes are observed in the large basinal cycle with the stabilization at the level of exhaustion of water resources in a water and salt balance extremely complicated for the functioning of the lower reaches.

This gives rise to very important tasks for WMC control in the arid zone. These are : constant control over the utilizations of water resources and reduction at all levels and stages of irretrievable water consumption ; uninterrupted planning for different temporal stages of the level of maximum utilization of water resources in the basin of each river, proceeding from the stabilization at a certain level of the basinal cycle ; taking into account the basin's mineral balance [temporal stages should reflect for each period (10—15 years) a certain technical level of WMC control system and the possibility of bringing the WMC up to the level over the next time period] ; setting of long-term limits for the utilization of local water resources ; determining for each temporal stage the indicators of the ecological efficiency of development, the possible ecological changes in the zones of influence of the river basin, particularly in the lower reaches, drainless reservoirs, etc.

From this point of view, the understanding of the interaction of the WMC with natural conditions in the arid zone is essential. Under the impact of runoff regulation, changes occur in the runoff's regime and volume and to a certain degree in mineralization. Changes also affect the channel and evaporation losses, the character of vegetation and plankton, as well as a number of other indicators. In the zone of reservior afflux the territory gets flooded. All these are generally known phenomena and there is a wide range of means and technical solution to combat their adverse effects.

But most of all the basinal cycle is affected by changes in the territorial cycles, which are themselves largely determined by the technical level of the irrigation systems. It is a well-known fact that the development of irrigated farming through greater humidification sharply increases the activity of all the biological processes in the former desert areas, including the energy potential, the activity of micro-organisms, biomass soil, intensity of infiltration, etc. All this accelerates soil-forming processes. In our works we demonstrated[1,2] that a correct choice of reclamation techniques taking into consideration soil demands and hydrological conditions ; the right combination of irrigation techniques and a complex of development measures—all this will lead to rapid soil productivity growth (an important ecological effect), with a minimal effect on ground waters and with minimal water intake.

The same works show that the creation of an optimal reclamation regime (a relationship between irrigation and drainage techniques that would ensure minimal water expenses per unit of harvest) also provides for the minimal interaction with the basinal cycle, due to :

—minimal intake of water from the river ;
—minimal salt exchange with the river, at a close-to-nil level ;
—minimal salt exchange between the aeration zone and ground waters ;
—minimal pollution of the river with regenerated water ;
—minimal removal from the fields of pesticides, herbicides and fertilizers.

The correctness of the method was clearly demonstrated by the experience of the development of the Hungry steppe, when the optimal reclamation regime was applied. In the case of the Hungry steppe the optimal regime in debit terms, with a 1 g/1 mineralization of ground waters, is the semi-hydromorphic regime with the water depth at 2m, with a 2—10 g/l mineralization—2.5 m, and more than 10 g/l— the semi-automorphic regime with the water depth at 3 m.

TABLE 15.4 : **Comparative Water Balance of a Zone under Irrigation**

m^3 per 1 ha (1972)

Item of balance	Old irrigation zone (acc. to N. Reshetkina & H. Yakubov	New irrigation zone
Precipitation	2 258	2 460
Duty of water	13 441	8 950
Inflow from outside	—	120
Overall inflow	15 699	11 530
Overall evaporation	7 842	8 500
Humidification increase in the aeration zone	—	600
Change in the ground water level	20	530
Drainage and water removal	7 877	2 130

With the application of deep subsurface horizontal and vertical drainage under a flushing irrigation regime, the Hungry steppe developed the semi-automorphic regime with ground water at a depth of 2.4 m (3 m in the case of vertical drainage). As a result the average gross irrigation duty of water amounted to 7.5—10.2 thous.m³/ha (the 1969 minimum was 6.28 thous.m³/ha) with the annual water consumption being 10.8—12.2 thous.m³/ha. Drainage and removal runoff in the same period was fluctuating from 0.91 to 2.89 m³/ha. The entire area saw a fall in salt accumulations and the disappearance of natural solonchaks, as well as the fall in the amount of saline land, with the salt removal rate from 3 to 18.6 t/ha (29.6 t/ha in 1969).

It can be said as a comparison that in the old zone of the Hungry steppe (Table 15.4), where on the land with surface drainage the average depth of ground water is 2—2.3 m, the irrigation duty of water is between 12.1 and 15.6 thous.m^3/ha with the overall water consumption being 15.2—19.4 thous.m^3/ha and drainage runoff—from 4.8 to 8.5 thous.m^3/ha. The total salt removal at a non-optimal regime fluctuates between 15 and 28 t/ha.

In the other irrigable regions of Central Asia with a non-optimal reclamation regime the total water consumption is even greater, while salt removal (Bukhara, Khoresm, Tashauz) in the past five years amounted to 55 to 68 t/ha.

On the basis of the above mentioned methods the Central Asian Irrigation Research Institute carried out an analysis of specific water consumption and draining in the area of Uzbekistan, considering the change in the runoff character of the rivers Syr-Darya and Amu Darya, as well as the change of these indicators in connection with the improvement of irrigation systems. The calculations were done in two stages for a long-term period : (1) bringing efficiency up to the criterial technical level (η_c=0.78 to 0.8) and switching over to the optimal reclamation regime ; (2) full automation of the inter- and intra economic networks (η_c=0.85 to 0.88), increasing the efficiency of irrigation to 75 per cent.

The calculations show that the proposed measures and particularly the optimization of reclamation regimes make it possible not only to bring down specific water consumption and increase the area of irrigable lands in the republic, but also to reduce the level of water mineralization in the Syr-Darya and Amu Darya rivers.

Thus, WMC management in the arid zone, on the basis of optimization of the basinal cycle, considered in the context of territorial cycles, ensures progressive socio-economic and ecological development for a basin, on the basis of sophisticated irrigation farming. These guidelines must also ensure the further development of the Central Asian agrarian-industrial complex. Local water resources are to be complemented by the year 2000 by part of the runoff of the Siberian rivers diverted to the region. The addition (18 km^3) will amount to a 150 per cent rise on the present resources.

FOOTNOTES

1. Irrigation complexes in Central Asia. Tashkent . Uzbekistan. 1983.
2. Water management complex in the irrigable zone. Moscow . Kolos. 1984.

Note : Both works are in Russian.

16

PROTECTION OF IRRIGATED LANDS OF TAJIKISTAN AGAINST SALINIZATION AND BOGGYING

E.G. Vaksman, S.I. Vasil'chikova and *P.A. Kerzum*

An optimal use of lands in agriculture and other sectors of national economy is a precondition for resolving the problem of providing population with food and industry with raw materials. Hence the special attention of our Government to an effective use and improvement of lands. For our mountainous Republic the problem of increase in soil fertility and of making productive the marginal lands are of particular importance.

The total area of the Republic is 14,255,000 hectares. Agricultural lands comprise about 31 per cent of the Republic's territory, including 24.3 per cent of pastures. All the other agricultural lands account for only 6.5 per cent of which 5.5 per cent are plowed lands, including 3.5 per cent of irrigated ones. Although the area of plowed lands has recently somewhat grown, with the rapid growth of population the share of plowed lands per capita has rather declined from 0.29 ha in 1970 to 0.19 ha in 1985. The decrease in the share of irrigated lands has been equally marked from 0.15 ha to 0.12 ha between 1970 and 1985, as the potential of their expansion in lowland areas have been practically exhausted.

Irrigated lands are the most valuable agricultural resource, particularly in the Kurgan-Tyubin region where fine-fibred cotton plants are grown. The total area of irrigated lands in

1980 comprised 6,276,000 ha of which 583,000 ha are plowed irrigated lands and 302 thousand ha are under cotton plantation.

It is irrigation which, mainly, provides for the high living standards of the Tajik people. Productivity of an irrigated hectare is almost 5 to 7 times greater than that of a dry one. However, supply of considerable amounts of water to formerly virgin lands necessarily leads to important changes in the hydrological regime, including many negative ones, for instance, the rise of the ground water table, salinization of soils and boggying. Due to discharge into rivers of sewage and drainage waters with greater concentrations of toxic salts, pesticides and herbicides, as well as of dissolved mineral fertilizers, the quality of water for irrigation in the downstream zone of rivers decreases. This deterioration of water supply consequently makes cultivation of agricultural plants complicated, and correspondingly, calls for higher financial allocation to fight against these negative phenomena. In this respect great attention is devoted to the problem of the environment protection against flooding, salinization and contamination of the ground and river waters and of soils alike. A system of nature conservation measures has therefore been developed and implemented.

Irrigated lands in the south of Tajikistan are located on the margin of muntainous regions of the water basin of the Amu-Darya river and the plainland spaces of Middle Asia. They are not a homogeneous massif, but are scattered in big and small valleys separated by southern endings of mountain ridges.

In the north of the Republic the irrigated massives are located among mountain ridges in the water basin of the Syr-Darya river where they transform from the central part of the Fergana Valley to vast flat plainlands cut by the Syr-Darya river. Some of their parts lie on the foot plainlands of the Kuramin and the Turkestan ridges.

All of the irrigated soils of Tajikistan, but for a few exceptions, are subjected to salinization and due to this their fertility diminishes. Salinization of soils is a clearcut and tangible manifestation of the natural geochemical process—a discharge of salts dissolved in water from mountains down to the plains and to terminal hollows. The following figures give some idea as to the extent of such salinization. Annually, almost 3 tons of salts per square kilometre, on the average, are washed out from soils and mountain rocks in the water basin of the Vakhsh River ; the Vakhsh River itself drains out about 10 million tons of salts per year. If all these waters of the Vakhsh River brought down every year are evaporated, a dense layer of salts, one metre in thickness, should cover the area of almost 300 ha. The Syr-Darya River in the region of Leninabad also carries about 10 million tons of salts annually. The Amu-Darya river brings down nearly 25 million tons of salts per year.

A considerable mass of salts with the help of irrigation water enters within the oases boundaries. For example, over 2 million tons of salts are annually brought down into the Vakhsh Valley. With evaporation of the irrigation waters the dissolved salts remain in soils, and ground waters. There have been cases when this process became catastrophic and considerable spaces of soils turned out to be useless because of excessive salinization of the soil.

During the last century and at the beginning of the present one, when the drainage network was missing on irrigated lands, the fertile land occupied only 40 to 50 % of the territory, the remaining part being saline. The surplus reserves of salts comprised millions of tons. Almost everywhere on the irrigated territory of Tajikistan drainage systems of a horizontal or of a vertical type were built to fight against this threatening phenomenon.

On an average, 23 running metres of horizontal drainage from 2.5 to 4 metres deep fall per every ha of the irrigated area in the Republic. Interdrain distances are mainly set within 100 to 400 metres. In particular cases there is built a fine horizontal drainage net, either provisional for washing periods or permanent for discharge of surplus water under extreme conditions (intensive pressure feeding of ground waters, great amount of precipitations, heavy clay soil-grounds, etc.).

Basically, for all irrigated oases of the Republic the discharge of salts by way of a collection and drainage network is more than the income with irrigation water. With the increase in remoteness of irrigation and as desalinization of soil grounds and ground waters increases, the difference between the income and discharge of salts decreases, thus for the recent years in the Vakhsh Valley, for instance, they have appeared to be actually equal. It has been noted that with the increase in density and length of the drainage net the discharge of salts from oases perceptively increases. Therefore, we have repeatedly recommended that for the first 10 to 20 years of active meliorative improvement and mastering of saline lands there should be built a somewhat lengthy drainage system than is required for the operational period. For example, for the Beshkent Valley to obtain the maximum amelioration effect it has turned out expedient to make the interdrain distances almost twice. Such an increase in density of a drainage system is justifiable economically.

Despite the widely branched drainage net, due to various reasons the condition of lands in 85 thousand ha is unsatisfactory. Plots with mean, heavily and very heavily salinized soils and plots, where the level of ground waters and their mineralization elements exceed the critical values (Table 16.1), are referred to lands of unsatisfactory conditions.

The excessive water expenditure on irrigation, which at present amounts to approximately 12 billion cubic metres per year, is one of the main reasons for the status quo of the meliorative efforts.

TABLE 16.1 : **Land areas with different depth values of the level of ground waters**

Regions	Depth values of the LGW, in metres			
	0—1	1—2	2—3	more than 3
Leninabad	5119	23393	11826	118874
Kulyab	2203	22418	19943	25625
Kurgan-Tyubin	10876	39364	49008	121018
Regions subordinated to the Republic	693	3639	4417	66442
Total for the Republic	18891	88814	85194	331959

Water expenditure is 2 to 2.5 times higher than the amount of water evaporated and used for transpiration by cultivated plants. This is due to a low efficiency factor (EF) of irrigated systems (0.45 to 0.60), an unsatisfactory planning of fields, an imperfect system of water use and the necessity for additional water supply for creating the washing regime of irrigation. Considering the total evaporation on lands used for cotton and alfalfa crop rotation, the expenditure of 10 to 14 thousand cubic metres per ha is an actual irrigational norm which is 35 to 45 per cent higher than the planned one.

Therefore in the midsummer period the ground water in a considerable area of land rises up almost to the land surface level and very often reach the root zone (Table 16.2). This complicates the execution of agrotechnical measures, prolongs vegetation period of cotton and of other cultivated plants, and serves as a cause for secondary salinization.

TABLE 16.2 : **The efficiency factor for irrigated systems of Tajikistan for the year 1983**

Regions	Irrig. area, in ha	Efficiency factor for water use EFWU	Efficiency factor for irrigated systems	
			interfarm	general
Leninabad	201208	0.83	0.90	0.63
Kulyab	70168	0.76	0.82	0.62
Kurgan-Tyubin	221083	0.74	0,76	0.59
Regions subordinated to the R.	78924	0.88	0.89	0.45
Total and average for the Republic	571383	0.80	0.83	0.59

Special services in the Republic investigate where lands are subjected to processes of salinization or boggying and recommend relevant measures for their improvement. More often, these are measures of a complex character and require considerable capital investments for construction (rebuilding of the irrigation net, drainage, field planning, etc.) perfection of labour organization and scientific observation of the irrigation regime. Initially turn works are carried out on plots where the mid-summer level of ground waters lies nearer than 1 to 1.5 metres from the earths surface. Every five-years, rebuilding of the irrigation net and meliorative improvement of lands is done on the area of 50 to 60 thousand ha. The volume of work to be done in the future is to be enlarged.

It is envisaged to complete the, rebuilding of the irrigation net in 10 to 25 years and to raise the EF up to 0.76 to 0.80. Automation and mechanization of watering practices will allow to decrease the infiltration losses on fields and the land surface water discharge by 20 to 30 per cent. On the whole, this will allow to liquidate the basic causes for secondary salinization of soils and for boggying.

On newly irrigated lands in side valleys and on the plainlands near the mountains where the grounds contain huge, although scattered, resources of salts, the ground is watered with the beginning of irrigation and the salts acquire mobility. As the ground water table rises, they move towards the surface, concentrate and are capable of salinizing the soil. To avoid this it is necessary to timely build the drainage net for the discharge of salts into river arteries.

Passing through the soil and grounds of the irrigated massif the salt mass differentiates, the non-toxic insoluble salts being retained in greater mass than the ones which are toxic for plants and are easily dissolved. Thus, mineralization of the returning waters is higher even with the poorer composition of salts as compared with the irrigation water. Further downstream the rivers, towards their deltas, this process gains force, until at some place the water becomes altogether useless for irrigation.

As is observed in the general geochemical scheme the irrigated massives represent transition zones on the way of salt masses from mountains towards plainlands and terminal hollows. Salinization of soils is a consequence of salt sedimentation along this way. It is not possible to stop this general natural geochemical process and to exclude ways of salt getting within the irrigated territories. But we are capable of rendering it totally harmless. The task of melioration of saline soils now, firstly, lies in ensuring the discharge during the shortest possible period of time, of the surplus toxic soils accumulated for centuries outside the boundaries of irrigated valleys and, secondly, in a systematic regulation of salt moving routes through hydrotechnical and agro-technical measures, letting them pass through their transition zones. This is harmless for agriculture.

These problems were solved in the past decades for the large valleys of the main rivers of Southern Tajikistan—the Vakhsh, the Pyandzh, the Lower Kafirnigan and the Kulyab rivers. The fact that a smooth thick layer of shingle which is well penetrated by water, provides quick "ventilation" of waterbearing horizons, has favoured the success of the melioration of the soils in these valleys.

The new lands being projected for irrigation in the Republic, are either salinized or contain considerable amounts of easily dissolved salts in the lower layers. The side valleys like the Dangarine, Jawan, Garautine, Obikiik, Beshkent along with some other valleys, where there are no smooth shingle horizons and the fine earth thickness is highly mixed with very poor water-penetrating properties of layers, are included in such lands. This has acutely complicated the conducting of melioration works for saline soils here, and has provided no possibility of applying here the whole complex of melioration measures recommended for the main valleys. Investigations and working out of new practical recommendations for the regulation of the water and salt balance in complicated hydrogeological side valleys are at present under way.

In recent decades there has been desalinization in considerable areas of salt marshes in the Republic as a whole. At present melioration and development of gyprum-bearing salt marshes of the Karlang massif is being carried out successfully. Desalinization of soils due to the drainage network has played an important role in the solution of this problem. The content of salts in soils and ground waters, which have accumulated for centuries due to the absence of drainage, has sharply decreased. Not only soils, but also underground waters are desalinized, the latter in their mineralization state having become suitable for the nutrition of cultivated plants. But alongwith successful liquidation of boggy lands and salt marshes, some plots are still taken out of agricultural rotation due to boggying and repeated salinization. A melioration of saline lands in the Vakhsh, Kyzylsu-Yakhsu and other valleys, and disregard for the drainage systems, drainage drilling holes, as well as for the cleaning of drainage installations, threaten the cotton harvest. Many drains and collector networks are silted up to the surface level. The drilling holes of vertical drainage work at half-productivity pace, or are stopped because of poor productivity and of the pumps being out of order. This leads to very grave consequences and there occurs repeated salinization and the whole fields fall out of agricultural turnover.

In the flood zone of the Kairak-Kum Water Reservoir, during the first two years after its filling about 2 million ha of lands irrigated by gravity were salinized. Thus, on the Chkalovsk massif the lowest lands began to be bogged and salinized as a result of the rising of the ground water table. We managed to correct the situation only by undertaking drastic measures for the building of drainage systems. The boggying of the massiff's lands has been stopped and the struggle against repeated salinization is going on successfully.

Data for 1980 obtained by the expedition on large-scale mapping of the "Tajikgiprozem" Institute show that due to uufavourable meliorative conditions of irrigated lands there still remain 93 thousand ha of salinized soils in the valleys (Table 16.3).

TABLE 16.3 : **Areas of irrigated lands salinized to different degrees in the natural and economic regions of the Tajik SSR**

in thousaad of ha

Natural and economic regions	Weakly salinized	Averagely salinized	Heavily salinized	Salt-marshes	Total of salinized soils
Kurgan-Tyubin	29.8	8.0	4.0	3.9	45.7
Kulyab	10.4	2.4	0.9	1.0	14.7
Leninabad	18.5	6.0	3.8	4.6	32.9
Total for the Republic	58.7	16.4	8.7	9.5	93.3

The salinization of irrigated lands result in certain losses of agricultural production.

All these saline lands in the Republic are located not in vast massives but in small plots either devoid of plants, or with suppressed cotton plants among healthy crops. As a result, crop capacity of cotton decreases. Conservation of saline soils, consequently, is one of the forms of useless embezzlement of land resources. Expenses on melioration of one ha of the long-time irrigated lands is 5 to 10 times less than the expenses on mastering of 1 ha of new massives for cotton. Therefore, first of all, it is necessary to do away with salinization of lands prepared for irrigation.

At present salinization of soils on new lands, before machine irrigation, should be considered as inadmissible. With the modern state of melioration science and technology, the fundamentals of which should be known to all those involved in irrigation and agriculture, it is quite possible to prevent salinization and boggying of soils with the help of timely measures. For this, it is necessary to enlarge and to properly maintain the existing drainage nets in valleys and to carry out their cleaning during the autumn and winter seasons.

Due to development of irrigation, waters with a higher content of mineral elements are often used ; such are those from collector networks or ground waters from drilling holes in the Asht, Khodzhent and Kulyab regions. The Vakhsh and Syr-Darya Reservoirs create possibilities for certain changes in the quality of irrigation waters. In order to avoid the loss of soil fertility, it is necessary to have a clear idea as to directions and scopes of changes in physico-chemical properties of mineralized waters, when they are used for irrigation. Permanent control over meliorative conditions of irrigated lands and over the quality of irrigation waters is executed by structural bodies of the Ministry of Agriculture and the Ministry of Melioration and Water Resources. On the basis of actual data on the regimes of ground waters and on salinization of soils, as well as on the forecasts made, they recommend and carry out measures directed to prevent repeated salinization and boggying of lands.

17

WAYS OF RATIONAL USE AND CONSERVATION OF THE WATER RESOURCES OF UZBEKISTAN

S.K. Ziyadullaiev

Uzbekistan is one of the constituent republics of the USSR. More than 18 million people, not only Uzbeks but people of other nationalities live and work on its vast area (450, 000 km^2). The problems associated with the steady increase of the well being of the population, its material and cultural level, the solution of the issues related to the dynamic development of agriculture and the demands of the population for food and other products is acquiring a paramount importance.

The basis for stable and secure farming in Uzbekistan is artificial irrigation. The natural conditions, centuries-old customs of the people, the abundance of heat and solar light make it possible here to grow on the irrigated lands heat loving cultures and to get high and stable harvests of cotton, rice, vegetables, fruit, grapes, etc. Irrigational construction helps to ameliorate large territories of waste lands converting earlier lifeless steppes into blooming orchards. In other words, irrigated agriculture is the basis for agricultural industry (95% of gross production).

However, the use of vast areas of irrigable land is difficult for lack of water resources. Thus, only 31 per cent of the 12.5 ml hectares of irrigable lands in the Uzbek SSR were irrigated in 1983.

The effective use of the favourable natural-climatic conditions for obtaining high harvests of cotton, vegetables and fruit ; the development of irrigable lands, the involvement of large labour resources of the population into useful work, all this depends mainly on the availability of water resources.

Water is distributed very unevenly on the territory of our country. Only 14 per cent of all the river run-off is formed in the south, including Central Asia where 12 per cent of the population of USSR live. If the country average of water per person is about 18,000 m^3 of the water runoff a year, this average in the southern regions is about 1.5 thousand m^3, or about 10-15 times less.

Working hard for obtaining water for irrigation, the farmers of Central Asia created a large cultural oases, but all irrigation was of a very primitive character until the Great October Socialist Revolution. During the years of Soviet Power, the irrigation of Uzbekistan has been greatly developed. Before the Great Patriotic War, in 1938-39, the working people of Uzbekistan, using the methods of people's construction, built major irrigation canals to meet the need for water. Thus, the Great Fergana Canal (270 km) was constructed in only 45 days. At present the length of the main irrigation system, the interfarm system and the intrafarm system in the republic is 160,000 km.

To completely use the potential water resources, to increase provision of water and to adapt the natural river regime to the requirements of water users in the Aral sea basin, a system of large and small reservoirs with a total volume of 60-65 km^3 performing seasonal and perennial run-off regulation was created. Most important of them are Toktogul reservoir on the Narin river, Andijan reservoir on the Kara-Darya, Charvak resesvoir on the Chirik, Chardaryin reservoir on the Syr-Darya, Nurek reservoir on the Vakhsh, Tuyamun reservoir on the Amu-Darya and others. The construction of Rogun reservoir on the Vakhsh and others has begun. A characteristic feature of the construction of the reservoirs is the fact that their waters are used not only for irrigation but for the production of electric power as well.

Due to the growth of power potential in the republic, it is possible to realize on a large scale machine irrigation on the area of about 1.6 million hectares. The largest objects of such irrigation system are the Amu-Karshin and Amu-Bukhara canals consuming on the average up to 50,000,000 kw of electric power annually.

As a result of the irrigation development the area of irrigated lands increased from 1.4 ml hectares in 1913 to 4 ml hectares in 1984. During the period of 1970-1983 it increased by 1,080 thousand hectares. The production of the gross product of plant growing increased two times while the water uptake for irrigation increased only 1.4 times. It means that the average annual water uptake from the irrigation sources per one hectare of irrigated land decreased while the efficiency of water usage increased. In fact, the production output per 1,000 m^3 of the water used increased 1.5 times during 1970-1983. Lately, the irrigated lands of the republic produced about 6 ml tons of raw cotton (more than 60 per cent of the amount produced in the country) including up to 600, 000 tons of fine-fiber cotton, more than 3 ml tons of cereals including 1.8 ml tons of corn, 555,000 tons of rice, 1.6 ml tons of fruit and grapes, 3.6 ml tons of vegetables, melons, water-melons and gourds and more than 30,000 tons of cocoons and other products.

At present, the water uptake in the republic is realized simultaneously from 250 large and small irrigation sources by means of 40 barrages and pumping stations and 228 water scooping headworks. But the needs for water already exceed the river run-off. Thus, the water resources of the main irrigation sources in the Aral sea basin will be completely used up by the national economy in 1993-1995.

Therefore, a set of measures is being taken in the republic to economically use all the water reserves available in order to increase agricultural production. They are : an increase in the efficiency of the systems by reorganizing the irrigation network ; further regulation of the river run-off of both large and small flows and a wide redistribution of water resources among basins ; introduction of new methods and techniques of irrigation using polimer pipes, flexible hoses, film, which will allow water to be spent more economically ; a decrease in the irrigation norms at the expense of growing drought-resisting kinds of cotton and other cultures ; desalinization and use of mineralized underground waters for whose removal 78,000 collectors and drains were laid ; the introduction of a complex of agrotechnical and meliorative measures. Works are being done to strengthen the irrigated plots, to straighten irrigation canals and to plan the irrigated lands. As a result of the above measures, the efficiency of the irrigation systems reached the average of 0.61-0.63 in the republic.

Regularly, beginning with 1950-55 the automation of certain water distribution objects (reservoir, water constructions, canals, pumping stations, etc.) was introduced in the republic and gradually the control of whole water distribution complexes in river basins is being realized. This kind of control is already functioning partially in the basin of the Zarafshan river and is being developed for the basin of the Syr-Darya. The systems with the centralized automation control of the complex of irrigation constructions ; facilities in river basins using the telemechanical water distribution ; mechanization of irrigation with optimal norms and providing a stable optimal meliorative state of the irrigated land are considered at present to be the most up-to-date form of the organization of this branch of economy.

In the past 20-30 years, technically perfect projects are used to develop vast lands in the Golodnaya, Karshi and Dzhizak steppes. For instance, when developing 300,000 hectares in the Golodnaya steppe, all the intrafarm irrigation canals were equiped with antifiltration coating (solid concrete facing, prefabricated ferro-concrete plates on polyethylene film, ferro-concrete trays). Drainage nets have been constructed everywhere (horizontal and vertical). This enabled a high efficiency (up to 0.8) of the irrigation systems to be reached. The further development of the lands of the Dzhizak and Karshi steppes is carried out using industrial methods employing the latest engineering achievements meeting the modern requirements of the scientific and technical progress. The irrigation network is built taking into consideration the application of modern methods of automatic control and monitoring, providing the optimal conditions for using water. Mud storages have been built in the Namangan and Kashka-Darya regions to combat the destructive spring floods in the republic. In other words, the irrigation of Uzbekistan is now a complicated multi-industrial system an independent branch of the national economy, the main purpose of which is to provide water to irrigated lands, industrial enterprises, power systems, communal water systems, fish farms and pasture lands covering millions of hectares. The refinement of this system is a multi-aspect problem, which, to a certain extent infringes on the interests of the economies of the zones to be reorganised. Its solution will require a lot of time and great capital investments, which, however, cannot prevent the fast realization of the necessary measures to further develop irrigation.

The radical solution of the problem of the provision of the lands of the republic of Central Asia with water is to transfer water to the Aral sea basin from the rich rivers of Siberia. At present, in accordance with a decision by the Party and the Government of the country, the compilation of a detail design of the main transfer canal is being completed.

An important element of the complex of constructions for transferring part of the Siberian river run-off is the main canal, Siberia-Central Asia, unique in length, capacity and parameters. Its distance from the head water intake from the Ob river to the Amu-Darya river will be 2,566 km, the capacity in the first stage will reach 1,150 m^3/sec. its width as to the water plane will be 200 m and it will be 20m deep. The main canal will have unique pumping stations, and the total height of lifted water along the canal will be 160 m.

The transfer of the first flow of Siberian water with a volume of 27.2 km^3 will make it possible to irrigate more than 4.5 ml hectares including about 800,000 hectares in Uzbekistan. The development of irrigation on the basis of Siberian water is a major socio-economic problem of increasing the employment and well being of the population. Its realization will create favourable possibilities to continue the development of the riches of desert and semi-desert territories of Central Asia and Kazakhstan. The increase of water resources in the region will improve the natural complexes and increase their biological productivity and decrease the dependence of the national economy on weather conditions. A large-scale production of agricultural products to supply the population with food and industrial raw materials will be organized on the newly irrigated lands, thereby considerably increasing the contribution of Uzbekistan to the solution of the Food Programme of the country, by increasing the production of cotton, cereals, vegetables, fruit, grapes and livestock products. This creates favourable conditions for an increased development of the processing branches of the agro-industrial complex, an improved distribution of the productive forces and an increase in the incomes of the population. Besides, the transfer of Siberian water will contribute to the development of different useful minerals of the Turgai river basin, the adjacent region of the town of Aktiubinsk and other territories and to the creation on this basis of a powerful energy complex.

Economic estimates have shown a high effectiveness of the transfer of the first part of Siberian water to the south of the country. This will not have an adverse impact on the state of the environment.

In future, the increase of water resources is thought to be obtained through transition, on a great scale, to drip irrigation and subsurface irrigation, to the control of the precipitation regime, a possibility of using glaciers and other measures based on the achievements of the scientific and technical progress.

We must point out with satisfaction that scientific projects widely carried out in Uzbekistan and their implementation open up great possibilities as to the use and conservation of water resources in the conditions of expanding irrigated agriculture and increasing water use for agriculture, industrial production and the improvement of settlements.

In the conditions of shortage of water resources the problem of their conservation in the process of exploitation acquires a special importance. In terms of the present day level of the scientific and technical progress the urgency of this problem is in part due to the increased industrialization of the national economy of the republic.

During the years of Soviet power, Uzbekistan has been converted from an outlying province of tzarist Russia into a republic having a diversified, technically equipped economy. The total volume of industrial output in 1983 increased 234 times (without cotton-cleaning industry 500 times) as against 1924, and 19 times (without cotton-cleaning 32 times) as against 1940. During the tenth Five Year Plan period alone the aggregate social product increased by 33 per cent against the Ninth Plan period, the national income by 29 per cent, the main production facilities 1.5 times. As to the output of all industrial products, the republic occupies a dignified place in the country.

The place of Uzbekistan in the specialization of cotton predetermined the creation and development of industries connected with cotton growing. Power, machine-building, chemical, textile, food industries are developing at a rapid rate. The development of the deposits of coal, gas, non-ferrous metals, construction materials and other kinds of mineral raw materials has contributed to the development of extractive industries.

The development of industry brought about a rapid growth of towns and settlements of urban type. 108 towns appeared in Uzbekistan only during the years of socialist construction. The population of the republic grew 4.4 times against 1913, including town population which grew 7 times.

The growth of industry and towns caused an increased volume of waste waters discharged into reservoirs and deteriorated quality of the water in them.

The main water conservation measures in the industries of the republic are directed now to the economy of pure water, decreased discharge of waste waters with complete purification. They include transferrence of the most water-consuming enterprises to the system of recycled and repeated use of water ; the development technological process using no or little water and the replacement of water cooling by air cooling. One of the most effective ways of the rational use and conservation of water resources is the introduction of circulating and repeated water supply system. From 1971 to 1984 the volume of circulating, repeatedly used water increased 3 times in the republic, which made it possible to decrease the specific consumption of fresh water per unit of industrial output almost 1.5 times. Already now the majority of enterprises of non-ferrous and chemical industries in the republic meet their requirements for water mainly at the expense of circulating water. The coefficient of water recycle in them is correspondingly up to almost 80 per cent.

The decrease of the pollution of water resources and diminished water intake are realized by using purified waste waters of some enterprises for providing technical water for others. For example, the leading enterprise of non-ferrous metallurgy of the republic—the Almalik mining-metallurgical combine—every day sends 30,000 m^3 of blowdown and purified discharge water to a chemical plant for secondary use in technological processes. This does not require capital reconstruction of the traditional foundations of modern industrial technology, but provides a sharp decrease in fresh water consumption and eliminates the discharge of contaminating substances into reservoirs. A new technological link is created in the water recycle system within a number of industrial enterprises.

The main measure to prevent the deterioration of the quality of the water resources of Uzbekistan is the purification of industrial and communal run-off. At present, more than 900 purification constructions function in the republic whose total capacity is 5 ml m^3 per day. More than 100 of such constructions were built only during the 10th Five-year plan period. The construction of new and the increase of the efficiency of the work of the reconstructed purification works will make it possible, in spite of the general increase of water disposal, to reduce the discharge of contaminated waste water into rivers to one-fifth.

A lot of work is being done in Uzbekistan to provide the population with high quality drinking water. While before the Great October Socialist revolution the main source of drinking water supply were aryks and wells which did not meet the sanitary requirements, at present, all the towns and settlements of urban type have water-supply. The length of the improved water-supply line is over 10,000 km. It increased by 4.5 thousand km on collective farms and state farms only during the years of the 11th Five-year plan period. In a number of settlements without water-supply, more than 13 thousand wells were drilled to provide the population with drinking water. Now Uzbekistan occupies one of the first places in the USSR in water consumption per town dweller and the provision of the population with centralized water supply.

It should be pointed out, however, that in spite of the measures taken, the irregularity of the development of water-supply in the republic still exists. The population of some rural settlements is not yet fully provided with centralized water-supply and water consumption does not always correspond to the level of the improved housing facilities. Our aims in this respect are clear : all the population of the republic should be provided with high quality drinking water irrespective of the place of abode. In this connection, additional measures to construct water-supply network, to conserve water sources, to improve the sanitary conditions of towns and rural settlements are to be developed and realized. Correspondingly, funds spent on water-supply increase from year to year. During the 10th five-year plan period only about 150 ml roubles of the capital investments of the state were spent on the development of the water-supply system, and over 188 ml during the 11th five-year plan period. A considerable part of the money goes to the districts of the KarakalpakASSR, Khorezm, Bulkhara and Kashkadaryin regions, where there is a shortage of drinking water.

The problem of water resource conservation becomes especially urgent as a result of the increased rates of the development of the agricultural production of the republic (12 times against 1913), its further industrialization and intensification, which means increased use of mineral fertilizers and chemicals protecting plants and, as a consequence, increased activities aimed at preventing the pollution of water by residual amounts of toxic compounds.

The practical solution of this problem is based on a complex approach taking into account the natural—climatic and regional conditions as well as the irrigation character of the republic's agriculture. The basis of the complex of corresponding measures being realized in the republic is the improvement of the agricultural system on the whole and technological processes for plant protection in particular. They are directed to the maximal increase in the efficiency in the use of fertilizers and pesticides and, simultaneously, to the prevention of their residuals from getting to water sources. This complex of measures is realized along the following lines :

—Improvement of agrotechnical methods of cultivating agricultural crops allowing a reduction, by a factor of 1.5—2 of the use of highly toxic compounds in the fight against pests, diseases and weeds and increased efficiency of the mineral fertilizers used.

—Strengthening the material-technical basis of all the agro-chemical services and departments responsible for transportation, storage and application of fertilizers and pesticides. The equipment of farms with storage facilities for the complex mechanization of all kinds of work and use of in-bulk transportation will considerably decrease unproductive wastes of mineral fertilizers and chemicals protecting plants.

—Control in the use of pesticides and mineral fertilizers in accordance with the developed cartograms on each farm; the creation of mechanized stations for filling sprayers and specialized lots for treating cotton seeds at a distance of 1,000 m and more from water sources and ponds; equipping these stations with washing facilities for tanks with closed water-supply.

—Improvement and expansion of the arsenal of mineral fertilizers balanced as to the content of nutrient substances and use of less toxic and less stable preparations in the environment with a high selectivity coefficient.

—Replacing entire aviation treatment near settlements and water sources by surface facilities using small-size methods considerably decreasing consumption of the liquid per unit area and increasing the efficiency of the preparation used.

—Wide introduction of the biological method of the protection of cotton from main pests, decreasing the volume of chemicals used by 12 per cent annually and the frequency of the treatment of plants by 10 per cent. An integrated system of protecting plants is being realized at a rapid rate. It will make it possible to retain the ecological balance in agrobiocoenose.

The realization of the measures aimed at rational use of water resources and their conservation will increase the efficiency of social production and provide for further development of the productive forces of Uzbekistan.

18

PRODUCTION, DISTRIBUTION AND CONSUMPTION OF POWER FOR RURAL DEVELOPMENT

The Indian Scenario

Satyesh C. Chakraborty

ENERGY AND ECONOMIC GROWTH

It is hardly possible for a society to achieve rapid economic growth without getting access to abundant and cheap energy-resources. This can be seen as a general law, for no instance can be cited to prove an exception. A more positive evidence is given in this regard by the fact that countries that are economically more advanced are also those consuming more energy per capita relative to the poorer socities. We may further observe that the periods of relatively rapid economic growth in these countries were also the periods when access to cheap energy resources was secured.

The nature of energy-resource that secured rapid economic growth had, however, varied according to the technology in use in a given society. Any review of the history of human civilization would bear testimony to this observation. For example, societies, using non-mechanical or primitive technology had achieved relatively rapid economic growth as and when these succeeded in using relatively high amount of living energy in the form of slaves and animals as distinct from the others. When tools or instruments with moving parts came into use.

the societies securing water-mills to tap energy of running water or wind-mills turned by the energy of moving air achieved relatively rapid economic growth in a distinctive fashion. In the same way, varying usages made of coal and steam differentiated success between countries in drawing advantages of the industrial revolution. Later, electrical energy, for advantages of easy transmission, secured regional spread of economic growth. Electricity could turn wheels as well as generate impulses for communication. It is clean and amenable to more versatile usages than, say, the water-mills, wind-mills or coal and steam. It is not surprising, therefore, that the societies achieving rapid economic growth are those which turned to producing electricity in preference to moving water or wind and coal. Later, with the introduction of internal combustion engines, petroleum appeared as a more convenient energy resource than coal. Volume per volume, energy packing is less in coal than in petroleum. Given the technology, petroleum can be transported easily and be used for generating mechanical, thermal and electrical forms of energy. Here again, societies achieved rapid economic growth by using increasing volumes of petroleum. Even the most modern energy resource, nuclear power, tells us the same story. Different materials thus emerged historically as energy resources matching the evolution of technology.

The above relationship between energy resource, technology and economic growth helps us to appreciate the reality as obtaining in India today. The sources of energy in this country can be grouped under four heads, viz., (a) living energy contributed by humans and animals, (b) thermal energy derived from vegetable and animal wastes, (c) thermal energy generated through burning of coal and petroleum, and (d) electrical energy produced by using coal, petroleum and nuclear heat. We are excluding for the present such energy sources as sunshine or bio-chemical reactions. Nevertheless, the list given above clearly indicates that the social base of technology in India is extremely mixed and ranges from the most primitive non-mechanical to the most modern nuclear techniques. Therefore, no simple strategy for securing access to energy resources is readily available. Even if the country wishes to enhance its capacity to produce electrical energy, for example, it has to be abundant enough and cheap enough to replace the energy sources related to more primitive technologies. The magnitude of the problem can be appreciated if we scrutinise Table 18.1 which indicates the relative order of the listed energy resources used in India. To make this comparison, we have converted all these sources into equivalents of coal.

TABLE 18.1 : **Relative size of energy sources of India**

Source	Coal equivalent (millions tonnes)	Relatlve Order (%)
Living energy	124.6	38.99
Vegetable & animal wastes	100.0	31.29
Coal used as such	54.0	16.89
Petroleun used as such	18.5	5.79
Thermal electricity	10.5	3.29
Hydro-electricity	12.0	3.75
Total	319.6	100.0

A careful examination of Table 18.1 would show that the social base of technology in India is primitive and dominated by the usage of non-mechanical tools and implements. This is given by the fact that more than 70% of the energy resources of India is suitable for use primarily for ploughing soil, threshing harvests, lifting water from wells, cooking food and transport by carts through the use of animal and human muscles and by burning animal and vegetable wastes. Since labour productivity cannot be increased without commissioning machineries and since without increasing labour-productivity India cannot hope to attain rapid economic growth, it will be necessary to enhance generation of energy from other resources. India has, however, rather restricted options to exercise.

Indian options on energy development

Energy resources required to drive machineries or to operate equipment are coal, petroleum and certain radio active materials. These are also called the conventional sources of energy. All of these are non-renewable resources. Amongst the renewable resources, hydro-electricity has been put to use in India. Other renewable energy resources like sunshine, wind, tides and geo-thermal gradients have not been used on commercial scales. These are the unconventional energy sources. It is necessary to assess how India is endowed with all these resources in order to appreciate what options are available to make energy available abundantly in all corners of this country.

India is relatively well endowed with coal than petroleum. Unfortunately, both the natural resources are unevenly distributed in the country. The same is true, when potentials of hydro-electric power generation are considered. However, the distribution of these three resources cover between them almost all parts of India. For example, the States of Kerala, Karnataka, Gujarat, Jammu & Kashmir, Himachal Pradesh, Sikkim, Arunachal Pradesh, Assam, Meghalaya, Manipur, Mizoram and Tripura are well endowed with hydro-power potentials. Unfortunately, these have little or no reserves of coal. In contrast, the States of West Bengal and Bihar have large reserves of coal, but very little of hydro-power. In contrast, the States like Tamil Nadu, Andhra Pradesh, Orissa, Madhya Pradesh and Maharashtra have both hydro-power and coal resources. Another contrast is provided by the States like Rajasthan, Punjab, Haryana and Uttar Pradesh, which have no coal reserve and potentials of hydro-power generation is quite poor. In matters of petroleum, the States of Assam contains the older fields. But the major contribution is now given by the off-shore wells located along the coasts of Maharashtra and Gujarat.

The above pattern of regional endowment of energy-resources does not, however, determine the pattern of regional consumption of energy. The pattern of consumption of energy has been primarily governed by the nature of technology in use in the different parts of the country. For the present, we should note that all the regions consume coal and petroleum in varying quantities and are dependent upon large-scale transhipment of these materials. Transport of materials across this vast country is expensive and this could be avoided to a great extent if these mineral resources could be used for conversion into electricity. We may also consider that electricity can be used with greater facility to support a larger range of productive activities than coal, it is for this reason that India has laid so much of emphasis on production of electrical energy by using coal. This has been integrated to a considerable extent with the stations producing electricity from hydro-power, diesel generators and atomic reactors. In short, electricity has been seen as the basic form of energy needed to establish equitable opportunities for economic growth across the regions of India.

Although electricity is a clean energy (in the sense of a non-pollutant), capable of transmission over a long distance at a low cost, amenable to secure coverage over any size of tract through dense dendrones of transmission lines and suitable for operating a large variety of plants and equipment, there are a number of other factors which restrict its usage as the only form of energy. For example, technologically it has not yet been able to substitute for coal in various kinds of pyro-metallurgy. Since India will need to produce metals in order to develop economically and to construct power generators and transmission systems, not all the available coal can be put to production of electricity. As the reserves of metallurgical coal in India is small, only the very inferior grades of coal has been ear-marked for power-generation, the intermediate grades being kept as reserve for future use in metallurgy with possible beneficiation through imported coal. Then, we should also admit that the electrically driven plants and machineries have to remain stationary near the power supply point and, therefore, cannot offer comparable advantages of roving machines, like cars, tractors, etc. These roving machines are run with internal combustion engines and require the usage of diverse kinds of hydro-carbon. This means that not all the reserves of petroleum can be ear-marked for power generation.

The above observations are given merely to indicate that there exists a strong lobby in India in favour of thermal power generation. This lobby consists of two interest groups, one working for use of coal and the other for petroleum to generate thermal energy. Amongst these two interest groups, the coal-lobby has got the support of the national policy makers. Today, almost all thermal power-plants use coal, except seven-stations running on oil and two on gas. Nevertheless, the petroleum lobby is a persistent force and is securing market for small captive-generators. Since the total demand for electricity exceeds supply, the wealthier consumers are acquiring such captive power plants run on diesel, kerosine or petrol. The lobby for hydro-power has been rather weak over the past years. This will be revealed from Table 18.2.

TABLE 18.2 : **Generation mix**

Year	Hydro-capacity MW	% share	Thermal capacity MW	% share	Nuclear capacity MW	% share
1960-61	1917	34	3737	66	—	—
1970-71	6383	39	9468	58	420	3
1979-80	11387	36	19280	62	640	2
1989-90 *	3000	37	50000	61	1800	2

*Projection

Weakness and strength of hydro-power lobby

The weakness of the hydro-power lobby has been conditioned by many factors, Of these, we shall highlight only four factors, viz., (a) regional orientation of rainfall, (b) regional orientation of hydraulic head, (c) competition amongst users of water, and (d) constitutional authority on river-systems. Some of these factors are amenable and the others are not.

Let us take, for example, an unamenable factor. In India surface run-off of water is primarily determined by the annual and seasonal pattern of rainfall. Very few rivers, fed by glaciers, are located in the Himalayas. Most of the rivers of India are non-perennial, being conditioned by extreme seasonality of rainfall. This means that the base-load capacity of any hydro-electric plant is insured by the size of an artificial reservoir constructed in a given valley. The capacity of these reservoirs are, in turn, determined by the volume of expected run-off.

The pattern of rainfall in India influences hydro-power potential in two ways. Regionally some tracts receive more rain than others. For example, the tracts receiving heavy rainfall are found in the eastern mountainous regions extending along the border of India and Burma and of India and Tibet. The other area of heavy rainfall is located along the western flank of the Sahyadri escarpment at the edge of the western coastal plain. This means that the opportunities for developing hydro-power is regionally variable and restricted. This limitation becomes more acute when we take note of the regime of rainfall. The length of the rainy season varies widely over regions and over the years deviation from normal rainfall is pronounced at any given place. For this reason, power production from hydro-electric plants varies from year to year and also between seasons.

The factor of available hydraulic head makes hydro-power generation a little more problematic. Greater this head is, the less will be the requirement of water to generate a given quantum of hydro-electricity. This advantage is not available in all parts of India. It is true that the hydraulic heads of the Himalayan rivers are good. But it is also true that these Himalayan rivers are now actively degrading the unconsolidated sedimentary rocks of this folded mountain system. As a result of this water in these rivers are highly charged with sediments making this resource difficult to use for hydro-power generation. The same is true for the mountains flanking the border between India and Burma. The only other region, which provides good hydraulic head, is the Western flank of the Sahyadri escarpment. Unfortunately, here the streams are short in length and are entirely rainfed. Unless big dams are constructed, hydro-power generation becomes an uncertain art.

Over the whole of the plateau region, all rivers are very old in age and have, in most parts, rather wide valleys. These rivers are rainfed and require dams to permit hydro-power generation. In a sense, the hydro-power potentials of these rivers are given not by good hydraulic heads, but by the volume of discharge that the reservoirs can sustain. In short, for hydro-power generation, these rivers must have expensive artificial reservoirs in their valleys. This raises the cost on account of displacement of settlements, farms and forests.

The above observations take us directly into the circumstances concerning conflicting demands for water. On account of seasonality of rainfall, future growth of agriculture depends on continued expansion of irrigation facilities. The annual regime of rainfall also causes floods. For these reasons, almost all reservoirs are designed to meet multiple objectives, namely, for irrigation, flood control, hydro-power generation, industries and urban-centres. Amongst these, objectives of irrigation and flood control conflict with that of power generation. The reason is simple to comprehend. To control floods, the reservoirs are to be kept empty to maximize its detention capacity. This compromises the objective of hydro-power generation. Similarly, for irrigation, water has to be released at regulated intervals from the reservoirs. If conservation becomes the means for optimising irrigation, then hydro-power generation must synchronise with the periods of water-release for irrigation. This is certainly a restraining factor for attaining steady generation of power. Urban and industrial demands for water does not, however, restrict hydro-power generation. But these restrict baseload capacity, if conservation of water remains an overriding consideration. These relationships between hydro-power generation and other consumptive uses may explain why the plants located on the Sahyadri escarpment have emerged as more productive compared to the others. In this tract, most of the hydro-power plants do not have to mitigate the constraining effects of other consumptive uses of water.

We may now examine the effects of devolution of constitutional authority over the river-systems in India on hydro-power lobby. In India, the State Governments are enjoying exclusive constitutional power to decide about the ways the river-water would be utilised. No other constitutional authority, not even the neighbouring State nor the Union Government can override this authority of a given State on the water within its territory. As a result, two types of problems make the planning process difficult to conduct. In the first instance, the co-basin States find it difficult to reconcile their contending demands on a single river-system to formulate a comprehensive and consistent plan on water-use. Failures to negotiate formally often lead to inter-state water disputes, which lend themselves, in turn, to sub-optimal resolutions after protracted confrontations. Second ly, the individual States, while formulating their plans find it difficult to avoid pressures of the local interest groups, who do not necessarily appreciate the imperatives of national economic objectives. This also leads to sub-optimal resolutions.

In spite of all that we have stated above, the advantages of hydro-power is palpably demonstrated. In 1981, for example, the hydro-power plants explained for some 36 per cent of the total installed capacity of all types of electricity production units. But, in that year, the hydro-power plants contributed about 40 per cent to the total actual production of electrical energy in the country. The reason behind this is that the thermal power plants based on coal, record incidents of break-down rather frequently. This is due to mis-match obtaining between boiler-technology and the quality of coal used in these plants.

Presently, 70 hydro-electric schemes with a total installed capacity of 10169.5 M.W. are under different stages of construction. In the Seventh plan, it has been proposed to increase the proportion of hydro-power in the installed capacity. The Union Government, through extensive dialogue with the State Governments, is trying to get this national priority honoured both in the State sector and Central sector plans.

Political-economy of power consumption

We have so far been discussing the problems of hydro-power generation. Since economic development cannot proceed without consumption of the generated power, it is necessary that we examine the realities concerning electrical-power consumption in the country. Table 18.3 is perhaps a convenient starting point in this regard.

TABLE 18.3 : **Electricity consumption % share of utilities**

Year	Sectors				
	Domestic	Commercial	Industrial	Agricultural	Others
1950-51	12.6	7.5	62.6	3.9	13.4
1960-61	10.8	6.1	69.3	6.0	7.8
1970-71	8.8	5.9	67.6	10.2	7.5
1980-81	11.3	6.0	58.6	17.5	6.6

Table 18.3 reveals two important dimensions of power consumption in India. In the first instance, it shows that the major consumer of electrical power is the industrial sector. This should be a normal feature of any country wishing to develop economically. What is perhaps more striking is the second feature of the above consumption profile, which is that consumption of power in the agricultural sector is increasing quite steadily. The importance of this feature can be better appreciated when we note that in 1950-51 the total power consumed in the agricultural sector was of the order of 293 GWH, which increased to 20865 GWH in 1980-81. This increase is indeed impressive.

However, we should ponder here for a while. We should note the fact that energy consumption in agricultural sector through the use of diesel powered machines had also increased phenomenally during this period. In fact, the total energy produced by these diesel powered engines in rural sector has been more than that from thermal or hydro-power stations. This again brings back the issue of relative strength of the petroleum-lobby in India. To appreciate this phenomenon, we need to examine the political-economy of energy consumption in India. Once again we need to unfold the pages of history.

From the last quarter of the 19th century, electricity came into use in India. But the objective of power-generation was to meet the specific demands of urban centres. Quite a large number of towns and cities came to use electricity generated for these exclusively by their own power-stations. These were not inter-connected by any power-transmission lines. Such exclusiveness in the territorial orientation of power consumption persisted till India became independent. Power consuming industries flocked to these towns and cities. The rural areas remained generally without any facility for energy-supply. This means that almost the whole of industrial and domestic consumption, as of 1951, was urban in orientation.

After gaining independence, the new nation went forward with plans of electrical power generation. In the absence of transmission grids, the additional power generated was consumed primarily by the older urban centres. Only in the decade of the 60s that the nation became conscious of developing power-grids. But here again, the States enjoyed the exclusive constitutional powers to generate and distribute electrical energy. The State Governments, in planning their own distribution system, were influenced by the urban-industrial interest-groups. Even during the mid-sixties, when a new agricultural policy required irrigation pump-sets to be energised, very few villages were connected to any dependable power-transmission system. So the petroleum-lobby stepped in by way of supplying diesel operated pump-sets. After 1964, special emphasis was put on rural-electrification and that too for energising irrigation pump-sets. The order of achievement in this regard is revealed from Table 18.4.

TABLE 18.4 : **Progress of rural electrification**

Year	Number of villages connected by power-line	Number of pump-sets energised
March, 1948	1,500 (100)	6,430 (100)
March, 1961	21,754 (1,450)	198,904 (3,093)
March, 1971	106, 774 (7,118)	1,571,000 (24,432)
March, 1981	272,625 (18,175)	4,330,437 (67,347)
March, 1985*	350,000 (23,333)	6,500,000 (101,089)

N.B. Figures within bracket refer to index number with base 1947=100.

* Provisional.

We may note that in Table 18.4, index numbers have been computed with base 1947=100 for number of villages connected to power line and of pump-sets energised. By comparing these two index numbers, we can observe that the rate of growth of the latter has been phenomenally more than that of the former. This means that as soon as a village has been connected to a power supply system, a very large number of the farmers commissioned electrically operated pump-sets. In the process, regionally differentiated agricultural interest-groups emerged over time, which started exerting influence on further plans of their respective state-governments to develop denser network of transmission lines. As a result, the spread of electrical transmission system became regionally variable. This is as much true for meso-regions as it is for micro-regions. For example, in Punjab, Haryana and Tamil Nadu almost all villages have been connected to transmission lines, whereas in Assam only 30 per cent of villagers enjoy such an advantage. Similarly, within the State of West Bengal, the District of Nadia has 96 per cent of its villages supplied with electricity, whereas in the District of Purulia only 26 per cent of villages enjoy similar privilege.

Such an inequality in the regional development of power transmission system has stimulated two distinct processes in energy distribution planning. The regions or sub-regions, which got connected to power-grids earlier, have succeeded in influencing later decisions for developing increasingly elaborate power transmission network and in securing larger quantities of power to themselves over the years. For example, the District of Nadia in West Bengal as of 1984 had 2.40 Km. of 11 Kv powerline per energised pump-set, while it was only 0.01 Km in the District of Purulia. Then the State of Haryana, having connected all its villages to power grid earlier, now draws substantial amount of power from the neighbouring State of Himachal Pradesh.

The institutional machanisms necessary to facilitate intertractal power transmission were laid in India in 1964 by establishing Regional Electricity Boards. There are five such Boards, the jurisdictions of each of these are given in Table 18.5. The job of these regional boards is to coordinate the activities of the otherwise autonomous State Electricity Boards under the overall guidance of the Central Electricity Authority. These Regional Boards have now succeeded in connecting the transmission networks of all the States under their jurisdiction with the objective of creating opportunities for dispatching surplus power from one tract to the other. These Regional Boards have also tried to inter-connect the power-plants of all kinds through power-grids within each State. The Central Electricity Authority, in turn, is trying to inter-connect the regional grids to establish an all-India grid and is sponsoring a number of centrally financed schemes for power-plants in different parts of the country.

TABLE 18.5 : **Jurisdiction of regional electricity boards**

Region	States covered
Northern	Haryana, Himachal Pradesh, Jammu & Kashmir, Rajasthan, Uttar Pradesh, Chandigarh and Delhi
Western	Gujarat, Madhya Pradesh, Maharashtra, Goa, Daman, Diu, Dadra & Nagar Haveli
Southern	Andhra Pradesh, Karnataka, Kerala, Tamil Nadu & Pondicherry
Eastern	Bihar, Orissa, Sikkim and West Bengal
North-Eastern	Assam, Manipur, Meghalaya, Mizoram, Nagaland, Tripura & Arunachal Pradesh

The all India power grid, we may mention, is still in the realm of a dream. Even the objective of the Regional Electricity Boards to share power between the States has not yet been realised for most regions. The reasons for non-fulfilment of the targets are many, some of which are related to the limitations of the technology of power-production and transmission and the rest to the consumer behaviour. It is necessary that we examine these in some details.

We may take up the issue of consumer behaviour first. The diurnal pattern of power consumption is marked by two peaks, one in the morning and other in the evening. The regions producing electricity by using coal find it difficult to meet the peakload demands. This can be met by the regions more easily, which have hydro-power stations, which can be commissioned with short gestation lag. For this reason, the Regional Electricity Boards having a good mix of thermal and hydro-electric plants recorded better results in the inter-State transmission of power. In contrast, the Regional Boards, which are entirely or primarily dependent on coal based power plants, generate surplus power only during night time, when there are very few consumer of such power. This is how consumer-behaviour has restricted the success of the plan for inter-State power transmission.

The problem of peak demand can be met either by having captive hydro-power plants or diesel operated generators. By captive plants we mean such a power-station which can be put on production without encumbrance from other competitive users of the input, be it water or diesel. If we bear this in mind, then we can appreciate why inter-state power transmission has been more successful in the Northern and Western regions compared to the others. In the Southern region, in spite of having a large number of hydro-power plants. the opportunities under reference are restricted because there are other competitive users of water. Hence, strict control has to be maintained on the release of water in this region for exclusive hydro-power production.

In this connection, we should mention that India is passing through a period of rapid technology transformation. For example, even during the fourth decade of the current century, a 60 MW power plant was considered to be a giant installation. As new power plants were established, India decided to go in for larger capacity plants, like 120 MW and 200 MW units. Currently, preference for 400 MW plants is gradually becoming pronounced.

The above objective is defendable in the light of benefits derivable from economy of scale. However, in the context of sustaining base-load production, the above advantage tends to disappear. When for maintenance a plant has to be shut-down, the consequent short-fall in power supply becomes difficult to meet. We have already mentioned about the mis-match obtaining between technology of boiler-production and the quality of coal in use. This has caused frequent breakdown of power-plants, non-fulfilment of the objective of inter-state power transmission, upsets in the consumption-schedules and consequent strengthening of the petroleum-lobby. Many of the relatively prosperous consumers have acquired diesel operated captive power-plants to maintain their production schedules.

The same has been India's experience with the transmission lines. In the fourth decade of the current century, 11 KV lines were considered economical to transmit power over the zones of consumption. At that time, the consumer tracts were small in size and were fed by local power-stations. As the need for transmission of power over longer distances emerged, India installed higher capacity transmission lines, like 33 KV, 66 KV, 100 KV and 200 KV, in stages. Currently, the preference is for 400 KV transmission line. This is explainable. The larger the capacity is, the lesser is the loss of electricity in transmission. Unfortunately, the sub-sector of electrical engineering industry in India has not been able to meet the demands for step-down transformers and switch-gears to meet the rising demand. For this reason, the very high tension power lines connect the power stations with the large industrial agglomerations. In the absence of suitable transformer production, these high tension lines have not been connected to the rural grids. Consequently, the petroleum-lobby has retained its grip over the economy by way of supplying diesel operated pump-sets to meet the growing needs of irrigation in the rural areas.

Changing pattern of power consumption in the rural areas

It is difficult to predict in what way India shall achieve rural economic development through increased use of electricity. Table 18.6 provides a glimpse into the future. It shows that even at the end of the present decade, per capita consumption of power will remain rather low in India.

TABLE 18.6 : **Growth of power industry & consumption of power**

Year	Installed Capacity (MW)	Energy Generation (GWH)	Per Capita Consumpiion (KWH)
1950	2302	7514	18
1960-61	5654	20123	38
1970-71	16271	61212	90
1980-81	33141	119226	135
1989-90*	82000	310000	320

*Projection.

Some indications on the ways power will be used in the rural tracts are available from the studies of consumer behaviour in areas where the progress of rural electrification has been good. These studies refer to the situations obtaining in the States of Haryana, Gujarat and Tamil Nadu.

As the national priority was for increasing food production through increased use of lift irrigation technology, the pump-sets emerged initially as the major user of electricity in the rural areas. Domestic consumption closely followed the pump-sets as the growing consumers. Then came the workshops engaged in the maintenance of farm machineries. After that street lighting in the villages emerged as a contender for power consumption. Along with it, came the air-conditioned ware-houses (cold storages). It is only recently that we are finding the small-scale and cottage industries emerging as users of power.

The above observation may not be seen as a model describing the stages in the sectoral spread of power consumption in the rural areas for all parts of India to replicate. Examples of deviation from the above pattern are many indeed. For example, dairy industry of Gujarat has become the second largest consumer of power after pump-sets. In Tamil Nadu, power-looms are more important than domestic consumers. In West Bengal, air-conditioned warehouses consume power next to the pump-sets in the rural areas.

The point to note is that the pattern of consumption of power in the rural areas will vary according to the character of the given territorial production base. There shall be competition between the diverse types of consumers. The more productive users will win the race. Nevertheless, the winner shall not be the same in all parts of the country at any given moment. We should finally admit that comprehensive development of the rural economy shall not obtain until we provide steady supply of adequate power.

Note : All tables have been constructed from *Manorama Year Book*—1983, Kottayam, Kerala, pp. 452-455.

19

UTILIZATION OF POWER RESOURCES IN THE TAJIK SSR TAKING INTO ACCOUNT ENVIRONMENTAL ISSUES

M.A. Burkhanova

Accelerated development of power industry in the Republic, which stimulates development of productive forces and higher level of social well-being, produces some negative impact as well, and this should be taken into account when formulating development perspectives for this branch of national economy. The major negative impact is produced by fuel-power industries. Increased concern for these issues resulted in the origin of a new scientific branch of knowledge—"enercology" i.e., studying interaction of power industry (energy production) and ecology.

Although 90 per cent of the power-producing facilities in power systems of the Republic are accounted for by hydro power stations, representing ecologically pure sources of power, in 1982 over 35 per cent of fuel resources consumed by industries, and 15 per cent of those consumed by all sectors of economy were utilized by two thermal power stations, and boilers servicing industrial and community needs. In all, there are 600 of such boiler units in the Republic at present 580 of them having low capacity. These boiler units with low capacity are the main pollutants (in comparison with large industrial units) because methods of effective purification cannot be applied in them.

It should be, certainly, taken into account, that these discharges differ in their chemical structure. The principal polluting agent which is discharged by thermal power stations and boiler units into the atmosphere is sulphureous anhydride which constitutes 56 per cent of the total urban industrial discharges and is the most dangerous pollutant. The only means employed to neutralize this agent are high chimneys, which only help in disseminating discharged sulphureous anhydride higher up in the atmosphere.

The main damage produced by sulphur discharges into the atmosphere is that to human health. There is practically a linear relationship between the number of hospitalized persons and weight concentration of sulphureous anhydride in the air. One can also find a direct correlation between losses of working time and expenditure on sulphur filtering equipment.

Other polluting agents discharged by power industry of Dushanbe are nitrogen dioxide (61 per cent of urban industrial discharges), carbon dioxide, and smoke gases.

From the point of view of ecology the most pure full utilized by the thermal power stations is natural gas. The main pollutants produced by them are oxides of nitrogen (they are, however, less, than in the case of burning coal or mazut). The discharge of sulphureous anhydride is however insignificant though in case of using coal or mazut they are much higher. Pollution of air by solid particles and fluorides is absent. It is, apparently, expedient, to increase to every possible extent the use of natural gas by thermal power stations within the urban area, instead of other kinds of fuel.

A well-known statement by D.I. Mendeleev is : "to burn oil is the same as to burn banknotes". Large-scale use of mazut for power production is costly and unprofitable. Along with ecological benefits, use of natural gas by thermal power stations is economically efficient : prime cost of 1 kilowatt-hour of electrical power produced by power stations using natural gas is nearly 4 times smaller than that of those using solid fuel. Great potential may be found in essentially new technology of burning gas, which completely excludes the intermediate stage of vapour production. Here we mean the magnetic-hydrodynamic technology of transforming thermal energy of gas into electrical power, ensuring, at the same time, deep and cheap extraction of sulphur oxides from discharged gases.

When developing the schemes for location of new thermal power stations in the Republic it is necessary to take into account the whole set of factors ; first and foremost, the ecological ones. Expected discharges of projected thermal stations should be tested via the ultimate possible concentrations in the zones of perspective construction of thermal power stations (this item should be, probably, included into project documents for stations). Protection of air basin from negative impact of newly constructed large thermal power stations may require legislative measures, ensuring environment conservation and limitation of thermal pollution.

Taking into account the inadequacy of fuel resources in the Republic, and shortage of fuel-power resources in Central Asia, the alternative schemes of fuel-power balance for the Republic should envisage substitution as much as possible, of low-temperature heat-supply (which consumes over one third of all fuel resources) by other ecologically harmless sources of power. This is especially important for rural mountain regions of the Republic, where transportation of fuel is 6-7 times more expensive than in urban settlements (for example, in Dushanbe transportation of I ton of standard fuel is 20 roubles, in the Mountain-Badakhshan Autonomous Oblast—140 roubles). Requirements of rural population in fuel are far from being satisfied, therefore, shortage of high-grade coal for communal needs of rural settlements is mostly compensated by use of firewood.

Since cost of production and transmission of electrical power in the Tajik SSR is low, cheap power produced by hydel stations should be used for low-temperature power supply for community uses. Requirements of small-scale dispersed consumers, particularly rural consumers, should be met not through construction of new boilers, using imported mazut and coal, but through electrical heating of water.

The national industry has developed production of various types of electric heaters with widely ranging capacity : from 1 kwt. to 4-6 thousand kwt. Production of electric boiler units with capacity 10 thousand kwt is being organized. To meet all its requirements, a family of 3-5 persons living in a city needs 100-200 litres of hot water daily, and that in a rural place—

300-400 litres. Therefore, an electric boiler unit with 10 thousand kwt capacity (or 8.6 Gcal/hr in thermal equivalent) may meet requirements of 4-8 thousand urban families, or 2-3 thousand rural families. This type of facility will be able to accumulate heat and thus benefit from utilization of electrical energy at night hours, when other consumers are switched off, and electric supply systems have surplus power.

Another ecologically harmless method of meeting requirements of heat and hot water should be the utilization of solar energy, which has been already sufficiently developed technologically. Despite comparatively high cost, dependence on weather conditions, and the need to duplicate power supply equipment by thermal-based capacities, direct transformation of solar energy into heat is economically paying for decentralized consumers in southern regions of the country. Climatic conditions of the Tajik SSR make it expedient to use solar energy for the following purposes : hot water supply, heating, cooling of buildings, drying, heating of greenhouses, etc.

The project design institute Tajikgiproselstroy of the Ministry of rural construction of the Tajik SSR has developed a design of solar houses with collectors on southern side. Calculations made for a rural house located in the Hissar valley in the Shahrinau region show that about 60 per cent of heat requirements can be met by solar energy. Moreover during the summer season such heliocollectors are able to cool buildings. This method is highly recommended because recent data demonstrates several negative factors of large-scale use of air conditioners : increased number of respiratory diseases in summer period, change of air composition in buildings (in particular, increase of carbon dioxide concentration, less content of ozone), high pressure on electric power supply systems.

The Tajik SSR is rich in solar energy. Annual direct inflow of solar radiation on flat surface under cloudless weather is 2,904.7 kWh per m^2 in Dushanbe, 2,912.1 in regions under Republic's authority and on the surface of the Kairakkum reservoir, 3,894.3—in the Mountain Badakhshan Autonomous Oblast and in the Kara-Kul lake region (249, 250 and 335 kcal/cm^2, respectively, in heat equivalent).

Our calculations show, that in the immediate future summarized requirements of economy of the Republic in fuel resources (coal, gas, oil, oil-products) will amount to $50{\cdot}8{\cdot}10^{12}$ kcal ($7{\cdot}10^{12}$—coal, $17{\cdot}5{\cdot}10^{12}$—gas, $25{\cdot}4{\cdot}10^{12}$—oil and oil products). If all fuel-consuming industries in the Republic are substituted to the maximum possible degree by electric-power-based technologies, their expected requirements in fuel may be met by production of 59 bln kWh of electrical energy. Taking into account the fact that the average thermal equivalent of solar energy in the Republic is approximately 280 kcal/cm^2, and that efficiency of transformation of solar energy is assumed to be 10 per cent, then the solar equivalent, which would meet the expected requirements in fuel is 182 km^2 (the area to be covered by solar energy collectors), corresponding to about 0.13 per cent of the Republic's territory.

Use of solar energy for large-scale production of electric energy may be expedient in the Tajik SSR in the more distant future with advancement of technologies, methods, constructive decisions, and higher economic efficiency of operation of heliostations. At present the Krym Solar Power Plant has the following economic parameters : capital investments are at the level of 1,000 roubles/kwt, prime cost of electrical energy—1.5-2 roubles/kWh.

Use of solar energy for heating and hot water supply is already economically profitable in the Mountain Badakhshan Autonomous Oblast, where transportation of fuel is especially expensive, and climate is very favourable, including high annual total solar radiation (1.4 times as large as in the region of Dushanbe agrometeostation), long period of daylight (8-9 hrs per day, compared to 7.4 hrs in Dushanbe), smaller number of cloudy days (7 and 20 days in the regions of the Kara-Kul lake and the Murgab via 41 days near Dushanbe agrometeostation). Calculations made in the Physical-Engineering Institute of the Tajik Academy of Sciences have shown, that to meet 100 per cent requirements of hot water and 40 per cent requirements in heating would require operation of about 1 mln m^2 of helio-collectors, and investment of about 5 mln roubles in the Mountain Badakhshan Autonomous Oblast.

One of the highly promising trends in development of helio-power industry is construction of combined solar-thermal boiler plants, which would operate heliocollectors in summer, and use the regime of preheating of water for hot water supply systems (regime of economizer). This would allow to economize nearly 60 per cent of annual fuel reserves, required for boiler operations in a usual regime. This type of boiler plants is efficient in regions with limited fuel resources. Thus, to meet part of the community requirements of Dushanbe, it is planned to construct a solar-thermal boiler plant as part of the network of heat supply and boilers under Ministry of Communal Industry of the Republic.

A highly potential technology to be introduced in rural regions of the Republic is wasteless animal-breeding cycle, developed by specialists of the All-Union Scientific-Production Institution "Solntse" (Sun). The main idea of this closed cycle technology is production of biogas—methane—from wastes of cattle life activities, fermented and humificated in special collectors heated by helio-reactors. This gas may be used for different purposes, including heating of helioreactors in winter. Processed agricultural wastes are transformed into a valuable organic fertilizer. Despite its comparatively high cost (1-1.5 roubles/m^3), production of biogas from wastes is a highly potential technology for large animal-breeding farms.

Production of biogas has become widespread in China and India. By the middle of 1980's in India there were over 80 thousand biogas reactors, although part of them were not in operation. Large biogas-producing units were constructed there recently, which can supply biogas to a whole village and other nearby settlements.

Hydro-power resources of the Tajik SSR are being intensively developed through construction of large and middle-capacity hydro power plants. Limited fuel resources and increased cost of organic fuel, combined with adequate availability of small-scale hydro-power potential should stimulate development of small-scale hydro power production in the Republic. Construction of mini-hydro-power plants is especially profitable in the mountain regions with decentralized power supply, which are now serviced by Diesel power plants, using expensive oil fuel. Because of that, cost of electric energy produced by Diesel power plants in the Republic amounts to

6 cop/kWh, while that produced by mini-hydel stations does not exceed 2 cop./kWh. Construction of small hydel plants in the European USSR is considered efficient if capital investments do not exceed 600-800 roubles/kwt, while in the regions of decentralized power supply it may be efficient even if they amount to 2,000—3,000 roubles/kwt.

To promote development of small-scale hydro power industry in Tajikistan (or, rather, to return to this trend of construction of hydel stations, which has played an important role in development of the Republic's economy) an inventory is being made of suspended and drafted out small hydel stations, assessment of chances to reconstruct them and put them into operation, and to modernize and equip them with modern technology. In the coming years it is planned to obtain a technical-economic report on development of small-scale hydro power industry in the Republic, which would explicate priority projects and capacities put into operation.

The principal advantage of utilization of energy of small rivers is the virtually complete absence of negative impacts on environment, while large-scale hydro-power plants may produce complicated ecological consequences viz., large-scale submergence of valuable lands under storage reservoirs, changes in climatic regimes, and agricultural conditions for cropping, quality of water, etc. However, in mountain reservoirs of the Republic all these negative impacts are minimal, because of their small surface area, insignificant filtration and evaporation. In recent years, some information has though been collected on the so-called "induced seismicity" due to concentration of considerable amounts of water in small areas. This requires to be investigated. Thus, publications of the Institute of seismo-resistant construction and seismology of the Tajik Academy of Sciences note increased seismicity in the zone of construction of theNurek water reservior, which puts certain constraints on the regime of exploitation of this reservoir and on the location of large hydro-power projects in future.

The least developed branch in the perspective fuel-power balance of the Republic is the utilization of wind power. Mean annual wind velocity within the Tajik Republic ranges broadly : from 0.8 to 6.0 m/sec. The higher above sea level, the greater is wind velocity, reaching its maximum at large elevations (Fedchenko glacier, Anzob pass). In some regions orographic factors favour formation of jet streams, reaching 5-6 m/sec (Leninabad, Faizabad). Annual maximum of days with heavy winds (above 15 m/sec) is 40-60, and is observed at high elevations and at bottlenecks of valleys (Aivaj, Leninabad, Shahristan pass, Fedchenko glacier). In these regions it may be expedient to construct altitudinal wind-stations with low capacity to meet local requirements (irrigation of mountain fields, supply of electricity to small rural settlements, etc.).

In the USSR experience of operation of wind power stations with capacity ranging from 15 to 5,000 kw is available. The reliability and efficiency of these stations are above those in other countries. Their drawback, however, is changing wind velocity. It is therefore, expedient to combine wind power stations as a supplementary source of power with active systems of solar-based heat supply.

An important source of environmental pollution is car traffic, which accounts for over 60 per cent of discharge of pollutants into the urban atmosphere. In the amount of carbon dioxide, discharged car traffic exceeds urban industrial plants several times. It also produces noise pollution. Negative effects of large-scale development of car traffic may he reduced by substitution of internal combustion vehicles by electromobiles.

Electromobiles have several technological advantages as compared to automobiles : higher efficiency, simple construction design, smaller number of parts and assembly units subject to high temperatures and contact pressure, lower prime cost of production (excluding cost of accumulator battery) and longer period of exploitation.

The principal shortcoming is small reserve of movement because of low power capacity of accumulator batteries. The recent advancements in design of electromobiles have brought the following results : experimental samples of electromobiles can develop speed up to 80 km/hr, can move for 7-8 hours without recharging, can carry 10—11 tons of load. Recharging of accumulators is possible during planned demurrage by simple switching on the usual electrical system. Large parts of electromobiles recharged at night may become regulating consumers, which would level night gaps in loading patterns of power systems, and thus increase efficiency of their operation. Taking into account the losses due to toxic discharges of cars with petrol engines, one can already state lower cost of transportation by electromobiles small carrying capacity with lead-acid batteries for small distances (30-40 km) than in cars with internal-combustion engines. The above supports the necessity to gradually increase use of electromobiles, especially in large cities.

20

ROLE OF HYDRO-POWER INDUSTRY IN THE FORMATION OF THE SOUTH-TAJIK TERRITORIAL PRODUCTION COMPLEX (ST TPC)

U.K. Kletselman

Among a whole set of factors, which promote formation of a Territorial Production Complex of national importance on a comparatively small territory of Southern Tajikistan, the primarily role belongs to abundant resources of hydro power available in this region. In combination with unique natural-climatic conditions, considerable resources of minerals, raw materials and labour they form the basis for intensive and harmonious development of the ST TPC.

Second in the country according to total resources of hydro power (after the Russian Federation), and the first according to hydro power resources per unit of area, Tajikistan (as well as Eastern Siberia) has the highest economic efficiency in hydro power production in the Soviet Union. Prime cost of electric power produced by large hydro power plants of the Republic is 1.5 times lower than in the neighbouring Soviet Republics (Uzbekistan and Kirghizia), 1.5-2 times lower than in the Volga region, Kazakhstan, Western Siberia, 4-4.5 times lower than in central regions of the USSR. Per unit capital investment in hydro plant construction in the Republic is the lowest when compared to the cost of hydro-plants constructed in other regions of East Siberia.

Outstanding economic efficiency in the exploitation of hydro power resources in the Tajik SSR is accounted for by great runoff discharges and high river gradients, together with availability of sites to construct very high dams. Thus, in per unit channel capacity the river Vakhsh surpasses any of the large Central Asian rivers, and also the Volga, Angara, Yenisey. It originates at 3,600 m above sea level, and before reaching the lowland falls down by 3,160 m. Pams and hydro power plants to be constructed on this river are located at bottlenecks of valleys and at outcrops of hard rocks.

Utilization of hydro power resources of the Republic means not only large-scale production of cheap electric power, but also guaranteed cultivation of most valuable agricultural crops under irrigation. Therefore, in all stages of development of productive potential of the ST TPC, high priority was attributed to integrated use of water resources. In the first years of the Soviet Socialist state the bias was towards construction of irrigation facilities. Indeed, the construction of the Vakhsh main irrigation canal and development of its vast valley, which was lifeless before, is comparable in scales and in economic importance at the national level to the largest new projects of the first five-year plans. It was a unique project of that time, which envisaged construction of canals several thousand km long and earth works of 26 mln m^3. Irrigation of the Vakhsh valley was one of the largest national projects, which allowed to achieve an extremely important national task i.e., self-reliance in cotton. By now about 200 canals withdraw water for irrigation from rivers of the Republic ; their total length reaches 28 thousand km, and equals the total length of all rivers of Tajikistan.[1]

Since the very beginning of the Soviet state and till now the development of economy of the ST TPC and patterns of its productive capacities are permanently linked with irrigated agriculture. The zone of irrigated agriculture accommodates most of population of the complex. Density of rural population is 100-500 persons and more per 1 km^2. In the zone of dry farming this index reduces down to 5-50 persons per km^2.

At all stages of the development of the productive forces of the ST TPC, irrigated farming was the organic basis of its territorial pattern of production and, predetermined, above all, high economic efficiency of development and location of cotton industrial complex within the ST TPC area. Acceleration of cotton output and the pattern of location of cotton-farming areas produced the decisive influence on the distribution of collecting units, cotton-cleaning plants and oil-mills. Location of cotton textile plants, clothing factories, several regional servicing plants for textile and food industries, and of non-productive branches, was due to the favourable conditions resulting from local resources of raw materials,and requirements of the population of agricultural regions. The chosen specialization of agriculture was the basic factor, which determined configuration and density of roads and other infrastructural facilities. It produced the decisive impact on the settlement system formed in rural areas.

In its turn, functioning of several industrial enterprises (hydro power plants, engineering repair works, production of chemical and construction materials) create favourable conditions for more intensive agriculture and the necessary irrigation and land reclamation activities. The same trend is pursued by most institutions in the non-productive sphere (mostly educational and scientific research organizations) and in infrastructural facilities.

In recent years a highly efficient use of water resources becomes more and more pronounced which incorporates irrigation of lands (formerly used for dry farming) by mechanized uplift of water in order to create a large horticultural-viticultural complex of national importance. Mechanized irrigation of vast piedmont tracks in the Republic to create a horticultural-viticultural complex is possible only through large-scale use of cheap electrical energy produced by hydel power stations. It should be specially emphasised that cultivation of new irrigated lands plays a decisive role in the further upliftment of the level of well-being of rural population. Growth of agricultural production in recent decades in newly irrigated lands of the Yavan, Ilyichov, Dangari and other regions can serve as an illustration to successful achievement of production-technological and economic tasks, and more so, of social tasks. Populated places created there do not essentially differ from urban settlements. This establishes the favourable background to overcome the urban-rural disparities, and to fulfil an important socio-economic task of continuous upliftment of the material and cultural level of the population of the ST TPC.

The development of the cotton and horticultural-viticultural complex in the ST TPC was greatly emphasized till 1960. The seventh five-year plan (1961-1965) started a new stage in the development of hydro power resources and of productive forces of the complex. A cascade of Varzob hydro power plants including three derivation stations had a total capacity of 25.4 thousand kw. and a cascade of two stations constructed in the Seventh Plan period on the Vakhsh main canal (Perepadnaya and Tsentralnaya Hydro Power Plants, with respective capacity 30 and 18.6 thousand kw) has a total capacity twice as large as the Varzob Hydro Power Stations. The Golovnaya Hydel Power Plant, with a capacity of 210 thousand kw., came into operation in 1962 (with a 94.5 mln m^3 water reservoir of daily regulation) and has become one of the highest-capacity hydro power plants in the Central Asian region. One can say with certainty, that construction of the Golovnaya Hydro Power Plant has given a new impetus to large-scale utilization of hydro power potential of the Vakhsh river. It was followed by the construction of a giant power plant viz. the 2.7 mln kw Nurek Hydro Power Plant (with 10.5 thousand mln m^3 water reservoir). In the current Five-Year Plan period the 600 thousand kw Baipaza Hydro Power Plant would be put into operation. Following the decisions of the XXVI Congress of the CPSU, the Rogun Hydro Power Plant is under construction within the South-Tajik TPC; this is a highly efficient multipurpose plant. The essential technological-economic parameters of the Rogun hydrotechnical unit are as below : [2]

Installed capacity	3.6 mln kw
Output of electric power	14 thousand mln kWh
Total volume of water reservoir	14 km^3
Construction height of dam	325 m
Increase in irrigated area	320 thous and ha
Capital investments per 1 kw of installed capacity	200 roubles
Prime cost of 1 kWh of electric power	0.08 copecks

It should be noted, that the Rogun Hydro Power Plant is to be put into operation in conditions of higher technological level and advanced economy of the region, and as a result, higher economic potential. Exploitation of the Rogun Hydro Power Plant would allow for involvement into the economic turnover of resources of more remote, mostly mountain regions of the ST TPC.

As revealed by the above, each new hydro power plant of the ST TPC was in its kind, a new step forward in the scientific-technological advancement of the hydro power industry. Thus, the Varzob Hydro Power Plant had 2-3 thousand kw generator units, while the Golovnaya Hydel Power Plant—35 thousand kw units, the Nurek Hydro Power Plant—300 thousand kw units, and the Rogun Hydro Power Plant, which is now under construction will have 600 thousand kw units.

The available projections indicate that besides the six hydro power stations currently operational or under construction on the Vakhsh river, two more stages of the Vakhsh cascade—the Shurob Hydro Power Plant (750 thousand kw, 3 thousand mln kWh) and the Sangtudin Hydro Power Plant (900 thousand kw, 4 thousand mln kWh) may have favourable technical-economic parameters.[3] As was correctly stated by M.A. Burkhanova, the advantage of the development of the Sangtudin site before the Shurob site is that it will allow for a daily redistribution of peak discharges of the Rogun and Nurek Hydro Power Plants, and will function as a counter-regulator of the runoff. Taking this into account, it may be found expedient to begin construction of the Sangtudin Hydro Power Plant in the Twelfth Five-Year Plan period, using the available infrastructural facilities and the teams of construction workers formerly employed at the Baipaza Project. Construction of the Shurob Project may be started when construction activities at the Rogun Hydro Power Plant become less intensive. This will allow for the maximum use of the material technological basis and of teams of constructors available at the Rogungesstroy (Administration of the Rogun Hydro Power Project). Implementation of the above discussed projects, and later on—projected utilization of hydro power resources of the Vakhsh right tributary—the Obikhingou river—support the prognosis for large scale increase in power generating capacities for a long-range period.

High potentialities available in the ST TPC for large-scale production of cheap electric power may have a two-fold influence on specialization of the region : first, through transmission of large amounts of electric power to other economic regions, and second, through formation of a power-consuming production complex of industries.

Studies by several scientific and project-making institutions have proved that large-scale transmissions of electric power beyond the boundaries of the complex decreases economic efficiency of cheap electric power (excluding long-range transmissions of peak power outputs, which are profitable). Therefore, development of hydro power base supposes formation of a complex of power-consuming industries within the region.

Studies of economic efficiency of a complex of power-consuming industries in Southern Tajikistan bring one to the following conclusion : the more power-intensive is production, the higher are advantages of the South-Tajik Territorial Production Complex as a region of location of the respective industries. Thus, in Southern Tajikistan a comparatively low-power-intensive production of nitrogen fertilizers is economically efficient if the total output does not exceed requirements of the region ; but more power-intensive production of caustic soda is economically effective output meets the demand of the Soviet Central Asian Republics and of Kazakhstan, while optimal output of synthetic rubber, plastics, aluminium and magnesium should be more than the requirements of Central Asia and Kazakhstan.

The formation of a complex of power-intensive industries on the basis of the Nurek Hydro Power Plant has, by now, come to the final stage. A new phase in development of this complex is linked with the Rogun Power Project. Thus, according to preliminary calculations, operation of a new alumina plant on the basis of cheap electric power produced by the Rogun Hydro Power Plant will be economically effective even if imported alumina is used. If alumina is transported for 5,000 km, and afterwards metallic aluminium—for 3,000 km, still low-cost electric power available in the ST TPC will considerably compensate for the extra transportation costs. Prime cost of 1 kWh produced by the Rogun Power Plant is expected to be 0.08 cop. if one takes it as 0.15 cop. per 1 kWh of the projected aluminium plant located close to the Rogun Power Project, and as 0.3 cop. per 1 kWh in a region of alumina mining (actually, cost of electric power will be much higher there). The economic parameters of aluminium production near Rogun Hydro Power Plant, which is a source of cheap power (variant I) viz. a viz., a conventionally taken region of raw material mining (variant II) are as below :

Parameters	Variant I	Variant II
—Prime cost of electric power, in cop./ kWh	0.15	0.3
—Consumption of electric power per unit of aluminium product, roub./t	24	48
—Distance of alumina transportation, km	5000	0
—Lossses on transportation of 2 tons of alumina in roubles required for production of 1 ton of aluminium	12.5	0
—Distance of transportation of finished aluminium km	3000	0
—Losses on transportation of finished aluminium, roub./t	5	0
—Total transportation and power supply losses per 1 ton of finished aluminium	41.5	48

The above data indicate that favourable parameters of the power component result in lower total losses on transport and power supply by 6.5 rouble per 1 ton of aluminium production if located close to the source of cheap electric power, via the variant of its location near a source of raw materials. Taking into account the probable organization of mining and processing of local alumina raw materials, as well as the ever growing demand for aluminium in the Central Asian Republics and Kazakhstan, one can justifiably state that commissioning of the Rogun Hydro Power Plant will make Tajikistan the region of the best technical-economic condition for aluminium production.

Efficient development of this branch of non-ferrous metallurgy will be furthered by the organization of deep processing of aluminium, supported by available labour reserves and by a wide range of consumers in the Central Asian economic region. For this purpose, in the coming years, construction of a rolling-mill should be envisaged within the territory of the Tajik Aluminium Plant, and later on—of a foil-rolling plant located close to the Tajik Aluminium Plant, in order to meet the requirements of the regional economy (and, first and foremost, of the agro-industrial complex, engineering, and construction) in these products.

Cheap electric power supply is also favourable for profitable large-scale complex of chemical industries in the ST TPC. The combination of industries projected there should allow to substitute, as much as possible, the comparatively more costly heat-based processes, by cheap electricity-based modern electro-chemical technologies.

This problem will be solved to a considerable degree by the full commissioning of the Yavan electrochemical plant, which uses sodium chloride from the Tutbulak deposit, limestone and dolomite of the Puskhur and Yavan deposits, electric power of the Nurek Hydro Power Plant (and, in future, of the Rogun Hydro Power Plant), and natural gas supplied by nearby sources.

In our opinion, the conditions created in the ST TPC are also favourable for production of the wood-spirit (methanol) and its derivatives. Methanol is widely used as a solvent in lacquer-dye-stuff industry, for production of antifreeze, isoprene rubber, pesticides and other items. But methanol is mostly used, both in this country and abroad, for production of resins and plastics. In the USSR these products account for 45 per cent of consumed methanol, in the USA for 35 per cent.

Requirements of Central Asia and Kazakhstan in plastics are great, and since resins and plastics are more easily transported than methanol, it may be expedient to process most of methanol produced in Southern Tajikistan into resins and plastics. Increased demand of the Central Asian Republics in plastics is accounted for mostly by natural conditions of the region. Hot climate, shortage of construction materials, especially of timber products, force to plan higher per capita consumption of plastics, than in other regions of the country.

As we have previously indicated vigorous development of power-intensive industries based on production of non-ferrous metals and chemicals in the ST TPC, will be the most efficient way to exploit the abundant water resources of the region, and will also allow the involvement of the local resources of chemical raw materials into the national economic turnover. The latter process would, in its turn, be followed by increased employment in these branches of industry—an important consideration in a labour surplus region, such as Tajikistan.

Large-scale development of non-ferrous metallurgy and chemical industry corresponds well with the existing pattern of economy in the region :

—production of chemical fertilizers, of pesticides and herbicides, and of synthetic forage would ensure higher productivity of agricultural labour, and would create a new basis for its advancement ;

—aluminium metal, synthetic materials and plastics available in the region would promote development of processing industries, which would turn part of the available raw materials into finished products and thus create new production combinations ;

—production of man-made fibres together with available resources of natural cotton and silk fibres would be beneficial for development of several textile industries ;

—cheap and highly efficient goods made of aluminium and plastics, would both replace several tons of metals and timber imported from distant economic regions, and promote use of low-weight and durable materials in construction industry, this being especially valuable in regions of high seismicity.

Effective large-scale development of hydro power resources of Southern Tajikistan is, therefore, only possible through creation of power-intensive industries, with low expenditure per unit of consumed electric power. However, it should also be taken into account, that large-scale industrial production units within South Tajikistan are distributed over the area characterized by low self-purification capacity of atmosphere. These power-intensive "key" units, which are now already operating in the ST TPC (although some of them have not yet reached their projected capacity) have become, together with transport, the major sources of pollution in the air basin. Location of power-intensive branches in agro-industrial regions requires special consideration of soil responses and of specific features of irrigated farming on adjacent lands.

Experience of location of power-intensive production units in Southern Tajikistan supports the need to thoroughly consider the natural-climatic features of the regions involved. The project-design institutions, which are engaged in development of the future power-intensive projects should be more concerned with specifics of climatic regimes, as well as with employment of the most advanced technologies both in production processes and in purification of sewage, and gaseous discharges, and in the regeneration of water and other useful components from waste, recycling. Technological decisions should allow to maintain concentration of pollutants (characteristic for these industries) in the air and water environments below the ultimate permissible levels. As for the currently operating power-intensive production units additional studies are, required which would produce recommendations on reduction of gaseous discharges, on organization of water recycling systems, on wasteless technologies and on regeneration and utilization of solid wastes.

As was previously discussed, intensive involvement of cheap hydro power resources of Southern Tajikistan into production, and, creation (with employment of available reserves of minerals and of manpower) of complexes of power-intensive industries on their basis, are in no way a hindrance to the cotton-growing and horticulture-viticulture complexes, which have developed previously in this area. On the contrary, construction of high-capacity hydro power plants solves the problem of power supply and, at the same time, ensures runoff management, which meets the needs of irrigation especially important for irrigation-based agriculture of Southern Tajikistan. Thus, in efficient combination with the newly formed power-production complex, the traditional economic complexes of Southern Tajikistan produce a new economic formation within this area i.e., a large territorial-production complex including several interrelated industries.

A TPC is formulated as a planned, deliberately formed combination of stable interrelated and interdependent harmoniously developing industries of the national economy[4] located within a comparatively limited area ; therefore, the task of elaborating a single plan for formation and development of a TPC is part and parcel of any preparatory and decision-making activity. Such planning should always bear an integrated, intersectoral, interdepartmental character, and its implementation requires efficient interdepartmental co-ordination and synchronous operation of many participants in the process of creation and operation of a TPC. A Program-based approach is one of the ways to solve these complicated problems.

At present the need for elaborating individual regional development programs specially for newly developing regions, is clearly perceived ; such programs become widely practiced, and are considered as "an important component of the national prospective plans of economic and social development".[5] The State Planning Committee (Gosplan) of the USSR has adopted the appropriate methodological recommendations.[6]

The need to employ the program-based approach in order to do away, first and foremost, with interdepartmental discrepancies is also stressed by practical experience of formation and development of the ST TPC. There, one can give examples of inadequate coordination of even the major complex-forming units of productions, employing well tested technological principles of creation and exploitation. In the ST TPC the main local consumers of electric power produced by the Nurek Hydro Power Plant—the Tajik Aluminium Plant and the Yavan Electrochemical Plant—were put into operation after several years of delay.

Inadequate implementation of the TPC projects, apparently is not due to the program approach. Experience of economic analysis and modelling of TPC's reveals, that the requirements and specific features of program-based organization may be most fully applied to the investment component of the TPC projects, which seek to introduce the most recent advancements of the scientific and technological revolution, implemented in new conditions and unique scales. Random examples may be given of several cases of construction in the South-Tajik TPC.[7] Thus, construction parameters of the Nurek dam and the tunnel-construction operations were unprecedented in the world construction practice. The range and schedule of many construction operations depended on finalization of scientific research, experimental-industrial works and project-making. All this should be taken into consideration by plan documents ; and schedules of commissioning of a power plant, and of supplementary projects should be determined by the appropriate scientific-engineering activities, provided that all institutions concerned, irrespective of their departmental status, act under a single management, and seek to achieve one common target.

The models, which were made for South-Tajik TPC[8] revealed, that the best way to interpret the dynamics of the program-implementation process, taking into account alternative variants and random factors, is the alternative net time-table. It displays deliberately planned stochastic (uncontrolled) and controlled variants of development of a program in time, as well as moments and situations, which require decision-making, including those borne by events outside the program (achievements of science and technology, changes in situations). The alternative may also display results of a TPC structure optimization from the point of view of its contribution to fulfilment of the ultimate target.

It should be stressed, that besides the important role of an alternative net as a tool for simulating dynamics of a program, the very process of its compilation is very important for specifying and bringing into order the ideas on the perspectives and potential of the program, on possible constraints, moments and situations, which require more attention and thorough preparatory activities.

In conclusion, it should be emphasized, that by now over 90 per cent of electric power is produced in the ST TPC by Hydro Power Plants ; those hydrotechnical facilities, which are already in operation, are the determinant link in the system of activities for expansion of irrigation systems and successful solution of other socio-economic problems. Therefore, it may be concluded that in this region hydro power industry is not only the major component of the power base, but also the most important prerequisite for a rapid an[illegible]monious development of the regional economy.

FOOTNOTES

1. "*Tajikistan nature and natural resources*".—Dushanbe : Donish, 1982, p. 266.
2. Yunusov, B.V., "*Hydro Power Industry of Tajikistan*".—Dushanbe : Ifron, 1975, p. 200.
3. Per unit capital investments for these hydro power plants are 253 and 210 roubles per kw, and prime cost—0.125 and 0.1 cop. per 1 kWh, respectively.
4. See : "Simulation of formation of territorial-production complexes." Novosibirsk, 1971, p. 16.
5. "On advancement of planning and more effective influence of the economic mechanism on higher efficiency of production and quality of work". Postanovkenie TsK KPSS and SM SSSR, iyul, 1979—"Planovoye khoziaistvo", 1979, No. 9, p. 8.
6. Methodical recommendations on elaboration of target complex programmes for solving regional problems, forming and developing territorial-production complexes)—"Ekonomicheskaya gazeta", 1980, No. 13, p. 6.
7. "Long-term programs of capital investments, Chapters II and IV"—M. : Ekonomika, 1974.
8. See : Rakhimov R.K., Bronshtein Ya.T., Kletselman U.Kh., Karimov D.Kh., "Investment simulation for the south-Tajik territorial-production complex".—In : *Metody i praktika opredelenia effektivnosti kapitalnykh vlozheniy i novoy tekhniki.* —M. : Nauka, 1974, No. 23.

21

INVESTIGATIONS ON THE CONSTRUCTION OF THE NUREK HYDRO-ELECTRIC POWER STATION IN CONDITIONS OF HIGH SEISMICITY

K.M. Mirzoyev, S.K. Negmatullayev, G.S. Seleznev

Construction of high dams in seismic conditions is connected with the solution of a whole complex of specific tasks which have been successfully resolved when erecting the dam of the Nurek hydro-electric power station (HEPS). High seismicity in the region of construction, intensive deformation of the earths crust, great and small faults and a series of other factors have been a cause for additional requirements in regard of providing safety of such a grandiose construction unit (height of the dam is 300 m, reservoir volume is 10.5 m^2).

The Institute of seismoproof construction and seismology of the Academy of Sciences of the Tajik SSR established in 1955, has been conducting detailed investigations in respect of seismicity, seismic regimes, structure of the earths crust and seismic tectonics on the water surface of the Nurek HEPS reservoir. These studies have enabled us to evaluate seismic danger in the construction region and to carry out works on optimum choice of the dam-to-be. A series of works on the evaluation and substantiation of seismic stableness of the adopted variant of the earth-filled dam of the hydro-junction have also been completed.

The region with the Nurek HEPS reservoir is located in the midstream part of the Vakhsh River and it is within the seismically active Vakhsh region. This region is—distinctly subdivided into two parts—the southern part is located in the Tajik depression, it has a powerful sedimentary mantle from 10 to 12 km in thickness, and the northern part is located within the southern Tien Shan, where consolidated palaeosoic rock come out into the surface.

In the northern part of the region, in the west to east direction, along the foot of the Gissar Ridge there stretches the greatest Gissar-Kokshaal fault, the activity of which greatly determines the seismic regime of all of Tajikistan, the Nurek HEPS region included. The Nurek reservoir region is situated in the northern part of the Tajik depression. Within it there stretches a series of ridges—the Vakhsh, Gulindan, Srikhku, Tian, the North Karatau, Sanglak, and Sar-Saryak ridges which in the south are oriented meridianally, and in the north change direction to the north-east. The absolute altitudes of these ridges vary from 1,500 m to 3,200 m, becoming higher in the direction from the south to the north and the north-east. Geological investigations of the midstream part of the Vakhsh River are described in papers [1,4] and in some other works.

The main epicentral areas stretch rather clearly along definite geological structures. Full coincidence of earthquake epicentres with marked geological faults, however, are not observed. Evidently, this is connected with insufficient precision in determining the coordinate axes of hypocentres of the territory under study, slope drop of faults into depth, and at times, with their rather close situation from each other.

On the basis of a complex of geological and geophysical and seismological signs a number of seismogenic zones have been singled out upon the territory of the seismically active Vakhsh region. Their characteristics are given in works. [5,6] The Gissar-Kokshaal, Ilyak and Ante-Pamirs (the Pamir-Alai) seismogenic zones are the main zones, and the seismic regime of the Nurek reservoir region is connected with them.

The Gissar-Kokshaal seismogenic zone is traced along the edge fault of the same name, covering the adjoining belt of southern slopes of the Gissar and the Karategin ridges and adjacent parts of the Tajik depression. The seismogenic zone is 25 to 30 km in width. This zone is the most active one in Tajikistan when its seismic data are taken into account. Here earthquakes with magnitudes of over 6 units occur more often than in other zones. The average number of earthquakes with K=10 for 16 years related to the area unit of 1,000 sq. km is equal to 34. Such powerful earthquakes as the Karatag in 1907 with K=17 (M=7.25), the Khait in 1949 with K=17 (M=7.4), the Faizabad in 1930 and 1943 with K=15 (M=5.7 and M=6.0), the Markansoui in 1974 with K=16 (M=7.2) the Alai in 1978 with K=16 (M=6.8) and others are known to have taken place here. The inclination on the repetition chart in the zone has the value of $\gamma = -0.45 \pm 0.03$. The mean repetition time of one earthquake with K=17 for the whole zone is equal to 50 years, and to 1,000 years for one and the same place. The maximum possible earthquake is the one with K=18 (M=8.0) the repetition of which for the zone as a whole is equal to 150 years. Earthquakes with summary effect of 9 points within this zone calculated from data obtained from all strong-force earthquakes occur once in 400 years on the average.

A seismogenic zone of 10 to 12 km in width can be singled out along the Ilyak-Vakhsh edge fault and it has the same name. Earthquake centres are distributed upon the whole of the earth crust with the near-vertical drop towards the north. The greatest number of them occur in the depth values of 20 km. In the eastern part of the seismic zone there occurred the Nurek earthquake of 1956 with K=13.6 (M=5.3) which was followed by a great many aftershocks. Seismicity greatly increases to the east. If in the western part of the zone the number of earthquakes with K=10 per unit of 1,000 sq. km for 16 years is equal to 32, then in its eastern part it counts 117. The inclination on the repetition chart in the zone is equal : $\gamma = -0.38 \pm 0.02$. The maximum possible earthquake here is evaluated to be K=15.5 (M=6).

The Pamir-Alai seismogenic zone can be singled out in the north-eastern part of the Tajik depression. The Gulizindak and the Sarikamar faults stretch within its boundaries. The most recent elevations here reach the values of 4,000 m. The number of epicentres with K=10 for the area of 1,000 sq. km for 16 years of observations is of a value equal to 28. The inclination on the repetition chart is $\gamma = -0.39 \pm 0.03$. The maximum possible earthquake in the zone is estimated to be K=15 (M=6).[5,6,7]

The seismic investigations conducted have shown that the dam region of the Nurek HEPS is located in the 8-point zone of seismicity. Moreover, manifestation of high degree activity of weak and average-force earthquakes is characteristic of these places. The earthquakes, strongest in force however, can occur in the zone of the Gissar-Kokshaal fault, where repetition of small earthquakes is several times lower, as compared with the Nurek HEPS reservoir region. The repetition period of the 8-point earthquakes in the dam region is equal to about 400 years.

Earthquakes with a strong-force are a rare phenomena. Up to the present time there is no actual record of maximum-force earthquakes for the Nurek HEPS region. Due to this there arises a necessity for experimental and theoretical calculations of possible seismic influences, namely for synthesizing a seismogramme of strong-force earthquakes on the basis of the study of spectrum and time characteristics of weak local and remote seismic shocks.[8]

Investigations of spectrum and time characteristics have been carried out on the basis of earthquake records registered by the seismic station CHISS—"Langar" in seismogenic zones. The strong-force earthquakes can bring about considerable acceleration in the Nurek HEPS dam region.[9,10] Influences have been calculated for the vertical component of acceleration, displacement and speed. In Table 21.1 the mean value of oscillation accelerations caused by earthquakes from the nearest seismogenic zones are given.[11] Values of the mean periods of repetition of every class of earthquake in seismogenic zones in years which can cause calculated accelerations for the given distances[5] are given in this table. Periods of repetition have been calculated with consideration of the zone area covered by dimensions of centres of different class earthquakes in every seismogenic zone with the focus located at distances given in Table 21.1.

Two regions with different types of earthquake centres at a distance of 30 km and 40 km, and in the Nurek HEPS dam region at a distance of 5 and 10 km are distinguished in the seis-

TABLE 21.1 : **Maximum amplitude values of synthesized records of accelerations with repetition periods depending on seismogenic zones**

Seismogenic zones :	Classes K	15		16		17		18	
	R in km	a	t	a	t	a	t	a	t
the Gissar-Kokshaal	30	13.4	250	50.0	800	200.0	1800	400.0	2400
	40			26.0	800	90.0	1800	300.0	2400
the Ilyak-Vakhsh	20			200.0	150				
the Darwaz-Karakoul	85	3.2	600	12.0	1500	34.0	1900		
the Ante-Pamirs	60	6.5	2000	30.0	4900				

a—cm/c^2 ; t—years

mogenic zone of the Gissar-Kokshaal fault.

The investigations conducted on spectrum and time characteristics of seismic oscillations produced by local earthquakes and forecasting on the basis of parameters and synthetic records of strong-force influences have shown that differences of earthquakes from various zones are rather great. Therefore when calculating seismic stableness of a construction unit it is not possible to restrict ourselves only to a synthetic seismogramme, it is necessary to have a set of typical influences determined for every place we are interested in.

Due to a lesser influence of absorption of high-frequency components of seismic oscillations with near-surface earthquakes (H=5 km) occurring in the vicinity of the Nurek HEPS, as compared with more remote shocks, the former ones despite their lower energy potential will exert greater seismic influences upon rigid assemblies of the dam and building of the Nurek HEPS.

The maximum amplitude of the accelerogramme from one centre zone has the value of 200 to 400 cm/c^2, that is the intensiveness of influence according to the present-day effective point scale corresponds to 8 to 9 points, whereas by accelerogrammes from other centre zones it reaches the value of 6 to 7 points.

The problems of seismic stableness of the earth-filled dam were being solved in a complex way, in the following general directions : nature observations, testing of physical models and analytical investigations.

The study of seismic stableness has been carried out at the stages of a project task and a technical project, starting from the year 1960. Works on substantiation of construction were then conducted by many organizations of this country : ISMIS of the Academy of Sciences of the Georgian SSR, GIDROPROJEKT named after S.Ya. Zhuk, VNIIG named after B.E. Vedeneyev, VODGEO and others.

The spectral method was used for evaluation of seismic loads for the first time in the practice of projecting earth-filled dams.[12,13] This was favoured by development of the method of displacement gore and its experimental corroboration on the basis of investigations on the earth-filled dam oscillations and on behaviour of different-scale physical models when subjected to seismic influences.[14,15] The conducted investigations with the use of the spectral method allowed to evaluate seismic loads with more authenticity and, consequently, to evaluate the stableness of the dam as a whole.

The task of the evaluation of the possible residual deformation of the earth-filled body of the dam was being solved by way of generalization of data obtained when investigating the dam's behaviour during earthquakes[16] and testing the different-scale physical models (from 1/300 to 1/50 with the model height of 1 to 6 m). Experiments on models ware carried out in laboratory conditions on the seismic platform and in field conditions with the help of explosions with different influence intensity (from 5 to 10 points according to the MSK scales).[15,17]

In order to effect systematic control over the state of the dam during earthquakes it was recommended to create engineering-seismometric service (ESS).[18] The ESS should provide for obtaining materials on oscillations of the dam during earthquakes with different intensities with the aim of checking mathematic patterns and correcting experimental data obtained on models as well as from other dams with weak influences.

The ESS of the Nurek HEPS dam envisages mounting of 29 measurement points, among them there are 5 base points, 8 ordinary points and 16 subordinate ones.[19] The experience gained in the investigations of oscillations of the earth-filled dam's and on the Dam of the Golovnaya HEPS[20] was used in working out the ESS project.

Engineering-seismometric observations in the range of the Nurek HEPS were started in 1970 and the dynamics of the dam has been under study since 1972. For this period of time the dam has risen from 120 m up to the project marking points. The period of the dam's own oscillations of the base tone has changed from 2.5 down to 1.0 Hz, whereas the attenuation index is within 4.0 + 11.0 per cent from the critical value. Definitions were made during various influences : microseisms, industrial explosions, tangible earthquakes (up to 5 to 6 points).

Experimentally determined period values of the dam at all stages of construction very well coordinate with the calculated data. There has also been obtained good coordination with the data gained in model investigations. Oscillations of the dam are of a clearly manifested spatial character : the prevailing frequencies are singled out for every one of the three directions (side, longitudinal and vertical). The forecast spectrum of the dam's own oscillations of the Nurek HEPS is given in Table 21.2.

TABLE 21.2 : **Frequencies of own oscillations of the Nurek HEPS dam**

Component :	Frequencies, in Hz		
	1st tone	2nd tone	3rd tone
Side	0.92	1.71	2.6
Longitudinal	1.51	2.1	2.86
Vertical	1.69	3.71	5.78

Attenuation of own oscillations is a value of great importance determining the dynamic behaviour of the construction unit. This value can only be determined empirically and that makes its evaluation for the construction unit under project more difficult. Determination of attenuation is done through summarizing the data obtained experimentally in the world practice. In order to do this we must analyse the increase factor of the dam's oscillations subjected to different influences.

The increase in the factor values by acceleration of the earth-filled dams oscillations (the height from 1 to 280 m).[19,20,21] The range of change of perturbation acceleration varies from 1 to 1,300 Gaul (cm/c^2). Analysis of the chart shows : the increase factor for the crest of the dam changes from 20 with weak influences down to 1 when the influences become stone. This information has made it possible to give values of attenuation which vary from 4 to 50 per cent in critical portions within the range of influences from microwave oscillations to destructive earthquakes.

Development of the system of instrumental observations for recent years has favoured obtaining a number of records of destructive earthquakes during which oscillation acceleration in separate fragments of time are close to, or even exceed, the value of gravity acceleration (g) : the Saint-Fernando (1971)—1.2 g ;

the Gazli (1976)—1.3 g ; the El-Centro (1979)—1.74 g—earthquakes. Probability of such acceleration values can also be judged by experimental data gained from extrapolation of accelerations from weak earthquakes towards destructive ones.

Calculation of the dam's stableness with the help of the normative method does not appear to be possible with very high acceleration values. In this connection a suggestion has been put forward to calculate the stableness of the earth-filled dam taking into account the second maximum strain in the deformation values allowed.[22]

It is accepted here that in the dam's zones where the equilibrium state is broken by the Coulombe-More law plastic fluidity starts. The latter is taken into account by way of introducing a reduced value of the elasticity module. Obtained residual deformation values ($\triangle_i$) of the dam are compared with the maximum ones ($\triangle_i^n$). The bearing capacity for the i-element of the calculated scheme of the dam (for instance, by the method of the final element) is determined from the expression :

$$K_i = \frac{\triangle_i}{\triangle_i^n} \tag{1}$$

and for the dam as a whole

$$K_3 = \frac{\sum^n F_i K_i}{\sum^n F_i}, \tag{2}$$

where F_i—is the area of the i-element for the flat calculation scheme, and n—is the number of elements.

In conformity with the elaborated method an evaluation has been made of the bearing capacity of the Nurek HEPS dam subjected to influences of an earthquake of the 15th energetic class (Magnitude 6)— the maximum possible from the nearest focus zone. Results of the calculation are given in Table 21.3. On the basis of analysis of calculated data one can say that with the given seismic influence the bearing capacity of the dam is

TABLE 21.3 : **Importance of the measure of use of the dam's bearing capacity depending on deformations**

Factor / Loads	towards the lower still water: maximum	towards the lower still water: average
in portions of the unit	0.134	0.127
in %	13.4	12.7
Total, in percentage	26.1	

exhausted by 26 per cent. The following values of maximum deformations have been used in the calculations : shingle and nucleus material—9 per cent, stone surfacing —18 per cent.

The investigations conducted have shown that seismicity of the earth-filled dam of the Nurek HEPS requires that a number of constructive measures are undertaken : they are—broadening of the dam's crest, additional load on the dam's slopes and crest with broken rock stones, "arming" of the crest zone, etc. Recommendations of the Institute have been taken into account when working out the design project of the dam.

Detailed seismological investigations of the water surface of the Nurek HEPS reservoir during a long period of time (up to the moment of filling it with water, during the filling and after it) have permitted us for the first time in this country to reveal the relationship between the changes in water level and the region's seismicity. The greatest influence of the filling of the water reservoir upon activity of seismic shocks has manifested itself within 15 km away from the axis of the reservoir in two opposite directions. The change in the number of earthquakes per year since 1955 within 60 km along the reservoir. The change in seismic activity in time is also indicated. Splashes of activity in 1972 and in 1976 when the water surface reached the 100 m and 200 m level are registered.[23]

Numerous maps of the earthquake epicentres in the reservoir region are prepared for individual stages of the rising and dropping of the water level for the period from 1972 up to 1979. These maps however cannot be presented here. They have allowed us to arrive at some conclusions .The earthquake epicentres firstly appeared on the periphery of the reservoir to the south-west and the south of the zone. Their depth, did not exceed 5 km. The first powerful splash occurred in November of 1972, some time after the water level had started rising in August. In December 1972 and in January 1973 seismicity started to gradually extinguish.

Resulting from rapid discharge of water (40m) in February and March of 1973, seismicity again noticeably increased, at the same time earthquakes started to occur not only on the periphery, but also under the reservoir itself. In August of 1973 a new splash of seismicity occurred in the reservior region and epicentres of earthquakes appreciably moved to the east (for around 5 km) from the original place.

A rapid rise of the water started in July of 1976, and in December of that same year the 203 m level was reached. Increase in seismicity here began in the middle of August. In January of 1977 after the drop in the water level there started a new filling of the reservoir with water up to the 220 m level, but this filling (slow in time), being not significantly higher than the former level, did not bring about noticeable increase in seismicity. This can be accounted for by preliminary removal of strains when the reservoir was being filled with water up to the 203 m level and by a slow speed of the filling.[24]

A dense network of American-made high-sensitivity seismic station has started functioning in the reservoir region since 1975. This has permitted us to considerably improve the measurements of the coordinate axes of the epicentres. This has also revealed the known and latent faults in the reservoir zone. Data on mechanisms of centres restore the general picture of movement along faults in the zone of agitated seismicity.[25]

Detailed investigations on seismicity in the process of changing the water level of the reservoir have made the choice of a satisfactory scheme of genesis of agitated earthquakes possible. The calculations allow to forecast periods of increase and decrease in seismic activity in the zone while the dam of the Nurek HEPS is in use and indicate the change in seismicity in other regions where dams for other HEPS are being planned.

CONCLUSIONS

Investigations on seismicity and seismotectonics of the Nurek HEPS reservoir region, as well as on seismic stableness of its dam, have made it possible to build such a grandiose unit in conditions of high seismic activity.

The greatest acceleration values of seismic influences (0.4g) with occasional repetition (equal to 5,000 years) are found in the zone of the Gissar-Kokshaal fault. Earthquakes of the energetic class K=18 (Magnitude M=8) occur in the seismogenic zone of this fault. In the vicinity of the Nurek HEPS dam earthquakes with a maximum-force have a low energy value (K=15, M=6). Weak and average earthquakes, however, are more repetitive, as compared with the zone of the Gissar-Kokshaal fault.

Weak earthquakes in the region of the dam under construction are peculiar to the small depth value of bedding and, due to this, to the increased level of high-frequency component of oscillations in their spectrum. This factor must be taken into consideration, for high-frequency oscillations can be destructive for rigid assemblies of construction units, for equipment of the HEPS and for water filled material of the dam's body.

In conformity with the results of scientific investigations and experiments on models, a number of constructive measures have been suggested providing for seismic stableness of the Nurek HEPS dam. These have been used in the process of projection and construction of the HEPS. Guidelines for the organization and creation of engineering-seismometric services (ESS) in areas of high-altitude dams, and for the project for the ESS on the Nurek HEPS dam have been worked out with the purpose of control over its behaviour during strong-force earthquakes. Scientifically substantiated methods of calculating seismic stableness of the HEPS-to-be are also elaborated.

Convincing illustration of the influence of engineering activity of man upon seismic activity in the Nurek HEPS region calls for a necessity of taking into account factors which effect construction works in seismic regions. The elaborated scheme of agitated earthquakes resulting from additional load and changing of the pore pressure in the earth crust satisfactorily explains the phenomena described and allows for forecasting possible changes in seismic activity in any seismically active zones which have different types of loaded states of mountain rocks.

FOOTNOTES

1. Gubin, I.E.,—*Regularities in Seismic Manifestations on the Territory of Tajikistan* (In Russian). Izd. AN SSSR, M. 1960.
2. Zakharov, S.A., *Tectonic Regioning and Structural Scheme of the Tajik Depression* (In Russian). Trudy Instituta geologii AN Tajikskoi SSR, t.5, Dushanbe, 1962.
3. Bunais, V.I., Reiman, V.M.—*On Seismic Characteristic of the Central Part of the Tajik Depression* (In Russian). "Trudy Instituta seismostoikogo stroitel'stva i seis mologii AN Tajik. SSR", t. VII, Dushanbe, 1960.
4. Babayev, A.M.,—*The Most Important Seismogenic Faults of Tajikistan* (In Russian). Sb. "Seismotektonika nekotorykh rayonov yuga SSSR", M., "Nauka", 1976.
5. Babayev, A.M., Mirzoyev, K.M.—*Seismogenic Zones of Tajikistan* (In Russian). Sb. "Seismotektonika nekotorykh rayonov yuga SSSR", M., "Nauka", 1976.
6. Babayev, A.M., Koshlakov, G.V., Mirzoyev, K.M.—*Seismic Regioning of Tajikistan* (In Russian). Dushanbe, "Donish", 1978.
7. Mirzoyev, K.M.—*The Main Seismicity Characteristics of Seismogenic Zones of Tajikistan* (In Russian). Sb. "Seismotektonika nekotorykh rayonov yuga SSSR", M., "Nauka", 1976.
8. Rautian, T.G.—*The Method for Constructing Synthetic Seismogrammes of Strong-force Earthquakes With Local Peculiarities Taken into Account* (In Russian). Sb. "Voprosy kolichestvennoi otsenki seismicheskoi opasnosti". M., "Nauka", 1975.
9. Napetvaridze, Sh. G., Negmatullayev S. Kh., Seleznev G.S.—Forecast and Observed Dynamic Characteristics of Dams under Seismic Loads (In Russian). Trudy Sovetsko-Amerikanskogo rabochego seminara "Projecting and Construction of large Dams in Seismically active Regions". M., 1977.
10. Nikiforova, M.M., Rautian, T.G.—*Typical Spectra of Earthquakes of the Nurek HEPS Region* (In Russian). Sb. 2 Seismostoikost plotin", vyp. 4, "Donish", Dushanbe, 1978.
11. Nikiforova, M.M., Golubyatnikov, V.L.—*Forecast of Seismic Influence for the Nurek HEPS Region* (In Russian). Izvestiya AN Tajik. SSR, Nr. 1502-80, Dushanbe.
12. Napetvaridze, Sh. G.(Editor)—*Guidance for Calculation of Hydrotechnical Constructions (Pressure and Non-Pressure) in the Light of Seismic Influence* (In Russian). Tbilisi, 1966.

13. Seleznev, G.S.—Determination of Seismic Loads for Dam built of Local Materials (In Russian). Doklady AN Tajik. SSR, Izd. "*Donish*", t. IX, Nr. 4, Dushanbe, 1966.

14. Seleznev, G.S., Shuser, R.S.—On Evaluation of Dynamic Parameters of the Dam Built of Local Materials (In Russian). Trudy TNI, vyp. 2, Izd. "*Irfon*", Dushanbe, 1967.

15. Vorontsov, S.L., Sagdiyev, T.G., Seleznev, G.S.—Experimental Investigation of the Nurek HEPS Dam on Models (In Russian). *Bulleten po-inzhenernoi seismologii*, Nr. 6, 1970.

16. Seleznev, G.S.—Classification of Seismic Deformations of Dams Built of Local Materials (In Russian). *Inzhenernaya Seismologiya*, Nr. 3-4, Izd. "Donish", Dushanbe, 1966.

17. Seleznev, G.S., Abduraufov, Kh. Sh.—Investigation of Spatial Oscillations of the Earth-Filled Dam of the Nurek HEPS on a Physical Model (In Russian). Izvestiya AN Tajik. SSR, Nr. 788-80, Dushanbe, 1980.

18. Sagdiyev, T.G., Seleznev, G.S., Zaslavsky, Yu. L.,—Questions of Organization of the Engineering-Seismometric Service on Dams Built of Local Materials (In Russian). Izd. "*Donish*", Dushanbe, 1968.

19. Negmatullayev, S. Kh., Seleznev, G.S., Simpson, D.W., Rojahn, C.—Engineering and Seismological Observations at Dams. *Proc. 2 Int. Conf. on Microzonation*, v. II, 1978.

20. Seleznev, G.S., Zaslavsky, Yu. L., Chalkina, G.I.—*A Prediction of Earth Dam Response During Earthquakes*, 5 ECEE, *Instanbul*, 1975.

21. Seleznev, G.S., Barysheva, N.N.—Spectral Analysis of Oscillations of the Dam during the Earthquake on April 21, 1978 (In Russian). Izd. AN Tajik. SSR, *Otd. phys.—mat., khim. i geol.*, n., Dushanbe, Nr. 1191-80, 1980.

22. Seleznev, G.S., Belgorodskaya, G.N.—Calculation of Seismic Stableness of the Construction Profile of ths Dam of the Nurek HEPS 273m in Height (In Rnssian). Izv. AN Tajik. SSR, Nr. 3566-80, Dushanbe, 1980.

23. Negmatullayev, S. Kh. (editor)—Agitated Seismicity near the Nurek Reservoir (In Russian). Izd. "*Donish*", Dushanbe, 1975.

24. Mirzoyev, K.M., Negmatullayev, S. Kh.—Agitated Seismicity in the Reservoir Zones with the Example of the Nurek HEPS (In Russian). Sb. Sovetsko-Amerikanskykh Rabot po prognozu zemletryaseniy, t.2, kn. I, Dushanbe, 1979.

25. Simpson D.W., Negmatullayev, S. Kh.—Induced Seismicity at Nurek Reservoir, Tajikistan, USSR. *Bull. Seism. Soc. Am.*, Vol. 71, Nr. 5, 1981.

22

DESERTIFICATION AS A GLOBAL PROBLEM AND THE SOVIET CONTRIBUTION TO ITS SOLUTION

V.N. Orlovsky

Due to scientific and technical progrees man is able to transform landscapes on a vast territory and influence the natural meteorological course. The more mankind utilizes natural resources, the more pressure it exerts on natural ecosystems, which results in an aggravation of the conflict between society and nature.

Trends towards a complexity in the relations of man with nature in the conditions of the scientific and technical revolution can be observed in some form and degree in all the vital aspects of the development of the modern world. That is why in choosing the methods and strategy for an integral development, a careful analysis should be made of present-day social, economic, political and natural conditions. Ecological problems are such an area of theory and practice the integral development of which requires concerted effort on the part of representatives of natural, technical and social sciences.

Among the major global ecological problems is the desertification of arid territories which make up some 25 per cent of the Earth's land. Over 200 million hectares of irrigated land (or 14 per cent of the world's croplands) is in arid zones. The rest is used under dry farming and pastures. More than 800 million people live there, which is some 20 per cent of the world's population.

Desertification is a complex and multi-faceted process involving both general geographic aspects and social economic and political aspects.

There are two factors which aggravated the desertification process and lead to desert expansion. The first factor is the fluctuation in the climate with its incredibly complicated interaction with the earth's surface and periodic hard droughts. The other factor is the anthropogenic one, i.e, the activity of man himself with his irrational methods of nature utilization. It is in man's psychology that the resources of the desert are inexhaustible and most often he gives little thought to his actions which coutribute to desert expansion and fresh losses of land.

Man has to survive in fragile ecosystems, in unpredictable and often rigorous climatic conditions under the burden of various social-economic problems. His activity leads to land degradation resulting from incorrect and excessive exploitation.

It has been estimated that out of the 45 revealed causes of desertification, 87 per cent involve man's irrational utilization of water, land, vegetation, minerals, while only 13 per cent of the causes are natural processes.

However, it is a fact that desertification goes hand in hand with an extensive agricultural and industrial development of resources in arid regions. Pasture areas being used too intensively and unjustifiably long, land being over irrigated without the construction of a drainage system, lack of crop rotation, application of modern digging and transport vehicles ; all this upsets the established balance in ecological systems. Anthropogenic pressure passes the critical mark and the territory under exploitation becomes a wasteland, soil becomes salinized and bogged, sand emerges to the surface and starts to shift, erosion becomes more intense, etc.

The problem of desertification first attracted global attention after the tragic events of 1968-73, when a severe drought hit the southern Sahara region, otherwise known as the Sahel, which contains among other countries Mauritania, Senegal, Mali, Bourkina Fasso (former Upper Volta), Niger and Chad.

According to U.N. estimates, the total area of anthropogenic deserts, which emerged not due to natural causes, is more than

9 million square kilometres. For example in southern Sahara alone, the advancing desert in south, robs the local population of some 100 thousand hectares of land annually. According to official reports by the authorities in Senegal, Mali, Niger, Cameroon, Chad and Sudan, the annual desert advance ranges from 1,5 to 10 kilometres. In six years millions of cattle died from lack of fodder and water. Deaths among the population had also been reported. Moreover, about 30 million square kilometres (i.e. another 19 per cent of land) are on the verge of desertification, threatening more than 100 states.

Experts say that in the past fifty years the Sahara absorbed some 650 thousand square kilometres of marginal lands which had been used for farming or grazing. According to estimates provided by Sudanese researchers, in their country the desert advanced south by as much as 100 kilometres in the past two decades.

Such magnitude of the desertification process is typical also of other continents. In Chile, for one, as a result of a prolonged drought the Atacama Desert was moving on a front of 80-60 kilometres at a rate of 2.5 kilometres annually. In Asia the Tar Desert expanded its boundaries for fifty years at an annual rate of one kilometre. This region of India and Pakistan annually loses 130 square kilometres of fertile cropland. In the space of 20 years $520 billion worth of agricultural produce was lost due to desertification. The rural population of regions affected by desertification rose from 57 million in 1977 to 135 million in 1983.

The total sum of subsidies designed to combat desertification amounts to $4.5 billion annually. Another $2.4 billion goes in aid for the countries affected. All in all, losses brought about by desertification are five times greater than the expenses on combatting it.

Desertification is especially active on the territories of developing countries. Hence, the conclusion that the problems of desertification are most pressing and threatening for these states. A study specially carried out in the Republic of the Niger in the regions of Etazer and Azavan which cover an area of 100 thousand square kilometres and which were badly hit by droughts in 1968-73, showed that the traditional economy of the Tuareg nomads was undermined to such an extent that it can hardly be expected to be restored to its original state.

The absorption by deserts of cropland and pastures in ecologically vulnerable regions on such a scale in the long run results in substantial food losses. According to preliminary estimates, the likely losses in food products through desertification, i.e. the decrease in the total grain yield in arid regions, amounts to 30 million tonnes annually. That is why some scientists are justified in saying that the cost of such grain far exceeds the expenses on any viable programme to combat desertification processes.

It is essential now to establish an exchange of experience in desert development and to take urgent steps for the available know-how to be applied so as not to simply halt the physical processes of desertification, but also to influence the population to inflict the minimum damage through economic and social activities on the fragile ecosystems of the arid regions.

The 1977 Conference and the 1984 Session of UNEP emphasized that in terms of the solution of the problem there were major scientific tasks and difficulties of social economic and political character. Besides, there is no quick solution to a problem such as desertification. It requires constant scrutiny and scientific analysis, long-term forecasting and planning.

In the present day the causes of desertification, their diagnosis and their possible effects, as well as the principal scientific and technical ways of early warning and prevention are generally known. However, the threat of an intensification of the process persists, and has become a world problem.

In sharing its experience of an integral approach towards the study and development of arid regions with other countries, the Soviet Union makes a certain contribution to the solution of the problem.

In the past 25-30 years in its arid regions the USSR carried out a full modernization of the irrigation network. Projects were drawn up for the regulation and complex utilization of the flow of the major rivers in Central Asia and Kazakhstan. The application of advanced technology in irrigating desert land (anti-filtration lining and pipes, subsurface horizontal and vertical drainage, spray irrigation, etc) saved irrigation water, reduced filtrational losses and secondary soil salinization. Work is being expanded to collect precipitation and to accumulate fresh water underneath takyrs. Large and small desalting kits have been built. All this will serve as additional sources of industrial and municipal water supply, as well as the needs of animal husbandry.

Cardinal changes have taken place in pasture animal husbandry, which is an efficient direction in desert development. Small nomadic cattle-breeding farms have been replaced by large state and collective farms, which have divided among themselves all the grazing land and utilize it on a scientific basis. Long-term plans have been drawn up for pasture utilization providing for the introduction of rotational grazing, the prevention of over-grazing, a season-wise allocation of the livestock and a progressive technique of degrazing and improving the pastures. Technical measures are carried out to develop the watering network, improve the quality of pasture vegetation and create emergency stocks of fodder.

In order to prevent the consequences of desertification connected with the anthropogenic destruction of desert vegetation and with deflation, the USSR has drawn up and is applying a whole complex of reclamation measures, such as the creation of green shelter belts around oases, regeneration of the vegetable blanket destroyed by construction works, forestation and sand-fixing by special plants and man-made shields. In addition to the above mentioned methods, physical and chemical methods are also applied in sand reclamation. Films from bitumen, nerozine, polyacrylamide and polymer compounds are used.

The expanding construction in the past decades of canals and reservoirs sharply increased the area of land under irrigation and the available water supply in deserts. For instance, Turkmenia's Karakum canal, 1,100 kilometres long and with a water intake from Amu Darya of some 400 m^3/sec has made it possible to irrigate over 500 thousand hectares of new land and to water 6 million hectares of grazing land located in the canal's vicinity.

In 1978 the Institute of Deserts of the Turkmenian Academy of sciences launched international educational courses on combatting desertification. Taking part in the courses were representatives of developing countries in Asia, Africa and Latin

America. The courses deal with the three following subjects : (1) Fixing of Shifting Sand. (2) Reclamation of Salinized Soil Under Irrigation. (3) Ecology and Pasture Productivity.

In the courses some 233 people from 45 countries have improved their skills. There were 87 graduates from 16 Asian countries, 119—from 21 African countries, 20—from 6 Latin American countries and 4 graduates from Spain.

We tried to choose lecturers with an experience of work in the developing countries and well versed in their social and economic peculiarities. In their lectures the professors drew parallels, whenever it was possible, with the developing countries. The courses themselves were chiefly held in Turkmenia, Uzbekistan, Kazakhstan and Azerbaijan which in the past developed economically and socially along similar lines with developing countries.

A full-length educational colour documentary was made. The film, which is called "The Desert : Which Way to Go?" and which has both a Russian and an English soundtrack, shows the wealth of experience the Soviet Union has in desert development and in combatting desertification.

On the basis of projects a special programme has been drawn up : "Evaluation, monitoring and prevention of desertification and its combatting in the droughty regions of the USSR". A whole series of scientific works has been published, as well as cartographic and methodics manuals in Russian, English, French and Spanish.

In this way the Soviet Union's scientific and practical experience in combatting desertification and in the rational utilization of resources of desert ecosystems enabled it to promptly join in the realization of the plan of action to combat desertification. This experience was passed over to representatives of foreign countries. In all this we see our contribution to the solution of this global problem.

High on today's agenda is the question of whether the world community, with its multi-national and multi-state structure and the existence of countries withdia metrically opposed socio-political systems, can bring itself to tackling the task of monitoring and management of ecospheric processes, processes which to a great extent determine the life of Earth and the lives on Earth.

23

WAYS OF OPTIMIZING AND INCREASING THE PRODUCTIVITY OF AGRICULTURAL USAGE OF ARID TERRITORIES

T.K. Vlasova

In the last few decades, due to the aggravation of the world food problem, the assessment of the possibilities to intensify agriculture and to involve to a greater extent arid territories into the agricultural turnover is acquiring a special importance. This scientific task is very important because the population of the arid territories of the world comprise to a great degree of a large portion of those who have not enough food or starve, and whose numbers are constantly increasing. It is expected that by the beginning of the next century, half of all the starving population of the world will be concentrated in the marginal zones of Pakistan, Bangladesh and China alone.*[1]

It is evident that in searching for ways of solving the food problem in the existing conditions of food production in the world the leading role should be given to social aspects, i.e., abolishion of the existing contrasts in the distribution of food products among individual countries and among different social layers within the countries of the world capitalist system. This requires radical socio-economic and political changes.

It is important to note that mass famine and poverty which are especially acute in developing countries, particularly in

*Contemporary evaluations of the number of the underfed and starving in the world ranges from 300 mln to 1 bil people (1,2).

countries whose territories have large arid regions are not only the consequence of the increasing population or unfavourable natural and climatic conditions but primarily of their colonial past and their unequal, dependent situation in the world capitalist market today. This can be illustrated by the fact that during the severest drought in the Sahelion zone in Africa, eight most suffering countries exported two-three times as many proteins as they imported them in grain.[2]

The most important way of solving the food problem in the developing countries is to increase per capita incomes and to expand food production. Many bourgeois scientists who quite rightly stress the necessity of introducing a new international economic order for the solution of the food problem often underestimate this by referring to the fact that "even in the countries where many people have to starve enough food products are produced".[3]

The increase of the volume of the agricultural production in the third world countries, however, would not only make them less dependent on food imports, but would make it possible for their increasing rural population to find jobs, to increase their living standard and purchasing power and to limit a number of negative consequences of the growth of largest towns.

In contrast to the acute necessity of obtaining self sufficiency in food products, the developing countries have shown a sharp decrease of the volume of the production of agricultural goods per head in the last two decades. While in the 50's the developing countries were net-exporters of grain, they became net-importers at the end of the 60's. In 1970 the third world countries imported 42 mln tons of grain, and in 1979 80 mln tons. The grain import requirements of these countries is believed to reach 125-150 mln tons by 1990.[4] These figures once again support the importance of searching for scientifically substantiated ways of expanding the production of food in the developing countries, in particular, in the countries whose territories consist largely of arid regions.

Taking into account the increasing degradation of the land resources of arid regions, which directly results in a decreased volume of agricultural production, the problem of finding possibilities and ways of intensifying agricultural within these territories and of searching more rational forms of its organization is acquiring an even greater importance.

In order to approach an estimate of the extent of increase in food production within territories with arid natural and climatic conditions, it is necessary to discuss a number of basic methodological positions.

It is known that an important feature of land resources as a recoverable means of production is the increased fertility due to correct cultivation. To increase soil fertility and yield growth, it is necessary to take a system of agricultural measures corresponding to the concrete local peculiarities and resources of a particular territory. It is not a rare case, especially in the profit oriented capitalist system of production to find that the load of agriculture on land resources exceeds the allowable norms. K. Marx said :

> 'any progress in capitalist agriculture is not only a progress in the art of robbing the worker but in the art of robbing soil as well, any progress in increasing its fertility for a certain period is at the same time a progress in the distruction of the constant sources of its ferility, (5, p. 509).

The indicator showing the intensity of the agricultural exploitation of a territory* which is closely connected with the state of land resources can serve as the indicator of the extent of load or anthropogenic impact on the natural environment in agricultural production. When studying this interaction, it is necessary to introduce a space-time aspect and take into acconut, in addition to the intensity and state of land resources, such factors as technical progress (reflected in the invention and use of new agrotechnology including those for the protection of nature) and the efficiency of agricultural production.

Some turning points are observed during the process of nature-society interaction in agricultural production when the intensity of agricultural exploitation of a certain territory at a

*This indicator includes the density of basic capital investments in fertilisers, domestic animals, purchase of technology, building wells, fences, etc. and other resources per unit of land used in agricultural production.

particular level of agrotechnology reaches its limit, after which a sharp deterioration of the state of land resources takes place. The volume of agricultural production decreases which brings about a decrease of its efficiency and, finally, a decrease of the intensity of the agricultural exploitation of the territory.

Such 'ecological-agricultural' crises can be revealed at different levels : district, country, region, continent. In particular, in Australia where it is possible to trace the relatively recent history of settlements, 'ecological-agricultural' crises have been observed during the entire period of agricultural exploitation of the continent. These crises were over when new agrotechnologies were introduced which were more rational in terms of nature protection. These in turn made it possible to increase again the intensity of agricultural exploitation of the territory, to make the state of land resources better and to increase production efficiency. This went on until negative (from the point of view of nature protection) features of the new agrotechnology were evident and the intensity level exceeded an allowable level. So, one can see that the development and maintenance of the former level of agricultural production were reached by using the hit or miss method. Experiments and mistakes which often preceded a chance success led to a deterioration of the general state of the land resources of the country. Nevertheless, mainly, in humid regions and natural zones of the country, optimal agrotechnologies and means of land exploitation both from the point of view of nature protection and economy were reached by the middle of the XX century. As to arid regions, the problem of achieving rational agricultural usage of lands, taking into consideration nature protection and economic efficiency both in Australia and the majority of other countries of the world, is far from being solved and is very acute.

It is not an exaggeration to say that the ecological problems arising out of land resource degradation has become specifically acute in the arid regions of the earth which are characterized by a weak resistance of their natural environments to the anthropogenic impact. As is known, the disturbance of the ecological balance in the environment of arid regions due to irrational economic activities results in the development of the desertification process.*[6]

Periods of natural aridization have been observed during all the history of the development of our planet. As to desertification, American scientist H.E. Dregne distinguishes three most marked crisis periods of its occurrence : (1) 1,000-3,000 years ago when vast territories of arid regions in Europe, Asia and Africa were subjected to soil erosion and salinization ; (2) 50-150 years age when the colonization of large territories by Europeans brought about soil erosion and overgrazing and, (3) the last 30 years when an increasing pressure on land in the developing countries resulted in the acceleration of desertification process of all kinds.[7]

Methodologically useful as this periodization may seem, we believe it more correct to unite the last two into one taking into consideration the fact that they are separated by a negligibly short period. The increased frequency of strong and perennial droughts can serve as a vivid indicator of the beginning of this period. According to V.A. Kovda, 'long droughts (5-7 years) were observed in the following years : 1880-1886, 1895-1903, 1911-1916, 1939-1945, 1958-1967, 1972-1980'. Catastrophic droughts raged in 1982-1984.

All this makes one assume that it is during this second period that desertification which earlier was of local character has become a global natural-socio-economic phenomenon on our planet.

The global and multifaceted character of this process is revealed, firstly, in the fact that it has begun to strongly influence the climate all over our planet. The latest materials of the World Weather Organisation stress that as a result of mass overgrazing, irrational agricultural techniques, cutting out wood and bushes for burning the albedo (the reflective capacity of the earth) increases, which, correspondingly, decreases the amount of precipitation. Besides, wrong methods of tilling

*The materials of the UN Conference on the problems of desertification give the following definition of this process : 'Desertification is a process which leads to a decrease of biological productivity with consequent reduction of plant biomass in relation to the potential volume of a particular region for domestic animals, harvesting crop and material well-being of the people.'

reduce the capacity of the soil to retain moisture thereby decreasing evapotranspiration. All this influence not only micro-climatic aridization but global atmospheric processes as well. The above phenomena, according to climatologists, particularly stimulate and strengthen droughts.[9] Thus, it can be concluded that major droughts are the result of global, but not local, climatic changes brought about primarily by desertification.

Secondly, desertification causes changes of the scale of whole natural zones : steppes and savannas in many regions of the earth, having lost their former bioproductivity, are acquiring the appearance of deserts and semideserts. Desertification has covered 60 per cent of arid, semiarid and subhumid territories, or 25 per cent of the earth's land surface.[10]

Thirdly, the global character and social acuteness of the process can be judged by the fact that 20 per cent of the population of the world have found itself under its impact.

After the working out by the UN in 1977 of the 'Plan of actions to fight desertification' according to which large funds were allocated and other long-term measures were taken, the rates of the development of the desertification process neither accelerated nor decelerated by 1985 : annually as prior to 1977, 6-7 mls ha. of new lands were found subjected to this distructive impact.[11]

It is noteworthy that an ever increasing number of the world population are experiencing a 'severe' degree of desertification. While in 1977 57 mln. people were subjected to desertification, in 1984 they are about 136 mln.[11, 12] At this rate of desertification, half of the land completely looses its productivity and the expenditures on its rehabilitation are not justifiable economically. Thus, the main part of the population living within the above territories are doomed to be undernourished or is subject to famine.

When analysing the available data (Table 23.1), one can clearly observe an increasing gap between developing countries and industrially advanced countries as to the number of people subjected to desertification. As to the territory covered by this process, developing countries also outstrip developed countries : in the mid 1980's, 70 per cent of the territory of the arid regions of the developing countries were degraded, while in the develop-

TABLE 23.1 : Rural population subjected to a 'severe' extent of desertification

(1977-1984) in millions of people

REGIONS	1977		1984			1984			
	agriculture	cattle breeding	agriculture	cattle breeding		cattle breeding	dry agriculture	irrigated agriculture	total
Countries of the Mediterranean basin					Mediterranean Africa	2	6	0.5	8.5
	5.9	0.9	11.5	3.0	Mediterranean Europe	1	4.5	0 5	6
Africa without Mediterranean region					Sudan-Sahelian Africa	7	20	0.5	27.5
	6.0	7.1	41.0	11.5	Africa to the South of Sudan-Sahelian region	4.5	20	0.5	25
Asia, Australia, Oceania, New Zealand					Western Asia	2	9.5	4.5	16
					Southern Asia	4.5	18	6.5	29
					China and Mongolia	1	2	3.2	6.2
	14·3	6.4	45.8	8	Australia	—	0.3	—	0.3
America	13.4	3.0	13.2	2.5	South America and Mexico	2	11.5	1	13.5
					North America	0.5	0.5	0.2	1.2
TOTAL :	39.6	17.4	111.5	25.0		24.5	92.3	17.4	134.2

ed countries 40 per cent of all arid lands were degraded.[11] If one considers the territories subjected to 'severe' desertification, the difference between the third world countries and developed countries is even greater.

Desertification is especially strongly spreading in the developing countries in the regions of *non-irrigated agriculture.* It is established that in 1984, 50-65 per cent of all the area of the dry agriculture system in the developing countries and 25-35 per cent in the developed countries were subjected to a 'severe' degree of desertification.[11]

The movement of non-irrigated agriculture to the semiarid zone, beyond the real agriclimatic borders and ecological boundaries of its development, is the main cause of desertification with this type of agricultural usage of territories. The main factor determining the necessity of using new often unfit lands is the increasing demands of the third world countries for food.

However, expanding arable lands in the semiarid zone of the developing countries on the old primitive agro-technological basis is an ineffectful method and irrational way of solving the food problem. The displacement of the agricultural border to drier areas tears away lands with best pasture resources earlier used by nomads in cattle breeding during dry months. This leads to the aggravation of the food problem because during droughts the more stable and established system of cattle breeding by nomads and semi-nomads provides the population with food in a better way than agriculture which is irreparably damaged by drought. As a result of ploughing up land, wind erosion takes place, which earlier was prevented by natural pasture vegetation. In addition, the crop yields in the semiarid zones in the developing countries are extremely low : anually 1 ha of land yields only 1-2 metric centners of grain, as a rule one of four years being productive.[13]

Another cause of the accelerated desertification of the territories of non-irrigated agriculture in the developing countries is the 'imaginary intensification' of the '*lea*' tillage which consists in shortening '*lea*' periods. As a result, the productivity of crops decreases as soil fertility has no time to restore. Long '*lea*' lands are strongly subjected to desertification in the form of wind erosion, in less moistured areas, and water erosion, in more humid areas. The reasons for using more 'inteinsive' '*lea*' tillage are caused not only by the considerable population growth but by the increasingly growing export of farm produce to the developed capitalist countries. This can be illustrated by the example of exporting the most important African food crop, peanuts, which is used by the importers as high-calorie feed for livestock.[2]

In the industrially developed countries, the areas subjected to desertification in the regions of non-irrigated agriculture have stabilized for the 7-year period under consideration and in many zones, especially in the countries of the temperate belt, even decreased. This phenomenon is partially due to the withdrawal of large masses of land from dry agriculture in marginal agriculture zones subjected to especially strong degradation. The withdrawal of large areas of marginal lands, including those within arid regions, from the agricultural production of the capitalist countries has lately become a persistent tendency which can be explained by a purely economic factor, i.e. by a lower efficiency of the modern highly mechanized agriculture on less cultivated and rich soils. As far as dry marginal zones are concerned, we can observe here a certain impact of both ecological and economic factors.

The states of many European and North American developed countries, keeping in mind a considerable contribution of the arid zones into agricultural production as well as the undesirable consequences of the withdrawal of the population and the decreased level of the economic activities in the region, are trying to prevent a decrease of the volume of agricultural production and to stimulate further development of these lands. The results of such policy have proved very promising sometimes. In particular, in the USA and Canada, large expanses of pasture lands were ploughed up and sown with cereals in the far west of the Great valleys in 1982-1984.[14] This, of course, increased water and wind erosion. So, as the prominent American ecologist H.E. Dregne points out, 'The American Administration finances farmers to do constant and irreparable harm to natural pastures.'

This harm, however, is much smaller, as we pointed out earlier, than that in the developing countries. It should also be taken into consideration that the advance of the dry agriculture border to the semi-arid zone in the third world countries takes place first of all due to the 'land famine', while in the developed countries this takes place in order to get still higher profits from food export.

During the period under consideration the territory subjected to desertification in the regions of irrigated agriculture, situated within the arid areas of the earth, has also increased but not to such a great extent as in the system of nonirrigated agriculture. It should be pointed out, however, that the negative ecological consequences of irrrigational exploitation (salinization, swamping, irrigational erosion) are more difficult to liquidate as they require larger capital investments. The ecological harm due to the salinization of 1 ha of irrigated area is estimated to be 3 times as great as that from dry land desertification.[14]

Secondary salinization and swamping taking place in certain conditions decrease the yields of cultivated crops and often makes the soils unfit for agricultural turnover. Not less than 200-300 thousand ha of irrigated lands drop out of agriculture every year in the world for these reasons, approximately the same amount becoming irrigated. As a result, there are at present about 26 ml ha of salinized unproductive lands on the earth which earlier were fertile.[8]

The areas of salinized and swampy lands in the territory considered in the developing countries are not more than in the developed countries, however, the differences in the 'severity' of the desertification is very great. It demonstrates the fact that the developing countries are not in a position to invest enough funds to fight against the degradation of irrigated land. The examples of vast areas subjected to salinization and swamping in the developing countries are the valley of the Indus in Pakistan and India, regions of irrigated agriculture in Iraq and Egypt, and in a lot of countries of Latin America.

A lot of publications have appeared in the last few years which only stress the negative, ecological consequences of the development of irrigated agriculture in arid areas. However, we must mention the great contribution of dam construction and the creation of areas of irrigated agriculture in the development of a particular country, in the general increase of its economy and the growth of self sufficiency in food.

In particular, 400 thousand ha of earlier unused arid lands were irrigated in Egypt as a result of the construction of the Aswan dam. In addition, it was possible to replace basin irrigation of 300 thousand ha by the year-round arable land, which allowed two-three yields per year from the land, in spite of a number of ecological problems. Moreover, the navigation conditions from the Aswan to the Mediterranian have become much better, and the hazard of overflooding the regions adjacent to the Nile has been averted. At present, the Aswan HES generates 10 bil. kwh electric power annually, which saves, on the average, 2 million tons of oil. The total cost of the project was 450 million of Egyptian pounds, including the accompanying construction of the infrastructure. The expenditures were paid back in less than two years, giving the annual profit of 225 million Egyptian pounds, a large part of which (140 mil. pounds) consists of the income from agricultural production.[15]

Thus, we believe that the development of irrigated agriculture accompanied with appropriate measures to fight against its negative ecological consequences is an important way of increasing the productivity of agricultural production within arid zones. Even in the countries of the Sahelian zone, the waters of such rivers as the Senegal and the Niger are practically not used for irrigation, which might considerably increase the volume of agricultural production in these countries, which badly need food. However, as we have already mentioned above, it is necessary, together with the introduction of irrigation, to form a system of deep horizontal drainage, washing out of salts, optional vertical pump drainage, hydroinsulation on the canals, etc.

The latest experience of the USSR in the development of irrigated agriculture is a successful example in this respect. Thus, the area of strongly salinized soils in the Tajik Republic, earlier making up about 35 per cent of the irrigated territory, now has decreased down to 9 per cent thanks to the introduction of a complex of the above type.[8]

The development of irrigated agriculture is especially efficient as part of a complex of other measures aimed at optimizing the agricultural usage of the territories of arid regions. All these measures must be based on the rationalization of the territorial organization of agricultural production, all the system of natural resources, ecological and socio-economic factors being taken into account.

Let us illustrate the latter point by the example of the Sahelian countries. It is known that the southern part of this region gets comparatively large amount of precipitation. Though droughts did not spare this more humid semi-arid zone either, it possesses a considerable potential of agricultural, pasture and forest resources which are far from being adequately used.[16] The latter is partially due to the fact that the development of these more humid territories covered with forest and bush vegetation requires considerably greater capital and labour expenditures.

The modernization of the agro-technology of dry agriculture as well as the development of more reliable irrigated agriculture here would make it possible to increase the yield of commercial agriculture. Here also fattening of the cattle brought from the semi-arid zone could be performed before slaughtering. All this could improve the provision of food in the semi-arid zone where the advance of the border of dry land agriculture does an irreparable harm to the environment and does not guarantee stable harvests.

If it were possible to arrange such food supplies from the semi-arid zone, the semi-arid Sahelian territory could practice extensive cattle breeding based on the usage of natural pastures.

In this way a gradual agricultural specialization of different natural zones would take place taking into account all the characteristics of resources and natural conditions. It is evident, however, that such an agricultural specialization within arid regions will become possible if it is stimulated by an appropriate price policy and market system. It is necessary to simultaneously introduce effective methods of the organization and expansion of the activities of agricultural services and to improve the information system of the agrarian sectors of the economy.

The rationalization of the territorial organization of the agricultural usage of the territories of arid regions will make it possible to solve not only the socio-economic problems but would help to meet the growing demand of the population for food and control the ecological problems as well.

FOOTNOTES

1. Falcone, W.P., Recent Food Policy Lessons from Developing Countries. *Amer. J. of Agric. Economics*. 1984,66, 2, pp. 180-185.
2. Bagramov, L.A., *Sovremenni capitalism i prodovolstvennaia problema*. M. : Nauka, 1984, 335 p.
3. Lappe, F.M., Collins, J., *World Hunger: Ten Myths*. Inst. for Food and Development Policy, 1979.
4. *World Development Report* 1980. World Bank, USA—116 p.
5. Marx, K., *Capital*, v.I—M. : 1953.
6. UN Conference on Desertification. *World Desertification Map*, 1977.
7. Dregne, H.E., Scale and Characteristics of Desertification of the Arid Regions of the World.—in *Mon. Fighting Desertification by Complex Development*, 1981, pp. 19-20.
8. Kovda, V.A., *Problemi borbi s opustinivaniem i sasoleniem oroshaiemich* pochv. M. : Kolos, 1984.—304 p.
9. Hare, F.K., Climate and Desertification. *WMO Bulletin*, 1984, 33, 4, pp. 288-295.
10. Lamb, R., Desertification—the Day Statistics. *WMO Bulletin*, 1984, 33, 4, pp. 287-288.
11. Mabbutt, J.A., A New Global Assessment of the Status and Trends of Desertification. *Env. Conserv.*, 1984, II, 2, pp. 103-113.
12. Mabbutt, J.A., The Impact of Desertification as Revealed by Mapping. *Env. Conserv.*, 1978, 5, 1, pp. 45-56.
13. Le Houerou, H.N., The Nature and Cause of Desertification. In : *Desertification Environment in and around Arid Lands*, 1977.
14. Dregne, H.E., Combating Desertification : Evolution of Progress. *Env. Conserv.*, 1984, 11, 2, pp. 115-121.
15. Biswas, M.R., Biswas, A.K., Complementary between Environment and Development Processes. *Env. Conesrv.*, 1984, 11, 1, pp. 35-44.
16. Skuri, M., Regionalnoie razvitie i problemi opustinivania aridnich i semiaridnich territori k seveu i yugu ot Sachari. *Priroda i Resursi*, 1984, XX, 1, pp. 11-23.

[illegible]

[illegible] and only the [illegible] of [illegible] population [illegible]

[illegible]

[illegible] Comparative [illegible]

[illegible]

[illegible] Comparative [illegible] and [illegible] Progress [illegible]

[illegible] Comparative [illegible]

[illegible]

24

WATER MANAGEMENT IN ARID AND SEMI-ARID TRACTS OF INDIA

Diagnostic Aspects

Sulabha Brahme

In India nearly 70 per cent of the total population (685 million in 1981) draws its sustenance from agriculture and allied activities. About 50 per cent of the total land area of the country (total area=3,287 thousand sq. km.) is under crop-farming and 4 per cent under pasturage and live-stock farming. Large tracts in the country are dependent for rainfall on the south-west monsoon which is not only concentrated in a brief period of four months (June to September), but also is quite unevenly distributed both in space and time (Fig. 24.1). Adequacy of rainfall or the net water balance in an area can therfore be considered as the main criterion for delimiting the agro-climatic regions. Adequacy of rainfall can be determined by comparing the precipitation received with PE (potential evapotranspiration) taking also into consideration the characteristics of the soil in the area, particularly its water holding capacity. Accordingly four main agro-climatic regions can be distinguished viz., the arid zone where a constant water deficit is typical ; the semi-arid zone which periodically suffers from lack of water ; the sub-humid zone and the humid zone. The arid and semi-arid regions

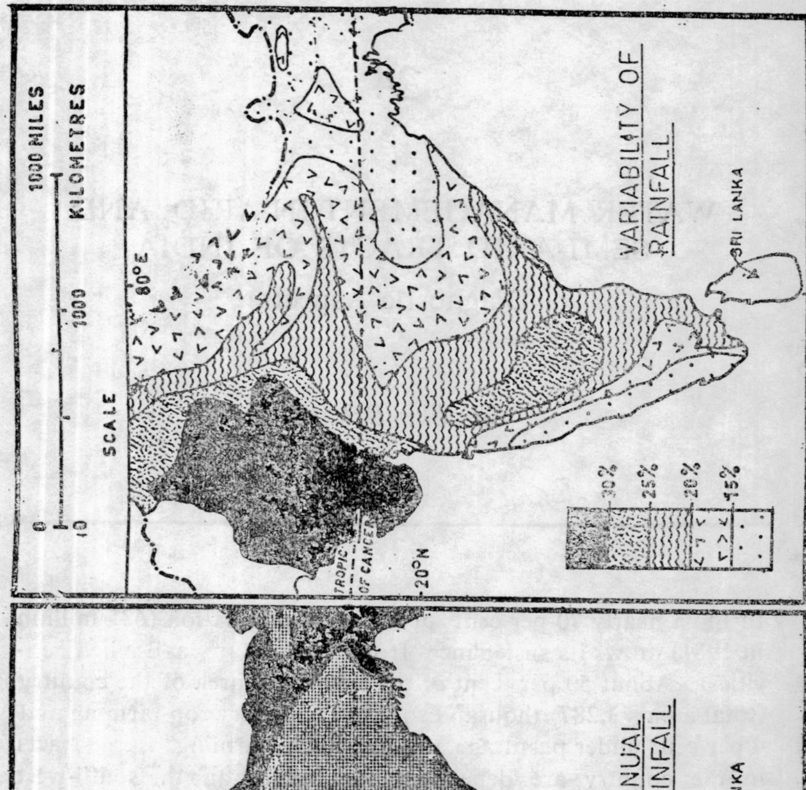
VARIABILITY OF RAINFALL
SCALE
0
10
1000
1000 MILES
KILOMETRES
80°E
TROPIC OF CANCER
20°N
SRI LANKA
30%
25%
20%
15%

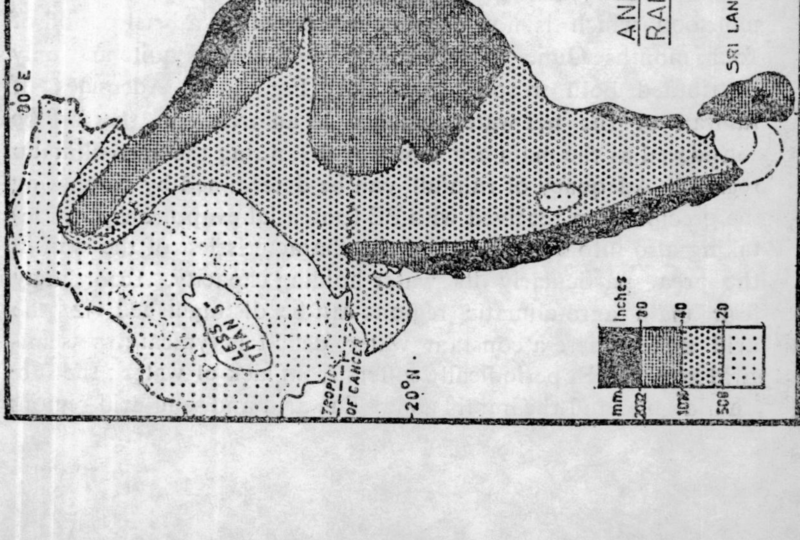
ANNUAL RAINFALL
80°E
LESS THAN 5"
TROPIC OF CANCER
20°N
SRI LANKA
Inches
80
40
20
mm
2032
1016
508

in India as delimited by the Irrigat ion Commission (1972) are shown in Fig. 24.2.

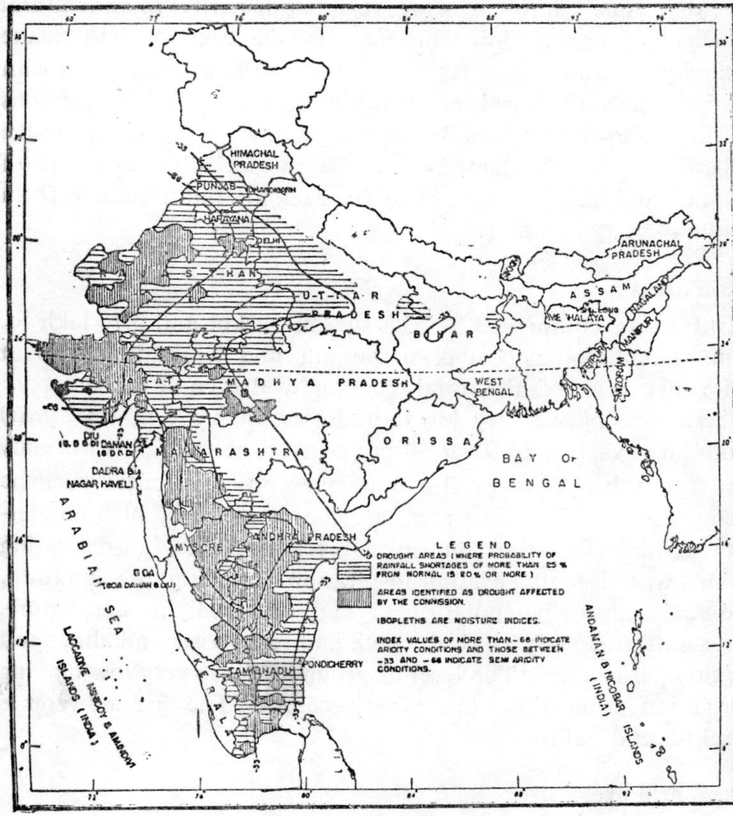

FIG. 24.2 : *Arid and Semi-Arid Tracts in India*

The Saurashtra-Kutch region of Gujarat, the western half of Rajasthan and parts of Haryana fall in the arid zone. Conditions very close to aridity prevail in the rain-shadow tract along the leeward side of the Western Ghats from Nimar in Madhya Pradesh to Mahbubnagar district in Andhra Pradesh.

Semi-arid regions comprise the Punjab plains, portions of West Uttar Pradesh and West Madhya Pradesh, Gujarat and eastern Rajasthan and in the south a long strip of peninsular plateau in the lee of the Western Ghats, stretching from

Maharashtra plateau through Mysore and Andhra Plateau down to Coimbatore plateau. As is indicated in Tables 24.1 and 24.2, the dry zone shows a wide regional disparity in agricultural efficiency[1]—a very low efficiency in the regions with acute scarcity of water (e.g. Rajasthan desert plain) in contrast with very high agricultural efficiency in the regions with enormous surface and underground water potential (e.g. North Punjab Plain, Tables 24.1 and 24.2.). Except the alluvial plains of Punjab and Haryana the entire dry area in India suffers from acute scarcity of water.

Arid areas

Arid areas comprise 3.17 lakh sq. km. of hot and 0.70 lakh sq. km. of cold regions (Ladak in Jammu and Kashmir) or about 11.8 per cent of the total geographical area of the country.[2] These areas have a very low rainfall (less than 375 mm per year) with large variability (over 50 per cent). The rainfall is not only indequate but also erratic and unevenly distributed over the crop season. The desert areas are characterized by high temperatures, large variations in diurnal temperatures, hot desicating winds with potential evapotranspiration exceeding precipitation, non-existence of perennial rivers and practically no agriculture. The soils are sandy alluvial, black and red, mostly alkaline and highly permeable. The level of groundwater is very low making irrigation from this source very costly. The groundwater is brakish and saline.

Semi-arid areas

The semi-arid region accounts for about a quarter of the total area in the country. In these areas, precipitation meets only about one-third to two-thirds of the evapotranspiration needs. Considerable variation in the number of rainy days and the distribution of rainfall in a year is noted in different parts of the semi-arid region. Irrigation facilities developed in this tract from rain-fed sources are unreliable; the groundwater situation is also not bright except for the Punjab plains. Medium to deep black, red and red-sandy, gray-brown and alluvial soils are the main soil types obtained in this tract. The soils are severely eroded and poor in fertility. Though rainfall is erratic

TABLE 24.1 : **Arid and semi-arid regions in India**

State	Total geographical area (000 sq. km.)	Total districts	Low rainfall area[1]			Percentage of irrigated area[2]	
			No. of districts	Net sown area (000 hectare) 1978-79	Percentage share in total sown area	In low rainfall region	All area
Andhra Pradesh	277	23	5	3924	34.6	22.5	35.8
Gujarat	96	19	11	6462	67.7	17.1	18.6
Haryana	44	12	10	3402	93.2	54.9	53.9
Jammu & Kashmir	222	14	2	110	15.2	71.8	40.9
Karnataka	192	19	9	6840	66.3	13.3	15.4
Madhya Pradesh	443	45	3	837	4.4	34.2	11.1
Maharashtra	308	26	7	7153	39.2	13.8	11.6
Punjab	50	12	9	3542	84.8	88.3	83.0
Rajasthan	342	26	20	13731	88.8	18.8	19.7
Uttar Pradesh	294	56	8	2488	14.2	64.7	43.5
All-India	3287	412	85	47961	33.5	31.2	27.5

Note : 1 Normal annual rainfall below 750 mm.
2 Cross irrigated areas/gross cropped area $\times$100 in 1978-79.

Source : Indian Agriculture in Brief, Nineteenth Edition, Ministry of Agriculture, New Delhi, 1982, pp. 192-199.

TABLE 24.2 : **Cropping pattern and agricultural efficiency in the dry agricultural zone in India**

Agricultural Meso Regions	Agricultural Micro Regions	Cropping Pattern	Agricultural Efficiency
2.1 Dry North-Western plain (Rajasthan plain & Punjab plain), Aravalli Hills, Saurashtra & Kutch peninsula	2.1.1 Rajasthan desert plain	Millets-oilseeds	Very very low
	2.1.2 Rajasthan semi-desert plain	Millets-wheat-oilseeds	Very low
	2.1.3 Punjab plain & its adjacent Ganganagar dist. of Rajasthan, Mathura & Aligarh dists. of Uttar Pradesh	Gram-millets-wheat	Very high/high/moderately high except low efficiency in two dists. in the South
	2.1.4 North Punjab plain	Gram-wheat-millets	Very high/high
	2.1.5 Aravalli Hills	Maize-wheat-gram	Moderately high
	2.1.6 Saurashtra and Kutch peninsula	Groundnut-millets-cotton	Low/very low/very very low efficiency except moderately high efficiency in Amreli dist.

TABLE 24.2 : (*Contd.*)

2.2 Dry Peninsular Plateau	2.2.1 Tapi-Narmada *doab* area	Millets-cotton-groundnut	High efficiency except low efficiency in Nasik district
	2.2.2 Upper Godavari basin	Millets-wheat-oilseeds	Low
	2.2.3 Upper Bhima and Krishna basin	Millets-groundnut-oilseeds	Low/very low except moderately high efficiency in Satara dist.
	2.2.4 Tungabhadra basin	Millets-groundnut-cotton	Low/very low except moderately high efficiency in Shimoga dist.
	2.2.5 Rayalaseema Plateau	Millets-groundnut-rice-cotton	High in the North and moderately high and very very high in the extreme South

Source : Economic Regionalization of India ; Problems and Approaches : Census of India 1961. Monograph Series Vol. I, No. 8, by Dr. (Miss) P. Sen Gupta and Dr. (Mrs) Galina Sdasyuk, 1968, p. 111.

and surface run-off from the soils is high, the relatively higher level of percipitation indicates greater feasibility of crop husbandry as compared to the arid areas. The yield levels are by and large below the all-India average.

Water utilization

Historical records bear testimony to the existence of a number of irrigation works in different parts of the country. The character of these works was largely conditioned by the physiographical features of the area in which they were located. In arid and semi-arid plains of North India perennial rivers like Indus and Ganges made it relatively easy to divert flood-flows through inundation channels. In the peninsula, where the rainfall is scanty, the practice of trapping storm water in large tanks for domestic and agricultural purposes was widespread. In areas where a high groundwater table permitted lift irrigation, wells were common.

With the advent of the British rule in India and the liquidation of a large number of princely states many ancient irrigation works and water storage tanks were neglected and went into disrepair. In the initial period the British paid little attention to this problem. However, the problem of irrigation soon came to the fore because of the repeated menace of widespread famines that took toll of thousands and lay waste vast stretches of agricultural land, adversely affecting the land-revenue collection. Political expediency and self-interest compelled the Government to consider preventive steps against recurrence of famines. Major "protective irrigation works" were taken up in the Punjab, and a few in Andhra Pradesh, Uttar Pradesh and Bombay Presidency. However, with the progress in commercialization of agriculture, the concept of protective irrigation work was pushed into the background. The Government became more concerned with the financial results. Even in the case of irrigation works constructed initially as protective works, the productive aspect attained prominence. This inevitably led to changes in the principles of Irrigation Water Management. For example, in the Bombay Presidency, establishment of sugar factories was encouraged by the Government in Godavari and Pravara systems[3] ; most of the stored water was used in the upper reaches of the canals to cultivate sugarcane and the areas most liable to famine were, consequently deprived of water supply which was originally meant essentially for those areas.[4]

There was only a limited expansion in the area irrigated by wells which was traditionally the major source of irrigation in many parts. Systematic surveys of subsoil water were carried out in the 1930's in Uttar Pradesh and Punjab and a significant progress in tube-well irrigation was achieved in the semi-arid areas of the Punjab. The tube-well construction programme received a new stimulus during the 'Grow More Food Campaign' launched in 1943.

With the advent of economic planning in 1951, irrigation received a high priority to bring about the much needed increase in agricultural production. The major projects taken up to benefit dry tracks included Bhakra Nangal (Punjab), Chambal Complex (Rajasthan and Madhya Pradesh), Tungabhadra (Karnataka and Andhra Pradesh) and Mula and Khadakwasla (Maharashtra). The viability of the projects is judged, on the basis of benefit-cost ratio ; the benefit being represented by the difference in the value of total annual agricultural production less the cost of cultivation before and after the introduction of irrigation, and the cost equals the annual interest (put at 10 per cent per annum) on capital, depreciation and expenditure on maintenance and operation. Schemes with benefit-cost ratio of less than 1.5 are generally not considered. As a result, the projects in tracts with difficult terrain and/or drawing on river flows of low dependability could not satisfy the criterion set for the acceptance of the project. In the development of irrigation facilities, even in the semi-arid regions, stress was put on commercial farming. The problems of semi-subsistence farming that provided livelihood to thousands of peasant families were not given due consideration.

Irrigation management

Irrigation Management Systems in India differ from region to region ; they are shaped by the local conditions such as the nature and extent of water resources, the soil-climate complex and the terrain of the irrigated area. The larger irrigation projects in North India e.g. Western Yamuna Canal (Haryana), the Upper Bari Doab Canal (Punjab) drew their supplies from perennial snow-fed rivers, providing for year round irrigation. The areas served by these projects are flat and the soils mostly alluvial. Under these conditions it was not necessary to put any restrictions on the cropping pattern.

In Maharashtra, on the other hand large storages have to be built to impound the monsoon participation. Unlike Karnataka plateau, the Maharashtra plateau is very uneven, furrowed with streams and studded with remnant ranges and hills. This topography does not permit a large command area. Canals have to negotiate through undulating terrain to command sufficient culturable land. Soils vary greatly, almost from field to field, in depth and texture. In the low rainfall belt, the erratic nature of the monsoon results in a varying demand for canal water from rotation to rotation. Moreover, multiple and variable crop patterns are common in Maharashtra. Under such conditions it is necessary to enforce regulatory measures to ensure maximum utilization of water during the monsoon season ; to encourage the cultivation of food crops with low water requirements during winter season ; to reduce to a minimum, the utilization of water in summer, and particularly, to restrict the area under sugarcane. To achieve this, a complex system of water management (viz. Block system) was introduced in the Decan. However, as the Maharashtra Irrigation Commission (1962) noted, it created problems of delays, frictions and irritations and gave rise to undesirable practices.[5]

Regulatory measures became necessary on the storage-supported irrigation projects in the dry regions of the Southern States for reasons similar to those in Western Maharashtra. For example, in the Tungabhadra Project, the area under heavy irrigation had to be restricted, so as to extend its benefit to a larger area. In addition, the commanded area had uneven terrain and black and red soils. For these reasons, areas suitable for heavy irrigation had to be identified and set apart for paddy and sugarcane. Consequently localization, i.e., fixing the ayacut and earmarking areas for specified crops requiring heavy irrigation, light irrigation and perennial supplies was adopted. In reformulating the irrigation management policy one has to keep in view the wide variations in terrain, soil, climate, water resources and requirements in different parts of the country. The operational problems, particularly the factors that make it possible for the vested interests to tamper with and defeat the regulatory system have also to be taken into account.

Surface irrigations projects

In the development of surface irrigation facility the Government takes the major responsibility but cooperation of the farmers in the command area has to be ensured to achieve efficient irrigation, water distribution and utilization. The preparatory surveys, selection of the site,[6] the design and construction of the dam and appertenance structures, main canal and distribution channels up to the outlets serving a block of 40 to 80 hectares are executed by the Government. Within the block the cultivators are required to construct the water channels to water their fields. This involves capital expenditure and co-operation of neighbouring irrigators (at least 51 per cent of the irrigators in the command of the distributary must give consent to such work). Long drawn legal battles in land acquisition often hinder the work of construction of field channels. The maintenance of field channels is also the responsibility of the farmers.

In the execution of the irrigation project, the drainage needs are often under-estimated or given a low priority. In the older projects proper provision of drainage system has been alttogether lacking. Impeded drainage and waterlogged conditions are created due to interception of natural drainage lines by canals, roads, embankments, non-maintenance of natural drainage line in the command area and seepage from irrigation system. In addition construction of field drain system is not done in time leaving a missing link between the field and the trunk drain system. Due to the above factors, there are considerable losses, and wastage of the valuable water stored for the purpose of irrigation.

Water loss is caused through evaporation, absorption and percolation and the extent of water loss varies with the soil type and canal system. The water management division of the Ministry of Agriculture and Irrigation, Government of India noted that in sandy loam, the surface losses are to the extent of 3 to 5 cu.m. per sq.m. of wetted parameter. Observations on losses made in the Upper Bari Doab canal in Punjab revealed that about 50 per cent of the water released is lost in transit—through main canals and branches (20 per cent), distributaries (8 per cent) and field channels (22 per cent).[7] In Gujarat, it was estimated that about 45 per cent of the water released was lost in transit.[8] Similar is the experience in Rajasthan. (Evaporation 10 per cent, seepage in canal and distributaries 35 per cent, field channels 20 per cent). About 45 per cent of the total evaporation loss occurred in the two summer months, viz. April and May ;[9] if irrigation is restricted upto March heavy losses during the summer months can be avoided and the quantity of water available for irrigation can be augmented. In Maharashtra the clay content of soil is high and hence the seepage losses on Godavari and Nira Canals were noted to be around to 10 to 15 per cent.[10]

In most parts of the semi-arid tract nearly 50 per cent of the water is lost between the canal head and the field. In addition there is a considerable wastage at the field level due to leaky or faulty field channels, growth of reeds and grasses in the channels, and wasteful methods of irrigation. In Upper Bari Doab canal, it was reported that of the total water released the estimated loss due to improper water management at the field was as high as 25 to 27 per cent. Wastage in the field to the extent of 27 to 30 per cent was noted in Gujarat.[11] In Maharashtra the farmers often resort to over-watering due to the unreliability of the canal water supply. There is a tendency to take all the available water to bring the soil profile to field capacity to ensure that the plants survive any shortfall in the water supply in the immediate future. As a result there is not only a considerable waste of water but persistence of this practice entails the risk of raising the water-table to plant root level thus making the land uncultivable.

While shifting from dry to irrigated agriculture it is essential to complete the works of land levelling and land shaping. Since proper land shaping cannot be organized for small fragmented holdings, consolidation of holdings is essential for preparing the land for irrigation. This work is often not properly executed and consequently proper application of water is not possible. The variations in economic and physical conditions between farms, and the mixed cropping pattern make water-use planning a difficult exercise. As a result the farmers do not often receive water in adequate quantity and at proper time. However, the big farmers who have the capacity and proper connections resort to pilferage of water. Due to such leakages, over-use and wastage of water in the upper reaches, the cultivators at the tail-end are often left without any water.[12]

A serious problem faced in the irrigation command areas due to seepage and leakages and lack of proper drainage network is the problem of waterlogging and salination of land which often accompanies it, gradually making the fertile soils useless for agricultural operations. It is estimated that about 3 million hectares of land are affected by waterlogging in the arid and semi-arid tracts. The problem is quite serious in Punjab,[13] Haryana, Maharashtra, and Rajasthan. Some of the newer irrigation projects like Chambal (M.P. and Rajasthan) started facing serious problems of salinity in large areas within a few years of the commencement of irrigation.[14] Poor maintenance of the distributaries and drainage channels, over-watering, cultivation of crops demanding heavy irrigation on deep black soils, etc., accentuate this problem.

It is often viewed that these problems can be resolved by correcting technical defects and improving administrative efficiency. However, it must be noted that these deficiencies cannot be corrected in isolation as they are rooted in the very socio-economic system, The failures in irrigation management need to be traced to their roots—the property structure in the society. The ownership of the agricultural land in India is highly skewed so also is the command over capital resources, access to modern inputs and credit and the capacity to manoeuvre the irrigation resources impounded at public costs. The influential big landowners in league with the local government functionaries like canal inspectors and sectional officers can alter the time-table for water supply, pilfer water from the canal and divert water according to their interest.[15] So long as the hold of the powerful land owning sections on rural economy and polity is not challenged, efficient use of irrigation water cannot be effected.

Groundwater resources

In India, the development of groundwater resources has been left almost entirely to the private initiative. No scientific assessment of the total groundwater resources is available and it is estimated on the basis of thumb-rule. State governments support the programme of groundwater exploitation on private account through promotion of rural electrification and extension of credit through Land Development Banks. The large land owners are obviously in an advantageous position to use these facilities.[16] The number of irrigation wells recorded a considerable increase in the past two decades. The traditional methods of lifting water from dug well e.g. bullock drawn *mhot* (a large leather bag), Persian wheel, etc., are being largely replaced by power driven (oil or electricity) pumpsets. Power pump-operated tube wells, where water is directly lifted from the ground aquifer, also increased in number. Some stipulations regarding the distance between two wells are laid down before sanctioning a loan but on the whole no effective control is exercised on the location of wells. Consequently adverse effects on water-table are noted particularly where tube well irrigation is widespread. A tube well imposes external diseconomies among users of common ground resources due to its considerably larger radius of influence as compared with a dug well. The radius and area of influence of a tube well varies with soil type of the water bearing stratum. In fine sandy layers with some silt, the radius of influence varies between 30 m. and 90 m. while in coarse sandy and gravel layers without silt and clay the radius of influence is the largest (between 300 m. and 600 m.). In such soil layers, the area of influence may vary from 30 to 115 hectares. It was noted in a study in Gujarat that as a result of the growth in the number of tube wells, water-tables have receded. The small farmers who depended on traditional human/animal power operated devices, lost access to groundwater as traditional devices are incapable of lifting water from greater depths and the small farmers do not have the means to go in for electrically operated pumpsets.[17]

Unequal distribution of economic benefits

The large farmers are exploiting a social resource like sub-surface water, using public funds at the cost of the small farmers. Unless a definite policy regarding the private use of groundwater resources is worked out the consequences will be disastrous in the dry tracts of Central and South India. If the rate of water utilization exceeds the recouperation rate, the number of dry wells and abandoned wells will increase. In Maharashtra today a situation has arisen where groundwater is being used to irrigate sugarcane crop while the village poor are forced to go for miles in search for a pailful of drinking water during the summer months.

The access to water is not as overtly unequal in the case of surface irrigation as in the case of groundwater. On paper all the farmers in the irrigation command *have* access to canal water. However, in practice, various factors work in favour of the large landowner and against the small peasant. The larger farmers are in a position to effect the necessary land shaping, levelling and other developmental works, they can also afford to dig a well or install a tube well in the command area. Thereby they not only secure supplementary water but also make the source more dependable. They can afford to go in for capital intensive commercial agriculture, using supplementary inputs like fertilizers, pesticide and timely weeding (weeds become quite a menace in irrigated agriculture). They can grow high value crops and ensure higher yield per unit of land. Many of the middle and particularly the small farmers do not have the land and capital resources to reap the benefits of irrigated agriculture in the same way. And when canal water is not dependable, they do not even go in for irrigated agriculture. The gains of irrigated agriculture are, thus, heavily weighed in favour of the large land owners.[18] Under conditions of water scarcity and scramble for water, the large farmers are better equipped to secure water through pilferage and corrupt practices because of their political connections, social position and economic strength. Consequently the smaller farmers are at a further disadvantage —they do not even get their rightful share.

Steep rise in land prices is noted in the irrigated tracts[19] and it becomes impossible for the small farmer to get any additional land. They even tend to lease out their land to large land holders and are at times forced to sell their land. It is also observed that when an irrigation project is underway rich farmers from irrigated tract buy dry lands at low prices and capture the potentially high value lands.

Irrigation ensures certain increases in the *total* production but high income levels are achieved largely by the big landowners. With the spread of irrigation the gap between the large and small farmer and between irrigated and dry agriculture has widened. The social objectives like increased employment, improved nutritional standards for the toiling masses are not given any consideration in irrigation planning. Ameliorative measures are introduced through programmes like Small Farmer Development Agency, Marginal Farmer Development Agency, and Drought Prone Area Programmes. However, as the beneficiaries lack the basic *land* rasource the programmes have proved to be infructious.

Reorganization of irrigation water management

In view of the need to achieve better utilization of irrigation water and for achieving freedom from hunger and malnutrition for the mass of toiling agricultural population, the management of water in arid and semi-arid tracts has to be drastically changed.

In arid and semi-arid regions water is the most scarce resource ; through careful conservation and utilization it can prove to be a life saving resource. The problem needs to be given high priority in India in view of the fact that considerable tracts of the country are semi-arid and the situation in some of these tracts notably Maharashtra is fast deteriorating. The benefits of irrigation are extremely unevenly distributed among the different sections of the landowners, Water resources are being used up in large quantities to cultivate crops like sugarcane that demand heavy irrigation,[20] whereas the orientation of the irrigation policy in semi-arid areas must be to attain *stability of yield on all farms* through protective irrigation. To achieve this there is an urgent need (A) to improve the effectivity of the present irrigation works and (B) to plan for equitable distribution of irrigation water.

(A) A comprehensive plan for improvement in the existing irrigation works has to be formulated to include (1) plan of afforestation and protection of catchment area so that the sources of irrigation are protected and the rate of siltation of reservoirs is reduced.[21] (2) Plan for improvement of canal network to check siltation, seepage and evaporation losses. Appropriate methods of lining of canal and distributaries will have to be selected in view of the site conditions. (3) Proper arrangements for drainage network. (4) Maintenance of canal and drains is most important but much neglected in India. Hence adequate provision for proper repair and maintenance has to be made.

(B) Even if the storage and delivery system is improved through the above measures and increase in the water availability is achieved by 60 to 100 per cent, the problem of proper use of water would remain intractable due to the individual property interests. Unless measures are found to overcome these obstructions, optimum use of the scarce water resources cannot be realised. For achieving rational use of surface water it is necessary to prepare a comprehensive plan for a river basin as a whole. Within the State, planning on water-shed and sub-watershed basis has to be undertaken. For each project, the Command Area Land Authority should be assigned the responsibility for works of land shaping, levelling, field channels and drainage network in the command area.[22] In order to ensure that private property interests do not hamper the overall planning, the Government should take over all the land in the command area on long term lease and all the works of development necessary for irrigated agriculture should be executed. Provision for all the families displaced due to the construction of reservoir, canals, etc., should be made through *allotment* of plots in the irrigated command on the condition that they personally work on the land allotted. Farmers' Associations for compact blocks (say of 40-50 hectares) can be formed to take the responsibility of irrigation management at the field level.[23] Irrigation systems cannot function satisfactorily unless farmers take up the field level functions that are performed today by the paid Government officials. Equitable distribution of water cannot be achieved unless farmers develop a high level of community organization and self-discipline. For regulation and operation of water distribution within the block the Association can employ trained local personnel. Today individual farmers spend considerable amount to pursue the *patkari* (overseer of canal) to release water out of turn and operate at cross purposes. Crop planning in view of the soil conditions, water availability and water requirements of different crops will have to be made for compact blocks so that supply of water can be made in a regulated manner. Measured water through furrow irrigation can help increase the effective use of water. Provision for training in proper cultivation of irrigated crops and supply of input on *time* (fertilizers, seed, etc.) will help increase the return per unit of water.

In arid regions, carriage of water through pipelines and trickle irrigation may have to be resorted to. Selection of crops that use water more efficiently e.g., barley, HYV wheat, sunflower, sorghum, bajra, beans, melon, pineapple would help attain relatively higher yield per unit of water used. Cultivation practices, e.g. cultivating crops in rows on the contour, thorough weed control, use of crop residue as mulch to reduce evaporation losses, etc., can improve the performance. [24]

For planning the use of groundwater resources systematic quantitative assessment of these resources is a prerequisite. Considering the rate of replenishment, judicious use of groundwater resources has to be planned in regions where rainfall is low and uncertain and geological conditions are unfavourable (e.g. the Deccan Plateau).

Conjunctive use of surface and sub-surface water has to be planned keeping in view the problems of rising water-table, waterlogging and drainage, in different command areas. [25] An integrated approach that plans for full use of canal water when available, use of groundwater in period of low canal water supplies and exclusive use of groundwater in uneven terrains is necessary. Combination of flow and sub-surface irrigation is an ideal solution for the problem of waterlogging. Exploitation of groundwater has to be regularized keeping in view the region-specific characteristics of rainfall, temperature, soil type and existence of surface water sources. It is necessary to place all the water resources under the control of one agency that should prepare a comprehensive water-use plan and provide technical advice so as to achieve optimum returns per unit of water used.

CONCLUSION

The strategy for agricultural development and irrigation water management in India has been production-oriented and relied mainly on the so-called "progressive farmers" ; this helped strengthen the dominant groups within the agricultural sector and increased economic polarisation, and marginalization of increasing numbers of working cultivators. Even though laws embodying socially desirable goals were enacted they were not implemented (e.g., land reform measures) as they were contrary to the interest of the dominant groups. Even when the small peasants come within the irrigation command area the threshold level for economic return to water (or fertilizer) is soon reached because of a large number of constraints e.g. small size of land holding, lack of proper contacts to ensure timely irrigation water supply, access to credit, technical knowhow and market information, etc.

To incorporate the vast masses of peasant workers in irrigated agriculture, to eradicate hunger and deprivation it is necessary to change the current development strategy. In the new strategy, irrigated land must be provided to all the working agricultural families (with or without land) from the area submerged due to the construction of the reservoir and the irrigable command area by rational allotment of irrigated lands. All the infrastructural facilities needed for the realization of the full production potential of irrigated agriculture must be provided on the basis of shared capitalization rather than monopolistic appropriation (as happens today). Farmers' Associations should take the responsibility of management of irrigation water distribution, crop planning and other agro-based activities and make appropriate investments in technical services, social facilities and agro-processing, etc. Sustained and organized efforts of agricultural labourers and peasant organizations can alone make a move towards such a reorganization of agriculture in the irrigated command areas. Steps taken in this direction will help resolve the conflict between those who lose their lands due to submergence and those who receive the benefit from the irrigation project. It will help remove absentee land ownership that is widespread today and secure the right of the tenant cultivator. This will help curb the power of the sugar barons and cotton kings and make it possible for the toiling masses to assert their democratic rights, the right to life with human dignity, and creativity.

FOOTNOTES

1. Agricultural efficiency for the present study is measured as follows :—
Let E_r denote the yield-efficiency of crop r in any district.
$E_{r_1} = \frac{Y_{r_1}}{Y_R} \times 100$ where Y_{r_1} indicates the yield of crop r_1 per acre for any aerial unit and Y_R the yield of the same crop for the country as a whole. The yield efficiency of each of the crops is weighted by its proportionate share of lands to the total cropped area in a district. The agricultural efficiency of a particular district may be measured as follows :—
$$Y_a = \frac{E_{r_1}.\ C_{r_1} + E_{r_2}.\ C_{r_2} + E_{r_3}\ C_{r_3} + \ldots}{C_{r_1} + C_{r_2} + C_{r_3} + \ldots\ldots\ldots\ldots}$$
Where Y_a indicates agricultural efficiency of the aerial unit, while E_{r_1}, E_{r_2}, E_{r_3}, E_{r_4} ... etc. denote the yield efficiency of crops r_1, r_3, r_2, ... etc. and C_{r_1}, C_{r_2}. C_{r_3} . . . etc. indicate the proportionate share of lands under crops r_1, r_2, r_2, to the total sown area in each district.
The Index of agricultural efficiency is calculated for each of the districts of the micro-agricultural regions. The indices thus obtained are arranged into seven groups at suitable class-intervals and ranked as below :—

Efficiency Index	*Efficiency Ranks*
Above 160	Very very high
140-160	Very high
120-140	High
100-120	Moderately high
80-100	Low
60-80	Very low
Below 60	Very very low

Economic Regionalization of India : Problems and Approaches, Census of India, 1961, Monograph Series Vol. I, No. 8, Dr. (Miss) P. Sen Gupta and Dr. (Mrs.) Galina Sdasyuk, 1968, p. 110.
2. *Development of Drought-prone Areas*, N.K. Jaiswal and N.V. Kolte, National Institute of Rural Development, Hyderabad, 1980, pp. 76-80.
3. *Drought in Maharashtra 1972 : A Case for Irrigation Planning*, Sulabha Brahme, Gokhale Institute of Politics and Economics, Pune, 1983, p. 32.

4. *Economic Aspects of Irrigation Water Management* (1967), in "Writing and Speeches of Prof. D.R. Gadgil on Economic and Political Problems", (ed.) Sulabha Brahme, Gokhale Institute of Politics and Economics, Pune, 1972, p. 100.
5. *Maharashtra State Irrigation Commission, Report,* Government of Maharashtra, Nagpur, 1962, pp. 119-123.
6. During the last thirty years of irrigation planning, it has been experienced that vested interests and political considerations have often interfered with the decision regarding the dam site ; this has led to indecision in relation to many of the projects vitally important for providing protective irrigation to dry tracts ; it also has meant that the best site was not always selected.
7. *Impact of Medium Irrigation Projects on Environment,* Rajasthan, Operations Research Group, Baroda, 1980, p. 8 : 44.
8. Estimated Water Loss in Various Irrigation Distribution Systems in Gujarat.

Irrigation system	Percentage loss in			
	Canal	Distri-butaries	Water courses	Wastage in the field
(i) Entire system unlined	15	7	22	27
(ii) Only canals lined	4	7	25	30
(iii) Canals and distributaries lined	4	2	26	32
(iv) Entire system lined	4	2	6	42

Lined canal effects substantial saving of water but entails an expenditure four to five times higher than the unlined canal. The decision regarding lining has to be taken in view of the estimated losses in transit, the risk of damage due to water logging as against the cost of lining.

Irrigation Agriculture in Gujarat : *Problems and Prospects,* V.N. Asopa, B.L. Tripathy, Indian Institute of Management, Ahmedabad, 1975, pp. 37-43.

For comparative data on Conveyance efficiency, see *The Economics of Irrigation,* Ian Carruthers, Colin Clark, Liverpool University Press, Liverpool, 1983, pp. 88-89.

9. *Impact of Medium Irrigation Projects on Environment, Rajasthan,* op. cit., p. 8 : 45-51.
10. *Report of the Irrigation Commission,* Vol. II, 1972, Ministry of Irrigation and Power, New Delhi, p. 244.
11. *Irrigation Agriculture in Gujarat,* op. cit., pp. 42-44.

12. "Even though the Pravara canals were designed to cover a culturable area of 157,000 acres, the area actually irrigated covers 60,000 acres only and that too only in the upper reaches of the canal, leaving the remaining area at the tail end with comparatively little benefit of irrigation. On the Nira Left Bank canal assured irrigation is spread over 213,000 acres leaving the tail end with 106,000 acres practically without any irrigation." *Maharashtra State Irrigation Commission, Report*, op. cit., pp. 46-47.

13. Punjab had the largest area affected by water logging which was estimated to be approximately 1.09 million hectares in 1958. Since then a number of drainage schemes have been carried out and water-logging brought under control. *Report of the Irrigation Commission*, Ministry of Irrigation and Power, New Delhi, 1972, Vol. I, p. 309.

14. *Report of the Committee of Ministers on Underutilization of Created Irrigation Potential*, Ministry of Irrigation and Power, Government of India, New Delhi, 1973, p. 139.

15. *Interim Report on Socio-Economic Evaluation of Mula Irrigation Project*, Ashok K. Mitra and P.V. Purandare, Gokhale Institute of Politics and Economics, Pune, 1982 (typed report), pp. 41-44.

16. (a) Construction of a well and installation of pumpsets involves sizable investment. Besides, there is uncertainty and risk in going in for investment in dug well. The capacity to bear risk and incur investment increases with the size of holding.

In a Micro-level Study in Anantpur District of Andhra Pradesh the following results were obtained.

	Size of holding (hectare)				
	Below 0.4	0.4 to 2	2 to 4	4 to 8	Above 8
Percentage of land-holdings reporting private sources of irrigation (well irrigation)	14.5	21.6	40.4	50.6	48.3

Farm Structure and Resource-use in Drought-prone Area, Vol. I, K.V. Patel, National Institute of Bank Management, Bombay, 1978, pp. 27-28.

(b) In five districts of Maharashtra *viz.*, Pune, Ahmednagar, Sangli, Satara, Solapur,—the major portion of which lies in semi-arid zone, the well-irrigation facility as noted in the Agricultural Census (1976-77) increased from 12 per cent in the case of small farmers to 41 per cent in the case of larger farmers. The distribution was as follows :

Size of operational holding (hectare)	Per cent land holders	Percentage share in total irrigated area	Percentage of land holders with well irrigation
Upto 1	29.2	6.3	12.6
1— 3	32.5	25.8	19.7
3— 5	15.8	21.5	27.7
5— 10	14.9	27.3	31.8
10 and above	7.6	19.1	40.8

Report of Agricultural Census, 1976-77, Maharashtra State, Part I and II, Government of Maharashtra, Bombay, 1980, pp. 128, 139, 150, 161, 172.

It must be noted that the large cultivators (with land holding above 10 hectares) form only about 10 per cent of the total agriculturists but own more than 40 per cent of the cultivated land and have a still larger share in farm investments (e.g., tubewell, tractor, etc.), whereas the small cultivators (less than 2 hectares of land holding) who are handicapped in a variety of ways form 40 to 50 per cent of the agriculturists in the dry agricultural zone.

17. *Irrigation Agriculture in Gujarat*, op. cit., pp. 69-70.

18. (a) *India's Green Revolution : Economic Gains and Political Costs*, Francine R. Frankel, Princeton University Press, Princeton, 1971, p. 39.

(b) *Seeds of Plenty and Seeds of Want : Social and Economic Implications of Green Revolution*, Andrew Pearse, Clarendon Press, Oxford, 1980, pp. 106-119.

(c) A Survey carried out in Niphad taluka, Nasik district, Maharashtra State in 1976 in a village where canal irrigation is extensive and 63 per cent of the net cropped area is irrigated, following results were obtained :

Size category of farmer	Average cultivated area per family (hectare)	Gross income per hectare (Rs.)	Net Agricultural income per family in 1976 (Rs.)
Small	1.0	1250	377
Medium	4.0	2640	4697
Large	12.0	4665	24465

Differential Impact of Agricultural Development : A Micro-study in Maharashtra State, Sulabha Brahme, Gokhale Institute of Politics and Economics, Pune, 1979 (typed), p. 468.

(d) In a study in Rajasthan it was noted that in a newly irrigated village near Kota the percentage increase in income between 1968-69 and 1971-72 was as follows :

Size of holding (hectare)	Percentage increase in income
Upto 6	9.3
6 to 15	11.9
Above 15	50.1

Social and Economic Implications of Green Revolution : A Case Study of Kota District, a Global—2 Report (mimeo), Bapna, S.L., Agro-Economic Research Centre, Vallabh Vidyanagar, 1973.

19. *Seeds of Plenty and Seeds of Want*, op. cit., pp. 114-116.

20. In Maharashtra State the area under sugarcane formed about 1.5 per cent of the total cultivated area and 13.5 per cent of the gross irrigated area in 1979-80. Sugarcane however consumed as much as 60 per cent of the water used for irrigation.

21. The effective life of storage reservoirs is getting reduced because of the high rate of sedimentation. The dead storage capacity is based on the assumption of sedimentation rates varying from about 14,287 cu. m. to 71,435 cu. m. per annum for every hundred sq. km of catchment area. Normally the life-span of a project is assumed to be hundred years. However, studies in recent years indicate that the observed rates of siltation are much higher than the rates initially assumed. Hence the urgent need to protect the catchment area through afforestation and other measures.

Siltation of Selected Reservoirs

Reservoir	Annual rate of siltation (in acre ft.)		Silt index (in acre ft. per 100 sq. miles of catchment area)	
	Assumed	Observed	Assumed	Observed
Bhakra (Punjab)	23000	33745	105	154
Tungabhadra (Karnataka)	9796	41058	90	382
Nizamsagar (Andhra Pradesh)	530	8725	6	104
Ukai (Gujarat)	7448	21758	31	105

Report of Irrigation Commission, 1972, Vol. I, op. cit., pp. 325-326.

22. *A Charter for Land*, B.B. Vohra in "Green Revolution : The Unfinished Task", Centre for the Study of Social Change, Calcutta, 1974, pp. 55-63.

23. Experience of the Pravaranagar Cooperative Sugar Factory (Ahmednagar District) operating successfully the distribution of water during summer months in all the villages within the jurisdiction of the factory is a pointer to the potential of local management, *Writings and Speeches of Prof. Gadgil*, op. cit., p. 105.
24. *More Water for Arid Lands : Promising Technologies and Research Opportunities*, National Academy of Sciences, Washington D.C., 1974, pp. 123-125.
25. *Maharashtra State Irrigation Commission, Report*, op. cit., pp. 144-146.

25

WATER MANAGEMENT IN ARID AND SEMI-ARID TRACTS IN INDIA
Prescriptive Aspects

Gurdev Singh Gosal

INTRODUCTION

Among the resources necessary for the development of arid and semi-arid tracts in the world, water plays a pivotal role, especially in the promotion and stabilisation of an agricultural economy. The task of water management in such areas hence, assumes an importance of its own kind. Water being scarce but a vital necessity, the major management problems in these tracts relate essentially to making the most effective use of the available water and developing suitable practices and techniques whereby production may be optimised under different soil, terrain and climatic conditions within the wide limits of the characteristics of these tracts. In view of the area to area and locality to locality (even field to field) variations in such resources, suggestions for the solution of these problems would have to be location specific. A scientific and judicious treatment of problems concerning water management in these areas, thus, calls for, among other things, a comprehensive assessment of the topographic, soil, climatic and groundwater resources, apart from the existing agricultural practices, at micro, meso and macro spatial scales as a pre-requisite. A remedial prescription can only follow diagnosis of the problem. The suggestions /observations made with regard to water-management in this paper are restricted to dry/semi-dry areas in tropical or sub-tropical latitudes in India, more especially the central and south-western Punjab where considerable amount of experimental research has been done by the agricultural scientists. The water management problems of cold deserts at high altitudes/latitudes are of a different nature.

Although the anxiety to utilise, gainfully, every drop of available water for optimising production is common in all arid and semi-arid tracts, ths strategies of water management in areas of irrigated and rain fed agriculture within them are different.

WATER MANAGEMENT IN IRRIGATION FARMING TRACTS

The discussion on problems relating to water management in areas of irrigation farming, and the solutions therefore, as discussed here are based mostly on the experiences of central and southern parts of the Punjab state. Some of the important issues relating to water management in these tracts are as follows (B.S. Sandhu, 1982, pp. 2-3).

(i) In central districts of Punjab, where, alongwith canal irrigation facilities, tube well irrigation based on large underground water reserves (of good quality) has been developed extensively during Post-Independence years. Here one finds a general tendency among the farmers to over-irrigate the crops resulting in a wasteful expense of the costly water resources. In the southwestern areas, on the other hand, which are either at the tail end of the canals or have poor quality underground water or both, the problem is generally of inadequate supply of irrigation water. Apparently, there is ample scope for developing optimum irrigation schedules especially for the major crops, not only for improving productivity but also for affecting economy in the use of water. Optimisation of canal water distribution in relation to irrigation needs of crops and regions is another important problem deserving immediate attention in these tracts.

(ii) In view of the distinctly higher remunerativeness and stable yields of paddy, there is a growing tendency to bring more and more land under rice cultivation. In this process, even highly sandy soil areas which are susceptible to large percolation losses of water are being increasingly put under this crop Thus unproductive and excessively high seepage losses, along with associated nutritional disorders occur on these soils, posing a serious problem.

(iii) As a consequence of high incidence of over-irrigation of crops and the prevailing slab-system of electricity charges for tube-well irrigation, the annual water drawal from the shallow acquifers of the central parts of the state seems to be in excess of the annual water recharge. As a result, the watertable in these areas has started showing signs of going down. This situation, if allowed to continue over a long period of time, is likely to seriously challenge the shallow tube-well irrigation resources which are the backbone of green revolution in this tract.

(iv) Losses of water arising from percolation in water courses and water application in the fields are alarming (20—40 per cent). How to reduce these losses through economically viable measures constitutes a significant area of investigation.

(v) Management of poor quality underground water in conjunction with or without canal water for crop production with sustained soil productivity is a major problem of the arid tracts of southwestern Punjab.

(vi) There are pockets of areas where water supplies are limited. How to make the best use of the limited water resources in such pockets is an issue which needs to be examined comprehensively.

(vii) Irrigation resource management under conditions of high water-table, soil salinity, and alkalinity, and sand-dune infested terrain is quite different from that for normal situations. There is a need to develop suitable water management practices for such problematic conditions.

(viii) In some areas water-table has been rising at an alarming rate. There is a need to trace the genesis of this phenomenon and find a remedial measure for it.

(ix) During the rainy season, frequent and excessive flooding of crops is a recurring hazard, the adverse effects of which should be investigated and removed as far as possible.

(x) Millions of tons of surplus crop straws are annually burnt by the farmers, polluting the atmospheric environment of the region. Positive and gainful use of these straws in edaphic environment, irrigation management and crop production needs to be investigated.

(xi) Application-oriented basic information relating to soil-water-plant-environment relationships, water and solar energy budgets of crop community and growth modelling in relation to water supplies is generally lacking. Effort should be initiated to cover this informational gap.

RECOMMENDATIONS FOR SOLVING SOME OF THE ABOVE PROBLEMS EXPERIENCED IN AREAS OF IRRIGATION FARMING

Irrational irrigation practices not only result in wasteful expense of costly and scarce water but also become instrumental in bringing a variety of damages and distortions in the quality of soil. Therefore, there is a need to evolve efficient and effective methods of using surface and ground water for irrigational purposes with minimum possible wastage. This urgency is becoming all the more pressing when the rapidly increasing water needs of the area are viewed against limiting scope of generating new water supplies.

Some promising approaches to minimise at-farm water losses and to increase water use efficiency are : (i) the development of optimum irrigation schedules for crops, (ii) uniform application of water in the field by suitable irrigation methods, (iii) lining of fields channels for reducing seepage losses and (iv) appropriate management of surplus crop residues for reducing losses due to evaporation, (B.S. Sandhu and S.S. Prihar, 1983, p. 1). In addition the consolidation of landholdings and the levelling of the arable land play a role of great importance in making optimum use ofwater and avoiding loss of water in irrigation farming. The Department of Soils of the Punjab Agricultural University has developed optimum irrigation schedules for several crops which economise water. These new (improved) irrigation practices are included in the recommended package of practices for *Rabi* (winter) and *Kharif* (summer) crops. These practices ensure high crop yields and also effect 20 to 60 per cent saving in irrigation water.

Irrigation Schedules of Crops

An optimum irrigation schedule is that time-sequence of minimum irrigations of appropriate depth to a crop which ensures optimum yield and permits minimum damage to the soil. Another favourable feature of these schedules is their non-monetary character and easy understanding for adoption by the farmers. For highlighting the significance of this recommendation in concrete terms, irrigation schedules of some of the major crops recommended for the Punjab areas are reproduced below (B.S. Sandhu and S.S. Prihar, 1983, pp. 1-8).

Wheat

Investigations have sown that a post-sowing irrigation depth of 6.8 cm is ideal for wheat on most of the Punjab soils. This depth also holds good for most of the other crops. The following irrigation time-table (given in Table 25.1) has been devised for timing irrigations to wheat sown on sandy loam or heavier soils after a heavy (10 cm) pre-sowing irrigation. The first irrigation should be relatively light and given about three weeks after sowing of the October crop and after four weeks to crops sown later. The subsequent irrigations are determined by the date of sowing.

A comparison of irrigation time-table mentioned in Trable 25.1 with the prevailing practice of applying 5 or 6 irrigations at specific stages showed that the new practice saves, on an average, two irrigations without any reduction in grain yield.

Many farmers tend to irrigate the crop even more frequently, applying 7 to 8 irrigations. Apparently in the over-irrigated areas the adoption of new irrigation time-table can save enough water to increase area under irrigated wheat by another 20-25 per cent. In case water supplies are limited, the optimum timing for one irrigation is at crown-rooting, for two irrigations crown-rooting and early booting and for three irrigations crown-rooting, tillering and grain-filling stages of the crop.

TABLE 25.1 : **Irrigation time-table for wheat***

Date of sowing	Second irrigation (7.5 cm)	Third irrigation (7.5 cm)	Fourth irrigation (7.5 cm)
	Days after the previous irrigation		
November 1—7	36	43	26
November 8—21	41	38	25
November 22 to December 5	44	30	15
December 6—20	35	25	15
December 21 to January 4	30	20	14
January 5—15	28	18	12

Note : 1. Advance the date of first irrigation on light soils and delay it to some extent on heavy paddy soils.

2. The indicated intervals for irrigation can be varied by 2 or 3 days on either side.
3. For each cm. of rain, increase the interval for the next irrigation by 5 days up to the end of January and 2 days afterwards.
4. If the date of irrigation falls around 15th March for crop sown before December 5, give a heavy irrigation of 10—12 cm. No further irrigation would be required.
5. For the crop sown after December 5, continue irrigation upto April 10. If, however, an irrigation falls in the first week of April, make it slightly heavier and no further irrigation should be required.
6. During March and April care should be taken not to irrigate on windy days to avoid lodging.
7. The time-table is not applicable if :
   (a) the crop has been sown without giving a heavy pre-sowing irrigation or
   (b) a hard impervious layer of lime concretions (*kankar*) or clay lies in the soil profile within one metre from the surface or
   (c) the soil is excessively sandy or saline.

Gram

In irrigated areas, the crop should be sown after heavy pre-sowing irrigation This practice permits deeper rooting and greater utilization of profile-stored water and, thus, reduces the

* B.S. Sandhu and S.S. Prihar : *Irrigation Scheduling to Crops in Punjab*, Department of Soils, Punjab Agricultural University, Ludhiana (1983), pp. 2-3.

post-sowing irrigation needs. This crop generally needs only one post sowing irrigation which should fall between mid-December and end-January depending upon the sowing time and rainfall. But in no case, this irrigation should be given earlier than 4 weeks after sowing. In a year of low initial profile-stored moisture and/or excessively dry season, another irrigation during the later half of February may be desirable. Excessive irrigation increases vegetative growth and depresses grain yield.

Toria, Sarson and Raya

These crops should be sown after a heavy (10-12 cm) pre-sowing irrigation. During post-sowing period, these crops generally need only one irrigation 3-4 weeks after sowing. If growing season is excessively dry, another irrigation around flowering stage may be given. This second irrigation can be advanced if there is a threat of frost. Compared with the earlier practice, the new irrigation recommendation saves 2-3 irrigations, but gives as much grain yield of raya.

Rice

Because of its high water requirements, the crop makes a heavy drain on water resources of the state. Farmers tend to continuously maintain standing water in rice fields. This practice is conducive to large deep percolation losses of water, particularly on coarse textured soils.

Recent experiments have shown that on non-saline sandy loam and heavier soils, the continuous submergence is desirable for only three weeks after transplanting (see Table 25.2). There-

TABLE 25.2 : **Effect of irrigation practice on irrigation water use and paddy yield (4 years' average) of rice on a sandy loam**

Irrigation practice	No. of irrigations applied (each of 7 cm)	Average paddy yield (Kg./acre)
Continuous submergence	25	2204
Irrigation applied 2 days after soaking of standing water	16	2212

Source : B.S. Sandhu and S.S. Prihar, 1983, p. 5.

after, the crop should be irrigated two days after the ponded water has soaked into the soil. Irrigation should be stopped 2 weeks before harvest for uniform and early ripening of the crop. Compared to continuous soil submergence, the new irrigation practice saves, on the average, 8-9 irrigations without reduction in paddy yield. Conversely, the practice ensures 20 per cent more area under rice with the same irrigation supplies.

Sugar Cane

The period April to June is very crucial for the growth of sugar cane. Both atmospheric (aerial) and soil environments during this period are excessively hot and dry for its optimum growth, hence the crop needs irrigations at 7-12 days intervals depending upon the severity of the prevailing weather. It is shown in Table 25.3 that as compared with 4 irrigations which is the usual practice of farmers, 9 irrigations during this period gave 35 q./acre (14 per cent) more cane yield.

TABLE 25.3 : **Mean (3 years) cane yield of sugar cane on a sandy loam soil as affected by irrigation during mid-April to June-end**

Irrigations applied	Mean cane yield (q./acre)
4	246
6	266
9	281

During the rainy season, frequency of irrigation is adjusted according to rainfall. If fields are subject to prolonged flooding, excess water should be drained, if possible. During winter, the crop should be irrigated at monthly intervals. To save the crop from frost, one irrigation is applied around mid-December and another in the first week of January.

Straw mulching of sugar cane crop is a very useful practice. It increases crop yields by 15-25%. The practice also economises 2-4 irrigations (B.S. Sandhu, 1982, p. 48). The beneficial effect of straw mulch on growth and cane yield of sugar cane is primarily attributed to considerable reduction in maximum soil temperature and reduced evaporation losses.

Groundnut

Groundnut is mostly a rainfed crop. It is sown with the start of the monsoons in July. Only about 20% of its sown area is irrigated. Investigations have shown, however, that crop sown after a pre-sowing irrigation in the third week of June gives 200-250 kg./acre more pod yield than that sown in July. Thus, wherever irrigation facilities are available, groundnut should be sown during the second half of June. During a normal rainy season in the central districts of Punjab, the crop generally requires two irrigations, one at pegging stage and the other at pod formation stage as is shown in Table 25.4. Where only one irrigation is available it should be applied at pod formation to June-sown and at pegging to the July-sown crop. But under low rainfall conditions, particularly in Bhatinda and Ferozepur districts, the crop may need one more irrigation. Another irrigation a few days before the harvest not only facilitates the recovery of pods, but also serves as a pre-sowing irrigation for the subsequent wheat or raya crop.

TABLE 25.4 : **Effect of post-sowing irrigation (mean 3 years) on pod yield of groundnut (Variety M-45)**

Irrigation practice	Mean pod yield (Kg./acre)	
	June-sown	July-sown
1 No irrigation	795	437
2 One irrigation at pegging	839	704
3 Two irrigations, one at pegging and the second at pod formation	1134	807
4 Three irrigations, one at flowering, second at pegging and the third at pod formation	994	784
Mean	941	683

Note : June-sown crop was seeded with a pre-sowing irrigation (B.S. Sandhu and S.S. Prihar, 1983, p. 7).

Savings in electricity and diesel consumption

As compared to traditional irrigation practices, new irrigation schedules bring about considerable savings in irrigation and energy costs. Area under irrigated wheat and irrigated rice is around 65 and 30 lac acres, respectively, in Punjab. Among irrigation sources, electric tube-wells, diesel tube-wells and canals roughly meet 25, 35 and 40 per cent irrigation needs of these crops. Assuming that about 50 per cent of the area under these crops are over-irrigated, the adoption of improved irrigation schedules on these areas would save 1,114 lac KWH of electricity and 346 lac litres of diesel. The saving in diesel alone would be worth Rs. 11 crores. These savings will further increase if improved water technology is adopted for other crops also. The saved water should be used for irrigating additional area. It is estimated that if new irrigation practices are followed, the existing irrigation supplies are sufficient to grow wheat and rice on an additional area of 9 and 4 lac acres, respectively.

Irrigation scheduling as a part of the process of water management in regions of irrigation farming is, therefore, a very promising area of research directed toward economising use of water on existing irrigated farmland and extending irrigation to additional areas, improving crop yields, saving of electricity and diesel, and protecting the soils against damages of various kinds.

Any amount of canal water found in excess of needs as a result of judicious exercise of irrigation scheduling in the central tracts of Punjab may be released for areas at the tall-ends of the canals in the arid south-western parts of the state where inadequate supply of irrigation water is a chronic problem. In areas of tube-well irrigation, where as a result of over-irrigation the water table had started going down, irrigation scheduling can help stop that trend.

Other measures

The desirability of constructing field channels in the irrigated areas covered under the Rajasthan Canal Project has been emphasized in a recent study (T.K. Roy, 1983). The main advantage of having field channels is that it reduces the loss of water occurring as a result of seepage, evaporation and uneven watering of fields. In some cases there may be uncontrolled watering resulting in some portions receiving excess water while the other portions not receiving any water. The amount of water saved by the construction of field channels as compared to field to field irrigation depends upon several factors like soil, level of the fields being irrigated enroute, length, alignment levels, soil of field channels and so on. All these factors make a quantitative assessment of losses varying in a wide range. It may even go up to 50%. But assuming a minimum saving in water of 10% due to construction of field channels, the benefit-cost ratio (in Rajasthan Canal Command Area) would be 1.68 (T.K. Roy, 1983, p. 105) which is very favourable.

The lining of field channels will further reduce considerably any loss of water due to seepage and will help taking water to the farthest fields in the area for irrigation. With a view to meeting the ends of social justice the costs of irrigation water should be uniform, irrespective of the distance of the fields/farms of the canals or its distributaries (also see E.J. Vander Velde, Jr., 1971). The lining of the Bhakra canal in Punjab has resulted in saving a lot of water which otherwise would have been lost due to seepage. This has enabled the canals to cover more areas in the arid tracts of the region for irrigational purposes.

Similarly, the use of underground pipes, instead of open surface channels, in tubewell irrigation areas may help conserve limited water resources by eliminating water losses resulting from evaporation and seepage (see also Leonard M. Cantor, 1967, pp. 51-2).

As has been illustrated with specific examples, the practice of straw mulching in areas of limited irrigation facilities in dry and semi-dry tracts has its own potentialities in conserving moisture for better crop performance.

Lastly, cropping patterns may be dovetailed with the availability of irrigation water and moisture present in the soil. Crops which require less water at critical stages of growth and can give higher yields per unit of water and area vis-a-vis per unit of time, may be encouraged.

WATER MANAGEMENT IN AREAS OF RAINFED AGRICULTURE IN ARID AND SEMI-ARID TRACTS

The problems of water-Management in areas of rainfed agriculture in the arid and semi-arid tracts are far more challenging than those of irrigated farming. Here farming practices become exceedingly strenuous even for achieving modest results. It is, in fact, a grim struggle for survival. Most of the suggestions on water management in dry and semi-dry tracts of rainfed agriculture in northwestern India have come from the research centres at Hissar (Haryana) and Jodhpur (Rajasthan). The utter inadequacy of rainfall and the highly variable occurrence of the monsoons both in terms of times and space, cause widespread distress, which apart from limiting the attainable potential of crop production, results in almost complete crop failures in two out of five years. However, based on work done at the two centres, suitable crop varieties and agro-techniques have been identified. Some of the techniques which hold promise for improving the yield of dry land crops in this region are given below (see Ranjodh Singh and S.S. Prihar, 1978, pp. 478-80).

Moisture conservation

Soil moisture in the seeding zone is the most critical factor under low rainfall conditions and the following cultural practices form an essential input of management :

(i) Increasing moisture availability by bunding of individual fields, preferably on contours.

(ii) Inter-row water harvesting carried out by making ridges and furrows on contours has been found to be a useful practice. It ensures more infiltration and uniform storage of moisture in the seed zone. The ridger-seeder developed by the Hissar Centre forms ridges and furrows and plants the crop in paired rows on ridges in one operation.

(iii) Initial tillage should be carried before the usual onset of rains for efficient absorption of rainfall in the soil.

(iv) Interculture operations, like mulch formation, after the effective rainfall are essential to minimise evaporation losses.

Other agronomic practices

(i) One of the major reasons of poor yields in drylands is the sub-optimum plant population. The problem has been solved to a certain extent by planting *kharif* crops on ridges and the *rabi* crops in furrows, and these operations can be done with the use of an implement called lister-seeder which has been developed at the Hissar Centre.

(ii) Consistent with the availability of moisture in the soil and the prevailing characteristics of land, soil and farm practices, suitable crops and crop sequence should be decided upon carefully. *Bajra* (pearl millet), *jowar* and *moong* are the important crops under normal low rainfall conditions. *Jowar* and *moong* crops are more drought resistant and perform better than *bajra* under late rainfall conditions. Transplanting of *bajra* has particularly shown promise under such conditions. Moisture in the seed-zone is more critical during the *rabi*, and it is recommended that the selection of crops be made on the basis of soil type and rainfall conditions during the preceding *kharif* season as given in Table 25.5.

TABLE 25.5 : **Soil type and rainfal conditions of selected crops**

Amount of *kharif* rainfall	Soil water storage capacity	
	High	Medium
Less than 200 mm	Taramira	Taramira
200—300 mm	Raya	Taramira
300—500 mm	Raya/Gram	Raya
More than 500 mm	Sarson/Gram	Raya

With a view to bringing stability to the farming economy in the arid and semi-arid tracts, it is essential to evolve more and more drought-resisting varieties of crops. This point need not be overemphasised as there is no other way of increasing and stabilising production in areas where water is so scarce and its supplies so erratic.

(iii) *Water Harvesting* : The western and southwestern parts of Punjab and Haryana and the western half of Rajasthan, where dry farming is prevalent under arid and semi-arid conditions, need to focus attention on improving their water management strategies. Here rainfall is too inadequate and variable for crops to mature to success and the land is usually kept fallow to increase soil water storage though the efficiency of the fallow is quite low. Inter-plot or inter-row water harvesting under such conditions offers good opportunities for augmenting soil water supply in the profile. In this technique, a part of the area is sown in strips a few metres wide. The remaining area is left in the form of slopes on both sides of the planted area. The rain water from the slopes runs on to the planted area and augments the water supply for the crop. This technique has been tried in a few places and has shown promise. Results obtained at Hissar and Ludhiana show that profile water storage was considerably improved and the yields were stabilised with this technique. Scientists of the Central Arid Research Institute, Jodhpur have emphasized the need to delineate dry regions with consideration for climate, soil and vegetation before a simple water harvesting technology for a location is developed.

TABLE 25.6 : **Comparison of conventional sowing with water harvesting**

Year	Rain (mm)	Crop	Yield Conventional	Quintal/Hectare Water harvesting Gross area basis	Net area basis
1972-73 (Ludhiana)	422	Maize (fodder)	50	46	77
1974-75 (Ludhiana)	213	Maize (fodder)	64	92	154
1968-69 (Hissar)	138	Bajra (dry matter)	3.9	15.9	31.8
1972-73 (Ludhiana)	100	Gram (grain)	1.6	7.3	12.0

There are still a lot many gaps in the existing know-how to improve and stabilise crop production in these areas. The programme of work undertaken in the All India Coordinated Research Project on Dryland Agriculture is likely to go a long way in achieving the objectives.

In the red soil areas of southern India, also suffering from dry conditions, terracing, contour bunding, graded bunding, ridges and furrows, etc., referred to earlier in the context of northwertern Indian areas, have proved helpful as soil and moisture conservation practices for better crop performance (Shri Niwas, 1985, pp. 10-15).

Further, timeliness and precision in the various farm operations (sowing, weed control, top dressing, etc.) are also among the key factors in dryland agriculture. For example, the time of sowing alone can make a lot of difference in production and productivity of dryland crops. Sowing time is crucial not only from the point of view of moisture availability for crop stand, establishment and growth of dryland crops, but has a long range effect on productivity. This has been examined and confirmed with reference to *sorghum*, *bajra*, *ragi* (finger millet), etc.

Securing and maintaining optimum plant population per unit area is the first requirement for obtaining higher yields. Under dryland conditions, soil moisture being a limiting factor, it is important that optimum number of plants are allowed to grow as per the availability of soil moisture in the profile (R.P. Singh and S.K. Das, 1984, pp. 2-19).

In drought prone areas, there is an urgent need to locate acquifers, both shallow and deep, which will provide a source of water supply for domestic use and for the livestock, apart from irrigation to adjoining fields. Optimum use of all available surface and ground water for providing life-saving irrigation must be made. It should be repeated that comprehensive surveys need to be conducted in all arid and semi-arid tracts to locate underground water reserves (mentioning the quantity and quality of water in each case) and their distribution plotted on maps before formulating strategies of utilisation and management of water resources.

Effective soil conservation and afforestation measures should be instituted in areas subject to drought in order to strengthen the capabilities to withstand/resist drought effects.

In drought prone areas, the utilisation of land for various productive purposes should be in consonance with the limitation of available resources. The development of appropriate cropping pattern involving drought resistant varieties is a task that should receive priority attention.

Long term strategies should concentrate on the development of agriculture, industries and other such economic activities in drought affected areas which are less vulnerable to shortage of water.

There is a need to evolve institutional arrangements and interactions that would elicit full involvement and co-operation from the drought affected public in conceiving, framing and implementing both short term and long term measures for dealing with drought conditions (*Hydrological Aspects of Droughts*, International Symposium 1979, New Delhi, Vol. 2, pp. 142-43).

Under conditions of drought, it is imperative to manage the available water resources in a manner that productivity per drop of water can be enhanced to the maximum extent possible. Every effort must be made to reduce losses through seepage and lack of proper water channels. Maximum advantage should also be taken of the available credit, subsidy and other facilities for launching dynamic programmes of water harvesting through individual and community farm ponds, tubewells and lift irrigation projects. Promoting efficiency in water use should receive the highest priority in employment generation programmes.

Finally, a massive information transfer programme through radio, television, local newspapers and through regular field extension staff has to be implemented with speed and efficiency. There has also to be a perfect co-ordination between knowledge transfer and input supply so as to maximise gains from science and technology at the farm level. The 'lab to land' programme launched by the ICAR as well as the National Training Programme of Rural Youth must be effectively utilized for the speedy transfer of appropriate technology to bring about agricultural transformation (*Hydrological Aspects of Drought*, International Symposium 1979, Vol. 2, pp. 188-89).

CONCLUSIONS

From all considerations of arid and semi-arid areas, water management emerges as an inescapably crucial factor both for improving and maintaining productivity of irrigated as well as non-irrigated agricultural lands.

In areas of irrigation farming, the development of optimum irrigation schedules may be singled out as the most promising measure not only for optimum production but also for conserving the scarce water resource for further extensification and intensification of irrigation agriculture, apart from reducing the cost of the water input. Other measures include the construction and lining of field channels, levelling of farmland to facilitate uniform watering of fields, use of underground pipes instead of open channels in tube-well irrigation areas, straw mulching and, last but not the least, the consolidation of landholdings.

In the rainfed agricultural lands, on the other hand, the development of drought resistant varieties, terracing and contour bunding of individual fields, inter-row water harvesting by making ridges and furrows on contours, tillage of the land before the onset of rains, surveys to locate good acquifers for developing irrigation facilities and mulch formation are some of the important measures for promoting and stabilising farm production.

For a comprehensive diffusion of the strategies of water management and of technical know-how, a massive information transfer programme through radio, television, newspapers and field extension staff has to be put into operation, effectively and thoughtfully. In essential terms, "Lab to Land" programmes have to be made a dynamic movement.

REFERENCES

Cantor, Leonard M. : *A World Geography of Irrigation*, Oliver and Boyd, London, 1967.

I.H.P., C.S.I.R. and I.I.T., New Delhi : *Hydrological Aspects of Droughts*, International Symposium, Dec. 1979, Vols. I and II (Proceedings), New Delhi.

The Indian Society of Agricultural Economics : *Role of Irrigation in the Development of India's Agriculture*, Seminar Series XIII, 1976 (Chapter 16 by R. Ghosh).

Niwas, Shri : *Soil and Moisture Conservation for Red Soil Areas*, Research Bulletin No. 1, Central Research Institute for Dryland Agriculture, Hyderabad, India, 1984.

Punjab Agricultural University : *Dryland Cropping in the Submontane Punjab (1971-81)*, Punjab Agricultural University, Ludhiana, January 1984.

Roy, T.K. : *Impact of Rajasthan Canal Project on Social Economic and Environmental Conditions*, National Council of Applied Economic Research, New Delhi, 1983.

Sandhu, B.S. : *Research Highlights of the ICAR Coordinated Project for Research on Water Management* (Ludhiana Centre) (1969-81), Department of Soils, Punjab Agricultural University, Ludhiana, 1982.

Sandhu, B.S. and S.S. Prihar : *Irrigation Scheduling to Crops in Punjab*, Department of Soils, Punjab Agricultural University, Ludhiana, 1983.

Singh, R.P. and S.K., Das : *Timeliness and Precision-Key Factors in Dryland Agriculture*, Project Bulletin No. 9, All India Coordinated Research Project for Dryland Agriculture, Hyderabad, India, 1984.

Singh, Ranjodh and S.S. Prihar : "Management of Rainfed Areas of Indus Basin," in *Land and Water Management in the Indus Basin* (*India*), Vol. I, National Symposium 1978—The Contributed Papers : Sponsored by the Indian Ecological Society, ICAR and Punjab Agricultural University, Ludhiana.

Vander, E.J. Velde, Jr. : *The Distribution of Irrigation Benefits : A Study in Haryana, India* : A doctoral dissertation submitted at the University of Michigan in 1971.

26

UTILIZATION AND CONSERVATION OF LAND RESOURCES OF THE MOUNTAINS OF CENTRAL ASIA AND SOUTHERN KAZAKHSTAN

A.M. Mamytov

Mountainous territories in the Soviet Union account for 28.5 per cent of its land resources. The share of the gross product of mountain areas in the nation's overall gross product does not exceed 10 per cent, despite the fact that the areas have fa: greater potential for increasing production. There is hence, a need for more intensive utilizatinn of mountain territories through greater crop yield, a cardinal change in the running of grassland farming, improvement of different farming systems and the expansion of areas under orchards and vineyards. Of special interest are mountane forests which cover 265 mln. ha or 41.6 per cent of mountain areas. They perform an important role in water and soil conservation.

In 1975 the USSR carried out a natural and agricultural regionalization of its land resources, which was to become the basis for a qualitative account of land resources, soil suitability classification and soil rating and the economic evaluation of land. According to this regionalization, the mountains of Central Asia and Southern Kazakhstan—Tien Shan, Pamiro-Alay and Kopetdag—comprise the Central Asian mountain region with a total area of 41,365 thousand ha. which is 1.8 per cent of the country's territory and 6.5 per cent of the total mountain area in the country. Agricultural land has an area of 19,456 thousand ha, which is 47.0 per cent of the region's territory, including 16,371 thousand ha. of pastures, which is 39.6 per cent of the region's territory. In Tajikistan and Kirghizia mountains account for over 90 per cent of the territory. The expansion of arable lands in the mountains is constrained.

In conditions of natural moistening, biological activity, comperatively speaking, is highest in the foothills and at low and medium altitudes, a bit lower at high altitudes and very low on plains. But once artificial moistening is applied, the productivity on the plains rises dramatically. According to A.E. Maltsev (1981), the relative bioclimatic potential rises here 20-fold, while in the foothills and at low altitudes it only doubles and at high altitudes it goes up by only one third.

The intensification of mountainous territories should proceed with due account for natural conditions through the improvement of agricultural and grass lands and pastures, the expansion of areas under orchards and vineyards as a basis for mountain forest reclamation and greater productivity of slope lands, as well as through the improvement of soil conservation measures.

Sheep-breeding, yak-breeding, horse-breeding and cattle-breeding are all developed in the mountain regions of Central Asia and Southern Kazakhstan. Mountain and pasture farming serve the interests of livestock-breeding.

As a result of natural and historical conditions, the ecosystems of mountain regions differ sharply from those of the plains. That is why the development of mountain territories has its peculiarities. In the foothills and at medium altitudes dry land farming is developed. Wheat, barley and lucerne, as well as some other fodder crops are grown there. 1.8 mln. ha. of land has been already developed for dry land farming (A.E. Maltsev, 1981). There are also reserves amounting to some 0.5 mln. ha.

The problems of dry land farming of Tajikistan have been studied profoundly by A.N. Maksudov (1964, 1965).

Dry lands have been used for a long time and they are often washed away. They give a yield of 1,000 kg. per ha.

These regions require soil-protecting crop rotation, conservation measures and equipment which would check erosion processes.

The ploughing of slopes steeper than 10-15° should be forbidden and perennial grass should be sown there instead. Soil should be tilled only after taking the local relief into account and only if conservation measures are applied which provide for the formation of a drainless drift, which would detain snow and water, substitute surface run-off and enhance soil absorption and soil's filteration of water. Experience has also shown the advisability of the rotation of annual crops and perennial grasses as well as of hole-digging.

Historically orchards have been concentrated in regions with a rough relief. in the foothills and at medium altitudes. Many mountain orchards have a long history and were created by grafting cultigens of fruit-trees to wild apple. There are such orchards in the Zailiysky and Jungarsky Ala Tau in Northern Tien Shan. The "Gorny Gigant" farm in Kazakhstan has mountain orchards in its possession with a total area of 2 thousand ha. Vast fruit plantations cover the slopes of the Kirghiz Ala Tau at an altitude of 1,200-300 in and the Chatkalsky and Fergansky ridges at an altitude of 1,400-800 m. The foothills of the Kirghiz ridge are being developed for the cultivation of sweet almond and '*unabi*' (A.S. Bulychev, 1979). Grapes with a high sugar content are grown at low and medium altitudes where it is warm enough.

Much work aimed at increasing mountain productivity, forest expansion, slope forestation to prevent erosion, development of gardening and vine-growing is being carried out by the Varzobskaya mountain botanical station of the Botanical institute with the Tajik Academy of Sciences, the Varzobsky forestry, the Southern Kirghiz forest and fruit station of the Forest section of the Kirghiz Academy of Sciences and others.

On a larger scale, proceeding from the oil and climatic peculiarities and from the structure of vertical zonality, botanists and forest experts in 1971 drew up scientifically founded principles for mountain development on the example of the Varzob river gorge of the Gissarsky ridge. Wild fruit plants are hardly affected by the dry climate and low temperatures. These plant resources are therefore widely used in selection work to obtain seeds for drought-resistant stocks in dry mountain gardening. An entirely new way of obtaining seeds has been devised at the Varzobskaya mountain botanical station, whereby seeds are planted in a permanent place, skipping the nursery stage.

A.A. Shakhnazarov conducted longterm studies on various ridges of Western Tien Shan, which produced a wealth of experimental data (1983). This data determined measures for forest reclamation on mountain slopes, the role of artificial forest in water conservation and environment formation and the economic efficiency of mountain reclamation measures.

The Forest section of the institute of biology does the monitoring of water balance components and their transformation under the impact of forest management measures in nut and fruit forests. It conducts studies aimed at introducing and acclimatizing trees and bushes in the spruce forest zone and works out measures to ensure a rational utilization and greater productivity of nut and fruit forests.

Mountain forests in the USSR make up 41.6 per cent of all the country's forest's while in Central Asia and Southern Kazakhstan they occupy a mere 3 per cent of the region's territory. At the same time the forests there are quite diversified, a fact which largely determined their present state and the methods of forest management in the region.

Central Asia's nut and fruit forests are in some way unique. With over 130 species of trees and bushes, they are in effect natural botanical gardens. Walnut grows on an area of 27 thousand ha, apple forests on 14.2 thousand ha. and pistachio trees cover 19.5 thousand ha. Hence, these forests are of immense value as keepers of an exceptionally rich genofund. The territory of this unique forest has been declared a state reserve and the Sary-Chelensky biospheric reserve was set up there.

Central Asia and Southern Kazakhstan are regions with developed livestock-breeding, mainly sheep-breeding, based on natural grazing. The total area of mountainous natural pastures is : Kirghizia—8,816.8 thousand ha., Tajikistan—3,347.9, Uzbekistan—6,204, Turkmenia—997 and Southern Kazakhstan—8,255 thousand ha.

Climatic conditions and huge areas under pastures provide for the development of pasture breeding which has its own peculiarities in mountain regions. In the mountains, unlike on the plains, chiefly a seasonal use of pastures is feasible, due to weather factors rather than due to pasture sward contents. Other factors include the length of the time the snow cover stays and the state the passes are in.

In the case of mountain pastures the cattle, as it were, goes up along with the spring, which is due to the vertical zonality of the mountains.

Natural pastures and hay in Central Asia and Southern Kazakhstan are the main sources of fodder for livestock-breeding which account for 50-70% of all fodder. But despite their great significance, the productivity of natural pastures is falling. Some 30-40% of the pastures are polluted and subjected to heavy grazing. As a result their yield has fallen sharply.

Research institutes in Central Asia and Southern Kazakhstan have set the major guidelines for a rational utilization of pastures. Interesting ideas were put forward by A.G. Mamedinov (1982), K.I. Isakov (1976), L.P. Lebedeva (1984), L.I. Popova (1963), V.S. Sharashova (1967), V.S. Sharashova and others (1964), A.S. Tsekanov (1979), H.Y. Yusufbekov (1968) and others.

L.P. Lebedeva was the first to carry out a study of the ecological situation in the region of mountain meadows in Soviet Central Asia. She also made a study of the living conditions of lion's foot meadow formations widespread in the subalpine zone of the central part of the Kirghiz ridge and the ridges of the Northern Tien Shan ; the change was determined in the plant cover depending on the economic impact, which made it possible to regulate the direction of processes and forecast the yield of highland subalpine pastures. The statistical models have been worked out of lion's foot and Jerusalem sage communities according to the number of shoots of species and productivity.

A.S. Tsekanov (1979) carried out a lengthy research which proved the necessity of a rationalization in utilizing natural summer pastures by providing rest for the plants without excluding them from the rotational grazing through the alternation of the early summer and autumn grazing and refraining from repeated sward removal in the vegetation period. Pasture improvement—both superficial and a more profound procedure involving the use of irrigation and fertilizers—affects all the links of biogeocenosis and preserves and enhances soil fertility.

The stations "Kabadian", on a gentle slope of the southern spurs of the Ak-Tau ridge at an altitude of 400 m, "Tamechet", on the crest of the Ranchon-Tau ridge at an altitude of 1,600 m, and "Anzob", in the central part of the Gissarsky ridge at an altitude of 3,373 m. above mean sea level, have made a study of the dynamics of growth and development and the biological peculiarities of fodder crops. They have also studied the productivity of phytocenoses, on whose basis the most feasible terms were set for grazing and mowing the swards of the basic types of pastures in Tajikistan (A. A. Madaminov, 1982).

Such measures as fertilization, removal of weeds and poisonous plants, fencing, and irrigation have proved to be effective everywhere.

The Soviet Communist party's Central Committee at its plenary session in October 1984 approved a long-term programme for development of reclamation and more efficient use of reclaimed land with a view to increasing food production.

There are all indications that in the future irrigation will be moving into the mountains. In conditions of developing irrigation on steep slopes and the development of sheep-breeding and other livestock-breeding, intensive irrigational and progressive pasture erosion would occur. Of great concern in this connection is the state of mountain pastures, which are rapidly degrading, while the forest area is shrinking.

Soil and plant covers are closely inter-related. Thinning of grass stands and the shrinking of forest cover in mountain territories contributes to erosional processes and leads to the emergence of gullies and mudflows. Tillage implements which do not comply with mountainous ecological conditions are another contributing factor in soil cover disturbance.

All this sets serious tasks for a rational development and utilization of land, its conservation and the development of advanced methods of irrigation and tillage, which would rule out erosion, degradation and other negative processes.

The exploitation of natural resources in mountain regions requires a more flexible approach, since the restoration of the disturbed balance in the precarious mountain ecosystems takes much more effort and time than in flat country conditions.

Because of the special geographic and geomorphological locations the mountains of Central Asia and Southern Kazakhstan are often the scene of large avalanches and landslides, Gravitational processes are especially violent here with mudflows and snow avalanches destroying everything on their way. All these phenomena inflict incalculable material damage. Erosion-wise too the mountains of Central Asia and Southern Kazakhstan are a most dangerous region.

High altitudes are chiefly dominated by precipitous slopes more than 40° steep. At medium altitudes there are steep slopes of 30-40° and at low altitudes and in the foothills the slopes are 10-20°. The average figure for Tajikistan, for instance, is over 26° (A.A. Sadriddinov, M.R. Yakutilov, 1981).

The figures for mountain soil erosion are : Tajikistan—72%, Uzbekistan—82% (Zakirov T.S., Kochubey M.I. and others, 1981) Kirghizia—92% (Djunushbaev A.D., 1984). With the rapid development of livestock-breeding, in particular of sheep-breeding, pasture erosion is becoming an acute problem. According to E.B. Aybasov (1981), excessive grazing results in the decline of the hydro-physical property of soil, an increase in the runoff and water and pasture erosion. The network of paths increases to reach 55 per cent of a slope's territory and the genetic horizons A+B are destroyed up to 25 per cent.

All this causes concern over the state of biological productivity of mountain territories. A whole set of anti-mudflow, anti-erosion, reclamation and managerial measures should be taken, such as the grassing of severely eroded slopes, the construction of hydrotechnical anti-mudflow and anti-erosion installations and a drastic improvement of natural pastures. Conservation measures should be worked out taking into account the exposition and steepness of the slopes. According to V.T. Tegisov (1981), at a slope steepness of 4-7°, slightly eroded soil emerges on the northern slope and moderately eroded on the southern slope. At a steepness of 8-11° it is moderately or severely eroded.

A special role in combating these phenomena is played by natural vegetation and forest reclamation measures. The role of forest vegetation and shrubs in water conservation and regulation, as well as in soil conservation extends far beyond mountain territories, since they grow in river basins which feed the irrigation systems of the agricultural zone and regulate the surface runoffs of large river basins.

A rational utilization of biological resources requires a strict account of the reserves being utilized and a rationing of their utilization, in order to obtain the maximum amount of produce at an optimum impact on nature.

We have entered a new stage in world mountain research, characterized by the staging of highly complicated experiments and the use of sophisticated methods. Mountains are in effect becoming a proving ground for science, a sort of natural laboratory. Biologists study the flora and fauna, pedologists invent new ways of mountain soil development, hydrometeorologists work on ways to combat avalanches and landslides, seismologists forecast earthquakes, geologists engage in mineral prospecting, physicians study the effect of mountain conditions on the human organism and archaeologists scrutinize the drawings of the cave-men. Geographers, geochemists, physisists and entomologists are also involved in research there. In short, science increasingly opens up the opportunities for a complex economic development of mountain territories.

In view of the high priority of studying mountain ecosystems, the Presidium of the USSR Academy of Sciences set up a Scientific Council to study the problem : "Complex study and development of mountain territories in Central Asia and Kazakhstan". It includes 70 topics and 8 sections and involves 26 research institutions in Kazakhstan, Tajikistan, Uzbekistan, Turkmenia and Kirghizia.

Within the framework of the Council's scientific research three issues of collected articles have been published and "Problems of Mountain Development", and "Ecological Aspects of the Problem of Mountain Conservation" is to be published shortly. The works deal with the state of and prospects for the natural biological mountain resources. their rational utilization and conservation.

The XXXIII session of the Council for coordinating the activities of the scientific academies of the Union republics noted that as a result of a joint effort on behalf of scientific institutions of the Academies of Central Asia and Kazakhstan, a number of significant results were obtained which later proved useful in the republics' economies. A geo-botanical study of mountain vegetation was carried out for Central Asia and Kazakhstan (Tien Shan, Pamir, Kopetdag). A preliminary account of the territories which could be used for pastures was prepared and a forecast was made on the grass yield on these territories. A study of the soils of mountainous Central Asia and Kazakhstan has been completed and a soil map drawn up.

In order to use the experience for a more effective complex study and utilization of the region's biological resources the efforts of the scientists should be pooled in the future too.

Another sub-project for mountain research is the : "Arid Mountain Ecosystems of Central Asia and Kazakhstan" of project 6a "Mountain Ecosystems" of the MAB Programme, which was formed at the decisions of the Third and Fifth joint Plenary sessions of the Soviet and Republican MAB committees. This sub-group includes representatives of republican MAB committees from Kazakhstan, Kirghizia, Tajikistan, Turkmenia and Uzbekistan, as well as representatives of the Scientific Council "Complex study and development of mountain territories in Central Asia and Kazakhstan".

The Kirghiz republican MAB committee has drawn up a draft programme of complex research on the sub-project : "Arid Mountain Ecosystems of Central Asia and Kazakhstan". The programmes were coordinated with the presidiums of the scientific academies in the republics involved. The programme of the sub-project includes 46 topics and four sections, on which work is being done by scientific institutions in Kazakhstan, Uzbekistan, Kirghizia, Turkmenia and Tajikistan.

The sections deal with the following problems : conservation of land and water resources in arid mountain territories ; the biological foundation for the utilization, transformation and conservation of plants in mountain territories of Central Asia and Kazakhstan ; the biological foundation for the utilization and protection of wildlife in mountain territories ; nature conservation, biosphere monitoring and the setting-up of preserves.

Unlike the Programme of the Scientific Council on mountain problems, the Programme of the sub-project "Arid mountain ecosystems of Central Asia and Kazakhstan" mainly involves topics dealing with scientific research in nature conservation and the forecasting of the state of the biosphere in mountain territories and the methods of preventing an adverse anthropogenic effect on mountain arid ecosystems. Organizational and coordinating work on the sub-project is to be closely linked in the future with the work of the Scientific Council "Complex research and development of mountain territories of Central Asia and Kazakhstan."

In the past few years the Scientific council on mountain problems, with assistance from the presidiums of the scientific academies in the Central Asian republics and Kazakhstan, held a number of plenary sittings in the cities of Frunze, Alma-Ata, Tashkent and Dushanbe. Coordination of scientific research, elaboration of scientific and technical reports, projects, and designs ; cooperation in preparing scientific publications, all this would considerably enhance the efficiency of research and will ensure greater introduction of the results of the research on these two programmes into the economies of the mountain territories of Tien Shan, Pamir and Kopetdag. In this way, experience is gradually being gained in conducting inter-republican regional research of mountain ecosystems, in compliance with the programme "Man and the Biosphere" carried out by the Scientific Council on mountain problems.

Although mountains foothills, valleys and plains are all physically and geographically interrelated, each one of them has its own peculiarities in economic development, utilization and application of tillage implements and machines. Everywhere there is a specific ecological situation in time and space.

Mountains possess immense natural resources including land resources. The latter are characterized by high complexity, having low contour, differing depth, stoniness and erosion on different slopes of mountains and foothills. They differ from lowlands in terms of the type and management of cultivated crops, reclamation techniques, the means of mechanization and electrification and, consequently, the specialization of production. In view of the importance and complexity of developing mountain lands a Coordinating Council has been set up at the National Agricultural Academy specifically to deal with the problem of mountain farming. The Council should pool the efforts of scientists engaged with this problem from various regions of the Soviet Union. They are to solve complex issues, such as increasing soil fertility, preventing soil erosion, the invention and introduction of new cultivation methods, as well as new machines to mechanize technological processes in farming and livestock-breeding in mountain conditions.

In its resolution under the heading : "The state and prospects for the development of research into the problems of agriculture in mountain regions" the Presidium of the Agricultural Academy notes that a major task is to provide the scientific backing for a complex of measures designed to increase productivity of mountain farming and of all the branches of mountain agriculture, which in itself is a large reserve in increasing output of produce. It is essential to have scientific institutions concentrate on the creation of a scientific approach towards running mountain agriculture, with due regard to the utilization of the natural and economic potential, highly efficient technological processes and the cultivation technique for the basic agricultural crops, chemicalization, reclamation, development of fodder production and livestock-breeding, the creation of machinery and technical means for complex mechanization and electrification, the solution of problems relating to the social development of mountain settlements. Ideas should be put forward on improving specialization, management and incentive in the output of produce.

Mountain research has today assumed global importance. Another indication of this was the international symposium held at Vratsa, Bulgaria, on October 24—9, 1983. The symposium— "The relationship : man—mountain ecosystems" dealt with the anthropogenic impact on mountain ecosystems, their conservation and reproduction in specific regions and countries and the search of ways and means to achieve harmony in man's future relations with mountain ecosystems.

At the symposium, scientists from different countries expressed the desire for cooperation in dealing with problems of the utilization and conservation of the planet's mountain ecosystems. Joint research is already underway. Soviet and Bulgarian scientists, for instance, are conducting a comparative study of the Caucasus and the Stara Planina mountains. A collection of articles has been published, prepared by the Institute of Geography at the Soviet Academy of Sciences, the French National Centre for Scientific Research and the Institute of Geography of the Alps at Grenoble University. The work— "Alps —Caucasus" (contemporary problems of constructive geography of mountain countries) contains the results of Franco-Soviet symposiums of 1974 and 1976.

International cooperation will make it possible to elaborate the scientific basis for an optimum anthropogenic impact on the utilization of biological resources of the mountains, especially pastures, forests, water and wildlife. The mountain systems of the world are extremely diversified' which makes an analysis of the structure of the vertical zonality of the world's soils of particular interest, since it is the type of vertical zonality, with its temperature and water regimes, that provide a scientific basis for regionalization and economic utilization. Large regions have already been singled out, taking into consideration the specific features of mountain territories of the Soviet Union. Regional councils for mountain territories of the Caucasus, the Crimea, the Carpathians, the Urals, Siberia, the Far East are to be set up along the lines of the Scientific Council on the complex study and development of mountain territories in Central Asia and Kazakhstan.

In view of the special significance of mountain ecosystems it has been thought necessary to organize working meetings which would be sponsored by the secretariat of the UNESCO programme "Man and the Biosphere" and where reports would be delivered and joint proposals put forward on the study of mountain arid-ecosystems.

Since mountain ecosystems are still largely undisturbed by man, they catch and preserve more solar energy in the form of phyto and zoo-biomass, a substantial part of which is utilized by man. If the utilization and conservation of mountain resources has a scientific foundation, they become more productive. Ecological research is expanding and is aimed at studying the processes of erosion and degradation of soils in mountain territories and the way they are affected by forest, bush and grass communities in order to preserve mountain ecosystems.

Mankind will continue unveiling the mysteries of the plants and wildlife of mountains to use them later as a genofund for creating new species of cultured plants and animals and increasing the resources of the biosphere.

The reasonable use of the advantages of socialist society serves as a scientific basis for increasing the natural and economic potential of mountain territories for the good of mankind.

REFERENCES

Bulychev, A.S., Ways of rational development of land in the lowlands of the Kirghiz ridge under sweet almond. National conference "Protective foresting and rational utilization of land resources in the mountains". Tashkent, 1979.

Isakov, K.I., *Pastures and grasslands of Kirghizia*. Frunze, 1976.

Maksudov, A.N., *Basic problems of dry land farming in Tajikistan*. Dushanbe, 1964, 1965 (vols. 1&2).

Madaminov, A.A., Ways of increasing productivity of mountain pastures and grasslands in Tajikistan. In : *Problems of mountain development*. Frunze, 1982.

Maltsev, A.E., *Natural conditions as a basis for agricultural utilization of water and land resources on the example of Central Asia*. Moscow, 1981.

Natural and agricultural regionalization of land in the USSR. Moscow, 1975.

Mamytov, A.M., *Mountain soils in Central Asia and Southern Kazakhstan*. Frunze, 1982.

Popova, L.I., Seasonal dynamics of the development of the main phytocenoses of the Verkhne-Narynsk syrts in Central Tien Shan. Frunze, 1963.

Khanazarov, A.A., *Soil erosion and forest reclamation in the mountains*. Moscow, 1983.

Tsekanov, A.S., The ecological and biological basis for the improvement of highland pastures in Inner Tien Shan. Frunze, 1979.

Sharashova, V.S., The structure and rhythmics of grass stands in soddy steppes and meadow steppes in Tien Shan. Frunze, 1967.

Yusufbekov, H.V., *Improvement of pastures and grasslands in the Pamirs and the Alay valley*. Dushanbe, 1968.

27

MODELLING OF THE INTERACTION OF NATURAL AND ECONOMIC SYSTEMS OF A MOUNTAINOUS REGION

A Case Study of the River Vakhsh Basin

Z.D. Usmanov and *O.P. Sapov*

The drainage area of the Vakhsh river is situated in the upper reaches of the Amu-Darya. It is a mountainous region having practically all the types of landscape characteristics of Soviet Central Asia—from high mountain ranges within the Pamirs to deserts on the right bank of the Amu-Darya.

Areas near the water divide in the highest ridges with peaks going up to 7,000 m are covered by glaciers and firn fields. All the large arteries of the basin are fed by the mountain valley types of glacier, whose lengths reach tens of kilometers.

In the middle part of the basin all the rivers are united into a single artery—the river of Vakhsh, which at a considerable distance flows with small tributaries in a narrow U-like valley.

In the lower part, the river valley sharply turns into large terraces merging with the right-bank terraces of the Amu-Darya, whose height above sea level ranges between 300 and 500 m.

Corresponding to orographic conditions, the climatic and vegetation belts change from the high mountain ranges to the valleys.

The geological structure of this territory is determined by geosynclinal belts of different ages like the Tien Shan, Alai, and the North Pamirs—Kun Lun in the north and the Tajik tectonic depression—in the south. There are also outcrops of diverse rocks, from Precambrian gneisses and crystalline shales and marbles, Paleozoic sedimentary, intrusive and effusive formations to Cretaceous-Paleogenic limestones, sandstones and clays. In the depressive parts of the basin considerable areas are occupied by thick Neogenic red-coloured sandstones.

Quaternary deposits are everywhere represented by loose conglomerates, sands and loesses. In the mountainous parts of the valleys they form powerful terrace complexes, and in depressions their thickness is often over 1,000 m.

The bedding of the parent rocks was formed during the Phanerozoic epochs of folding. During the recent times complex block folding dislocations developed within the Tien Shan and the Pamir parts of the Vakhsh basin and linear folding-erosional structures in the Tajik depression.

In the process of an intensive tectonic genesis, it is quite common to come across ruptures of different ranks ranging from deep and wide fractures cutting the Earth's crust for hundreds of kilometers, to near-surface faults expressed in individual reversed faults, faults and overthrusts.

The altitudinal jumps resulting from intensive and very recent uplifts created conditions for the formations of practically all the known types of relief from micro to macro forms, from the glacial-nival relief in high-mountain areas to the plane one in the lower reaches of the Vakhsh river.

The complex geological structure and a sharply dissected relief under corresponding climatic conditions, have led to the formation of quite a variegated soil cover. The soils of plains, foothills, middle and high mountains are represented by numerous varieties from light sierozems, light-brown carbonate and leached soils to high-mountain meadow, desert and cryogenic ones.

Vegetation and the animal world of the Vakhsh basin, having formed under the influence of general continental and arid climatic conditions, are also distinguished in their diversity—from the herbs of the Alpine meadows to haloxylon of the deserts, from the Pamirs yak to the desert monitor, it includes a considerable number of endemic forms.

The contrasting orography and the continental climate have conditioned an increased dynamics of ground waters associated with the period of spring rains and summer melting of glaciers and with the corresponding floods on the rivers. In the basin of the Vakhsh river two hydrodynamic zones are distinguished—the upper one with the capacity of up to 200 or 300 m., with fresh hydrocarbonate waters of good quality, and the lower one corresponding to deep horizons of artesian waters with increased mineralization and with capacity of up to several kilometers.

The Earth's crust in this region is not a stable substratum for natural processes. Tectonic movements, which have resulted in quite a complex geological structuring of the regions, continue to the present date. According to highly accurate measurements, the current vertical and horizontal dislocations of individual blocks of the Earth's crust along fractures can be measured in centimeters a year and, reach amplitudes in meters during a century.

Everywhere in the Vakhsh basin one finds human settlements. In the high-mountain part, due to scarcity of lands suitable for building, there are only individual villages (*kishlaks*). Their scanty population is mainly engaged in cattle breeding, organized on the principle of free grazing of domestic animals.

In the middle part of the region the number of *kishlaks* is much greater, however the population of each of them is not numerous and ranges from a few dozens to two or three hundred people. A single anthropogenic environment provides a cascade of water storage reservoirs and hydro-power plants on the Vakhsh river. This is quite a powerful nature-transforming force whose impact rapidly spreads about the whole mountain region.

The lower reaches of the Vakhsh river is one of the most densely populated regions of south-west Tajikistan. The spectre of anthropogenic impacts on nature here is especially diverse—from alienation of lands for transport and electric transmission lines to stripping work in mining industry and pumping of ground waters ; from construction of irrigation networks, development of virgin lands and greenery plantations to the change of soils' chemical composition and pollution of atmosphere by industrial emissions, etc.

Even a short description of the Vakhsh basin shows that, as a single whole, this is a large natural-economic complex, characterized by a great diversity in its components. Economic systems rapidly developing in it are a powerful indicator of the impact on nature, which is capable of turning the region into an environment hardly suitable for the life of people.

The complexity of direct and feedback links among the nature forming components excludes the possibility of planning a harmonic development of the region on the basis of intuitive prerequisites and requires the creation of a special instrument for forecasting. On the modern level of knowledge, this role may be fulfilled only by an imitation model of the dynamics of the natural-anthropogenic complex of the Vakhsh basin. In its final form such a model, realized with the help of special computers, should fulfil the functions of a "machine of knowledge" of a mountain region.

In this report the first results obtained from the study of this problem are presented. Natural environment, developing according to its objective laws, is considered as the basis of the "machine of knowledge". Anthropogenic impacts are interpreted as disruptions brought in from outside. With such an approach to the study of this problem, it becomes possible to foresee different ways of the evolution of the region's nature depending on the character of planned anthropogenic impacts. An analysis of different scenarios allows to choose acceptable variants, which provide for an efficient functioning of the economic systems and preservation of the environment favourable for man.

The use of a systems approach makes it possible to formulate the structure of the "machine of knowledge" on any level of detail, while elaboration of programmes for its component parts fills it in with a definite content.

AN AGGREGATIVE PORTRAIT OF THE NATURAL ENVIRONMENT OF A MOUNTAIN REGION

On the most generalized level of the hierarchical ladder is the description of the portrait of a region, as well as the planet which includes the lithosphere, hydrosphere, atmosphere, and the organic world (flora and fauna). Evolution of these components is conditioned by two types of impacts caused either by physical fields of the Earth or by influence of the Cosmos. Due to the fact that physical fields in the basin of the Vakhsh river are sufficiently studied, they will not be taken into account in the further presentation of the material, while the influence of the Cosmos is presented by rythms discovered in global natural processes and by solar activity on the surface of the lithosphere and in the Earth's atmosphere.

The generalized portrait does not reflect the specificity of the region. With this purpose, it is necessary to get to a more detailed level of its description, on which form and content (composition) should be distinguished for each component.

In the composition of lithosphere we distinguish bedrocks and quaternary rocks. Bedding of these rocks within the region determine the inner form of the lithosphere, while its surface form is characterized by relief. The latter is represented by three gradations : macro-meso- and nano-reliefs, because they differ in their influence on the dynamics of the natural portrait of the region and in their reaction to the impacts of nature-forming components.

Hydrosphere includes glaciers, watercourses, water basins, ground water and precipitation, whose spatial distribution is determined by the forms of lithosphere. Two other components, viz., atmosphere and organic world, are not presented in detail, but are used in aggregative form. The list of components is supplemented by soil and solar activity. The latter is considered to be component because the degree of its manifestation in the region in great measure depends on the state of the environment.

Thus, 16 components are used for the chosen level of the description of the portrait of the region's natural environment (see Table 27.1).

CHARACTERISTIC SCALES OF THE TIME OF NATURAL PROCESSES

Even on a strongly aggregated level of description, the natural complex of the region is seen as quite a complicated dynamic system. Significant changes of each component of the system are manifested in different periods of time. For instance, the organic world is sensitive to seasonal variations in climate. A considerable restructuring of macrorelief, which influences the state of the region's nature, goes on during thousands of years. Different kinds of metamorphism of bedrocks embrace time intervals in hundreds of thousands or in millions of years.

Thus, the evolution of the components of the natural environment goes on with different rates. When observing the dynamics of the region through "small" time intervals, the changes in its states are registered by means of rapidly evolutionizing components. In "large" time intervals the dominating role belongs to slowly evolutionizing components. In every definite moment the portrait of the region's natural environment represents the result of the previous evolution of all its components taken together.

Let us consider the following characteristic scales of time:

1. Day
2. Season
3. Year
4. Decade
5. Century
6. Millennium
7. One hundred thousand years
8. One million years and more

The three first scales are most illustrative. With their help many natural processes are described, which are associated with the periodic movements of the Earth in the solar system, in particular, the rythms of activation and impoverishment of the manifestation of life in living matter.[1]

Day is determined by the period of the full revolution of the Earth around its axis.

Season is an interval of time, during which the Sun moves between two points of the ecliptic (the spring and autumn equinoxes, the summer and winter solstices).

Year is the time of a complete revolution of the Earth around the Sun.

For denoting the other time scales the decimal system of chronology is used. Each of them corresponds to one or several characteristic rythms in the natural processes, whose periods are comparable with the above decimal scale. Thus, scales from 4 to 8 should not be used literally.

"Decade" is the time interval corresponding to half of the 22-year cycle of solar activity.[2] The influence of this cycle is discovered in the outbursts of seismic and volcanic activity,[3] in stage-like development of mountain glaciations,[4] in changes of climate,[5] and in life activities of organisms,[6] etc.

"Century" symbolizes a secular, 80 or 90-year cycle of solar activity, characterizing the dynamics of the group of spots.[2,5] In the nature of the Earth, this cycle is, for instance, manifested in dendrology[7] and in rythmical changes of the concentration of radiocarbon in the dated samples of wood.[2]

"Millennium" is the interval of time comparable to the 900-year period of the mutual perturbation of the planets of the solar system,[8] with 1850-year cycle of seismic and volcanic activity of the Earth,[3] etc.

The scale of time is comparable in tens of thousands of years, for instance, 26,000-year period of the precession of the Earth's axis.[9] However, we do not use it because the natural rythms corresponding to it are not yet substantiated well enough.

"One Hundred Thousand Years"—corresponds to the shortest period of the change in polarity of the Earth's magnetic field. It is comparable, for instance, with the 40,700-year summer geological-climatic rythm,[4] with the cycle of significant glaciations, repeating every 50,000—100,000 years[10] and others.

"One Million Years and More" characterizes geological scales of time. The main rythms of mountain formation (the last of them : Caledonian, Hetcynian, and Alpine epochs) go on for about 200,000,000 years. In the geological literature they are linked with the cycle of the "galactic year—the time of the full revolution of the solar system around the centre of the Galaxy.[11]

A CONCEPTUAL MODEL OF THE INTERACTION OF A REGION'S NATURE FORMING COMPONENTS

Under point I, a definite level of the description of the portrait of a region's natural environment is formulated. On this level a conceptual model of the interaction of a region's components is represented in the form of a square table with the dimension 16×16. In its rows and columns the following components are denoted by ordinal numbers : 1 to 7—the principal components of lithosphere ; 8—soil ; 9—organic world ; 10 to 14—the main states of water ; 15—atmosphere, and 16—solar activity. Elements A_{ij} are given on the points of intersection of lines and columns ; full number meanings from 1 to 8 are awarded to them, which correspond to one of the characteristic intervals of time of point 2, in whose scale the registered change of j-component under the influence of i-component is manifested. The main diagonal represents the time when the components influence themselves, i.e. self-limitation, under which we understand the ability of the component to return to the state of equilibrium. The figures A_{ij} and A_{ij}, symmetrical in respect to the main diagonal, characterize mutual interaction of the i-and j-components.

Each of the chosen components of the natural complex of a region represents by itself a complex object characterised by a great number of properties and studied by one or several sciences, which at present are disconnected both methodologically and terminologically. That is why, considering the impact of one component on the other, we singled out from the first one a definite property, which caused considerable general changes of the other component through a corresponding process. The ordinal number of the time scale, during which these changes had been registered, was entered into the table of interaction.

Let us consider, for instance, the influence, of macrorelief on glaciers. The geometrical form of its surface and the geographical location are the major properties of macrorelief. Out of the whole variety of the processes of macrorelief impact on glaciers we choose vertical uplifts, whose influence on the state of glaciers is considerable. In the Vakhsh river basin these uplifts go on with the rate of several cm a year. Thus, a significant change in the state of glaciers may be expected in the scale of "century". That is why in Table 27.1 element $A_{5,10}$ is given the meaning of 5.

If one takes into account the change in the geographical location of macrorelief due to continental drift, this process will manifest itself in reforming of the state of glaciers into the scale of "one million years and more".

Thus, Table 27.1 should be considered as the first approximation to the description of the interaction of natural environment components within the limits of the "machine of knowledge" of a region's integrated development. The figures given in Table 27.1 are tentative and may be specified depending on the chosen components.

Table 27.1 forms the basis for :

—choosing components and processes necessary for the elaboration of short-term and long-term forecasts of the evolution of a region's natural environment ;

—organizing project interdisciplinary research ;

—formulating standards of monitoring organization.

ANTHROPOGENIC IMPACT ON THE NATURAL PORTRAIT OF A REGION

In the prehistoric time the relations of man with the environment remained within the limits of the natural evolution of biogeocenosis. With the development of social production, man becomes "... a unique agent, whose power grows with the course of time". This fact is illustrated by comparison of Tables 27.2 and 27.3. Each of these two tables supplements Table 27.1 with five following lines numbered through 17-21 and gives the notion about the impact of anthropogenic components on the components of natural environment. For denoting the degree of impact, time scales of point 2 were used with implication that these impacts in each of the tables remained unchangeable with time. For illustration, figure 8 ("a million years and more") is omitted in the tables and a blank square corresponds to it.

Tables 27.1 and 27.3 taken together describe a conceptual model of the dynamics of natural environment under the impact of anthropogenic components. Taking into account a continuous growth of the intensity of anthropogenic impacts, one should bear in mind that compilation of such a table is expedient for definite moments of time.

The clarification of the feedback impact of natural components on the anthropogenic ones gives the possibility to expand the table into a new one with dimensions of 21×21, which will evidently describe the conceptual model of the interaction of natural and economic systems of a region.

TABLE 27.1

	1	2	3	4	5	6	7	8	9	10	11	12	13	14	15	16
1. Bedrocks	6	5	5	6	6	5	4	8	6	5	5	4	4	6	1	8
2. Occurrence of bedrocks	5	4	5	6	7	6	4	3	3	7	4	3	2	2	5	5
3. Quaternary rocks	8	8	8	8	6	5	2	3	6	8	2	3	4	1	8	1
4. Occurrence of quaternary rocks	8	8	7	8	7	5	4	5	5	8	1	3	3	1	8	8
5. Macrorelief	7	7	7	6	7	6	8	6	6	5	6	8	8	6	6	7
6. Mesorelief	7	7	5	6	4	8	4	5	5	8	6	5	5	6	6	6
7. Nanorelief	6	8	5	4	7	4	5	3	3	8	1	3	3	8	8	8
8. Soils	6	8	5	8	8	8	3	4	2	8	8	3	2	4	1	1
9. Organic world	6	8	5	8	8	4	3	2	1	8	4	4	2	2	1	1
10. Glaciers	4	4	3	8	7	4	3	8	1	3	1	2	3	1	1	1
11. Streams	4	8	2	6	7	6	3	3	3	2	4	2	3	8	1	2
12. Water basins	3	5	3	8	8	5	3	3	3	8	4	3	3	1	1	1
13. Groundwater	6	8	3	8	8	5	3	2	2	8	2	3	3	8	2	8
14. Precipitation	4	8	3	8	8	7	4	3	2	2	1	1	2	8	1	1
15. Atmosphere	5	8	3	8	8	8	3	4	2	2	1	1	2	1	1	1
16. Solar radiation	4	8	4	8	8	8	8	1	1	1	8	1	8	1	1	4

TABLE 27.2 : **Impact prior to the beginning of Christian Era**

	1	2	3	4	5	6	7	8	9	10	11	12	13	14	15	16
17. Population			6				5	5	4		5	5				
18. Industry			6				5									
19. Agriculture			5				5	4	4				6			
20. Transport			6				6	6	6							
21. Building	6		5				4	5	4		5	5				

TABLE 27.3 : **Impacts in our time**

	1	2	3	4	5	6	7	8	9	10	11	12	13	14	15	16
17. Population			4				4	3	3		4	4	4			
18. Industry	4		4		4		4	4	3	2	3	3	4		1	
19. Agriculture			4				4	2	2		2	2	2	3		1
20. Transport	4		4				4	2	2		3	3			1	
21. Building	4	5	4	4		4	3	3	2		4	4	2	2		1

"MACHINE OF KNOWLEDGE" OF A REGION'S INTEGRATED DEVELOPMENT

The table with the 21×21 dimensions is in fact a principal scheme of the "machine of knowledge" of a mountainous region. The use of systems approach makes it possible to specify this scheme up to any necessary hierarchical level of description of not only the whole table, but also of its individual parts. The detailed scheme represents by itself an "assembly scheme" for creating a "machine of knowledge". Its units are completed by the available and specially elaborated imitation models.

At the present time, within the limits of the "machine of knowledge" of the Vakhsh basin there is enough data for the full programme of the water-erosional-accumulative block. It includes an imitation model of water exchange within the cascade of water storage reservoirs on the Vakhsh river, which is designated for forecasting changes in the water level of reservoirs in certain regimes of their exploitation. Water removing at the exit of the cascade is the initial source of information for an imitation model of water distribution among the consumersin the Vakhsh valley. This information directly pertains to the imitation model of the dynamics of the ground water level in the lower reaches of the Vakhsh river.

Two other imitation models are designated for forecasting the process of silting in water storage reservoirs due to alluvial sedimentation and the change of their shores due to abrasion, crumbling, and landslides.

For the programmes of the "organic world" block, we created imitation models of the dynamics of ecosystems of the Nurek water reservoir and "Tigrovaya Balka" nature reserve.

For determining short-term tendencies in the development of anthropogenic components an imitation model was elaborated for forecasting changes in the main economic indices of the region's economic system.

For the "agriculture" block we built imitation models for evaluating bioproductivity of cultivated landscapes, dynamics of the growth of a cotton-plant bush and for a short-term forecasting of the population dynamics of the cotton field insects.

An imitation model was also built of the atmospheric pollution by industrial emissions.

In conclusion, we would like to note that, with further accumulation of imitation models and with the uniting of them into a single system, the necessity arises to design special computers, with the help of which the "machine of knowledge" of an integrated development of a region will be realized in full measure.

FOOTNOTES

1. Vernadsky, V.I., *Biosfera* (Biosphere). —M. Mysl, 1967, pp. 222-376.
2. Vitinsky, Yu. I., *Solnechnaya aktivnost'* (Solar activity).—M. Nauka, 1983, 192 p.
3. Maksimov, E.V., Problemy oledeneniya Zemli i ritmy v prirode (Problems of glaciation of the Earth and rythms in nature)—M. Nauka, 1972, 296 p.
4. Shnitnikov, A.V., Glavneishiye ritmy v prirodnykh yavleniyakh verkhnego pleistotsena i golotsena (The most important rythms in natural phenomena of Upper Pleistocene and Holocene)—V sb. "Ritmichnost' prirodnykh yavleniy. L. Gidrometeoizdat, 1971, pp. 35-38.
5. Kuznetsov, A.D., Loginov, V.F., Kosmicheskiye vozdeistviya na atmospheru (Cosmic impacts on the atmosphere).—L. Politekhnicheskiy institut, 1984, 157 p.
6. Chizhevsky, A.L., *Zemnoye ekho solnechnykh bur'* (The earthy echo of solar storms). M. Mysl, 1976.

7. Siren, G., Hari, P., Long term geophysical cycles in Scandinavia. *J. Interdiscipl. Cycle Res.*" 1972, 3, N 3—4, 425—427.
8. Ryabov, Yu. A., Dvizheniya nebesnykh tel (Movements of celestial bodies).—M. Fizmatlit, 1962, 215 p.
9. Astronomicheskiy, Kalendar', (Astronomical calendar). Postoyannaya chast', M. Nauka, 1981, 704 p.
10. Emiliani Cesare, The cause of the ice ages. *Earth and Planet. Sci. Lett.*", 1978, 37, N 3, 349—352.
11. Lungersgauzen, G.F., O periodichnosti geologicheskikh yavleniy i izmenenii klimatov proshlykh geologicheskikh epokh (On periodicity of geological phenomena and change of climates of past geological epochs). Sb. "*Problemy planetarnoi geologii*" M., 1963, pp. 7-49.

28

ECONOMIC-GEOGRAPHICAL PROBLEMS OF MOUNTAIN AGRICULTURE IN TAJIKISTAN

H. Mukhabbatov

At the present stage of socio-economic development of the country all necessary preconditions have been created to increase efficiency of agricultural production. Involvement of new agricultural resources into the economic cycle would also contribute to achievement of higher efficiency. In other words, an important task is to draw into productive sphere the weakly developed natural-economic zones, which would accelerate advancement of cropping and animal-breeding. By these zones we mean the mountain territories, which have huge areas and considerable potential for agriculture (fertile lands, rangelands, meadows, etc.). Rational use of natural resources of mountain areas is a means to increase production of cropping and animal-breeding and to achieve targets put forward by Plenary Session of the CPSU Central Committee in May, 1982 and by the Food Programme of the USSR.

Tajikistan is a mountain Republic and is one of the high altitude regions of the globe. Mountains account for 90 per cent of its area. Glaciers and ice fields for Tajikistan accumulate great volumes of precipitated moisture, which feed rivers of Central Asia, and thus form the basis of irrigation of cotton fields and other agricultural lands in this vast arid tract of the country.

Mountain regions of the Republic have about 10 per cent of the population of Tajikistan. In the recent past their share in the population of the Republic was much greater. Depopulation of mountains has taken place mostly in the post-war period, when a considerable part of mountain population has moved to valleys, where new irrigated cotton-growing areas have been developed. This development, though economically feasible, was a forced process, because in this period the velleys (especially the Vakhsh valley) did not possess the necessary labour resources.

In the post-revolutionary period the mountain areas as well as Tajikistan has moved a long way on the path of development and have leapt from backwardness to progress, from feudalism to socialism omitting capitalism. Mountain areas have undergone fundamental economic and social transformation. The insularity of the mountain areas and the separation of mountain villages (*kishlak*) from the external world for the long autumn-winter months have become things of the past. A broad network of schools, cultural-educational institutions, public health services have been created in mountain regions. Population of these regions benefits from modern means of transport and communication, electricity supply, and other achievements of modern civilization and scientific-technological progress.

However, the economic potential of mountain areas of Tajikistan is not yet great. Their role in the gross product of the Republic and in its total income is rather small. Agricultural output of mountain areas is about 10 per cent of the total for the Republic and the industrial output is below 5 per cent.

By now nearly all valley lands fit for irrigation have been developed while population continues to grow rapidly. Shortage of free lands, which may be used both for increase of cultivated areas, and for industrial and residentia construction, as well as for other social and cultural projects in the velley regions may impede economic and social development. According to specialists, in future this problem may become even more acute. All this makes the problems of development of mountain areas extremely urgent.

Economic development of mountain areas is, actually, an extremely labour-intensive venture, requiring substantial capital investments. Therefore, it is necessary to find the most effective ways to overcome the nature-borne difficulties of economic development. Nearly all mountain areas of Tajikistan are remote from the main railway lines, and usually communicate with economically more developed zones by automobiles through low-quality roads, which are sometimes not operational throughout the year. All this results in high transportation costs. As a rule, expenditure on construction of industrial and social projects, especially of transport and water management facilities is much higher in mountains than in valleys. Areas fit for cultivation are rather scarce in the mountains. They are mostly represented by small plots in river flood-plains and alluvial fans. It is much more difficult to introduce machinery there, than in the valley areas.

Mountain and foothill territories are characterized by vertical zonality of climate, soils and vegetation, producing, together with dissected relief forms, extreme variety of natural conditions and resources. Of the natural factors, producing fundamental impact on agricultural production, one should stress the dissected relief. This accounts for such negative factors as erosion of soils, mozaicity of lands, their complex configuration, abundant rock debris, different productivity of similar soils on slopes of different aspect and inclination. While the average slope gradient of agricultural lands in the USSR is from 2 to 4° in Tajikistan, over 88 per cent of cultivated lands have slope gradients above 10°. 2/3 of ploughed and pasture lands in the Republic are under permanent threat of erosion. This considerably hinders use of agricultural machinery, and decreases its efficiency. The greater the slope gradients, the higher are losses for transportation of seeds, fertilizers, fuel and other materials.

Of all the cultivable areas of the Republic located on slopes above 10°, 25.0% are accounted for by plots below 1 ha, 37.0% from 1 to 3 ha, 28.0% from 3 to 10 ha. Especially heavy fragmentation is peculiar for areas in the Mountain-Badakhshan oblast. Another important factor, which influences agricultural practices and labour efficiency in agriculture is height above sea level. Altitudinal distribution of the territory of Tajikistan is as follows : 36.2% below 1,000 m above sea level, 20% from

1,000 to 2,000 m and 43.8% above 2,000 m.

It should be noted, that climatic conditions do not prevent the cultivation of many crops, including heat-loving crops, on high elevations. Thus, in some natural-economic zones, cereals are grown up to 2,200 m, and higher. In the south of the Republic vineyards are found up to 2,000 m, and in the Botanical garden located in the Pamirs up to 2,320 m. An interesting phenomenon is that at different elevations the same crops ripe at different dates, even within one administrative region. Since long, citizens of mountain regions used these specific natural phenomena for selection of crops.

Now there is a need to scientifically develop patterns of crop distribution and of agricultural specialization depending on vertical zonality. Vertical zonality, steep slopes, mozaicity of fields make it difficult to use machinery in mountain agriculture. The higher one goes above the sea level and the steeper are the slopes, the economic efficiency of agricultural machinery becomes lower. Experiments have shown, that with every 100 m of elevation the capacity of the motors reduces by more than 1 per cent.[1] Tests carried out by specialists have demonstrated that at elevations 2,000 m above sea level, the capacity of Diesel engines gets reduced by 17 per cent. However, a low percentage of cultivated lands in mountain regions is mostly due to relief factors, specially steep slopes and small fields and varied microrelief. A diversified relief results in mozaicity of cultivated fields. Thus, the cultivated area in the mountain regions of the Pamirs consists of 4,600 plots, ranging from 0.01 to 8.3 ha.

Soil patterns are also determined by vertical zonality. Dissected relief and slope gradients result in the disturbance of this zonality by soil intrusions. Mountain soils are stony and in the Komsomolabad and Kalikhumb regions stony lands are widespread. Abundance of stones increases filtration capacity and impedes erosional processes, but accelerates depreciation of agricultural machinery.

Mountain agriculture considerably differs from lowland agriculture in farm practices, methods of animal-breeding, agricultural machinery and irrigation techniques. In most mountain regions of the Republic labour efficiency is very low, because cultivation is performed mostly by hand tools. A considerable natural resource potential of mountain areas is not utilized, or is inadequately utilized because of difficult conditions of work. As a result of higher labour expenditure, prime cost of agricultural production in mountain regions is much higher than in the lowlands. This creates economic inequality of mountain and lowland farms.

However, despite all drawbacks, reserves of mountain areas allow for 2-3 times higher gross output, if the necessary amount of capital investments are provided. It should be noted that some products of agriculture can be produced only in mountain environments.

Increased potential of the Republic, advancements of economic conditions for agricultural production on the basis of scientific-technological progress create the objective prerequisites for accelerated development of mountain territories and for their increased role in the economy of Tajikistan.

Mountain regions possess high potential for the development of agro-industrial complexes. Of large economic significance may become large-scale fruit production of mountain regions, which would meet requirements of the whole country.

There are considerable areas of slope lands, which may be used for fruit plantations : they are estimated about 1 mln ha. At present these lands are used, with little exception, for dry farming of cereals. An interesting experience in the use of uneven slope lands has been in the Hissar zone. Several years ago these lands were either not cultivated, or, when cultivated, produced low yields (maximum yields of cereals were 4-5 q/ha, average income—90-100 roub/ha). A substantial portion of the mountain slopes is within the zone of non-irrigated fruit-growing, especially for viticulture. It includes the northern part of the Kuliab oblast, the Hissar valley and some areas in the north of the Kurgan-Tiube oblast. Grapes grown in the foothills and the mountain zones of the Republic belong mostly to table and currants varieties and have the highest saccharine content in the country—up to 30 per cent. Investigations of climatic regimes in the Hissar valley have revealed that many areas in this hilly terrain are favourable for viticulture. Thus, in the state farm named after Rasulov, average yields in 1983 on hilly areas were 120 q/ha, while some brigades gathered up to 150 q/ha.

Widely known beyond the limits of the Republic, and even abroad became the varieties of apricot grown in the north of Tajikistan. But those grown in the upper reaches of the Zeravshan river and in the western Pamirs are of no inferior quality. Dried apricots and currants are in great demand far beyond the limits of the Republic due to their high saccharine content and delicious taste. In mountain areas production of dried fruit is the optimal and the most convenient form of marketing. Construction designs of solar dryers for fruit and grapes are already available. An important task now is to speed up the construction of facilities for solar drying of production in fruit and grape-growing farms.

In southern Tajikistan, especially in the Vakhsh zone, slope land may be planted by subtropical species (pomegranate, persimmon, figtrees), and even by lemon-trees, if protected from frosts for which artificial heating is not required. Estimated foothill and mountain land areas in the Vakhsh zone, which may be used for these crops are about 130 thous. ha. Full utilisation of these lands can provide, according to very modest assessments, a 1-1.2 mln tons increase in output of most valuable fruit.

Experience gained in the last decade shows, that the high mountain climate of the Garm zone is rather favourable for horticulture. A great contribution to the cultivation of formerly barren lands and mountain areas was made by the state farm named after the 50th anniversary of Tajikistan, located in the Garm region, and specializing in cultivation of trees for horticulture. There, seedlings are grown on the basis of new technology. It allows a growth of 500 to 1,000 trees per 1 ha, instead of 100-150. This is profitable both from the point of the economy, and of intensive exploitation of machinery. The collective farm started these activities in 1975, when the first seedlings were planted over 40 ha using the technique of stepped orchard. This state farm has contributed much to the increase of the number of local varieties of apples and pears ("*khubani*", "*maliki*", "*shokhi*", "*noshpati*"), as well as to the introduction of foreign verieties like "crimson", "royal", etc. At present the total area of orchards in the state farm is over 800 ha and average yields are 180-200 q/ha.

Besides the state farm mentioned above several other state farms are specializing in growing fruit. According to preliminary estimates, by 1990, production of apples and pears in the Garm zone can be increased up to 60,000 tons. This would meet the requirements of high-quality apples and pears of the Republic, as well as of some other economic regions of the country.

Mountain regions are also favourable for growing of potatoes. Production of potatoes has increased threefold during the last 15 years i.e., from 51,200 tons to 158,000 tons. The yields grew from 78 q/ha in 1965 to 158 q/ha in 1983.[2] High mountain state farms gather annually 300-340 q/ha of potatoes. In some brigades the potato crop in 1983 reached 400-420 q/ha. Potato-growing is beneficial for animal-breeding. It was calculated, that along with the main product, each hectare under potato crop can give a yield of forage (non-standard potatoes and green parts) which is equivalent to average yield of a hectare of alfalfa crop. In mountain conditions profitability of potato production is 15 times higher than of beef-production (and 6 times higher than beef-production using industrial technology).[3] This aspect is very important for solving the major problems of socio-economic development of rural places in mountain and high-mountain areas. According to assessments made by the Institute of Economy of the Tajik Academy of Sciences, index of efficiency of potato-growing in the mountain zone exceeds from 2 to 30 times the corresponding index for any other agricultural crop, except for tobacco. However, labour intensity of tobacco-growing is 10 times greater, than that of potato production.

There is also some potential of vertical expansion of potato crop. In the recent years potato fields have occupied lands higher and higher along the slopes of the Karategin, Turkestan and Zeravshan ridges, and of the ridge of Peter the First. On the mountain plateau of Jilondi in the Jirgatal region, which is 3,000 m above sea level, average yields of potatoes for many years has been 150-180 q/ha. Now, accurate assessment of high-mountain lands fit for potato-growing, and scientific recommendations for their use are urgently needed, both because of intensive development of potato-growing, and in connection with orchard-growing in mountain zones of the Republic.

An urgent problem to be solved is the development of the infrastructure for production and of storehouses and road network. There is no doubt, that construction of storehouses on farms is highly desirable. However, all storehouses, which are now available in the mountain regions are designed only for storing seed stocks. As for commercial potato produce, all of it is delivered to places of consumption directly after harvesting. This results in considerable damage to them. Therefore, it is necessary to undertake construction of a wide network of potatostorehouses using local construction materials. Supply of this product to regions of consumption in accordance with requirements of the retail net, will reduce losses to a minimum, and ensure more balanced use of cargo traffic round-the-year.

No better is the situation of horticultural economies in the mountain regions. One can often observe that the crop, produced with so much effort, is not able to reach its buyer because good roads and specialized fruit storehouses are not available. In mountain areas it is necessary to construct storehouses for potatoes and fruit, which would be capable to keep about a half of the harvested crop, as proposed by the Food Programme. These storehouses should be based on the most advanced technology, using active ventilation and artificial cooling. Along with construction of storehouses, optimal use of potato and fruit production, and their better supply to consumers should be ensured by construction of canning plants and of juice-producing shops.

It is necessary to further advance the traditional animal-breeding, in the mountains which is hampered by limited forage resources. In this connection, the problem is to increase in every way possible the resources of forage, to prevent degradation of rangelands, and to reclaim them in order to increase their productivity.

Scientific institutions should be given the charge of developing recommendations for a considerable increase in productivity of rangelands. This would require comprehensive studies of rangeland areas. Similar studies should also be carried out for areas which are listed in land surveys as cultivable. Under specific reclamation activities part of them may be used for forage production. Such studies will be especially important for the Mountainous Badakhshan oblast.

In future further studies will be required to select high-yielding rangeland plants, to develop techniques for radical and surface reclamation of rangelands and to introduce agricultural practices of growing wild forage plants for grazing and hay-making. It is especially important to develop technique for reclamation of autumn-winter rangelands for sheep on slopes in order to produce upto a thousand units of forage and more from one hectare.

Application of mineral and organic fertilizers is the most reliable and tested way to raise productivity and forage capacity of mountain rangelands. The studies carried by the Institute of Biology of the Kirgiz Academy of Sciences at 1,700-3,400 m above sea level have shown, that application of mineral fertilizers (nitrogen and phosphorus) in amounts 60 kg/ha gave a 2.5-4.0 increase of yields of high-mountain rangelands. Further experiments have shown the importance of sheep manure for higher productivity of rangelands. According to specialists, a 2.5-3.0 mln sheep live-stock can annually reclaim 50-60 thousand ha of rangelands without any additional expenditure.

At the same time all efforts should be made to considerably develop production of forage under irrigation, uplift productivity of forage crops, utilize agricultural and industrial wastes for forage, and create meadows, where possible. An urgent problem is to upgrade cattle, structure of live-stock, and to advance the breeding systems.

The Tajik mountains are rich in certian species of fruit-bearing and officinal plants : various nut-trees, almond-trees, barberry, sweetbrier, Hippophae rhamnoides, Ephedra, etc. According to preliminary assessments, total area of wild fruit-bearing plants is over 100,000 ha. Besides upgrading feeding diet, they have valuable officinal properties. In the past years mountain forests thinned out because of over-exploitation. As a result, these rare fruit-bearing forests can no more protect slope soils from erosion. It is therefore, necessary to take care of the propagation of these forests.

Tajikistan is a highly potential region for the development

of large plantations of walnut. Suitable lands are available in all zones of the Republic at altitudes from 800 to 2,300 m. Especially high is the potential for walnut plantations in mountains of Central Tajikistan and Western Pamirs. Expansion of areas under walnut is very profitable since it is in high demand (1 ton of walnut may give from 7 to 7.5 q of valuable officinal oil).

Pistachio-trees do not require very specific environmental conditions. Their nuts are very valuable and contain 70 per cent oil and 23 per cent proteins. Pistachio growth is usually spread from 600 to 1,400 m above sea level, and occupies 80,000 ha. Pistachio is in high demand in food industry and perfumery. Profitability of pistachio-growing depends greatly on employment of suitable agricultural practices.

Areas of Hippophae rhamnoides exceed 2,000 ha. Its plantations are spread in flood-plains of the rivers Pianj, Shakhdara, Zeravshan, Surkhob, Kamarou, Sorbo, etc. Officinal properties of this plant are widely known. However, we often find that many forests of H. rhamnoides are left without care and maintenance.

Plantations of Ephedra equisetina are abundant. They always cover slopes with stony soils. Forests of E. equisetina are used as sources of valuable officinal raw material. To replenish them, it may be expedient to plant ephedra on mountain slopes with gradients of 20° and more. These plantations would serve both anti-erosion and water protection functions. One should also note, that because of non-rational exploitation and cattle grazing many valuable and officinal species (barberry, cataway (zira), sweetbrier, St.-John's-wort etc.) are destroyed, and areas under them have become smaller. Annually hundreds of tons of medicinal wild fruit and berries are wasted. It is necessary to undertake urgent action in order to conserve them and to increase their productivity.

In Tajikistan, where the mulberry-tree serves man from times immemorial, there is not a single organization, which is directly engaged in harvesting and growing of edible mulberry. Ancient medical books has informed us of the medicinal properties of mulberry. Thus, the book "*Makhzan-ul-avdia*" (treasury of medicinal remedies) reads : mulberry is the fruit of a glorious tree, it renovates blood, cleans spleen, benefits liver and organs of respiration". Medicinal properties of mulberry were described in detail in "Canon". For ages skillful *dekhans* (peasants) were selecting new species. Now they count over 50 (bedona, balkhi, marvorid, nabori, shakhtut, etc.), and each has its own properties. In war times people ate fresh berries and kept dried berries for winter. Areas under mulberry-tree should be expanded, since this may be rather profitable for farms. The mulberry-tree is also very decorative, and can grow on barren stony lands.

It is of extreme importance, to develop and persistently implement a system of nature conservation activities in mountain regions. Priority should be given to prevention of soil erosion in mountains and to consolidation of the soil layer on eroded lands. The most effective tool for this purpose is planting of perennial species.

Afforestation and restoration of forests in mountains should be promoted in every possible way. Unfortunately, unplanned felling is still going on in mountain gorges, while the rates of forest reclamation activities are very low. It appears necessary to develop a programme of forestry development in mountain regions of the Republic, which would accelerate afforestation and creation of forest-orchards.

Thus, possessing huge reserves of natural-climatic, water, and land resources, the mountain areas urge for their most rational and integrated use to meet the demands of the national economy. Implementation of the above proposed measures, which seek to develop the mountain economy, would not only promote agricultural efficiency but also the overall level of productive forces of Tajikistan.

FOOTNOTES

1. I.M. Khokhlov, Aktualnye voprosy razvitiy a zemledeliya izhivotnovodstva v gornykh raionakh Sovetskogo soyuza (Urgent problems of cropping and animal-breeding in mountain areas of the Soviet Union). Tbilisi, 1975, p. 12.
2. Narodnoye khoziaistvo SSSR v 1983 g. Statisticheskiy yezhegodnik (National economy of the USSR in 1983. Statistical yearbook). M., 1984, p. 236.
3. Problemy effektivonsti proizvodstva (Problems of efficiency of production). "*Donish*", t. VI, Dushanbe, 1981, p. 99.

29

PROBLEMS OF THE DEVELOPMENT OF MOUNTAINOUS REGIONS OF THE USSR WITHIN THE FRAMEWORK OF THE PROJECT "MOUNTAIN ECOSYSTEMS" UNDER UNESCO "MAN AND BIOSPHERE" PROGRAMME

Y.P. Badenkov

In recent decades (and especially in the period after the Second World War), under the conditions of scientific and technological progress, of population growth and insufficiency of foodstuffs, the problem of development of new territories and/or intensification of the development of historically used ones acquires an ever greater importance. This process is directed to an utmost use of biospheric resources—food, energy, mineral, and recreations.

Naturally, this process is also characteristic of mountain regions of the world which occupy 25 per cent of the dry land. Though 10 per cent of the world's population lives in mountainous regions, 40 per cent of this population depends to some extent on the resources concentrated in mountains. This general situation undifferentiated by regions is as ineffective as the mean temperature of patients in hospital. A number of regions and countries of the world, such as Nepal, Switzerland, Equador and others, and a number of Union Republics in the USSR—Kirghizia, Tajikistan, the Transcaucasian Republics, in many respects, if not completely, depend on the development of resources of mountains.

The process of intensification of natural resource use has its negative side as well : exhaustion of renewable resources, degradation of ecosystems, deterioration of the quality of natural environment, etc.

Depending on geological-geomorphological, natural-climatic and socio-economic diversity of mountain ecosystems, the character of developmental problems and the ways for their solution differ in different countries and regions of the world. However, it should be noted that the set of such problems for all the mountainous regions is common and may be, without distinguishing regional priorities, outlined as follows :

—deforestation-desertification,
—erosion,
—increase of the danger of natural hazards : mudflows, landslides, floods,
—overgrazing and degradation of pastures,
—regulation of flow and interruption of water balance,
—development of mining industry and of transport—disturbance of the ecosystems' sustainability,
—recreational development,
—changes in settlement systems (depopulation and population growth),
—transformation of traditional (cultural and historical) links,
—disturbance of the aesthetics of mountain landscapes,
—nature conservation and organization of a network of reserves.

This list may probably be enlarged, but in general it seems to be sufficient for characterizing the situation in the mountainous regions of the world.

However, when tackling the problems of regional development, some of them come to the foreground, others are of minor importance or are at present in an embryonic form. And this is natural, as an enumeration of the mountainous regions of the world shows how diverse are their natural, socio-economic and political conditions and corresponding problems of development. There are Arctic and sub-Arctic mountains (Spitsbergen, Alaska, Khibini and others), the mountains of

Europe (Alps, Balkans, Carpathians), the highest structures of Asia (Hindu-Kush, Himalaya, Pamirs), the greatest mountain system of the American continent (Cordilleras and Andes), the mountains of Africa (Atlas, Ephioshi, Dragon and Ruven-Zori). However even if this diversity of natural-climatic and socio-economic conditions are taken into account, the set of developmental problems remains to be quite general. In short, this may be illustrated by two mountainous countries occupying extreme positions in the levels of economic development: Switzerland and Nepal. The former is one of the most developed countries, the latter-one of the most underdeveloped in terms of living standards.

Nevertheless, these two countries have one problem in common : interrelation (autonomy and interdependence) of the development of mountainous and plain territories. Although there is a basic difference between the two (Nepal is an agrarian country, Switzerland a highly industrialized one), population density in mountainous and plain areas is quantitatively comparable (95 prs./sq. km in Nepal and 25 to 50 prs./sq. km in Switzerland).

However, it should be underlined that the problem is *Common*, but its acuteness and ways of solution are not. The economic potential (without the historico-political aspect of the problem) determines the level, the scale and the strategy of regional development of these countries. Nevertheless, let us emphasize once more that the problems of erosion, soil degradation, flow regulation, and tourism "boom", are the problems of ecological-economic contradictions which exist in both the countries although on different levels. Probably this commonness of the problems and the experience of corresponding scientific elaborations in such developed countries as Switzerland, Federal Republic of Germany and others serves as a basis for an active scientific collaboration of scientists from the Hindu-Kush-Himalaya region within the framework of the International Centre for Integrated Mountain Development (ICIMOD).

Mountain ecosystems occupy large areas in the USSR (35 to 40 per cent of the total, of which 12 per cent are over 1,500 m in altitude). 20 per cent of the population of the USSR lives in the mountains.

Differing in structure, lithology and the history of geological development and being situated in different natural-climatic zones, mountains represent a diverse and contrasting set of types of mountain ecosystems. The Arctic mountain deserts of the Novaya Zemlya and of the Polar Urals, the volcanoes of Kamchatka, of the Kuril islands and of the Caucasus, the mountain structures of the Chersky and Verkhoyansky ridges, the Altai, the Sayan mountains, the Tien Shan and Pamirs. This list far from being complete gives a notion about the diversity of the mountain ecosystems of USSR.

Differences in the resource potential, economic development, and the national traditions of the population, supplement the specificity and the originality of the development of the country's mountainous regions. There is a certain "specificity" in the matter of development of mountains in the Soviet Union, conditioned by the factors enumerated above. The mountain ecosystems of the north-east of the country are intensively developed for the purposes of mining, while their agricultural use is limited due to harsh natural-climatic conditions. In the south of the Far East, mineral and forest resources are intensively developed (the Sikhote Alin ridge, the Dzhungdzhur).

The development of resources is most profound and integrated in the regions that have long ago been historically developed : the Carpathian mountains, the Caucasus, Soviet Central Asia with its agricultural, mining and recreational development. The latter region is quite intensive and embraces those regions that have formerly not been used for these purposes (the Sikhote Alin mountain land, the volcanic mountains of Kamchatka, etc.). For instance, in Kirgizia during a short period (from 1970 to 1978) the number of tourists increased 12 times and reached about 2 million whereas the total population of Kirgizia is only 3.5 million.

The intensive development of the resources of mountains leads to the aggravation of ecological problems such as expansion of erosional processes and decrease in the ecosystems' productivity. It is especially true of mountain pastures. According to N.A. Gvozdetsky, in mountainous regions of

Soviet Central Asia and of South and South-East Kazakhstan, up to 30 or 40 per cent of the pastures are littered with half-eaten plants and are eroded. This has brought about a 2 or 2.5-time decrease in productivity. The same phenomena are also characteristic of the mountains of the Caucasus. The erosion-prone lands occupy about 2/3 of the country's area (in the Asiatic part they are 4 times as large as in the European one), while a considerable part of them pertains to mountainous regions.

An active development of irrigated agriculture in the arid regions of Soviet Central Asia made the problem of insufficiency of water resources more acute despite the fact that mountainous regions are well provided with them. Let us note that within the Pamirs there is a large nival-glacial system (with the largest glaciers of Fedchenko, RGS*, Garmo, Medvezhiy and others) with the total area of over 100 sq. km and containing colossal reserves of fresh water.

Soviet glaciologists actively work on the two problems most important for the national economy : study of the processes of glaciers and the dynamics and management (regulation) of their run-off.

The above review, though most general and far from complete, gives an idea about the importance of the problem of development of mountainous territories both on global and on regional (national) levels.

ORGANIZATION OF RESEARCH IN THE USSR WITHIN THE FRAMEWORK OF THE PROJECT MAB-6A "MOUNTAIN ECOSYSTEMS"

Research work on the study of nature and development of mountains in the USSR are carried out by numerous scientific organizations of the Academy of Sciences of the USSR, those of the Academies of the Union Republics' and by Universities and other institutions. One of the projects uniting and coordinating this research is the Project "Mountain Ecosystems and their Rational Use" (MAB-6a) of the UNESCO Programme "Man and Biosphere", which is under way since 1974.

At present the scale of research on the problems of mountainous regions has considerably broadened and a Leading Centre

*Glacier of Russian Geographical Society.

of the Project has been created uniting six regional Working Groups. Till the last days of his life (March 1985) the Director of the Institute of Geography of the USSR Academy of Sciences Academician I.P. Gerasimov was the Chairman of this Centre. After his death, the Chairmanship went to Prof. V.M. Kotlyakov who is at present the Corresponding Member of the Academy of Sciences of the USSR, Head of the Glaciological Department of the Institute of Geography and Vice-President of the Geographical Society of the USSR. Coordination of work on different regions of the country is realized by the following Working Groups :

—"The Caucasus" (Head—Prof. E.D. Kobakhidze).

—"The Crimea-Carpathians" (Head—Corresponding Member of the Ukrainean Academy of Sciences M.A. Golubets).

—"Soviet Central Asia" (Head-Academician of the Academy of Sciences of the Kirgiz SSR A.M. Mamytov).

—"The Urals" (Head—Corresponding Member of the Academy of Sciences of the USSR V.N. Bolshakov).

—"Siberia—the Far East" (Head—Prof. V.R. Alekseev).

—"The Altai-Sayan Mountains" (Head—Prof. V.S. Revyakin).

The research work under the MAB-6a Project are carried out on the following problems :

—theoretical bases of the development in mountainousr egions ;

—regularities of the formation and development of natural complexes and their individual components (relief, climate, water resources, glaciers, soils, vegetation, fauna, etc.) in different altitudinal belts ;

—scientific substantiation of a rational use of natural resources and conservation of nature in mountainous regions ;

—study of natural hazards in mountainous regions (avalanches, mudflows, landslides, etc.) and delineation of hazard-prone zones ;

—study of problems caused by the development of agriculture, industry, transport and different systems of landuse in mountainous lands ;

—monitoring of the mountain environment ;
—problems of recreational use of mountainous lands ;
—the impact of economic activities of man on mountain ecosystems and the main problems of ecological-economic planning ;
—systems of settlement and human ecology in mountainous lands.

Studies under the MAB-6 Project are undertaken by numerous organizations in different regions of the country and dozens of expeditions are organized for this purpose every year. Regional and All-Union conferences on mountain problematics are held, whose materials are published in the form of collective volumes and monographs.

There are a number of observation and experimental stations carrying out long-term studies in mountains : the North-Caucasian Scientific Station of the Institute of Geography of the USSR Academy of Sciences, the Martkon Station of the Tbilisi University, Stations of the Moscow University in the region of Elbrus (the Caucasus), in the Carpathians and Khibin Mountains, the Tien-Shan Physico-Geographical Station, etc.

Specially mentioned should be the efforts at *international cooperation*, which is realized both on multilateral and bilateral bases. *Multilateral cooperation* is organized within the framework of the Projects of UNEP, UNESCO-MAB and with the countries of COMECON—Bulgaria, Poland, Cuba. The MAB-6 Project is closely linked with the Project of UNEP "Mountain Agriculture", which is under the scientists of Georgia and the People's Republic of Bulgaria. Regular courses on the problems of mountain agriculture are organized in Georgia for specialists from developing countries.

Scientists of the Soviet Union have long-standing and fruitful contacts with the Commission on Mountain Geo-ecology (Chairman-Professor B. Messerli, Switzerland) of the International Geographical Union. There are good prospects for cooperation with the International Centre for Integrated Mountain Development (ICIMOD) of the Hindu-Kush-Himalaya Mountains.

Bilateral cooperation is a traditional form of research undertaken by Soviet scientists with their colleagues from other countries. The work organized in the form of joint field symposia is especially effective. As an example, it may be mentioned that a series of Soviet-French and Soviet-Bulgarian field symposia resulted in the publication of substantial monographs "The Alps—the Caucasus" and "The Caucasus—the Stara Planina" (1980, 1981). It seems that in this context a perspective should also be developed for joint Soviet-Indian research by the way of organization of analogous field symposia. We should probably also discuss the question about organization of biosphere reserves in analogous regions of both our countries, which would carry out research according to coordinated programmes and maintain a steady system of exchange of information and specialists. These biosphere stations may be looked upon as specific scientific-methodological centres of research on the whole spectra of the problems of development of mountainous territories.

In conclusion, it is necessary to emphasize that both the UNESCO Programmes "Man and Biosphere" and the MAB-6a Project "Mountain Ecosystems", besides having academic aspects of research, have a strictly practical orientation, i.e., scientific research should build a basis for the strategy of integrated development of mountains and suggest a set of alternatives to the persons and organizations making decisions.

30

DEVELOPMENT OF NATURAL RESOURCES AND CREATION OF TERRITORIAL PRODUCTION COMPLEXES (TPC)

A.I. Zavulunov

The Tajik Soviet Socialist Republic possesses enormous natural resources which can be used to provide higher development rates for the national economy. The republic is particularly rich in mineral resources which allow mining industries to be developed.

Of primary importance for increasing the efficiency of the mining industry and the development of natural resources on the whole is the creation of territorial-production complexes. The creation of such complexes makes it possible to achieve high economic effects, as natural resources are developed at lowest cost and in close contact with operating enterprises as well as with those under construction. TPC's have common sources of both natural material and labour resources. As to the non-ferrous metals prospected, Leninabad region occupies one of the leading places not only in the republic but also in Middle Asia and hence it possesses a reliable mineral-raw material basis on which to create TPC's.

The great role and importance of natural riches of Northern Tajikistan were mentioned, in particular, as far back as the 1930's at the First Conference on the Study of the productive Forces of the Tadzhik SSR held in Leningrad. Speaking at the Conference, Academician A.E. Fersman said, 'Three large regions of mining industry have been contemplated now, namely, the remarkable Khodgent region, the region of the middle flow of the Zeravash river, and, finally the Darvas region.'[1]

Later he wrote, 'The first region is the gate of Fergana, a region where the rich Kara-Nasar with its lead, zinc and silver determines the main lines of the future, these metals being joined, on the one hand, by coal resources of Shuraba, Samgara salts and, on the other, by greatest possibilities of agriculture'.[2]

The necessity of creating new complexes in the republic was stressed at the XIX Congress of the Communist Party of Tadzhikistan and at the XXVI Congress of the CPSU. The report of the Central Committee of the Tadzhikistan CP at the XIX Congress of the Communist Party of Tadzhikistan pointed out that among other things to be done . . . 'it is necessary to give prominance to designing the *Saravshan mining complex* on the basis of the deposits of non-ferrous and rare metals, coal and construction materials, the building of the *Adrasman industrial complex*, based on the development of Bolshoi Kanimansur deposits.'[3]

Thus, there are all grounds for creating and forming new complexes in this region having rich mineral resources and favourable geographical and economic conditions and, particularly, the availability of work-force.

Research and design organisations are doing research and developing design documents on the creation of the North-Tadzhik TPC on the basis of exploiting Bolshoi Kanimansur deposits. It is also planned to establish the Zeravshan complex on the basis of the deposits of non-ferrous and rare metals, coal and construction materials. The main goal of the new complexes will be a complete and all-round development of the natural resources of these regions and provision of the national economy of the country with products of the mining industry.

This paper discusses the peculiarities of the creation of the North-Tadzhik TPC.

The literature in Economics treats the notion of a territorial-production complex in different ways. We believe that the best definition is given in the official document on recommendations and methods : 'the TPC is a specific unity of technologically and economically interconnected, proportionally developing enterprises and plants subservient to different ministries and administrative bodies, concentrated on a limitted territory and using its resources and a unique infrastructure. The TPC include specialised enterprises with their factories, providing rational employment for the work-force, as well as the infrastructure, energy and construction bases, transport and social and cultural facilities.'[4] According to A.E. Probst, these complexes may be of two kinds : first, a primary and at the same time locally most limited form (covering rather small territory), secondly, regional TPC's, covering more or less large areas of the country's territory.[5]

In our opinion, the complexes which are planned to be created in the north of the republic will be local, with mining being the main specialisation. They will be based on mining and enrichment integrated plants which will constitute 'the core' of the complexes. But alongside with industries of productive specialisation, the complexes will have :

—branches of productive infrastructure and enterprises serving the economy and population (construction, transport, communications, light industries, construction materials production) ;

—branches of non-productive, social infrastructure (housing, culture, education, health service, social welfare, etc) meeting the needs of the population.

The planned North-Tadzhik TPC is situated in the northern and north-western part of Leninabad region and covers the right bank of the Syr-Darya river. It comprises Khodgent, Asht and Matchinsk district (39 per cent of the territory of Leninabad region) with a population of 306.4 thousand people, one fifth of the region's population.

The creation of the complex must provide the following :

—the most rational employment of the rapidly growing work-force of the region and the area in the public sector ;

—improvement of the branch structure of industry by primarily developing industries based on the use of local mineral and raw material resources ;

—maximal effective use of the latest achievements of science and technology for creation of the complex (when designing and constructing) ;
—combination of the interest of industrial development with social problems ;
—improvement of the environment and creation of comfortable conditions of life for the Soviet people on the basis of the concept of ecological compatibility of industry and the biosphere.

A number of plants of non-ferrous metallurgy are functioning on the territory of the future complex. The largest of them, not only in the region but also in the republic, is the Adrasman lead-zinc combine. Even now we have economically rather developed Adrasman subregion in which, together with non-ferrous metallurgical plants, other industries have been highly developed : low-voltage instrument plants, large-panel construction, plants of facing and non-metalliferous materials, a silicalcite plant, and a combine of subsidiary plants. Light and food industries are represented by the Kairakkum carpet combine, Khodgent ginning house, Asht Association of craftswomen working at home, Gafur wine plant, Khodgent brewery and meat-packing factory, Kairakkum combine of grain products, etc.

The exploitation of the deposits of Bolshoy Kanimansur urgently requires the construction of an ore-concentrating plant and this, in turn, will involve simultaneous development of other industries. Thus, during the development of the complex, machine-building enterprises can be located here producing electrotechnical output of interbranch purpose. Construction materials industry will be highly developed.

When the combine for extracting and processing non-ferrous ores on the basis of Bolshoy Kanimansur is built, a great amount of stripped rock suitable for the production of concrete and non-metalliferous construction materials will be created. The use of the simultaneously obtained limestone and possibilities to establish additional quarries for its extraction on the adjacent deposits will provide this raw material for the development of concrete industry not only in Leninabad region but also in the adjacent regions of the Uzbek, Kirghis and Kazakh Soviet Socialist Republics. Thus, favourable raw-meterials conditions are created for building up concrete industry capacities which, according to the estimates of Kharkov Yuzhgiprocement Institute, are necessary to fill the gap in the expected cement shortage in Middle Asia. The development of cement industry does not fully satisfy the needs of Leninabad region for cement. Bearing in mind the fact that Adrasman region has deposits of limestone, clay marls, it seems worthwhile for the Ministry of construction materials of the USSR to consider a possibility to include in the perspective scheme of the development of the industry of constructive materials, the construction of a cement factory in Adrasman with the capacity up to 2 m tn. The latter possesses high quality raw material resources and work-force. In addition to limestone, possibilities are created when stripping the deposits to effectively extract, in great amounts, tens of millions of cubic meters, of non-metalliferous materials—rock waste, gravel, sand, etc. The acquaintance with the scheme for the development of enterprises of non-metalliferous materials of the USSR shows that future needs of West Siberian and Kazakhstan regions for these non-metalliferous materials cosiderably overtakes their possible production capacities. Therefore, instead of dumping millions of cubic meters of non-metalliferous constructive raw materials on the territory of the future complex, it would be expedient to envisage the construction, on this basis, of a factory producing respective materials to be sent in future to the above mentioned regions of the country.

The development of heavy industries (non-ferrous metallurgy, construction materials, etc.) provides, in general, for the employment of men. In order for women work-force to be employed in the complex it is necessary to build enterprises of light industry. When developing branches of this industrial unit, of primary consideration should be its high consumption of labour and materials. Of no less importance is also the consideration of the possibility to build in the region small-size enterprises, as well as the transportability of ready products from the region, and raw materials to the region.

It is planned to reconstruct and enlarge the Kairakkum

Carpet Association, which will allow its capacity to be increased from 10.8 million m^2 to 15 million m^2 of carpets and carpet products per year. The expansion of the Association will also require additional work-force. As to light industry, it is worthwhile to open in the settlement of Adrasman affiliated branches of the enterprises already functioning, for instance, a clothing shop affiliated to Leninabad clothing factory, an association of crafts-women working at home under the ministry of local industry, which will result in a higher employment of the able-bodied population of the settlement, especially women. At present, there is an affiliated shop of Asht factory employing 70 home-workers. It is necessary to enlarge it. A great amount of women work-force will be used in the complex to be created in various public services (an everyday-service house, a bath-laundry combine, etc.).

Particularly developed in the region will be the food industries which are directly connected with the development of those branches of agriculture which supply them with agricultural raw materials. These are such industries as fruit-and-vegetable (canning) industry and wine production. A canning factory is planned to be constructed in Asht with the capacity 20 million conventional pots employing 120 people and even more in future. The expansion of the raw base at the expense of growing vines in Asht region makes it possible to plan the construction of a winery in the settlement of Asht with the capacity of processing 10.000 to of vinegrapes employing 110 people. Salt industry will develop at high rates due to practically unlimited salt deposits, easy access, and favourable conditions of exploitation. Asht salt factory is planned to be enlarged by constructing a salt briquetting shop with the capacity of 20.000 tn.

The development and construction of state food enterprises will be accompanied with considerable development in the region of cooperative industry. In this sphere, an increased production of grain products is envisaged. The production of confectionery will not increase during the period as the increased demand for production in the region is planned to be provided by state enterprises. The production of non-alcoholic drinks by cooperative industry is also planned to be increased. Canning industry is planned to be greatly increased.

The number of public catering enterprises and retail trade are planned to grow both within cooperative industry and the department for the supply of workers under the Ministry of non-ferrous metallurgy of the USSR.

The planned development of the region requires the expansion of the suburban agricultural base. The needs of the population for gourds and potatoes, fruit vinegrapes and to a considerable extent whole milk and meat should be satisfied by the local production capacities. There are already specialised farms on the territory of the complex but they will not be enough in future. Suburban farms should be created in Asht, Khodgent and Matchinsk regions. Specialists believe that this will involve a considerable change of the production structure of agriculture and of the direction of its specialisation. The creation of a large subsidiary farm is recommended on the new irrigated lands of Asht region. It will be able alongside with the supply of whole milk and meat, to produce great amounts of vegetables and early potatoes for public catering for the workers of the combine and for children's organisations. As to the rest of the population of the complex, it should be supplied by the whole agricultural-industrial complex of the republic.

The improvement of its transport service is of great importance for the development of the North-Tadzhik TPC. At present only automobile transport is used in the region, but due to the development of new deposits in the region of Bolshoy Kanimansur and the construction of a large mining-enrichment combine and other enterprises it is expedient to consider questions of servicing the complex by different transport means including railways.

The creation of the North-Tadzhik TPC in Leninabad region will also solve problems of social significance and economic development of new territories, employment, construction of social-cultural centers and housing. In addition to the funds which will be allocated for these purposes under the plan for the development of the social infrastructure of the republic, the construction of clubs, cinemas, cultural palaces for new industrial objects of the complex is also envisaged.

The formation and creation of the complex will make it possible not only to sharply increase the significance of Leninabad region in the economy of the republic, but will add to the general contribution of Tadzhikistan to the settlement of economic problems of the country.

The USSR has acquired a great experience in the effective use of natural and work resources and in the creation and formation of new TPC's on their basis. This makes it possible to develop individual regions of our country in an effective way. Territorial-production complexes, being territorial organisations of public production, allow their natural, energy, productive and labour resources to be used to the utmost. They also create favourable conditions for increasing the productivity of social labour and the efficiency of public production.

REFERENCES

1. *Problemi Tadzhikistana*. Len., 1933, v. I, pp. 10-11.
2. Ibid., p. 11.
3. *Communist Tadzhikistana*, 1981, Jan. 24.
4. Metodicheskie ukazania krazrabotke gosudarstvennith planov economicheskogo isocialnogo razvitia SSR.—*M. Economica*, 1980, p. 740.
5. Probst, A.E., *Problems of Socialist Industry Distribution*. M., 1971, p. 90.

31

PROBLEMS OF DEVELOPMENT OF A REGIONAL COMPLEX IN KIRGHIZIA

K.O. Otorbaev and *A.Y. Biyalinov*

The territorial development of the Soviet economy, the experience and achievements in building socialism in formerly backward regions, one of which is Kirghizia, are convincing proof of the complexity and diversity of regional economic tasks in a country such as the USSR.

In accordance with the basic economic law, socialist development involves constant satisfaction of man's growing demands and the raising of the standard of living of all the members of society. The regional aspect of social progress involves the process of ensuring a systematic growth and levelling of living standards in each zone, region and Union republic. This problem should be tackled-with, keeping in mind the natural differences, since according to Marx, among individual countries, and even regions there will continue to exist a certain inequality in living conditions, which although can be brought to a minimum, can never be fully eliminated.

It follows from what we have said that efficient regional development requires specialization of a region's productive forces in the country's economic system. Thus, regional development of a complex is a balanced and coordinated development of the largest possible amount of industries producing a wide range of use values and in this way directly effecting living standards. On the other hand, the existing "inequality in living conditions" demands of a region to specialize in certain products, conditions for whose manufacture are the most favourable there. Of course, both should contribute to greater efficiency of production.

An important feature of regional development in the USSR is the functioning of different territorial production units economic regions, Union republics, districts) within the framework of a common economic complex of the country.

The 1977 Constitutions says that the Soviet economy is a unified complex involving all the links of public production, distribution and exchange on the territory of the country. This complex includes highly developed productive forces and mature production relations, as well as an appropriate economic mechanism. Its creation became possible due to the successful implementation of Lenin's policy. The focus was on the alignment of the formerly backward outlying regions of Russia with the level of development achieved by the central regions. In that period Kirghizia's economy was developing at rates far exceeding those of the country as a whole. Thus in the period, 1922-84, the republic's industrial output grew 747-fold while that of the nation grew 551-fold.

It should be said however, that such accelerated regional development was made possible through national support, since at the time the republic had no sources of accumulation of its own. This was done with due significance given to the rational utilization of the republic's natural, labour and material resources. This particularly holds true for labour resources, since Kirghizia is one of the leaders in the country as regards the amount of manpower and its growth rate. The natural increase in population and therefore the inflow of labour resources is twice as high here. Appropriately enough, the most developed industries in Kirghizia are light industry and engineering and metal-working industry. During the period between 1924-83 the output of light industry grew 230-fold, of engineering and metal-working 240-fold. The large agricultural base of the republic gave a boost to food industry, whose output grew 210-fold.

These three are the dominant industries, producing 77% of

the total industrial output. Other industries too, however, have made headway. The production of building materials, for example, grew 1,349-fold in the same period. There was also some development of power industry, fuel production, forestry and wood-working industry, non-ferrous metallurgy and of some other industries. At present industrial production involves some 130 industries manufacturing over 3,700 items. In this way, regional policy in this country ensured increased growth rates for Kirghizia's industrial production, brought her economic development close to the national level and changed the structure of public production where industry has emerged into the forefront. Ninety per cent of the republic's territory is mountainous, and this has an inevitable effect on the whole of the economy, specifically on agriculture. Hence livestock breeding, which largely involves the use of natural pastures, is the leading branch of agriculture, providing 60 per cent of its gross product. In sheep population Kirghizia has the third place after the Russian Federation and Kazakhstan, while in the number of sheep per farmland unit it holds first place. The average amount of sheep per 100 hectares in the country as a whole is 45, while in the case of Kirghizia the figure is 119. In Kirghizia 100 hectares of farmland give 0.33 tonnes of wool and 1.3 tonnes of mutton, the highest figures in the country.

Pastures take up most of the land in the republic, with only a small proportion used for plowing ; the croplands are situated chiefly in valleys. Crop production is concentrated in the Chuya valley and in the foothills of the Osh district. The main crops here are sugar beet, cotton, tobacco, and cereals. Crop production has recently switched over to the production of seeds of sugar beet and lucern. Kirghizia is expected to become a major supplier of these.

Regional peculiarities have also had a great impact on the development of transport. Due to natural factors the most developed in Kirghizia is road transport, which deals with 97 per cent of cargo transportation, while only 3 per cent falls on railways and river transport. Railways could be built only in the Chuya valley and in the foothills of the Osh district. Besides, their length was limited, which confined rapid industrial growth to these regions alone. Hence, the bulk of Kirghizia's economic potential is concentrated here. Economic pressure per unit of area is very high in these regions, several times higher than in the rest of the republic.

The local peculiarities in the development of the republic's productive forces affected the territorial shaping of its economy. Two major economic regions have emerged in the republic. The North Kirghiz and South Kirghiz regions have sharply differing natural, climatic, demographic, economic and social features and different levels of economic development. The North Kirghiz economic region includes the regions of the Chuya zone, of the Issyk Kul, Naryn, and Talas districts. It accounts for 56.6 per cent of the Republic's population and 62.8 per cent of its territory. It provides 73.4 per cent of the gross industrial product and 64.3 per cent of produce. Inside the North Kirghiz region itself several economic sub-regions emerged, which can develop further. They are the Chuya, Issyk Kul, Naryn and Talas sub-regions.

The South Kirghiz economic region can be split into the Osh-Jalal-Abad, Lower Naryn and Kamajay-Haydarkan subregions. The region specializes in non-ferrous, food, light engineering, and fuel industries, cotton and tobacco growing and livestock breeding.

Among Kirghizia's economic sub-regions the most typical is the lower Naryn region. It accounts for 13.2 per cent of the republic's territory and 10 per cent of its population. The subregion's share in the gross industrial product amounts to 5.8 per cent, and it accounts for around 11 per cent of the republic's produce. The leading industries in its economy are power industry, electric engineering, non-ferrous metallurgy, sheep breeding, cotton growing and vegetable growing. A relatively small subregion, it has on its territory plants, water-power stations with longterm storage reservoirs and mineral deposits. This provides favourable conditions for emergence and development of the Lower Naryn territorial-industrial complex. Such a complex would lead to the creation of a region highly developed in all aspects. The sub-region's level of economic development already exceeds the republic's average, and is expected to rise still more due to rapid industrial growth.

Within the South Kirghiz economic region the least developed is the Kamajay-Haydarkan subregion. It accounts for 8.5 per cent of the republic's territory and 6.4 per cent of the population, only 31.7 per cent of which lives in urban areas. In industrial and agricultural production the subregion's share is insignificant 2.8 per cent and 3.1 per cent respectively. In per capita production output the subregion holds the last place in the republic. But having said that, it should be noted that the economic role of the sub-region can be hardly overestimated, since it is the leader in the country's production of antimony and mercury. The sub-region also plays an important part in meeting the republic's needs in meat, milk, wool, tobacco and canned vegetables.

A characteristic feature in the development of the economic complex of the Kamajay-Haydarkan subregion is the stabilization in the scale of industrial production. This was brought about by the exhaustion of certain deposits of minerals and coal, which led to the closing down of a number of plants. In view of the shrinking of the raw material base for extractive industries, it is our belief that new plants should consist of light and food industries. This should prove instrumental in solving both economic and social problems engendered by the curtailment of the extractive industry.

Another poorly developed economic sub-region is the Naryn sub-region, which specializes in livestock breeding. It accounts for 25.3 per cent of the territory and 6.4 per cent of the population of the republic. Its share in the republic's industrial and agricultural output is 1 per cent and 9 per cent respectively.

The sub-region's low development rate was largely due to its location high up in the mountains, which hampered the exploitation of the large amounts of mineral deposits available there. But with the increased economic capabilities and demand in raw materials and fuel, it would be expedient to create on the territory of the Naryn subregion a North Kirghiz mining-ndustrial complex. Most favourable conditions are available for this, such as ; the concentration of non-ferrous metal ore deposits, coal, building materials on a relatively small area of 120-140 square kilometres ; the proximity of the Naryn and Kokomeren river with their substantial water-power resources nse network of roads.

In scale and economic priorities an important role in the development of the territorial organisation of the republic's productive forces belongs to a complex exploitation of water-power resources, deposits of non-ferrous and rare metals, marble, as well as of unique recreation resources in the area of lake Issyk Kul. This together with the further development of the economy of the Chuya valley will be the basis for the shaping in the region of a territorial-industrial complex. This will provide a boost for the industrial centres already existing within the complex—the Kara-Balta, Frunze and Tomak centres, for the emerging West-Chuya and West-Issyk Kul industrial centres, as well as for the Issyk Kul national resort.

The emergence of a territorial-industrial complex would lead to an additional increase in the region's gross social product of 11.7 per cent with agricultural output jumping by 27.7 per cent and industrial output by 8.2 per cent. It would accelerate the rates of economic and social growth of Kirghizia as a whole and would enhance her role within the national economic complex.

One of the most dynamically developing and promising regions is the Talas economic sub-region, which accounts for 13.1 per cent of the republic's territory and 7.2 per cent of her population. Rapid industrial growth increased the sub-region's shares in the republic's industrial output from 0.7 per cent in 1975 to 2.2 per cent in 1980. The subregion's share in agricultural output which is 9.6 per cent is also significant.

In the past years the general level of the subregion's economic development has markedly increased, which was largely due to industrial production growth. For instance, in the period 1971-80 alone industrial output grew 5.4-fold, which far exceeds the rates of growth of agricultural output. The sub-region's industrial pattern too has undergone major changes. The leaders in the field are now : power industry—44.8 per cent, food industry—19.6%, light industry—9.4 per cent and building material production—11.3 per cent. However, most of these industries, with the exception of the power industry, are represented by small enterprises. In agriculture the leading branches are livestock breeding, tobacco growing and grain farming.

The Talas economic region is rich in minerals, most of them untapped. Deposits have been discovered there of iron pyrite and facing stone which could engender respective industries. New types of production can be also developed here with the framework of the agro-industrial complex. This requires more efficient processing. It is expedient to organise the already existing industries viz., building materials and shoe and clothing industries.

The pattern of the territorial structure of the republic's economy and of its regions and subregions largely depends on a rational relationship between the levels of development of material production and of social infrastructure. This is due to the increasing influence of the latter on most of the indicators of the subregions' economic growth, as well as to certain problems related to social development which were brought about by a high birth rate and rapid population growth. Certain regions experience a shortage in housing, children's pre-school facilities, modern hospitals, shops, catering services, etc.

An analysis of the economic development of each particular sub-region in Kirghizia has brought to light a number of common features :

—coinciding directions and levels of development of the basic industries and the social infrastructure of both the existing and emerging economic complexes within regions ;

—unequal development of different elements of the social infrastructure ; priority in most of the economic sub-regions is given to the development of health service, education and of housing and communal services ;

—insufficient (taking into account the population growth) growth rate of social infrastructure capacities, especially in economic sub-region specializing in farming and livestock breeding, with a dispersed population, low level of urbanization and of industrial development.

It should be noted that problems relating to the development of social infrastructure are being tackled increasingly successfully. The latest trend is towards the evening out of the different levels of infrastructure development, particularly of the elements that directly influence living conditions. If we also take into account the increased overall level of infrastructure development within the republic's economic sub-regions, then we can state that social factors of economic growth are increasingly being taken into consideration when drawing up plans and in long-term pre-planning scientific research.

When drawing up the economic parameters for Kirghizia's long-term development, prominence was given, aside from problems of industries, to territorial problems of social infrastructure development. The basic principles for long-term planning were : the fullest possible development of the entire complex of industries making up the social infrastructure ; accelerated development of its priority elements ; housing, health care, children's pre-school education, services and recreation. If we take the territorial aspect, priority should be given to rapid and complex development of the social infrastructures of industrialized economic subregions, characterized by a high level of urbanization. These same principles should be implemented in the regions, territorial-industrial complexes and towns taking shape and developing in conditions of labour shortage, in particular skilled labour shortage.

The problem of rapid and proportional development of the social infrastructure, although becoming a major factor in the growth of production efficiency and economic and social development of territories, cannot be solved quickly and in one way, due to the diversity of concrete temporal and spatial conditions. The decisive role here is, of course, played by planning. It should zero in on estimating the levels of development of this or that element of the infrastructure, proceeding from the final goal-reproduction of the population and labour resources. In other words, orientation should be towards the indicators of an optimally functioning economy, rather than towards the actual achieved average indicators, as is the practice. Hence, the need to meet as far as possible the growing requirements of the population, rather than aim at an even distribution of economic facilities over a region's entire territory.

The level of infrastructure development has a direct effect on the participation of the able-bodied population in social production. Fuller utilization of labour resources, the ensuring of maximum employment and the implementation of the right to work are prerequisite to the realization of the basic economic law of socialism. On the other hand, this has a profound social significance, since the moulding of a new man—a builder of communism, can succeed only by way of labour in the sphere of social production, where apart from creating material and spiritual values, he asserts himself as a personality.

In this context fuller employment is a major issue of Kirghizia's regional development. According to census estimates, only 71.2 per cent of the republic's able-bodied population are involved in the economy, which is over 10 per cent less than the national average (81.8 per cent). That is why it appears expedient for Kirghizia to pursue the road of extensive development through new construction, which would create new jobs. New plants should be built, if possible, in farming zones, which are areas experiencing an inflow of labour resources. According to the 1979 census, 69.3 per cent of the republic's population live in rural areas. 34.4 per cent of the able-bodied population are involved in farming, while the national average is 21 per cent. Meanwhile, broad and complex application of mechanization, introduction of scientific production methods—concentration and specialization—all this reduces the overall number, as well as the share of the population involved in farming. A specific feature of the indigenous population is their low mobility, a factor also to be taken into account when building new facilities. Therefore, it would be more rational to build small and medium-sized special-purpose plants, shops and branches in the rural areas.

Thus, to solve the problems relating to Kirghizia's complex regional development, an effort aimed at creating an interrelated network of territorial-industrial complexes of different classes and types is required which would have a balanced economic structure, and which would contribute to the maximum utilization of natural, economic and demographic preconditions for development. The industrial and territorial proportions of development have to be specified in order to increase the efficiency of the functioning of economic systems, which in its turn would leads to better living standards in Kirghizia'.

32

THE USE OF NATURAL RESOURCES OF THE TAJIK SSR ON THE BASIS OF ITS NATURAL LANDSCAPES

K.V. Stanyukovich

For many years the Academy of Sciences of the Tajik SSR has carried out work on the study of the Republic's nature and natural resources. Every specialized institute of the Academy studies nature and natural resources of Tajikistan in its own field. Within the Academy, Council on the Study of Productive Forces (SOPS) takes an active part in elaboration of long-term schemes of economic development of the Republic and of its territorial-production complexes. When creating new gigantic industrial complexes one needs to determine where new settlements and industrial enterprises are to be located, and where agricultural-recreational zones are to be created. For this, natural landscapes should be studied, classified and landscape maps compiled. This information is also necessary for implementing effective measures directed to nature conservation and rational use of natural resources. In this age of technical progress and space research, changes in nature are so rapid and profound and sometimes they go on in such unexpected directions, that they bring about irreversible changes in natural landscapes of a catastrophic character. In order to control such changes in natural landscapes, they should be well studied and classified.

This classification is based on natural regionalization (Stanyukovich, 1968), which divides Tajikistan into two natural regions : Front Asiatic and Central Asiatic. Both of them have their own types of belting and specific natural belts. Every belt, in its turn, is characterized by specific landscapes. Thus, we present here description of 52 principal landscapes by belts.

THE FRONT ASIATIC REGION

This region occupies all Tajikistan except the East Pamirs. The following belts are characteristic of it :

Plain lowland belt, very hot, with desert and ephemeral vegetation, fine-fibered cotton plants on gray-brown light and typical Gray soils (Sierozems)

At present and in future this is the belt of the most intensive subtropical agriculture with mass development of cotton-growing, ditch plantation of citric plants, growing of pomegranates, fig-trees, persimmon, and other heat-loving plants.

A. *Humid landscapes with ground humidification*

A flood-plain landscape of "tugay" thickets (forests, of river valleys, local) of Turanga and oleaster ; three species of Elaeagnus in combination with tamarisk (Tamarix) bushes ; willows (Salix) and overgrowth of tall herbaceous vegetation such as reed, plume grass, imperata, solonchak and boggy vegetation on the shores of water reservoirs and low over flood-plain terraces of perennial rivers. Soils types are alluvial-meadow, forest, meadow-boggy and solonchak. There are also found pastures, hay-fields, and areas of irrigated cultivation.

B. *Arid landscapes with atmospheric humidification*

Landscapes of ephemerals on alluvial and proluvial-alluvial foothill plains and *terrace surfaces*. They are weakly dissected or hardly dissected at all, and have a profusion of bluegrass (Poa bulbosa vivipara), desert sedge, xerophytic perennial wormwoods (Artemisia) and annual saltworts on gray-brown soils and light gray soils (sierozems). Spring and winter pastures and cultivated lands are also characteritsic features.

Landscapes of sandy deserts with haloxylon, saltwort (Salsola Richteri) and solonchaks. These abound on half-fixed and fixed sands of lowlands and on weakly dissected alluvial terraces. The greater part of the territory is good for sowing when irrigated.

Landscapes of alluvial-proluvial on slightly sloping *lowland* plains with vegetation of karabarach species, Russian thistle (Salsola kali) sarsazan zeidlitia and on Hammada deserts on solonchaks : They also occur partially on gray land and gray-brown desert soils, which may be used for irrigation when washed out.

Landscapes of saltwort-sagebrush (*Salsola-Artemisia*) *deserts*; These consist of Sogdiana and finely dissected wormwoods and oriental saltwort on gray-brown soils and light sierozems of proluvial slightly sloping and flat lowland plains. Development for irrigated agriculture is possible here.

Landscapes of sagebrush deserts with Sogdiana and finely dissected wormwood on light and typical sierozems in proluvial sloping lowland plains : With irrigation they may be used for sowing.

B. *Anthropogenic landscapes*

An anthropogenic landscape on alluvial and proluvial-alluvial lowland plains : These are weakly and moderately dissected ; are occupied by villages and towns and have sown areas and orchards on irrigated lands. They have an abundance of fine-fibered cotton plants.

Foothill-plain and dyry belt, hot, with shibliak (xeropyllons thin forest) tall herbaceous-ephemeral and desert vegetation, and early ripening cotton plants on typical and dark sierozems

This belt is favourable for intensive settlement and agriculture and early ripening cotton plants are grown here.

A. *Humid landscapes with ground humidification*

Tugay landscapes (river-valley forests, much changed by man) on flood-plain terraces of rivers and on foothills and lowlands plains. Among the trees, willow, oleaster and turanga predominate and among the shrubs—desert thorn (Lycium), sea buckthorn and tamarisks. Meadows are sedge and cereal-herbaceous ones. Tall herbaceous vegetation of gigantic cereals, reed and plume grass is also found. Soils consist of alluvial meadow-tugay with many conglomerates. The landscapes are used as pastures and are mainly occupied by settlements, orchards and irrigated fields.

B. *Arid landscapes with atmospheric humidification*

Xerophytic thin forest-shibliak of different density with Amygdalus bucharica, pistachio, Calophaca on dark sierozems and on alpine-cinnamonic carbonate soils : The relief is slightly undulating, on hilly with gentle (rarely, steep and stony) mountain slopes.

Landscapes of tall herbaceous vegetation with ephemeral couch grasses and plants of Hordeum bulbosum on mountain foothills and the sloping and hilly relief of the piedmont area on dark sierozems : There also exist Crateagus thickets and Amigdalus bucharica. Couch grasses with hay plant (Prangos Pabularia) and sheep's fescue are also met with. The area may partially be used for dry farming (boghara) and for irrigation agriculture.

C. *Landscapes with undeveloped or disturbed soil-vegetation cover*

Landscapes of rocks and taluses on red beds. They consist of slopes and crests of different steepness. Soils are primitive and not fully developed and are rich in gypsum. The vegetation has a predominance of xerophillous small-leaved, rough and partially thorny bushes (thorny almond), dwarf mimosa (Prosopis L.) combined with bean caper plants (Zygophyllaceae), Hammada saltwort (Salsola arbuscula). The lands are unproductive.

D. *Anthropogenic landscapes*

Anthropogenic landscapes of this belt on plains and in foothills are more humid, making possible boghara cultivation. Soils are dark sierozems ; relief is more rugged and the vegetation consists of shibliak, plants of Hordeum bulbosum group and couch grasses (Graminae). Cotton plants of medium ripeness and other subtropical plants grow easily.

Middle and low-mountain belt, warm, with broad-leaved forests, bushes, steppes and deserts ; vineyards and melon fields ; cattle breeding on dark sierozems and mountain brown soils

The area is potentially favourable for intensive settlement, for building towns, resorts, university cities and industrial centres.

A. *Humid landscapes with ground humidification*

Landscapes of flood-plains in low and middle mountains on flood-plain and low flood-plain terraces : Soils are alluvial-meadow and alluvial-forest. Arboreous species consist of willow, plane-tree (Platanaceae), walnut (Juglandaceae), ash (Oleaceae), apple-tree and cherry plum (Acer turkestanicum). Against the background of the meadow, bushes are quite common. Hay fields, pastures, wood-cutting fields, vegetable gardens, and orchards abound here.

B. *Humid landscapes with atmospheric humidification*

Landscapes of broad-leaved forests on mountain slopes with more or less flat relief : these have slopes of U-like valleys with fragments of erosional and socle terraces, partially covered by blankets of deluvium and coluvium. Soils are alpine-cinnamonic typical and leached. In forest glades and dry slopes cinnamonic calcareous is found. There are many woodless meadow glades. Walnut and maple forests are widespread in the lower part, higher up changing into maple-juniper ones. Extensive terracing and creation of highly productive forest-orchards is possible.

Landscapes of umbelliferous species, hay plants (Prangos pabularica), camomile and rosarium plants on mountain slopes with patches of talus and rocks : They occupy vast areas on the Gissar-Darvaz mountain slopes and are met with on slopes of different expositions. They have Alpine-meadow-steppe soils. The grass stand consists of tall herbaceous vegetation of the umbelliferous family—hay plant (prangos pabularia), Cocand, Karatau, and Kukhistan camomile and others. Hay fields and pastures are also found.

Landscapes of Rosaceae are common on steep and gentle

slopes. They appear in the place of felled broad-leaved forests. Soils here are cinnamonic-leached and typical alpine cinnamonic. Dominating fauna species are Canadian dog rose (Rosa canina), Caprifoliaceae, June berry (Amelanclier), hawthorns (Crataegus), colutea, barberries (Berberis) and others. Hay fields and pastures abound. Reforestation and, in many places, terracing and plantation of forest-orchards are possible.

C. *Humid-arid landscapes with atmospheric humidification*

Landscapes of juniper forests consist of a continuous alteration of juniper thickets (on soils of juniper forests) with patches of sheep's fescue steppes (on alpine-fine earth-steppe soils) and ephedra overgrowth on talus. The relief is of medium steepness. Mountain slopes are covered by fine-earth blanket. In the lower part of the landscape, which is often of belting strike, there is the predominance of hemispheric juniper, in the upper part of the Turkestan type. Pastures, wood cutting and medicinal plants are also found.

Steppe landscapes are most common on the northern slopes, usually on skeletonless and fine-earth-detritus light-cinnamonic soils of gentle ridge slopes. The vegetation consists of sheep's fescue, crawling blue glass (Poa bulbosa), Kirgiz, Caucasian and Lehman feather grass (Stipa) and geranium. Pastures are quite common.

Landscapes of estragon (*Artemisia dracunculus*) *steppes* are formed in the place of sheep's fescue steppes due to overgrazing. Alpine light-cinnamonic soils are common here. Relief of mountain slopes of medium steepness is present. Pastures are very overgrazed.

D. *Arid landscapes with atmospheric humidification*

Middle-mountain vakhan-sagebrush desert and steppe-desert landscapes on very steep mountain slopes. Soils are skeletal light-cinnamonic, carbonate, alterating with rocks and taluses. Vegetation is xerophytic and rarefied. Vakhan wormwood predominates together with Acantholemon pamiricum and with Stipa badakhshanica and caucasica grasses in more humid parts. The territory can hardly be used due to steepness and rockiness of the relief.

Mountain-desert landscapes of ridge slopes with Vakchanica-hammada vegetation on thin stony-detritus sandy soils of the Vakchan ridges' southern slope are found with poor pastures.

E. *Landscapes with undeveloped soil-vegetation cover*

Landscapes of rocks and taluses are found in the lower part of medium-height mountains. Depending on the substratum and the region of location, vegetation varies very much. In places, where taluses and rocks are devoid of skeletonless soils, mosses and lichens predominate in the vegetation. At the foot of the taluses there are many bushes : Amygdalus bucharica, nettle trees (Celtis), different species of June-berries (Amelanchier med.) and dog roses, and on the taluses themselves—grapes (Vitis vinifera), virgin's bower (Clematis), and hay plant (Prangos pabularia). These are unproductive lands.

E. *Anthropogenic landscapes*

Anthropogenic landscapes of the lower part of the medium-height mountains are mainly found on terraces above the flood-plain of mountain valleys, on remnants of plantation surfaces, debris cones and on the flattest parts of slopes, with cinnamonic typical and light cinnamonic stony soils. There are fields, villages and on slopes, cultivated hay pastures. On gentler slopes—irrigated or boghar agriculture is practiced.

Middle-mountain, cool belt of decidiuous and juniper forests, steppes and mountain deserts with cattle breeding, cultivation of grain crops and vegetables on alpine light-cinnamonic and alpine-cinnamonic meadow-steppe and steppe soils

The conditions here are favourable for oasis settlement, cattle-breeding, cultivation of vegetables and grain crops.

A. *Humid landscapes with ground humidification*

Landscapes of floodplain parts of valleys with diverse meadow and tugay vegetation on alluvial soils both on recent alluvium and on a mature soil cover, including natural vegetation : birch and maple groves, sea buckthorn, (Hippophae rhamnoides) thickets, and many kinds of willow and dog roses grow on a rich meadow blanket. Hay fields, pastures, villages, agricultural lands abound.

B. *Humid landscapes with atmospheric humidification*

Landscapes of meadows of a Himalayan type with tall and diverse herbaceous vegetation on high-mountain and alpine meadow and meadow-steppe soils of dark colour : Such landscapes are common on slopes of U-like valleys of different steepness with fragments of erosional and socle terraces, often covered by blankets of deluvium-coluvium. Predominant species are evergreen thorn (Cornus), liguliflorous plants, and catmints (Labiatae). Hay fields and pastures are also found.

C. *Humid-arid landscapes*

Landscapes of thorn grasses (Cousineta psathyrostachydis) are common on stony slopes of dry medium-height and high mountains in places of overgrazing. Relief consists of slopes of denudational and erosional ridges. Soils are desert-steppe and light cinnamonic. Predominant species of vegetation are Cousinia Fedtchenkovii, verticilatus splendida sarawschanica and coronatus.

D. *Arid landscapes with atmospheric humidification*

Landscapes of Artemisia-Korshinsyi and Artemisia-Lehmanniana *deserts* on steep mountain slopes of northern exposition. Soil cover consists of desert-steppe character. In the vegetation abundant are feather grasses (Stipa badakhshanica, turkestanica) and sheep's fescue (Festuca sulcata), i.e. steppe species as well as cushions of Acantho-lemon pamiricum. Pastures are mostly difficult of access.

Landscapes of Artemisia-Korshinskyi as well as Artemisia Lehmanniana deserts with a considerable participation of thorny cushions of Acantho-lemon on steep mountain slopes difficult of access. Here the soil cover is of high-mountain-steppe soils and a considerable part of the landscape slopes consists of rocks and taluses. Slopes are mainly of southern expositions.

E. *Landscapes with undeveloped and disturbed soil-vegetation cover*

Landscapes of taluses in the upper part of medium-height

mountains are quite diverse. In the area of Sarez lake they are mostly lifeless. In Shugnan, in rocks common are : Acantholemon elecampane (Inula shmalgauseniana), currant (Ribes pubescens) and others. Humid stony taluses are characterized by communities of *evergreen thorn* (cornus), hay plant (Prangos pabularia), catmint (Nepeta), Ferula Grigorjevii, etc. These are unproductive lands.

F. *The anthropogenic landscape in this belt is not well distinguished*

High-mountain hemicryophytic, moderately cold, with cattle breeding, rugged alpine relief with high-mountain meadows, steppes and cushions on high-mountain meadow-steppe and zang soils

Only sporadic settlement is possible, in some places—seasonal. It has a belt of pastures.

A. *Humid landscapes with atmospheric humidification*

Landscapes of high-mountain hemicryophytic meadows have medium-height grasses, steppes and cushion plant formations in high-mountain relief of an Alpine type. This landscape occupies large territories in all the west Tajikistan area. Soils are alpine-meadow and alpine-steppe. Summer pastures are found.

B. *Humid-arid landscapes with atmospheric humidification*

Landscape of high-mountain, have hemicryophytic steppes with a considerable admixture of herbs edelweisses (Leontopodium alpinum), cinquefoils (Potentilla) with cushions of oxytropises on gentle slopes with skeletonless matter on fine earth, rock debris and alpine-steppe soils. Herbs found are estragon (Artemisia dracunculus), scorzonera, Adonis and cereals, (Graminae) fesculs, etc. Summer pastures are found.

High-mountain, euxerophytic, cold, cattle breeding belt with meadow-steppe cushion pants association vegetation on high-mountain-meadow-steppe soils of the alpine relief of Tajikistan

B. *Humid landscapes with atmospheric humidification*

Landscapes of cobresia on slopes of medium steepness ;

Vegetation comprises of a continuous cover of Cobresia capillifolia with participation of Alpine herbs of starwort (Aster), edelweisses (Leontopodium alpinum) and oxytropis. Soils are alpine-peat-boggy, meadow-steppe and meadow. Summer pastures abound.

High-mountain alpine landscapes of the Gissar-Darvaz ranges have rugged relief in the process of rejuvenation. The landscape consists of continuous alteration of rocks and taluses on slopes and in small fine earth valleys and slopes. Vegetation and soils are in various stages of formation and destruction. Soils are alpine-meadow, alpine-steppe, zang, in some places—saz peat-boggy. Vegetation ranges from one species—fumitory (Corydalis Fedtchenkoana) and bifora (Bifora Fedtchenkoana)—to cushion plant associations of oxytropis savellanica and oxytropis immersa, Cobresia meadows and steppes of Poa Litwinowiana. Summer pastures which are in considerable measure are difficult of access.

Alpine landscapes of the West Pamirs type : Relief consists of a complex of sharp-peak narrow water-divide ridges and surfaces of slopes of different steepness. A large part of the area is occupied by taluses and rocks. Vegetation grows in depressions, where skeletonless material accumulates, and on alpine-meadow, alpine-desert-steppe, and peat-boggy high-mountain soils. Vegetation consists of cushion associations of zibbaldias and Oxytropis melanotricha with Potentilla pamirica, in some places—There is a predominance of onion (Allium Fedtchenkovii), Poa Litwinowiana, sedges and cobresias.

Nival belt of lifeless rocks and glaciers

Nival landscape of the Fedtchenko type : Glaciation here is almost continuous and glaciers are often of a dendroid type. Relief is created by erosional and exaration activity of water and glaciers. The firn line from the side of the East Pamirs is between 4,800 and 5,000 m. In the north and west—between 4,200 and 4,400 (4,400) m.

Nival landscapes of the Gissar-Darvaz type. Glaciation here is discontinuous and the relief rugged with crests, peaks and slopes of ridges, reworked by exaration processes. The firn line in the Gissar-Darvaz range is at 3,700 to 4,200 m and *in* the West Pamirs—at 4,800 m. Vegetation and soils are absent ; there are some small patches of them only in the lower part of the belt.

THE CENTRAL ASIATIC REGION

In Tajikistan it occupies only the East Pamirs and, due to great heights, is only represented by high-mountain landscapes of upper belts.

High-mountain hemicryophytic, moderately cold with cattle breeding with desert-cushion plant association vegetation on high-mountain-desert and desert-steppe soils pastures

A. *Humid landscapes with ground humidification*

Landscape of saz vegetation is common on the floodplain terraces of rivers and lakes, in the broad high-mountain valleys of the East Pamirs. Ground waters are close to the surface. Soils here are meadow-boggy and boggy with a thick peat horizon. Microrelief consists of many hillocks ; vegetation is mainly represented by Carex orbicularis and Carex melanantha. There are very good pastures and hay fields in some places.

Elymus landscapes on floodplain terraces of rivers and lakes of the East Pamirs. Permafrost is close to the surface and thermokarst is sharply expressed. There are takyr saline weakly humous soils ; sometimes above the takyr there is a layer of sand. Mainly Elymus vegetation is found with sedges, Poa tibetica, sea blite (Suaeda), etc. Pastures are also present.

C. *Humid-arid landscapes with atmospheric humidification*

Landscapes of high-mountain blue-grass (Poa) steppes on high-mountain gentle northern slopes of the East Pamirs ridges. Soils are Alpine-steppe and skeletonless. In vegetation Poa relaxa is dominant, other plants are cushion plant, Acantholemon plants, oxytropises and alpine herbs of edelweisses, Stellaria and others. Summer pastures are found.

Landscapes of high-mountain fescue (Festuca sulcata) steppes are met with on gentle slopes, on fine-earth and skeletonless debris and alpine steppe soils. Vegetation is rarefied and low ; quite common are such cushion plants as Oxytropis savellanica and cryophytic herbs. Summer pastures are also found.

D. *Arid Landscapes*

Landscapes of rarefied low grass hemicryophitic *steppes* are common in broad valleys and depressions of the East Pamirs covered by sandy blankets. Very rarefied vegetation of feather grasses (Stipa orientalis and glareosa), Ptilagrostis, Iris tianschanica and cushions of Oxytropis Poncinsii are found. Alpine desert, sandy, AC are the main-soils. Summer pastures are present.

Landscapes of rarefied grass Christolea steppes in combination with Eurotia are common on desert-steppe primitive soils, on levelled surfaces of secondary water divides, and gentle slopes with fragments of erosional terraces, often covered by moraine deposits of a debris character.

Eurotia desert high-mountain landscapes are found on the bottom and the terrace-like surfaces of valleys and on gentle slopes of ridges of the East Pamirs. Alpine-desert soils of different mechanical composition are common. Vegetation is extremely rarefied and poor in species composition. Associated plants are Stipa glareosa, orientalis, and caucasica, and Acantho-lemon diapensioides of cushion plant association. All-year-round pastures may be used for sowing grass.

Landscapes of small feather grass Eurotia deserts occupy debris cones and ridge slopes over the river Alichur valley. Soils are alpine-desert, sandy-loam and sandy. In the vegetation cover Eurotia is accompanied by tansy (Tanacetum pamiricum), Stipa glareosa, orientalis and caucasica. When irrigated grass may be sown.

Landscape of small feather grasses, tansy (Tanacetum) and eurotia deserts on sandy fans of the right-bank tributaries of the Alichura river have Alpine-desert soils. When irrigated the area may be sown with grass.

Landscape of Artemisieta rhodanthae-eurotia vegetation is met with in the region of Rangkul and Aktash, where there are outcrops of calcareous rocks. Levelled relief is of the East Pamirs type. Alpine-desert are strongly carboniferous. Rosiflorus wormwood predominates with a considerable admixture of eurotia. Cushion plant association is quite abundant. Pastures are also found.

C. *Landscapes with disturbed or undeveloped soil-vegetation cover*
Landscapes of unfixed sands in the high Pamirs exist in the region of Shadput and Rangkul. These landscapes are the product of the overflowing of alluvial deposits on the Akbaital and Oksu rivers. They have unfixed ridgy and hammocky sands and in some places—gigantic barkhans. One of the latter, in Shadput reaches 150 m in height. These are unproductive lands.

Landscapes of taluses and rocks in dry high-mountains of the East Pamirs occupy large areas. The movement of taluses differs in intensity and their vegetation is extremely rarefied. Common here is Artemisia rutifolia and santolinifolia, march cinquefoil (Comarum) and Roemeria. Of the eucryophytic plants characteristic are such short bushes as tea-plant (Thea kuriliana and honeysuckle (Lonicera Semenowii). Lands are unproductive.

High-mountain eucryophitic cold, cattle-breeding belt. Gentle, more seldom-rugged, alpine relief with deserts and cushion plant associations on alpine desert, more seldom desert-steppe soils. summer pastures

A. *Humid landscapes with ground and atmospheric humidification*
Landscape of short-grass eucryophytic meadows and cushion plant associations occupy depressed elements of relief near the foot of slopes crests and on small patches of fine earth in valleys. Soils are Alpine-meadow primitive and zang. Vegetation is of a typically meadow eucryophytic character. In dry places, patches of ayania and cushion plants occur. Summer pastures are found.

B. *Arid-humid and arid landscapes with atmospheric humidification*
Landscapes of cushion plant associations of the East Pamirs are present on gentle slopes and flat tops of secondary water divides, with fine and smooth dissection. Soil cover consists of unformed alpine-meadow and peat soils in depressions and of alpine-desert ones under cushion plants. Vegetation consists of saz of Carex melanantha and in drier places (the greater part of

the landscape), cushion plant associations of Oxytropis melanotricha and savellanica and of Dryadanthe tetrandra. On the driest slopes one finds ayanias. Summer pastures are poor.

C. *Arid landscapes with atmospheric humidification*

Landscapes of high-mountain ayania deserts exist on gentle slopes and secondary water divides, as well as on island uplands and their slopes. Soils are soft, unformed and of alpine-desert character. Vegetation has a predominance of ayania tibetica and patches of cushion plant associations. Very large areas are occupied by rocks and taluses. Very poor pastures and unproductive lands are characteristic.

D. *Landscapes with undeveloped vegetation and soil cover*

Kryophytic taluses and rocks. Soils are not developed. Vegetation is of no significance. Lands are unproductive.

Nival belt of lifeless glaciers and rocks

Nival landscape of the East Pamirs type is situated at heights above 4,800 to 5,000 m. In the lower part the relief is often smoothed, in the upper one—sharply alpine. The firn line is at the height of 5,000 and 5,500 m. Glaciation is discontinuous, there are many lifeless outcrops of rocks and taluses. Vegetation and soil cover are absent.

CONCLUSIONS

The following conclusions may be drawn from the characteristics of the above landscapes widespread within Tajikistan.

In the lower hot belts, within the plain lowland landscapes irrigation cultivation of the following subtropical cultures should be expanded and intensified as much as possible : cotton plant, citric plants (in trenches), persimmon, pomegranate, fig and geranium. Provided the lands are irrigated aboundance of light and heat here makes it possible to get great yields of these cultures.

As there are practically no plain lowlands left unused, which are suitable for agriculture, low mountain landscapes, shibliak and others, should be more intensively involved in economic development for the purposes of developing boghar horticulture and viticulture, while landscapes of broad-leaved forests should be used for creating in the low and medium-height mountains of the Gissar-Darvaz, a belt of forest-orchards (of fruit-bearing, woody, Amygdalaceal, pip fruit and caryocarpous species). There is the necessity to organize protection and control, as well as rationalization of economic use of pastures in medium height and in high mountains, which very rapidly degrade because of overgrazing.

In the same belts and on the same landscapes a wide network of resorts, rest houses, sanatoria and academic towns may be created.

REFERENCE

Stanyukovich K.V. Atlas Tadzhikskoi SSR. Karty "Rastitel'nost", "Geobotanicheskoye rayonirovaniye", "Prirodnoye rayonirovaniye". (Atlas of the Tajik SSR. Maps : "Vegetation", "Geobotanical Regionalization", "Natural Regionalization"). Iz-vo GUK, Dushanbe-Moskva, 1968.

33

INTENSIFICATION OF REGIONAL RESOURCE-USE UNDER CONDITIONS OF HIGH RURAL POPULATION DENSITY

K. Umarov

Tajikistan belongs to those regions of the USSR which show the highest natural growth rates of population. In the period 1958-1984 its population increased 2.2 times. To compare : in the same period national population increased by 31.0 per cent, that of Byelorussia—by 22.6 per cent, of the Baltic Union Republics by 27.3 per cent.

The high growth rates in the Republic are due to traditional patterns of demographic behaviour of the indigenous Tajik population combined with the effective implementation of social programmes in the period of socialist construction and development. Such activities include : organization of the highly effective health care service for the population and the world's most progressive system of social guarantees and insurance.

Stability of high natural growth rates is accounted for by high ratio of rural population and by limited scales and weak dynamics of urbanization in the region. In 1959 rural areas had 67 per cent of population of the Tajik Republic, in 1980—66 per cent.

The studies show that rural areas of the Republic are characterized by surplus labour resources and have the highest density of population in the USSR. However, labour surplus in rural areas does not at all mean unemployment. It does not and cannot exist under the socialist system. Labour resources are above the actual requirements of the agrarian-industrial production, and of rural social infrastructure enterprises.

In the zones of irrigated farming density of rural population comes close to 150 persons per sq. km. In the Hissar valley density of urban and rural population is above 1,300 persons. Especially high growth rates of rural population density are in the suburban zones of large cities. In rural settlements located around Dushanbe, Leninabad, Kurgan-Tyube, Turzun-Zade, population density is 2.5—3.0 times above the average for the Republic.

The population growth rates of rural peripheral areas are 1.4—1.5 times higher. The same trend (although less clearly pronounced) is observed in the main cotton-growing regions of the Republic. The rates of growth of cropping area are however, behind those of rural population. As a result, there is a growing "pressure on land" : in 1959 there were 0.59 ha of cropped area per rural person, in 1980—only 0.28 ha. To compare : the national average of cropped area per rural person is 2.2 ha ; in the Ukrainian SSR, 1.9 ha ; in the Byelorussian SSR, 1.6 ha, and in the Estonian SSR, 2.2 ha. According to this parameter Tajikistan has a less favourable position, than other Central Asian Republics. In the Uzbek SSR in 1983 the above parameter was 0.41 ha ; in the Kirghiz SSR, 5.29 ha and in the Turkmen SSR, 0.59 ha.

Rates of growth of cropped areas due to development of new virgin lands were not high in Tajikistan, because of its limited scales and lower efficiency as compared to the Kazakh, Uzbek, and Turkmen Union Republics, which in the period 1960-1983 increased, 1.26, 1.36, and 2.2 times respectively. Tajikistan—experienced an increase of only 1.12 times.

These data indicate the complicated character of the situation from the point of view of socio-economic functioning of the region's rural sector. There is a high and stable natural growth of rural population in the region and the potential for development of new irrigated areas is limited. This results in higher ratio in agricultural production of the element of *aggregate demographic expenditure of the society*. Some portion of the growth in agricultural production goes to maintain the rural population at the current levels of consumption. Another portion of gross agricultural output goes to provide for growing demand of rural and urban population of the region, to participate in the inter-Republics' exchange, and also to replenish the national emergency reserves. The two latter cases deal with expansion of the Republic's contribution to higher levels of well-being of population of the whole country, which should be equivalent to contribution of other regions as components of a single national economic complex to uplift of the population well-being in the Tajik SSR.

The existing level and dynamics of agricultural production requires radical and, at the same time, thoroughly investigated and scientifically sound measures. The main attempt should be *to intensify the use of regional resources.* It should be stressed, that here we mean all resources—both human and natural-economic ones. In other words, *it is only the integrated approach, that may ensure* achievement of the targets required by the society. There can be no other approach since partial decision-making and implementation may solve some problems, but may aggravate other ones. Therefore, it appears necessary to implement measures for intensive use of regional resources through elaboration and realization of integrated target programmes. Such programmes, taking into account all the integrated features of the Tajik SSR (production, economic, demographic, social, settlement patterns, geographical, ethnic features, etc.) should clearly express relationships of all components of regional resources in the process of their use. They should aim at optimization both of targets and of means to achieve them.

Intensification, which provides for increased return per unit of production investments with full preservation and even improvement of environmental quality contributes to solution of the most important problems of socio-economic development of the Republic, and of its agrarian sector.

However, more intensive use of regional resources does not at all mean rejection of extensive development, i.e., increase of production output through "expansion of the field of production" (K. Marx). More so because refusal of this way of increasing the volumes of production hampers solution of the most important socio-economic problems faced by the region. In the Tajik SSR extensive development of production is necessary to create a large number of new employment opportunities in industry, agriculture and other branches of the national economy and to ensure cent per cent employment of economically active population. This is the most important constitutional conception of the socialist state. However, in specific conditions of today, the strategy of extensive development of agriculture and other components of agro-industrial production is not able to ensure the necessary growth of production efficiency and environment conservation. Expansion of the "field of production" should be carried out on intensive basis through the use of the most recent achievements of science and technology. The return from each newly created working place should be higher, than from those already in operation ; each new machine should have a higher capacity than that of the same designation already in operation ; each new hectare of newly developed land should give higher yields with lower costs as compared to agricultural area which are already under cropping. All this requires to review the methods of organization and management of production and in some cases to completely abandon traditional technologies and ways of using scientific-technological achievements.

More intensive use of regional resources is not possible without achieving a higher efficiency in the use of the "human factor". This is not only because man is the main productive force of the society. Development of people's potentialities is the best pre-condition for higher efficiency of regional resource-use.

As campared to other types of resources, intensive use of labour resources suggests intensification of conditions for their reproduction. Experience accumulated in Tajikistan and other labour surplus regions of the country reveals that intensive use of labour force based on the extensive type of population reproduction does not provide the requested efficiency, but sometimes reduces efficiency of the use of the material component of productive resources. This, in particular, may be the reason for a phenomenon which is paradoxial at a first glance : that is shortage of skilled labour alongwith general labour surplus in the region. Low level of spatial mobility of rural population, lack of industrial skill, inadequate professional and social awareness of people, and some other factors represent the direct results of the predominantly extensive type of reproduction of labour resources in rural areas.

More intensive expanded reproduction of labour resources promotes gradual formation of favourable conditions for solving the tasks of :

(a) increasing mobility of rural population, redistribution of surplus rural labour from the rural sector (agro-industrial production and social infrastructure of rural places) to regions of new development (the centres of the South-Tajik territorial-production complex, virgin lowlands, as well as foothill and mountain areas), in small and medium-size urban places of the Republic, and to labour deficient regions of the country ;

(b) gradual transformation of the demographic behaviour of rural population in the region and gradual development of rational attitudes of couples to reproduction ;

(c) formation in each individual of a careful, scientifically sound perception of nature, sharp turn from the now predominating consumption-biased perception of natural resources to a common desire to restore the disturbed ecological balance, and to increase resources for recreation ;

(d) to make population more culture-oriented. Formation of rational requirements is a most important factor in increasing efficiency of production intensification and in relaxing society-nature contradictions.

Awareness of the need to intensify the conditions of life of rural population in the labour surplus region is the most urgent requirement of to-day. The most important measures are the following.

I. *Organized resettlement in less populated regions of the country*
Under high mobility of rural population this process may be only welcome if it answers the needs of the society. However, under low rural population mobility, organized resettlement in other regions, even if demanded by the society's requirements, meets serious socio-psychological opposition. The latter is of extreme importance, and should be prevented by deliberate action.

II. *Significant increase of capital investments*

To ensure full employment and a socially adequate level of well-being it is urgently necessary to develop the economy in new areas. As an example, one may mention development of foothill and mountain areas and the creation of horticultural-viticultural state farms in the newly developed areas. Unplanned activities are also taking place. In the recent years one may observe spontaneous migration of population from labour surplus cotton-growing rural places to mountain regions. In some places the old settlements, which were formerly considered to have low development potential, are revitalized and have gradually become permanently inhabited by people. There are certain grounds to suggest, that this will become a large-scale phenomenon in the near future. It has an objective character and requires corresponding planned control. Organization of life and work of people in developing mountain areas would, naturally, require large-scale capital investments. To develop one hectare of irrigated land in mountain areas, 5-12 times as much investment, is required as in lowland areas. For each new employment these figures are still more impressive, since the conditions of creating modern production and social infrastructure are especially difficult due to specific natural features of mountain areas.

Still, the present-day economic potential of the Republic does not yet ensure large-scale development of mountain areas. In case such an attempt be made, it would result in sharp decrease of the accumulated funds and limitation of the regional resources for consumption. Besides, all the machinery, technologies and organizational structures for development of newly irrigated lands are designed for lowland areas. Experience of developing mountain areas reveals, that they do not respond to local specifics, and produce negative ecological impacts. Such efforts require essentially new systems of machinery and technology, and this may take a considerable period of time.

III. *Implementation of birth rate control programmes*

Drastic methods are not desirable, and do not bring the required results. Besides, they do not correspond to the principles of democracy. The socialist society would never adopt such methods, since they radically contradict its fundamentally humanistic nature.

The only possible way out is to implement indirect methods, which would finally produce modification of demographic behaviour of population and would decrease birth rates. These include creation of facilities for leasure-time activities, optimal employment of women in the sphere of production, formation in all groups of rural population of aspiration to gain knowledge, desire to master new advanced labour skills, to develop broader scientific and social-political outlook, etc. Effects of indirect methods of birth control are also characterized by a large time lag.

This brings us to the conclusion, that conservation of the inertial variant of socio-economic development of rural areas in Tajikistan is undesirable ; it would decrease efficiency of regional resources, and would produce some negative economic, social and ecological effects. Other alternatives of development are desirable in the rural areas with high population density.

Our task is to attempt to answer the question ; whether it is possible to create an economic mechanism flexible enough to prevent the aforesaid negative effects of intensification of the use of regional resources aimed to solve the problems created by the existing demographic situation.

These negative trends are not at all inherent in the social system of the country. They are produced by failures of the practice of planning and management of the economy and also result from ignoring the objective laws of social development. A certain influence is also produced by the inertial style of administration at lower levels and hesitation in making bold but sound decisions. Of certain importance is also the sprawl of rural and urban places, leading to withdrawal of cropped areas, environmental pollution (in limited scales), negative effects on quality of life (great distances of journeys to work and to culture and servicing places, large-scale use of chemicals in food production, widespread introduction of synthetic fibres in cloth production, etc.) Land erosion is intensified. Thus, before diversion of the Vakhsh runoff to the Yavan and Obikin valleys, the maximum width of the Yava-Su canyon was hardly reaching 40 m, whereas now it is 80-100 m in many places. This resulted in withdrawal of 5-7 thousand ha of land fit for irrigation. The only factor, which produced this situation was erroneous construction of vertical drainage. The same can be said about the ecologically valuable juniper forests in Central Tajikistan. Absence of timely measures to provide the rapidly growing population with fuel resulted in sharp decrease of areas under juniperus forests. Excessive "pressure" of domestic animals on rangelands in some foothill areas results in increased erosion and lower natural productivity.

All this highlights the need for radical changes favouring more intensive use of the regional resources. The most important of them is implementation of measures to reduce "pressure on land", i.e. to achieve not only relative, but also absolute decrease of rural population. The principal means to reduce "pressure on land" is stimulation of population migration. It is a widely held opinion, that the indigenous population of the Central Asian Republics is characterized by low mobility because of many ethnic and socio-psychological factors. However, with gradual development of urbanization, advancement of communication, increase in educational level of people, and of their outlook, this argument becomes groundless. The general laws of sociology and the more specific laws, which control territorial mobility of people, act everywhere. In rural places of Tajikistan new stimuli for migration are gradually pavingt their way. According to one of the latest sociologically surveys carried out by the Council for Study of Productive Forces of the Tajik Academy of Sciences, 30 per cent of the interviewed active rural labour claims to be a potential migrant. Over 50 per cent of them are young people below 30 years of age.

Now there exist actual ways to stimulate rural migration. Such as :

(1) Creation of more attractive conditions of life in small and average-size urban places of the Republic which require accelerated rates of socio-economic development. Accerelated creation of new employment in such settlements is justified by economic expediency of priority distribution of the units and organizations of the first and third blocks of agrarian-industrial complexes.

(production-technological servicing of agriculture, processing of agricultural raw materials, storage, transport, etc.).

(2) Organized recruiting of graduates from rural schools to continue their education in professional-technological schools (PTS) of the Russian Federation, Ukraine, and other Union Republics. The experience of recruiting rural youth to PTS of the Russian Federation indicates that a considerable part of these young people stay for work in places where these PTSs are located.

(3) Large-scale training of rural population in construction activities ; this is an important precondition for employment of population in northern regions using shifting method, and may create favourable background for future selection of new areas of residence by rural population.

(4) Overall distribution of the method of contracts by teams of workers in rural areas, and introduction of the corresponding articles in Statutes of collective farms and interfarm enterprises and organizations. The contracts by teams of workers may become a stimulus for migration, if combined with the progressive methods (shchiokinsky method) of labour organization.

(5) Organized development of commuting from suburban farms through agreements of rural and-urban Soviets of the people's deputies.

The "exogenous" factors of reducing "pressure on land" also include rational redistribution of population within the Central Asian economic region. In Tajikistan effective potential for economic development of virgin lands on plains is practically exhausted. Uzbekistan, Kazakhstan and Turkmenia possess vast tracts of land, which may be developed with relatively low investments. The Food Supply Programme of the USSR plans putting into operation newly irrigated lands.* It would be implemented owing to a cascade of dams which store water in Tajikistan and which have already been constructed, or are now under construction. The national interests require mobiliza-

*Prodovolstvennaya programma SSSR na period do 1990 goda i mery po yeyo realizatsii (Food Supply Programme of the USSR for the period up to 1990 and measures to implement it). Materially maiskogo plenuma TsK KPSS 1982 goda. M., 1982, pp. 67-68, 72-73.

tion of resources for development of the sectors and branches of material production, which are most effective, and most comprehensively meet the social requirements with lowest expenditure. In this connetion, the administrative boundaries should not be an important bar for persuing the national interests. More so because according to the USSR Constitution (The Main Law) all land and water resources are the national property, i.e. the property of all Soviet people.

These considerations account for the expediency of organized diversion of the surplus labour resources from cotton-growing valleys of Tajikistan to cotton and rice-growing farms in the virgin areas of Uzbekistan, Kazakhstan and Turkmenia. High efficiency of this sort of activities is also accounted for by the existing production experiences and labour skills of the population. Thus, stimulation of labour-migration from the southern regions of Tajikistan, specializing in growing fine-fibre cotton, to the southern labour-deficient regions of Uzbekistan and Turkmenia, which are in future to become important producers of these varieties of raw cotton, may be of high economic, as well as social importance, as long as the losses (because of changing place of residence, acclimatization, and social adaptation) will be reduced to the minimum.

The history of cultivating virgin lands for cotton crop gives some examples, which illustrate organized inter-Republic migration. Thus, when, in the 1930s, a new major area of fine-fibre cotton production was developing in the south of Tajikistan, immigrants were represented mostly by peasants from densely populated Fergana valley of the Uzbek SSR. This was an important factor for accelerated development of virgin lands in the Vakhsh valley of Tajikistan, because all immigrants came from traditionally cotton-growing families.

Efficient functioning of the agrarian sector in the region is promoted by large-scale use of achievements of science and technology. Active introduction of modern technologies is the only way to ensure effective use of land all the year round. In the southern and central regions of the Republic two cereal crops are quite possible with average yields 100-150 q/ha. Many farms cultivate such high protein crops as Brassica and perko as participants in cotton crop rotation system. Yields of green crop reach 250-450 q/ha in the most advanced brigades of farmers. Overall introduction of such practices is important for a sharp rise in output of animal-breeding. This requires efficient use of machinery ; higher level of mechanization and automation of production practices; adoption of the most progressive methods of production and labour organization ; use of achievements of the biological sciences, especially of genetics and selection, and advancement of seed production. In this connection, it is necessary to make every effort to counteract the possible negative influence on the natural environment of more intensive use of land resources. In particular, considerable advancement should be made in application of fertilizers to agricultural crops and in chemical protection of plants. However, taking into account the very specific situation in these regions, it appears urgently necessary to seek for principally new approaches, methods and, technologies for their economic development. We mean here principally new agricultural and construction machinery, new forms of cultural and domestic servicing of people, etc.

Thus it may be beneficial for solving the majority of socio-economic and ecological problems in mountain regions to introduce there cent per cent electrification, higher level of electricity consumption in production and domestic activities, as compared to valley regions and cities. This may, in particular help to completely stop the use of wood fuel for domestic purposes (not through more widespread use of coal, oil, or gas) and to conserve the unique flora of mountain regions.

However, construction of major hydro power plants would hardly solve this problem effectively, since even in future, transmission of electric power across deep gorges and high-mountain passes would be economically of low-efficiency. It would be more efficient to construct a large number of minor hydro power stations in every populated valley. However, equipment for such plants is still not produced in the USSR. It is also paying to produce and install in mountain areas the facilities for using power of biogas, sun, and thermal waters.

There are diverse ways to make the use of natural resource more effective depending on the local situation. Their efficiency is closely linked with local initiatives and with the enthusiasm of the local planning and administrating bodies. Some failures in use of regional resources have produced certain problems and difficulties, but they cannot be referred to as irreversible. What is important, is that the factors, which produced these problems are known now, and have been objectively assessed. All this gives grounds for optimism, for confidence, that these problems would be solved by deliberate planning.

34

MANAGEMENT OF NATURAL RESOURCES AND LONG-TERM FORECASTS

A Case Study of the Tajik SSR

K.M. Saidmuradov

Solution of urgent economic problems and advancement of developed socialism in our country, its Union Republics and economic regions, in a great measure depends on an efficient and purposeful management of natural resources in long-term perspective, i.e. on their rational use and comprehensive location of production in different natural-economic zones.

The economy of any region, including that of Tajikistan, comprises of many sectors whose development depends on natural factors. In particular, the availability of proved commercial reserves of mineral raw materials is a basis for location of mining industry, while the availability of water resources in the region serves as a basis for development of hydroelectric industry and as a source from which the water needs of settlements and industries are satisfied. At the same time, unfavourable natural conditions and the low quality of natural resources require much labour and capital investments.

Hence, in the long-term forecasts of development and location of productive forces elaborated by research institutions of Tajikistan (The Scheme of Development and Location of Productive Forces of the Tajik SSR for the period till 2000, the Scheme of Development and Location of Productive Forces of the South-Tajik Territorial-Production Complex for the period till 2000 and others) an important part is assigned to scientifically substantiated inventory and evaluation of the impact of natural factors on the development of material production in a spatial context. Combination of the elements of natural resources and natural conditions, which are always in a complex interaction, often predetermine specialization and efficiency of location of certain industries in the region.

The experience of long-term forecasting of the development of productive forces in Tajikistan shows that a thorough inventory of vegetation, mineral raw material and hydro-power resources in great measure determines the rational development and location of both material resources and of social infrastructure.

The vegetation resources of the Republic are very diverse and rich. The vegetation cover of Tajikistan provides pastures, fodder, wood, a number of useful medicinal, food, tanning and dye plants. It serves as raw material for pharmaceutical, dye, tanning, and wood-working industries. All the vegetation resources of the Tajik SSR, both in its wild and cultivated flora are distributed strictly by belts.

The principal belts of Tajikistan are : very hot, hot, warm, moderately warm, moderately cold, and cold.

I. The lower plain belt, very hot and dry, has a wild flora which is poor in vegetation resources. Short-grass ephemeral deserts, used as winter-spring pastures, as well as sage-brush and solonchak deserts occupy large areas here. Due to the dryness, productivity of this vegetation is very low. But then cultivated flora of this belt, grown with irrigation is the basis of the Tajik agriculture. Fine-fibered cotton is highly productive here. Also, widely developed is the trench culture of citric plants, as well as plantations of subtropical cultures (persimmon, pomegranate, fig, geranium) quite possible are several harvests a year from one and the same area.

II. The next hot piedmont-plain belt is richer in precipitation and its wild vegetation is represented by ephemeral tall couch grasses and different types of shibliak. There are productive spring pastures and in some places—even hay fields. The shibliak vegetation, which is also widespread here, produces fruits (for instance, *pistachio nut*) ; *sage-brush* and *Salsola*.

Deserts occupy smaller areas here. With irrigation very high yields may be obtained from many cultivated plants. Early-ripening cotton plants are quite productive, there are extensive orchards, fields of melons and plantations of a number of sub-tropical cultures. In some regions boghar cultivation is possible, for instance, in the place of some shibliaks boghar viticulture develops.

III. The low-mountain warm belt, depending on precipitation, has a very diverse vegetation. Here in the Gissar-Darvaz, where the mean annual sum of precipitation reaches 1,000 or 1,500 mm (and even up to 2,000 mm), quite common are maple-walnut forests, rich shibliak thin forests, steppes and meadows. The rich natural vegetation is the source of nuts and other fruits, medicinal, tanning and dye plants. Large areas, occupied by thin forest, may be turned into forest-orchards. Cultivated vegetation may be grape-cucurbitaceous (when irrigation is practiced), grain-vegetable or fodder. There are many good summer pastures, the climate is very healthy, specialization may be both in livestock breeding and field-crop cultivation. But labour investments are needed everywhere : in forest plantation, in improvement of pastures, and in creation of local food-processing industry. Areas with desert and dry-steppe vegetation are quite considerable in this belt as well.

IV. Middle-mountain cool belt in different regions of the Republic is occupied, depending on precipitation, by quite diverse vegetation. Here we have decidious and juniper forests, meadows, steppes and deserts. Forests give timber, but the areas occupied by them are small and they should be expanded as much as possible, both as the source of timber and as the means of fixing slopes and combating erosion. In this belt, everywhere with suitable relief cultivation and vegetable growing are possible, mainly with irrigation, as there are few territories with sufficient precipitation for boghara agriculture.

In this belt steppe and desert pastures are good, but they need careful management. Cattle-breeding and cultivation of grain crops and vegetables are the major kind of economic activity here.

V and VI. High-mountain belts with the alpine, meadow-steppe and cushion plant vegetation : All of them are summer pastures, some difficult of access. Cultivation and the growing of vegetables is possible only in the lower part of the desert belt of the Pamirs. Because snow is absent all-year-round, grazing of cattle is possible here.

Mineral raw materials are one of the most important elements of natural resources here. The degree of investigation and development of the mineral raw materials in great measure determines the industrial potential of different regions. That is why, the problems of supply of mineral raw materials is one of the most complicated economic problems.

The growing need of the economy of our country in different minerals are met by all the Union Republics. A certain contribution to the creation of the All-Union mineral raw meterials base is made by Tajikistan as well. Our Republic supplies considerable amounts of antimony, mercury, lead, zinc and other kinds of mineral materials.

The transformation of Tajikistan—formerly backward margin of tsarist Russia—into a Republic with developed agriculture and industry in great measure has become possible because during the years of Soviet power different kinds of mineral resources have been discovered here. At the present time about 300 deposits of them are proved, reserves of 50 kinds of minerals are estimated, about 100 deposits are exploited in which about 36 kinds of mineral products are extracted.

The important characteristics of the principal kinds of fossil minerals is as follows.

An important place in the mineral raw materials base belongs to *fuel-energy resources* (coal, oil, gas).

Coal reserves are estimated in seven coal fields, of which 6 contain bituminous coal and 1 lignite. Shurab coal field produces up to 900 thousand tonnes of coal a year.

In future the main role in coal mining industry will be played by a large, Fan-Yagnob deposit of high-quality coals, of which 80 per cent are cooking. The exploitation of it will start at the beginning of the Thirteenth Five-Year Plan period. Development of the other, smaller deposits is possible in a more remote future.

Deposits of oil and gas are found in the north and in the south of the Republic. Of 14 discovered fields 13 are exploited.

The oil and gas deposits, usually of medium capacities, are associated with Paleogen and Cretaceous strata. More significant deposits are found in Jurrasic rocks at the depth of 5 and 7 km.

Ferrous and alloying metals are represented by iron and tungsten. A small Chokadambulak complex deposit of iron is situated in the north of the Republic ; in its ores, besides iron, there is bismuth, cobalt, copper, lead, zinc, silver, and gallium. The deposit is profitable, but due to its being small-scale, it is not considered to be the primary object for exploitation.

For the development of *tungsten industry* the Maikhurin deposit in Central Tajikistan has been prospected. Of its ores, besides tungsten, zinc, copper, cadmium, and indium may be extracted. The exploitation of this deposit is planned for the Thirteenth Five-Year Plan period.

The main role in the mining industry of the Republic is played by *non-ferrous and rare-earth metals* (lead, zinc, copper, antimony, mercury, tin, bismuth, aluminium, and strontium).

Lead and zinc are the leading minerals and its reserves in Tajikistan occupy an important place among the Republics of Soviet Central Asia. The largest deposits are located in North Tajikistan : 6 of the 24 of them are exploited. In future several other deposits in the regions of Altyn-Topkan and Adrasman may be mined.

Deposits of antimony are concentrated in the Zeravshan-Gissar mountain region. The largest of them at Dzhizhikrut has been mined by the Anzob Concentration Plant since 1950. A number of discovered deposits (of antimony and mercury-antimony) both near the Plant and farther from it may become an additional base of the Plant.

Mercury is extracted as a by-product in the Dzhizhikrut field. Quite significant also is the deposit of mercury in Konchoch. Its development is retarded because of the absence of an effective scheme of processing.

Features of tin ore mineralization are found in Central Tajikistan and in the Pamirs. In Central Tajikistan, of some interest is the Mushiston field, which is being explored at the present time. In the pamirs tin ore mineralizations are concentrated in two ore knots.

Small *reserves of bismuth* are found in the ores of copper-bismuth, polymetallic, gold and magnetite deposits. Quite significant may be the deep horizons of the deposits at East Kanimansur, whose exploitation is planned beyond the present century.

Nepheline syenites found in Turpi may in future serves as *raw materials for production of aluminium.* Their processing will allow to extract alumina, cement and chemical raw materials (potash, erevanite, metasilicate of sodium and of calcium). To use this deposit, it is necessary to improve the technology of extracting alumina.

Deposits of strontium are found in two separate regions : in the Fergana valley and in the Tajik depression. Their development in the near future is not planned.

Noble metals (gold and silver) have been known in Tajikistan since ancient times. *Gold* forms both primary and placer deposits. As by-component it is present in the tungsten, copper-bismuth, and polymetal deposits. It is extracted from golden ore proper and placer deposits and, as by-product, from complex ores.

The main part of the *reserves of silver* is in the north of the Republic in ores of polymetallic, copper-bismuth and true silver deposits. Isolated deposits of silver are also found in Central Tajikistan and in the Pamirs.

Of the *mining raw materials* of the Republic, the principal minerals are boron and fluorspar.

Boron ores are found in the Pamirs. The principal boron minerals are represented by danburite, more seldom—by datolite and axinite. Technical conditions of mining these ores are not complicated. At present specialists work at improving the technology of processing these ores for purposes of obtaining boric acid.

Deposits of fluorspar are know in North and Central Tajikistan. The deposit of Takob, which is being prospected now, will serve as the main raw materials base for the Takob Combine (at present it uses important raw material). Of considerable interest for the further development of the raw material base of the fluorspar industry is the deposit of East Kanimansur (its deep horizons), on which geological prospecting work is being carried out.

The Republic possesses great reserves of *mineral raw materials for chemical industry,* including rock-salt and carbonate rocks (limestones and dolomites). By its reserves of salt of industrial categories (3.6 billion tonnes) Tajikistan occupies the fourth place in the USSR and by the reserves of category C_2 (71 bill.t.) the first place. The Kamyshkurgan and Khodzhamumin deposits produce between 25 and 45 thousand tonnes of table-salt and fodder-salt a year. The Tutbulak deposit is exploited by the Yavan Electochemical Plant, which in the near future will get a sister plant producing 120 thousand tonnes of "extra" salt a year.

If needed, the salt of the Khodzhamumin deposit may be used in chemical industry. Of the limestone and dolomite deposits the Yavan Electochemical Plant mines the Puskhur one, while the Chinar and Yavan deposits are reserved for the future.

Tajikistan is rich in *building materials* used in industrial and residential building. Ore deposits of building stones, gypsum, raw material for air-slaked lime, sandy-pebble material, clays and loams for production of bricks, porous clay filler, agglopo-rite, vitreous sands, sands and sandstones for concrete and cilicate products, mineral dyes, and cap stones have also been discovered. There are over 140 proved deposits. For the present the total proved reserves of building materials can fully meet the requirements of building organizations.

Among the numerous minerals a specific group may be distinguished, that is trim (noble spinel, amethyst, scapolite) and odd-work (lazurite, jasper, ophite, serpentine, decorative marble) stones. Most valuable of them are deposits of noble spinel and lazurite, which on small scales are used by industry.

The Republic is exclusively rich in *mineral springs* differing in degree of mineralization (from fresh to brine), in temperature from cold to very hot), in chemical and gaseous composition (carbonic acid, hydrosulfide, siliceous, radonic, nitric, and methanoic), and in the contents of balneologically active elements. They are known in all the regions of Tajikistan. On the basis of some highly thermal springs (Khovotag, Obi-Garm, Khodzha-Obi-Garm, Yavroz, Garm-Chashma and others) resorts have been built which are famous beyond the Republic's borders. Medicinal-drinking water is bottled from the mineral springs of Sangkhok, Shaambry and others.

New resorts may also be organized in the Gissar valley, where mineral waters have been discovered by drilling, and in the Pamirs, where huge amounts of cold and highly thermal mineral waters have been found, which possess excellent baleological properties. The Aksukon Lake (North Tajikistan has medical muds on the bottom. The mud is used by the local mud-baths and partially is transported to the resorts of Tajikistan and Uzbekistan. The reserves of mud allow to considerably enlarge the Aksukon mud-baths and to increase the volume of mud taken by other resorts.

It can be concluded from the above description that in the Republic numerous deposits are prospected and exploited the Dzhizhikrut mercury—antimony deposit. These are polymetals, coal, oil, gas, many deposits of different building materials, trim, odd-work and facing stones, mineral waters, and medical muds. Deposits of strontium, bismuth, fluorspar and other kinds of mineral raw material are waiting to be developed.

The proved reserves of minerals made it possible to establish non-ferrous metallurgy, gas-and-oil industry and the industry of building materials. In the following decades the rates of industrial growth will require a sharp increase in the output of mineral raw materials. And, on the whole, the proved reserves should not only provide for the up-to-date development of mining industry, but also for its future progress beyond 2000. Already at present in Tajikistan part of the discovered deposits are planned for the development of some industries in the remote future.

But the generosity of nature is not unlimited, and the mineral riches are not renewable. That is why we should be careful and economical about our natural wealth. Rich and easily accessible ores have practically been worked out, and now it is the turn of poor ores and those difficult of access. The exploitation of mineral deposits becomes ever more complicated. The growing needs of the economy for different kinds of mineral raw materials can be met not only by putting into operation new deposits, but also by a fuller and more effective extraction of useful components from them.

Ores of non-ferrous metals of the Republic are multi-component. Alongside lead and zinc, they contain many valuable by-components : copper, gold, silver, bismuth, cadmium, selenium, tellurium, gallium, germanium and others, whose role sharply increases with technological progress, with the development of nuclear, jet, rocket and radio-electronic technologies.

Unfortunately, so far there have been considerable losses of useful components during extraction and processing of ores, although recently at the concentration plants of Tajikistan the number of extracted components increased. But still the level of multiple use of mineral raw materials remains low. Together with lead and zinc extracted from the ore into the concentrate are only those by-products which are approved by the USSR State Catalog. As a rule, these are : copper, gold, silver, bismuth, and cadmium.

Of great significance for the economy is the problem of elaboration of technological schemes for extracting by-products not only from standard ores, but also from refuse dumps and wastes of concentration plants. For storing them, quite expensive hydro-technical structures—tailing reserves are being built, which occupy considerable areas.

The use of waste materials from concentration plants and of strippings also resolves the problems of diminishing and liquidation of the sources polluting the environment. The level of losses in the process of mining is the indicator of rational organization of work. The taking out of ore bodies should be organized in such a way as to minimize the losses of useful components and not to allow exhaustion. From the point of view of the environment, sewage waters from concentration plants are particularly dangerous. Introduction of water recycling with purification of sewage waters will, in addition, decrease the losses of valuable components. Large scales of industrial, residential, hydro-technical and road building in the Republic provide a reliable guarantee for the use of by-products from concentration plants.

Creation in the Republic of a number of territorial-production complexes allows to solve the task of rational and comprehensive use of deficient kinds of mineral resources, which are acutely needed for the economy of our country. Thanks to the prospected and exploited deposits of minerals, North Tajikistan turned into an economically developed and densely populated region. One of the most important tasks here is the creation of a mining complex on the basis of prospected silver, polymetallic, bismuth and fluorspar ores. Mining will become one of the leading industries in the production specialization, which will considerably raise the economic potential of the Republic. The current research allows to predict, already at this stage, that this region will, in the foreseeable future, become one of the most developed regions of the country.

A territorial-production complex based on mining and processing of mineral resources will form in the Zeravshan valley. The creation of this complex has become possible not only, thanks to the availability of mercury-antimony and gold-containing ores, but also due to great reserves of high-quality coals in the Fan-Yagnob deposit mentioned above. Development of this field wlll allow to meet the requirements of the Republic in fuel. Besides, an industrial energy complex may be created on its basis.

Discovery of a number of deposits of valuable minerals (tin, silver, chemical raw materials) within the highest mountain region of the country, the Pamirs, makes it possible to speak about the possibility of creating territorial-production complex here.

Deposits of trim and odd-work stones have been discovered and are exploited in West Pamirs. Spinel and lazurite are the most important among them. In recent years a new province of coloured stones has been discovered in East Pamirs with ruby, tourmaline, topaz, spodumene and others. Besides, in this region there are deposits of limestone, an excellent facing stone. All this shows that in future the Pamirs may become an important supplier of precious, odd-working and facing stones.

Expansion of the mineral raw materials base of the Pamirs is also possible, thanks to discovery and prospecting of non-traditional kinds of mineral (radio-ceramic) raw material. Thermal springs possessing most valuable balneological properties is one of the wonderful riches with which nature endowed this mountain region. Only on one of them (Garm-Chashma) a high-mountain resort has been built. Some springs are used by local people for sanitary-hygienic and medical purposes. In future a significant role in the development of the Pamirs will be played by these reserves of mineral waters and construction. On their basis, high-mountain resorts of not only local, but also Republican scale can be built. Besides, the thermal waters of the Pamirs may be widely used in organization of greenhouse-hotbed farms and for central heating of many settlements.

The development of the Pamirs has already begin. Building materials are mined and mineral waters exploited. The first consignment of marble plates for facing new stations of the Capital's subway has already been transported from the Pamirs to Moscow. Thus, mining industry is one of the important components in the development of the highest mountain regions of the country—the Pamirs.

The developing South-Tajik Territorial-Production Complex is also worth mentioning. Alongside other factors, an important role in its creation has been played by mineral resources. Rock-salt and limestone served as a basis for the Yavan Electo-Chemical Plant. In the near future a new plant will be put into operation, which will produce "extra" salt. Within the South-Tajik TPC great reserves of rock-salt for the development of chemical industry are found in the Khodzhamumin deposit. The further growth of the industrial potential of this TPC also depends on the development of tungsten production on the basis of the Mankhurin deposit.

The South-Tajik TPC is rich in mineral waters. Alongside the prospected thermal springs, where a number of resorts have been built, within the TPC there are considerable positive reserves of mineral waters, in particular, in the Gissar valley. Thanks to it, this valley may become "a valley of resorts".

In the scientific forecasts made by Tajik specialists, an important place is given to the problems of rational use of water resources. Thanks to abundance of feeding resources and to great absolute altitudes, Tajikistan has a dense river network. There are 947 rivers of over 10 km in length. The hydrographic river network is within the basins of two rivers—Amu-Darya and Syr-Darya. The main part of the Amu-Darya basin (80 per cent) belongs to the Tajik SSR. The Tajik SSR, as well as the whole region of Soviet Central Asia, is located in the arid zone of the Soviet Union. Nevertheless, the Republic is well provided with water.

Reserves of the underground waters in the Republic (prognostic and in operation), estimated by 46 deposits, comprise 5.4 cu km, of which 1.6 cu km are not connected with the surface run-off. By now, one third of the operational resources of the underground waters has been extracted and used. Further increase of water intake may lead to a corresponding decrease of the surface run-off in the Republic. That is why only 2.5 cu. km of the underground run-off is recommended to be used of the total prognostic exploitational resources.

The level of the current water consumption in the Republic is much lower than the available reserves of water resources. However, the level of water resource use in different main river basins differs. Most strained are the economic water budgets in the basins of the Kafirnigan, Yakhsu and Kyzylsu river basins, as well as in a number of other smaller basins, where already at the present time there is deficit of water resources during the crop growing period. To guarantee water supply to agriculture and rapidly growing industrial and residential areas, there is a need of measures to regulate the run-off of these rivers with construction of irrigational water reservoirs.

Besides regulation of river run-off, very important are inter-regional and interbasin transfers of the run-off, which make possible development of large areas of virgin lands. The most significant of such projects has been irrigation of the Yavan and Ibikiik valleys (the irrigated area of about 30 thousand ha.), as well as development of the Dangarin valley (in perspective the irrigated areas will comprise 60 thousand ha.). Provided the river of Zeravshan is regulated for many years, its water resources (which at present are partically completely used outside the Republic) could be used for irrigation of 100 thousand ha. of lands in the Uratyubinsk and Ganchinsk regions of the Tajik SSR, some of which are used at present and others can be used in future.

In the present stage of the development of water economy in Tajikistan, hydroenergetics is the leading element of the water economy complex ; it takes upon itself the main material responsibilities for river run-off regulation and development of new regions. Besides, a considerable share of lands with machine uptake of water in the general structure of the developed lands makes hydroelectric plants also important in the meeting of the energy needs of the Republic's water economy.

The potential hydro-power resources of the rivers over 10 km in length comprise 32.3 million kw, while the technical resources are 19.3 million kw. Most of the potential and technical hydro-power resources of the Republic are concentrated in the Vakhsh basin. Seven rivers of the Republic have a mean annual capacity of 500 thousand kw, and 62 per cent of the total hydro-power potential. Over 16 per cent of the economically effective hydro-power resources are used now in Tajikistan, having increased, as compared to 1975, almost twice.

Regulation of the run-off of the Republic's principal river is primarily done in the interests of the water supply to the whole Soviet Central Asia. Sixteen water storage reservoirs of multiple use have been built in the basin of the Syr-Darya river and the regulation coefficient of its run-off has reached 0.94—0.95.

In the Amu-Darya river only seasonal regulation of the run-off is done at present. When the Rogun Hydro-Power Plant is put into operation, the regulation coefficient of the Amu-Darya will reach 0.9. For fully regulating the Amu-Darya run-off, an additional regulating body of about 6 cu. km should be created in its basin. According to data of designing institutions it would be most expedient to accumulate this volume of water in the Dashtidzhum water reservoir on the Pyandzh river having a capacity of 10.2 cu. km. This task should be solved synchronously with the lowering of the Sarez lake level in order to prevent the clogged up waters to break through.

Alongside the regulation of the run-off, of large rivers in the Republic, quite economically effective is a multiple use of small rivers in the mountainous and piedmont regions. Their waters are used for the development of arid territories in the low-mountain zone, which is the main reserve of the expansion of irrigated agriculture in the Republic.

To increase water supply to different sectors of the economy of Tajikistan there is need to pay more attention to the rationalization of the use of water and to protect it against pollution. For this, primarily unproductive expenditures of water should be reduced bringing the volume of consumed water to a fixed standard. In industry it may be achieved by introducing closed systems of water supply and prohibiting discharge of unpurified sewage water into rivers. In the residential sector there is need to accelerate construction of improved systems of water supply and sewage disposal, as well as of purification plants in cities and villages. In agriculture the main task is to improve the technical level of irrigation systems. Over 50 per cent of currently irrigated lands in the Republic are those of old irrigation with the coefficiency of the irrigation systems of 0.54, while in newly irrigated areas and on lands with a reconstructed irrigation system the coefficient increases between 0.7 and 0.9.

The problem of improving the management of the Republic's water economy should be named as the general problem of rational use of water resources.

Thus, the perspectives of development and location of productive forces and the indices of their efficiency in considerable measure depends on definite regional natural conditions and available resources. Their inventory in the current and long-term planning is obligatory.

Long-term forecasts of the economic development of the Tajik SSR show that in future, this region will be in a relatively favourable position in terms of its natural resources. Abundant and economically effective hydro-power resources will make possible not only construction of large hydro-power plants, but also solution of the whole complex of problems in electrification, in creation of new productional combinations, in irrigation of new lands, and, finally, in a considerable increase of labour productivity and living standards of the Republic's population. At the same time, the use of mineral raw materials and fuel resources in future will require development of mineral deposits mainly in mountain regions difficult of access.

35

FINE-FIBRE COTTON GROWING IN THE CENTRAL ASIAN REGION

B. Sanginov

Cotton is an important industrial crop providing raw material for many industries like textile, food, chemical and paper. Of special value is the fine-fibre of the species Gossypium barbadense used to produce cord, very strong threads, percale, yarn, baloon and parachute cloth, cambric, voile etc. Cotton seeds contain about 20 per cent vegetable oil. This oil is used to produce soaps, glycerine, stearin, technical oils and other products, while cotton cake and husks are a valuable fodder in livestock farming. 8,620 m of cloth are produced from 1 ton of fibre of the Soviet cotton kinds 108-F, and 15,150 m from the kinds 9647-1, 8386-V, Ash-25, the cost of the latter being 1.5-2 times as high as that of the former. Besides, the purchase prices of fine-fibre kinds of raw cotton are 1.5-2 times as high as those of medium-fibre cotton. Let us add that fine-fibre cotton economically is more profitable for both farms and industry.

The main directions and measures to increase cotton production in Central Asia and the Caucasus were outlined at the early stages of Saviet power, in 1918 and 1920.

Due to the fundamental reconstruction of agriculture, factory mixtures and loads were fully replaced by new selection high-yield kinds. Their district-wise distribution was carried out taking into consideration the natural-historical conditions of cotton growing zones and textile industry requirements. The cultivation of the Gossypium barbadense species started in our country in the 30's. Today, the USSR is the leading country in the world in the gross production of varieties of the species.

The Communist Party and the Soviet government give every support to the development of cotton growing. The decision of the Central Committee of the RKP (b) of June 18, 1929 set the task of freeing the USSR from the cotton dependence on the capitalist countries. Very soon this task was accomplished. Of great importance to the development of home cotton selection and seed-growing was the decision of the Soviet of People's Commissars of August 29, 1934 on Measures to Improve Cotton Seed-Growing.

The decisions of the XVII Congress of the VKP (b) greatly promoted the works aimed at developing and growing the most valuable cotton kinds earlier uncultivated in the country.

Of the 50 cotton growing countries in the world only the USSR has achieved such high and stable rates of cotton production. The cotton crop of fine-fibre varieties particularly sensitive to heat has been successfully developed. Implementing the decisions of the XXYI Congress of the CPSU, the farms of the cotton growing regions of the country have achieved great advances in increasing the production of raw cotton. Its storage grew from 118,000 tons in 1918 to 8.6 ml tons in 1984, and that of fine-fibre cotton from 6.6 thousand tons in 1931 to 1.2 ml tons in 1984. This was feasible due to the growth of the mechanization of cotton production.

Of outstanding importance for the successful development of home cotton growing was the fact that it relies on the collective and state-farm system, and on the scientific achievements and efficient union of theory and practice.

An important milestone in the further development of Soviet cotton growing is the wide introduction of new methods of cotton growing, chemicalization, and complex mechanization of all processes. Cotton varieties having zero or shortend branching types allowed plant density and crop-capacity to be increased. The quantitative growth of cotton production is accompanied with the fundamental improvement of its quality, which is particularly important for the textile industry.

The development of cotton selection and seed growing and the introduction of advanced technology of cotton growing in the Soviet Union has resulted in the complete replacement of factory mixtures by the Soviet high-quality varieties adapted to our soil-climatic conditions. Of special importance for the improvement of the qualities of Soviet cotton is the development of the crop of fine-fibre varieties. It made it possible to work out a wide variety of textiles and goods from the home cotton.

The high quality of the fibre of the Soviet fine-fibre cotton compared with the fibre of foreign varieties of this type is convincingly proved by a lot of data, specially by the comparative estimation of the fibre quality carried out by ZNIHBI.

All the other cotton producing countries of the world cannot compete with the Soviet Union in the quality of fine fibre cotton grown in the USSR.

As a result of all the work aimed at improving the lands, increasing the level of agrotechnology, stimulating the interest of cotton growing republics of the country, the production of fine-fibre cotton has considerably increased, mainly through increasing the crop-capacity. Of special importance is the in-

Country	Cotton variety	Technological fibre properties			
		staple mass length mm	linear density m tex (number)	breaking load, gc	relative breaking load gc/tex
USSR	Ash—25	39.5	7740	4.5	34.8
	8386—V	41.0	8000	4.7	36.5
	9647—I	40.8	7700	4.7	37.4
	6249—V	40.3	7280	4.7	34.2
	6465—V	40.4	6800	4.8	33.0
	7318—V	40.1	7150	4.7	34.1
	S—6037	41.3	7170	4.5	32.2
Egypt	Guiza—45	39.1	9140	4.5	41.0
	Guiza—47	35.3	6530	5.0	32.6
	Guiza—66	35.6	6350	5.2	32.2
	Ashmuni	30.9	5590	5.1	28.2
	Karnak	37.3	7690	4.6	34.9
	Dendera	32.7	7650	4.1	31.1

creased production of the cotton varieties mentioned, which is explained by their importance for the national economy.

The development of the crop of Soviet fine-fibre cotton varieties started after the victory of the Great October Socialist revolution when cotton growing acquired an exceptionally great importance in the Central Asian and Trans-Caucasian republics.

The selection work with fine-fibre cotton was directed towards creating varieties with high farming and technological properties, resistant to diseases and pests and suitable for machine harvesting.

The first selection institution which organized the study of cotton on the scientific basis was the All-Union Research Institute for Cotton Selection and Seed Growing named after G.S. Zaitzev. Today there are a number of institutes, experimental stations and other enterprises dealing with fine-fibre cotton selection.

Different climatic conditions in which selection and seed growing were developed greatly influenced the formation and adaptability to local conditions of the Soviet varieties of fine-fibre cotton compared with late foreign varieties. The introduction of first valuable Soviet varieties 23-V, 2 and 3, 35-I and others into production provided for increased harvests compared with foreign varieties. In addition, the technological properties of the fibre of these varities were not inferior to the fibre of foreign varieties.

The achievements of the Soviet selection made it possible to have six strain changings with fine-fibre cotton.

The requirement of the cotton industry for cotton fibre and its actual provision in % of the total volume (data of ZNIHBI for 1983)

	Cotton variety , %			
	1	2	3	Total
Requirement	4.0	5.5	4.5	14.0
Provision	6.7	6.3	2.0	15.0

The improvement of the properties of cotton fibre in the USSR as to its staple, strength, fineness and breaking length considerably influenced the productivity of labour and the capacity of equipment in spinning and weaving industries. The better quality of cotton fibre provided for the output of finer and more beautiful fabrics having high durability and strength. The actual sown areas, raw cotton stored, crop-capacity of cotton varieties in the USSR and in individual republics are presented in the following table (data of the Ministry of Agriculture of the Tadjik SSR).

Republic	Gross harvest (purchases) thous. tonnes	Crop capacity center/ha
In the country on the whole	9221	28.9
including		
Tadjikistan	880	28.8
Uzbekistan	593	31.4
Turkmenia	1231	23.2

Narodnoye khozyaistov SSR v 1983 g.M. : Financy i statistika. 1984 pp. 232, 233.

These data show that the cotton industry regularly gets the necessary amount of fine-fibre raw cotton it needs particularly the most valuable I and II grades.

During the years of Soviet power in Tadjikistan, a highly machanized agriculture has been developed with an emphasis on cotton growing. Tadjikistan is the main producer of fine-fibre cotton in the country. The crop occupies an area of 108,000 hectares. In 1984 the cotton growers of the republic harvested a record crop : the country recieved over 932,000 tons of cotton, the average harvest capacity exceeding 30 centners from each hectare. To compare, let us recall that in 1929-1933 the average fine-fibre cotton harvest capacity in Tajikistan was only 2.3, in Turkmenia 5.1, in Uzbekistan 6.8 centners per ha.

After the Great Patriotic war, the crop capacity of the fine-fibre varieties in Tajikistan steadily increased due to the development of a staple cotton based on irrigation, mechanization and chemicalization. The increase in its crop capacity exceeded the crop capacity of the Soviet cotton variety of the species Gossypium horsutum by 6-10 per cent.

Alongwith the growth in the crop capacity the area sown with fine-fibre cotton expanded. In 1960 175.9 thousand hectares were sown in Central Asia, while in 1983 over 430 thousand. This contributed to the growth of the gross yields of fine-fibre varieties of raw cotton in the country as a whole. The collective—and state—farms of the region possess great potentialities to increase the crop capacity of Soviet fine-fibre cotton varieties. Advanced farms get, irrespective of weather conditions, from 33 to 40 and more centners from each hectare annually.

The crop capacity of fine-fibre varieties in the Southern zone of Tajikistan, Vakhsh valley, exceeds considerably the average crop capacity of Soviet cotton. This is explained, partially, by biological peculiarities. At present, a series of cotton-harvesting machines have been developed, which can pick raw cotton of fine-fibre varieties as well as varieties of Soviet cotton. This is of great importance for decreasing the cost of raw cotton.

Let us add that during the whole period of the development of Soviet cotton production, the Communist party and the Soviet government have set such prices of raw cotton which might stimulate the development of this branch of the national economy.

Irrigated agriculture in the conditions of hot climate, little content of organic substance in the soil with long-term tilled-crop of cotton brings about a quick loss of soil fertility and a sharp deterioration of soil meliorative state.

Alfalfa is an effective soil fertility restorer. It should be combined with a correct crop rotation, introduction of manure and a wide use of intermediate-sideratinal crops contributing to the suppression of pathogenic germs of cotton.

Alfalfa accumulates about 20-25 tonnes of root mass for 2-3 years, increasing the content of humus in the soil by 0.4—0.5 per cent of weight, which corresponds to 10-15 tonnes of humus. In crop rotation, alfalfa is a powerful factor in the fight against the weeds of cotton fields and plant diseases. It helps the soil to get rid of wilt infection. In salty soils, alfalfa plays an important role as an indispensable meliorative crop.

Several studies by Central Asian scientists show that alfalfa sowing in the system of 10-crop—rotation of cotton and using intermediate crops provide for an increase of crop yields by 5-7 per cent compared with the old tillage system.

At present, optimal schemes of crop-rotation including cotton in the proportion from 66 to 75 per cent (3 : 7, 2 : 8, 3 : 9) have been introduced to the cotton growing collective—and state-farms of Central Asia.

In order to increase the efficiency of crop-rotation, to maintain a high level of soil fertility and to get stable high yields of raw cotton during all the rotations, deep (38-40 cm) ploughing is performed to close up the alfalfa layer 50-60 cm deep.

The problem of increasing the rates of the extended reproduction in agriculture is connected also with rapidly increasing scales of chemicalization. It has great potentialities to increase the yields of all crops including cotton.

During the years of Soviet power, a powerful industry of mineral fertilizers has been created in our country. The delivery of mineral fertilizers to agriculture increases from year to year. This will make it possible to use mineral fertilizers in the production of cereals and fodder crops.

As a result of many research works carried out by research institution and experimental enterprises as well as advanced practical works, a system of fertilizers for both individual crops and crop rotation was developed and the best ways of using them were also recommended.

The use of mineral fertilizers together with correct agrotechnology increased the yields of fine-fibre cotton in the USSR.

It has been established that 50-60 kg of nitrogen and potassium and about 15-20 kg of phosphorus are spent on 1 ton of raw cotton. Soviet fine-fibre cotton varieties require more nutrition as their vegetative mass exceeds the reproductive mass more considerably than that of the cotton varieties of species Gssypium hirsutum. As a result, the use of nutrients per unit of yield of raw cotton for fine-fibre varieties increases by 25-30 per cent. The effectiveness of the fertilizers depends on the right relation between nitrogen, phosphorus and potassium. The data of research institutions and the experience of advanced farms show that the best ratio of nitrogen, phosphorus and potassium in the cotton growing farms of Central Asia providing for an additional increase of yields should be considered as follows : 1 : 0.7—0.8 ; 0.5. This ratio allows the cotton growing farms of the country to get annually high yields of raw cotton having high technological properties of the fibre. The results of many field experiments show that the introduction of 225-300 kg/ha of nitrogen and 150-210 kg/ha of phosphorus guarantees stable raw cotton yields of 40-45 centner/ha and over.

The main task of the further development of cotton production is the increase of crop capacity and fibre quality. To carry it out, the cotton growing regions of the Soviet Union are introducing a series of measures to increase the quality of agriculture, to rationalize the use of land, to introduce the system of crop rotation and the best varieties of fine-fibre cotton having a set of economically valuable properties, to effectively use mineral and organic fertilizers, to improve the protection of plants from diseases and pests and, to introduce complex mechanization. The results obtained in cotton production are the results of the agrarian policy of the Communist party and the high efficiency of the socialist system of agriculture.

36

TIGROVAYA BALKA (TIGER VALLEY)
A Unique Nature Reserve

G.N. Sapozhnikov

> "Many people will be, probably, surprised to know, that our country has jungle. The word "jungle" comes from the Hindu "jungal", which means impassable bamboo thickets and dense tree-shrub growth with gigantic grasses and lianas along rivers and in river deltas. Very similar to jungle is the growth in flood-plains of major rivers of Central Asia— the tugai".—*Roald Potapov*, 1962.

Tajikistan is a mountain country. Mountains account for 93 per cent of its area. The South-western part of Tajikistan differs radically from the rest of its territory. Geologists identify this region as a South-Tajik depression. A powerful water stream—the river Vakhsh crosses the central part of the region ; its lower reaches located in dry subtropics are the site of a unique nature reserve—"Tigrovaya balka" (Tiger valley), which has become known all over the world.

Some fifty years ago, the tugais were widely spread along rivers of Central Asia, including flood-plains of the rivers Kafirnigan, Vakhsh, Kyzylsu, Pianj, which drain the south-western Tajikistan. Most areas formerly covered by tugai vegetation are now under cultivation. Tugais were preserved only in the lower reaches of the Vakhsh river in the reserved valley "Tigrovaya balka", and as a narrow belt along the river Pianj separating the USSR and the Democratic Republic of Afganistan.

"Tigrovaya balka" is the first nature reserve organized in Tajikistan.

Vigorous development of the Vakhsh valley in 1932 required creation in lower reaches of the Vakhsh of a nature reserve. This idea was suggested by scientists working in Tajik complex expedition. The nature reserve was to include the tugai areas and the Kash-Kakum desert (Flerov, Gromov, 1935).

In 1937 the State game inspection of the Tajik SSR organized a special expedition charged with the task to select an area in the Vakhsh valley to be turned into a reservation. This expedition recommended to organize a nature reserve in the valley "Tigrovaya balka" in the lower reaches of the Vakhsh river.

The "Tigrovaya balka" nature reserve was established on November 4, in 1938, by a Decree of the People's Commissariat of Agriculture of the Tajik SSR in order to preserve the natural complexes spread in southern deserts and flood-plains of Central Asian rivers, to protect rare animals, and to carry out comprehensive scientific research. At present the nature reserve occupies about 48 thousand hectares.

As has been mentioned above, the nature reserve is located in the south-west of the Republic, somewhat to the north of the Vakhsh and Pianj confluence. It has an elongated configuration (40 km long from the south-west to north-east) and includes flood-plain tugai forests along both banks of the Vakhsh lower reaches, sand desert areas of Kash-Kakum, Bori-Tau mountains, as well as the Khoja-Kazian low mountains which are the southern off-shoots of the Aruktau ridge.

The nature reserve is connected with the capital of Tajikistan—Dushanbe—by a good highway (the distance is about 200 km).

All the south-western region of Tajikistan, where the nature reserve is located, is a vast lowland, which spreads far to the south of the USSR boundary, up to the Bandi-Turkestan and Hindu Kush ridges (Geller, 1958). Absolute level of the Vakhsh valley within the nature reserve area is 323-325 m above sea level. Some parts at the left bank of the "Tiger valley", which merge with the Kash-Kakum sands reach 530 m, and only the Khoja-Kozian mountains reach as high as 1,000-1,200 m above sea level.

The flood-plain terrace has flat relief with depressions. Dead lakes of horseshoe shape and dense growth of aquatic plants occur frequently. The concave shore is always higher than the convex one. Some of the lakes (in particular, the Alla-Kul lake, which was formed in 1975-1976) are up to 2 km long and 10 km deep. Dead lakes result from division of river channel on branches, and from river wandering. The configuration of river banks often changes, and parts of river channel or branches are separated from a new channel by fresh sediments. If this part of the old channel still has a connection with the river, back waters are formed. If it is completely separated from the river then dead lakes are formed.

Upper terraces of flood-plains are characterized by desert communities. In "Tigrovaya balka" both sand and clay deserts are found. They were formed in the process of erosional lowering of the river level and the resulting decrease of the ground water level, all this prevented "irrigation" of areas with flood-plain vegetation by flood waters. The tugais die away, and are replaced by desert landscapes with specific plant and animal species (Kerzum, 1950).

Southern offshoots of the Aruktau ridge (Khoja-Kazian mountains belong to the typical low-mountain relief forms of the south-western Tajikistan : foothill stony trains, dissected slopes and smoothed water-shed summits.

Soils of the Vakhsh flood-plain terrace are represented by the alluvial-meadow type. In low mountains of Khoja-Kazian serozems are common.

In general, the climatic regime in the "Tigrovaya balka" nature reserve may be described by the following characteristics : long hot summer, short winter, large amplitude of day temperatures, and scanty precipitation falling mostly in winter-spring seasons. South-western dust winds—"afganets" are not rare in "Tigrovaya balka".

The nature reserve includes practically all landscape complexes found in the South-Western Tajikistan : mountains (low mountains up to 1,200 m high), semi-desert piedmonts, deserts and tugais. Using this sequence of landscape types we will describe the typical vegetation and animal communities protected in the nature reserve.

Mountain or low mountain and piedmont landscapes : They are found on the Buri-Tau hill and on the offshoots of the Aruk-Tau ridge—on Khoja-Kazian mountains located along the right bank of the Vakhsh. Three elements are clearly distinguished in the low ridge structure of the south-western Tajikistan : foothill stony trains, large dissected slopes with outcrops of indigenous rock, and less dissected, somewhat smoothed watershed summits.

Typical soils of low ridges are the serozems. Light serozems are spread up to a height of 500 m and sometimes reach even up to 600-700 m. Above these altitudes dark serozems are spread, representing the upper boundary of the serozem belt (Kuteminskiy, Leontieva, 1966).

Water is scarce on the ridges of the "Tigrovaya balka" nature reserve. Permanent streams on ridges are absent. Of great importance for watering of wild animals are temporary reservoirs of rain water in depressions of stone blocks, which are most often met along gorges, and sometimes on slopes (Sapozhnikov, 1965, 1976).

Faunistic complexes of ecosystems of piedmont and low mountain landscapes are rather specific. Several species of rare and disappearing wild animals, which are not to be found in other landscapes of the "Tigrovaya balka" nature reserve, and which have been listed in Red Books, inhabit these areas.

These include, above all, Ovis orientalis vignei Blyth, or as this species is often erroneously called even in specialized publications—Ovis ammon bocharensis Nasonov, 1914 (Sapozhnikov, 1976).

As reported by observers, Ovis orientalis vignei Blyth was preserved as a small population in the Buri-Tau massive (no more than some tens of specimens). In 1949 a warden of the nature reserve found remains of such a specimen in reeds in the vicinities of the Kabanye lake ; it has, apparently, descended from Buri-Tau and perished of unknown reasons.

In the 1930's and 1940's Ovis orientalis vignei Blyth were rather numerous in the Khoja-Kazian mountains (Chernyshev, 1958).

In rock ecosystems of these mountains another wild ungulate species was once found—Capra sibirica Pallas, 1776.

The foothill ecosystems along the right bank of the Vakhsh were in the past inhabited by herds of a most beautiful antelope—Gazella subgutturosa Guld., 1780, which now is to be found only in desert landscapes of the Kashka-Kum sands on the left bank.

The birds inhabiting low mountains include the following rare species of predators : Gypactus barbatus L., 1758, Circactus gallicus Gmelin, 1788, and also a desert partridge (Ammoperdix griseogularis Brandt.)

Rare reptiles inhabiting mountains and low mountains include Varanus griseus Dandin, 1803, Naja oxiana Eichwald, 1831 and an extremely rare snake—Boiga trigonatum Schneider, 1802). The latter is the only representative of this species in the fauna of the USSR. In Tajikistan only a few specimens have been reported. In general, this species is quite inadequately studied.

Still, the principal "reserved" landscapes in the "Tigrovaya balka" nature reserve are the landscapes of ancient desert, which occupy about 5-6 thousand ha on upper flood-plain terraces, and landscapes of tugai ecosystems, covering 17-18 thousand ha along the river Vakhsh.

Tugais are communities of defoliating xeromesophytous small-leaved mesothermic trees adapted to variating moisturing regimes. Annual rythm of this type of vegetation includes a short winter non-growing period, and a long summer vegetation with different periods of flood moisturing and the corresponding aspects of associated grass plants (Staniukovich, 1982).

Starting from its origin in the form of Gramineae vegetation on young alluvial sediments, replaced by tree-shrub plants, which are characteristic for mature flood-plain (tugai) vegetation, and then by groupings of halophytic or ephemeroid plants—each phase of tugai development is a result of changes in soil and hydrological conditions of flood-plain (changes in ground water level, increase or decrease of salt concentration in soil, etc.).

In combination with climate and hydrological regimes, soil conditions determine plant composition of tugai, finally producing a certain faunistic pattern. Abundance of forage and reliable shelters is favourable for many animals inhabiting tugais viz., insects, birds, reptiles, amphibia, rodents, ungulates, which in their turn, ensure abundance of predators.

Changes in tugai vegetation produce corresponding changes in fauna. Animals also directly or indirectly affect evolution patterns of tugais (Chernyshev, 1958).

Round-the-year moistening of vegetation in the reserve is provided by high level of ground waters on flood-plain terrace which are continuously replenished and refreshed by river run-off, as well as periodical floods. A specific feature of the ecological regimes is the extremely dry air because of long summer drought. This contrast of humid soil and dry air is a peculiar condition for formation of a tugai vegetation (Molotkovskiy, 1982).

5 principal types of ecosystems can be identified in tugais of the "Tigrovaya balka" nature reserve, each having its peculiar type of vegetation.

Reed ecosystems. An inherent element of the tugai landscape is the reed growth. It accounts for about 9 per cent of the total tugai area. As a rule, reeds form impassable thickets with live as well as fallen dead plants. The most exuberant growth of reeds is along banks of rivers, lakes and dry dead lakes. With the course of time reed growth becomes much more sparce because of salinization of upper soil layers.

Highly valuable as shelters for wild animals, reed growth is of little value as forage lands. It is only in spring that young shoots of reed are used as forage by porcupines, deers, wild-boars and some other animals. Reed thickets unbroken for many-years are rarely visited by animals (Sapozhnikov, 1973).

Meadow ecosystems are spread on 18-19 per cent of the tugai area. The tugai meadows include the following plants: Erianthus ravennae, sugar cane, liquorice, wormwood, Meilotus, Alhagi, etc.

As a shelter, the meadows are not of high value for wild animals, but they are perfect feeding grounds.

Ecosystems of Elaeagnus angustifolia L. forests

These account for 14 per cent of the total flood-plain growth. These forests are composed of exclusively Elaeagnus angustifolia L., and have an unbroken tree cover hence grass plants are nearly absent. But at forest edges the following grasses are abundant: Glycyrrhiza glabra, Erianthus ravennae, Alhagi,

Trachomitum, et al. E. angustifolia L. ecosystems represent the best type of habitat for animals. Fruit of E. angustifolia L. are of high nutrition value for mammals and birds inhabiting this nature reserve.

Ecosystems of poplar (turang) forest
These occupy over 25 per cent of the area. Poplar (turang) tugai seldom forms thick growth and its forests most often have park-type patterns of tree distribution. Undergrowth is most often absent, or consists of rare shrubs of Tamaricaceae. Deers, wild-boars, hares, porcupines come to turang (poplar) tugai to accumulate fat, and these are followed by predator mammals—jackals, reed cats, wolves.

Ecosystems of Tamaricaceae
These account for 34 per cent of the total area of flood-plain forests of the "Tigrovaya balka" nature reserve. They are spread over the most highly salinized grounds with shallow ground waters (1.5-5 m below surface). Grass cover pattern in Tamaricaceae shrub ecosystems is mostly a mosaic one, becoming denser near shrubs. Tamaricaceae ecosystems are the typical habitat of Lepus tolai and pheasants are less often observed here. Sparced growth of Tamaricaceae is used in spring as fattening grounds by deers, wild-boars. Places of their laying are often observed in thick growth of tamariks.

As was mentioned above, *landscapes of deserts* include the sands of Kashka-Kum, which represent an area of hillock-ridge-fanned sands ranging in height from 2 to 8-10 m. Vegetation is represented by a clearly formed unbroken shrub layer of mixed composition, 0.2—0.4 coverage and a height of 1.5-2.0 m. These include, first and foremost, the Haloxylon, several species of Calliganum and Salsola. In some plots Zygophyllaceae and some other shrub species are sometimes numerous.

Grass vegetation is characterised by a few species with predominance of small grasses. The grass cover mainly consists of Carex physodes, Poa bulbosa L., Artemisia seopaeformis Ledeb, and some other species.

Special attention should be paid to dead lakes. As a rule, they are surrounded by practically unbroken circle of reeds. Unlike reeds, cane does not form any noteworthy growth. In all lakes Typha is very rare. In submerged species the dominant are Myropphyllum and Potamogeton. Sometimes Najas is also found. The whole bottom of the Kabanye lake is covered by a thick growth of Ceratophyllum (Molotkovskiy, 1982).

Animals of tugais and deserts

Fish fauna in the water bodies of the flood-plains of the "Tigrovaya balka" nature reserve is comparatively poor and is represented mostly by Cyprinidae. Cyprinus carpio, Barbus brachucephalus, Putilus, Aspius, Siluridae are also found [there (Maxunov, 1968).

The dominant species is Cyprinus carpio, sometimes reaching 8 kg. in weight. Sheat-fish is common both in lakes and in the river Vakhsh.

Lakes of the Vakhsh flood-plain are inhabited by a very interesting representative of the fish world—Gambusia affinis holbrooki—killer of Anopheles larva. It was brought to low reaches of the Vakhsh in 1983. The species has propagated, and now is numerous in all lakes.

One should also note the Pseudoscaphirhynchus kaufamanni (Bogdanov, 1874)—the most ancient fish of Central Asia. This rare endemic species with considerably reduced area and population was included into the Red Book of the USSR, and also Red Books of the Uzbek and Tajik SSR (Krasnaya kniga SSSR, 1984).

Herpetofauna of tugai and desert landscapes in the nature reserve is rather varied. Snakes are often met, among them three species are dangerous for man: central-asian cobra, Vipera lebetina L., and Echis carinata Schneid. Naja and Vipera lebetina L. inhabit both tugais and deserts. Echis carinata Schneid is found only in the sands.

In diversity, the leaders among vertebrates are birds. In winter considerable population (up to 10-15 thousand) of waterfowl accumulates on dead lakes. However, the first-rate beauty and honour of the "Tigrovaya balka" is the Tajik pheasant, or black-golden pheasant (Phasianus colchicus bianchii). According to annual surveys the population of pheasants ranges from 1,000 to 2,500 birds (Sapozhnikov, 1982, 1984).

Tugais of the "Tigrovaya balka" were initially inhabited by 34 species of mammals, now there are only 33. The lord of jungles, the Turan tiger (Felis tigris virgata Matschic), has virtually disappeared. Its traces were observed for the last time on March 23, 1953 (Saposhnikov et al., 1984). The other predators inhabiting this nature reserve include the steppe wolf, jackal, karganka-fox, stripped hyena (very rare), reed cat and badger.

In the desert and its margins small groups of Gazella subgutturosa Guld. can be met, their present-day population, however, does not exceed 150-200 specimens.

The most valuable ungulate species in the nature reserve is khangul, or Bukhara deer. Its population somewhat increased in the recent years and reached a maximum of 450-500 specimens in 1976.

The vertebrates in the Red Book of the USSR, which now inhabit "Tigrovaya balka" include the following species :

Fish

1. Pseudoscaphirhynchus kaufmanni

Reptiles

1. Varanus griseus (Red Book of IUCN)
2. Boiga trigonatum Schneider
3. Naja oxiana Eichwald (Red Book of IUCN)

Birds

1. Plataleo leucorodia
2. Phoenicopteri
3. Circaetus ferox
4. Crypaetus barbatus

Mammals

1. Lutra
2. Hyaena hyaena
3. Bukhari (Red Book of IUCN)
4. Gazella subgutturosa Guld.
5. Ovis orientalis vignei Blyth

The "Tigrovaya balka" nature reserve is a unique natural body, not only in the Soviet Union, but on the entire globe. It has preserved the memory of the thick impassable growth of tree-shrubs, i.e. tugais which had existed in comparatively recent past in vast areas. The scientific and educational role of the nature reserve is invaluable. This preserved area of tugai enables us to appraise the impact of human occupance on nature and allows us to study the anthropogenic evolution of global landscapes.

REFERENCES

Chernyshev, V.I., Fauna i ekologiya mlekopitaiushchikh tugaiov Tadzikistana (*Fauna and ecology of mammals in tugais of Tajikistan*). Tr. In-ta zoologii i parasitologii AN Taj. SSR, t. LXXXY. Stalinabad : Izd-vo AN Taj. SSR, 1958.

Flerov, K.K., Gromov. I.M., Ekologicheskiy ocherk mlekopitaiushchikh doliny nizhnego Vakhsha (Ecological essay on mammals in valley of the lower reaches of Vakhsh).—Mat-ly po parazitologii i faune Yuzhnogo Tajikistana. *Taj. kompl. eksped.* 1932 g., vyp. 10. M. 1935.

Geller, S. Yu., Relief.—In : Sredniaya Azia. M. : Izd-vo AN SSSR, 1958.

Kerzum, P.A., Pochvy (Soils).—In : *Sovietskiy Tajikistan*. Samarkand, 1950.

Krasnaya kniga SSSR (Red Book of the USSR). Redkie ?i nakhodiaschiesia pod ugrozoi ischeznoveniya vidy zhivotnykh i rasteniy. T.I., M. : "Lesnaya promyshlennost", 1984.

Kuteminskiy, V. Ya., Leontieva, R.S., Pochvy Tajikistana (*Soils of Tajikistan*). Vyp. I. Dushanbe : Ifron, 1966.

Molotkovskiy, Yu. I., Rastitelnost. Zapovednik "Tigrovaya balka" (Vegetation. Nature reserve "Tigrovaya balka).—In : *Tajikistan* (Priroda i prirodnye resursy). Dushanbe : "Donish", 1982.

Potapov, R.L., V "Tigrovoy balke" (In the "*Tiger valley*"). Zapiski zoologa. M. : Gosgeografizdat, 1962.

Sapozhnikov, G.N., Okhrana vodopoiev dikikh zhivotnykh v Yugozapadnom Tajikistana (*Protection of watering places for wild animals in South-Western Tajikistan*). Tr. IV Vsesoiuzn. soveshch. po okhrane prirody. Minsk, 1965.

Sapozhnikov, G.N., Zapovedniki Tajikistana (*Nature reserves of Tajikistan*). Dushanbe : "Donish", 1973.

Sapozhnikov, G.N., Dikie barany (rod Ovis) Tajikistana [Wild sheep (Ovis species) in Tajikistan]. Dushanbe : "Donish", 1976.

Sapozhnikov, G.N., Zapovednik "Tigrovaya balka" ("Tigrovaya balka' nature reserve)—In : *Tajikistan* (Priroda i prirodnye resursy). Dushanbe : "Donish", 1982.

Sapozhnikov, G.N., O zapovednikakh i zakaznikakh Tajikskoy SSR (In reserves and sanctuaries of the Tajik SSR).—In : *Prirodnye resursy i zapovednyi fond Tajikistana.* Vyp. I. Dushanbe : "Donish", 1984.

Sapozhnikov, G.N., Yakovlev, Ye. P., Neranov, I.M., Rasprostranenie i chislennost nekotorykh vidov mlekopitaiushchikh i ptits Tajikistana (*Distribution and population of some rare species of mammals and birds of Tajikistan*). Ibid. 1984.

Staniukovich, K.V., Drevesnaya i kustarnikovaya rastitelnost (Tree and shrub vegetation). In : *Tajikistan* (Priroda i prirodnye resursy). Dushanbe : "Donish", 1984.

Zapriagaeva, V.I., Dikorastushchie plodovye Tajikistana (*Wild fruit-trees in Tajikistan*). M.—L. : "Nauka", 1964.

INDEX